HOMER
AND HIS
ILIAD

HOMER
AND HIS
ILIAD

ROBIN LANE FOX

BASIC BOOKS

New York

Basic Books
Hachette Book Group
1290 Avenue of the Americas, New York, NY 10104
www.basicbooks.com

Printed in the United States of America

Originally published in 2023 by Allen Lane in the United Kingdom
First US Edition: October 2023

Published by Basic Books, an imprint of Perseus Books, LLC, a subsidiary of Hachette Book Group, Inc. The Basic Books name and logo is a trademark of the Hachette Book Group.

The Hachette Speakers Bureau provides a wide range of authors for speaking events. To find out more, go to hachettespeakersbureau.com or email HachetteSpeakers@hbgusa.com.

Basic books may be purchased in bulk for business, educational, or promotional use. For more information, please contact your local bookseller or the Hachette Book Group Special Markets Department at special.markets@hbgusa.com.

The publisher is not responsible for websites (or their content) that are not owned by the publisher.

Set in 12/14.75pt Dante MT Std

Typeset by Jouve (UK), Milton Keynes

Library of Congress Control Number: 2023944145

ISBNs: 9781541600447 (hardcover), 9781541600454 (ebook)

LSC-C

Printing 1, 2023

For H.J.R.

σὺ γάρ μ᾽ ἐβιώσαο, κούρη.

When a small casket was brought to him, which seemed to those who were taking over the possessions and baggage of Darius to be more precious than anything else, he kept asking his friends which of the things worthy of high esteem seemed most fit to be deposed in it, and when many of them made many suggestions, he said that he would depose the Iliad there and keep it safe.

Plutarch, *Life of Alexander*, 26.1, on Alexander's decision after winning the battle of Issus in November 333 BC.

We worked in rotating shifts, two men, three men, swinging the corpses like a haul of fish from the sea . . . No person should ever have to witness so much death . . . It'd been like a dream through which I'd walked unharmed, grateful, of course, but numb and puzzled by it all. It reminded me of passages in Homer of gods and goddesses coming down from mount Olympus to the bloody battlefields at Troy to help their favourites, wrapping a mist or cloak around them and winging them to safety.

Oliver Stone, *Chasing the Light* (2020), p. 43, on a night battle on Vietnam's border with Cambodia, 1–2 January 1968.

Contents

Contents

Preface

Like its heroes, the Iliad has earned immortal glory. I first met part of it in Greek more than sixty years ago and soon went on to read it all. It is its own best advertisement, but great questions remain, how, when and where it was composed and what accounts for its extraordinary power. This book gives answers to those questions. It is based on long familiarity and love.

I have not presupposed knowledge of the poem. Throughout I have aimed to give sufficient context for this book to be readily intelligible to readers who, as yet, know little or nothing of the Iliad's text. My hope is that they will end by wanting to engage with it, perhaps eventually in Greek. Much has been written on it, and more will be, so that no general view of it can be entirely original, but in most of my chapters I have things to say which even its experts may find unfamiliar.

I believe most of the Odyssey to be by Homer, poet of most of the Iliad, but I have referred to it only sparingly. As it was composed after the Iliad and in awareness of it, I have imagined my readers to be in the position of the Iliad's first audiences, bowled over by what they had heard and wondering, for several years, what its great poet would compose and perform next.

I have applied two differing methods. The first three parts of the book present hypotheses and support them with evidence, inference and analogy. The fourth and fifth parts are appreciations of Homer's poem. Selection and emphasis make them more than just a summary for readers who are intrigued by the poem's fame but know little or nothing of its contents.

I have many debts over many years. I never forget that like many hundreds of Etonians before me, I was fortunate to be taken through the Iliad and Odyssey by Richard Martineau. His fluent, improvised translation while we followed the text in Greek imprinted the poems for ever after in our hearts and minds. I never imagined I would then teach them myself, but they have marked the beginning and end of my teaching in Oxford, framing it as if in a ring-composition. I began teaching the Iliad in 1973, an exciting time to start on it as Jasper Griffin was beginning to give his transformative lectures on Homer, his mind and art. After nearly forty years of teaching ancient history, I returned to teach it again in 2016, having learned so much meanwhile from the fine teachers of Homer who had been my colleagues in New College, Bryan Hainsworth, Denis Feeney, Peter Wilson and Jane Lightfoot, whose expert grasp of the poem guided my return and continues to inspire her many pupils.

The translations in this book are my own, made in prose while respecting wherever possible the sequence of Homer's verses. I am grateful to Anthony Cheetham, who first urged me to write a short book on how Homer's poems came about. This one is its descendant, longer, however, and different. I am also grateful to my publishers, Stuart Proffitt and Lara Heimert, for their close reading and penetrating comments, and to Alice Skinner for detailed observations too. Bernardo Ballesteros, Armand D'Angour, David Elmer, Alan Johnston and Irad Malkin kindly read and improved chapters on which they have particular expertise. Jonathan Keates and my colleague Stephen Anderson read a version of the entire book and commented on it most helpfully. Clara Robins and Jan Preiss assisted with notes and bibliography. Claudia Wagner has helped me find pictures. Mark Handsley has been an admirable copy-editor throughout.

From the Arctic to central Asia, Los Angeles to the plains of Kenya, the Iliad has been the constant companion of my travels, often adding to what I have encountered. Since 1977, my centre of gravity has been New College in Oxford, where I am the heir to two previous authors of books on Homer. One is David Margoliouth, a masterly scholar of Greek and especially Arabic, whose book on Homer and Aristotle, published in 1923, claimed to decipher the first seven lines of the Iliad and reveal eight lines of iambic verse concealed in them in which Homer declared himself to be from the island of Ios. This virtuoso undertaking has persuaded nobody. The other is Gilbert Murray, whose *Rise of the Greek Epic*, published in 1907, accepted that 'It seems on the whole safest to regard Homēros as the name of an imaginary ancestor worshipped by the schools of bards called Homeridai'. This book takes the opposite view.

When I began, I feared that writing a book on the Iliad might temper my love of it. It has done the opposite, alerting me to ever more details, artistry and interconnections on each rereading. With his typical passion and clarity Gilbert Murray concluded his Preface by stating that it was 'only an attempt to puzzle out a little more of the meaning of a certain remote age of the world, whose beauty and whose power of inspiration seem to shine the more wonderful the more resolutely we set ourselves to understand it'. I agree. He wrote those words in a September in New College, as I write these, in a library he never knew beside a garden whose contents he never knew, either. They, too, are part of my life's work.

Robin Lane Fox, 14 September 2022

Prologue
Enigmatic Homer

Homer's Iliad is the world's greatest epic poem. In my view it is the world's greatest poem, despite the existence of the Odyssey. In antiquity, most people agreed. Verses from the Iliad survive on about three times as many ancient papyri as those with verses from the Odyssey, a sign of its pre-eminence.[1] Its subject is the anger of the hero Achilles during the Greeks' siege of Troy and its harrowing consequences for the battles, loves, suffering and losses of the heroes while they fight in the active presence of their gods. The city of Troy was a ruin in Homer's lifetime and the intense action of his poem was only a brief part of a siege which was said to have lasted for ten years. Homer made it speak to us all. 'Everyone, from the beginning,' the philosopher Xenophanes already remarked c. 500–475 BC, 'has learned from Homer'.[2]

'Everyone' cannot be taken too literally: many women and members of poor families would not have known Homer's poems, especially if they were slaves, persons to us, but objects for those who bought and sold them. 'Everyone with leisure or education' was a more plausible claim. The Iliad rapidly became known across the not-so-small Greek world: it was admired in south Italy long before the 230s BC when the ruler of Sicily, Hieron, owned a preposterously large ship with a sequence of floor mosaics depicting the entire story of the poem. By then, the Iliad also had admirers in the nearby Latin-speaking world. In the 20s BC it shaped the second half of Virgil's great Latin epic, the Aeneid. Episodes from it continued to be represented in mosaic, sculpture, painting and many minor arts throughout the Roman empire. The most recent example is the big mosaic floor of a villa in Roman Britain, laid out in c. AD 370–400 and uncovered in Rutland in 2021. Three of its panels show Achilles' battle with Hector and its aftermath, one of which displays him dragging dead Hector behind his chariot, a scene derived from the poem's final books.[3]

The Iliad then became translated into every major European language, including English from the 1580s onwards. In 1829 Nikolai Gnedich finished its first translation into Russian and even imitated Homer's complex metre. In 1902 his Iliad was the one book that Trotsky had with him when he escaped from exile in Siberia. A year later, for his first published article, he used Homer's phrase 'untouchable hands' to describe what revolutionaries would one day turn on the ruling czar. Lenin made him take it out.[4]

In the next year, 1904, the entire Iliad was translated into Arabic verse by Sulaiman al-Bustānī, a Lebanese Catholic in Cairo. In 2004 Egypt's Supreme Council of Culture celebrated this version's centenary, reissued it despite its abstruse style and supported yet another translation, by ʿAhmad Etmān.[5] A translation of the Iliad into Japanese appeared in 1940 and one into Chinese began in the 1940s too. Full-scale imitations are rarer, but in the 1970s Moufad Zakaria composed an admired Iliad of Algiers, eventually 1001 Arabic lines long, evoking his country's history and its resistance to foreign domination. Homer's name and fame still influence popular poetry as far afield as Peru. In Colombia in 1990, the Ministry of Culture arranged for books to be distributed by donkey to rural villages, but a Spanish translation of the Iliad was the one book never given back. Villagers felt it related powerfully to their experience of fighting wars in which 'mad gods', one of them explained, 'mix with men and women who never know exactly what the fighting is about, or when they will be happy or why they will be killed'.[6]

In Europe, meanwhile, modern poets and novelists have preferred to exploit parts of the poem's back-story or its minor characters, whether king Priam's groom or its Greek and Trojan women. The most powerful transposition of the poem's plot is Michael Hughes's *Country*, published in 2018, which sets it in Northern Ireland during the recent troubles.

As these indirect tributes recognize, the Iliad itself is something we could not possibly now compose. It is at least 2600 years old, but it is beyond our ability. It remains overwhelming. It makes us marvel, sometimes smile and often cry. Whenever I read it, it reduces me to tears. When I leave it and return to everyday life, it changes the way in which I look on the world. My book sets out to explain why the Iliad is beyond us, yet why it is still so profoundly moving.

I will start by considering the poem's beginning, in order to give a sense of what Homer could contrive. It sets the context for what I will then pursue, the questions of where, how and when such a poem is likely to have been composed. They might seem easy to answer, given the poem's fame, but they already challenged the ancients. Their dates for the Iliad varied between what our numbered chronology would call *c.* 1050 BC and *c.* 680.[7] Modern scholars' dates range widely too, from *c.* 800 BC, still often regarded as a Dark Age in the Greek world, to *c.* 640 BC during its archaic period. Another view is that the Iliad continued to evolve until as late as *c.* 550 BC as performances of it spread ever further among Greek listeners.

Even the first surviving mention of Homer by name is uncertain. In his *Guide to Greece*, composed in the 130s AD, the learned Greek author Pausanias ascribed a mention of Homer to someone transmitted in later manuscripts of his text as 'Calainos', otherwise unknown.[8] The name is generally, but in my view uncertainly, assumed to be a copyist's mistake for Callinos, a well-known poet who was active in Ephesus *c.* 650–640 BC. If so, his would be the earliest known mention of Homer by name. However, 'Calainos' is said to have credited Homer with an epic poem about Thebes when he 'came to make mention of' verses from it. Such a mention, which its author 'came to' in a sequence of others, would be rather odd in a poem, but if Callinos really was the author of it, it would date Homer well before *c.* 650 BC.[9] The Theban epic poem was not in fact by Homer, and if Callinos thought it was, his mistake implies that Homer was not his contemporary, but someone further back in the past.

In the face of such early uncertainty, some modern scholars have wondered if the name Homēros was invented and bestowed later in antiquity, enabling several poems of unknown authorship to be bundled under one fictitious name. This view was first expressed by a French clergyman, François Hédelin, in 1664, but already in antiquity the meaning of the name had been discussed: was it based on a Greek word in the Aeolic dialect meaning 'hostage' and if so was it a clue to a turbulent event in Homer's own life? Did it mean 'blind'? Modern guesses have gone further: was it based on words meaning 'fitting [words] together' or 'assembly', or, even more wildly, was it derived from a non-Greek word, the west Semitic *'omēr,* meaning a speaker?[10] None of these ingenuities is necessary or convincing. The Greek name Homēros is not unique to the poet and in need of special explanation for that reason. Other people bore it in antiquity, though no other Homēros happens to be attested in our surviving evidence before *c.* 250 BC.[11]

VICO

In 1730, in Naples, the profound thinker Giambattista Vico gave a new twist to the notion that Homer was a fiction. He was so struck by the difference between the 'refined' customs of the Odyssey and the 'wild and savage' customs of the Iliad that he inferred that they went back to two different poets, up to four centuries apart, who had been composing in different parts of the Greek world. He concluded that the Homer of the surviving epics never existed, but that he was an idea or invention of poets of the individual songs which constituted them: 'the Greek peoples were themselves Homer', Vico maintained, developing his contention that early poetry was the repository of the thought and past of early peoples.[12] His views, expressed in Italian, were ignored in German and in English.

Since Vico, illiterate poets in oral poetic cultures elsewhere in the world have indeed been found to look back to a named master poet whom they believe to have lived several generations before their own, a singer with unique talents and an impressive style of life, whether Choibang in inner Mongolia or Blind Huso in southern Yugoslavia. These forbears are credited with very long lives and grandiose talents, but on one modern view, they have been invented by their followers: might Homer have been invented likewise in a Greek poetic culture which was still essentially oral? In fact, these past singers were real people, as was Homer. Eventually he was honoured as a god in many parts of the Greek world: 'Homer a god, not a mortal' was such a cliché that someone wrote it on a potsherd while learning to write in Karanis in Egypt *c.* AD 250.[13] Homer was the name of a master poet, details of whose life had been forgotten. They were then supplemented, like Choibang's, with legends.

Surely his birthplace, at least, would have been remembered, places being easier to retain than dates before numbered systems of chronology existed in the Greek world? However, it, too, was controversial. The earliest known claimants to it are all east Greek places, in the east Aegean or on the west coast of what is now Turkey. The Iliad never mentions any of them, but the silence is not significant, because its plot was set during the Trojan war and it was anachronistic for the poet to refer to Ionian cities which had been settled by Greeks long after that war supposedly ended. The bigger problem is that their claims to Homer only become known to us long after his lifetime. By *c.* 480 BC one such claimant was Smyrna, modern İzmir on the Aegean coast of Turkey.[14] Another famous one was Chios, the island just off Smyrna's coast. In the 520s BC a Greek poet tried to pass off his own poem, a hymn to Apollo, as one by Homer: to do so, he presented Homer obliquely as a blind man from Chios.[15] By then, Chios's claim to him was evidently very familiar.

As for blindness, it can indeed be an attribute of a skilled oral performer: in the first decades of the twentieth century, Blind Lemon Jefferson and Blind George Blake were guitar-playing geniuses in the American South who also worked with orally transmitted songs. However, there were other grounds for ascribing blindness to Homer. In antiquity Greeks sometimes thought that the gods gave special insight and talent to people whose sight they took away. There seemed to be a clue in the Odyssey. One of the oral poets presented in the poem is described as blind:

Prologue

0.   (The Muse loved him greatly and gave him both good and bad:)
     (She took away his eyesight, but gave him sweet song.[16])

These verses encouraged a belief that Homer had been blind too. In due course people wondered when he had lost his sight: was it before or after he composed his poems? It was not a trivial question: if he had been blind early on, he could not have written down the Iliad when he was composing it. Here too opinions divided, because the truth was unknown.

In the absence of evidence from Homer's lifetime, all we know is that as time passed, ever more cities competed for the distinction of being his first home. Around 100 BC, three short poems about the claimants were inscribed on the base of a marble statue of him, put up in Pergamon, two of which alluded to Smyrna, Chios, Colophon and Kyme, all sites along the Aegean coastline of modern Turkey, as competitors for the honour and compared them to dogs fighting over a bone, whereas Zeus alone knew the answer. At a similar date seven claimants were arranged in a neat line of hexameter verse, the metre of Homer's poems: one version of it listed 'Smyrna, Rhodos, Colophon, Salamis, Ios, Argos, Athenai [Athens]'.[17]

The tiny Aegean island of Ios is a surprising candidate but in the mid fourth century BC it had already asserted its claim by issuing silver coinage struck with an imagined portrait of Homer. It is the earliest portrayal of an individual Greek on a Greek coin, but it was modelled on portraits of the god Zeus and had no knowledge of Homer's real features.[18] Even Aristotle, c. 330 BC, gave space to the claim that Homer had been conceived on little Ios and had returned to die there. Aristotle studied Homer very carefully and wrote a book on *Homeric Problems*, and if he himself supported Ios's claim, he dated Homer's conception there to what we would calculate as c. 1050 BC.[19] That date related him to stories of the first Greek migrants who went to settle in Asia after the Trojan war, but it was not based on sound historical evidence. It was far too early, but in Ios's calendar one of the months came to be named Homēreon. Homer's supposed tomb was shown on the north-west of the island,

6

as it still is near modern Plakōtos, where a festival in his honour is held each year on 15 May.[20]

When Homer composed, nobody was yet writing literary texts in Greek prose, let alone biographies of contemporaries. History writing had not been invented. As a result the questions of this book's first three parts, where, how and when the poem was composed, have remained difficult to answer conclusively. The question of how it was composed is best addressed by looking outwards, beyond the text, to poems composed far in time and space from Homer's. They suggest possibilities which desk-bound scholars never fully realized. The dating of Homer's poem also requires an outward turn, to evidence found in other contexts by archaeologists and the many problems of interpretation which it poses.

In the book's fourth and fifth parts I will address a separate question, why the Iliad still has such power. Here, my question has all the evidence needed to answer it: the poem itself. Even so, answers are not easy to pin down in words. I will address it through what I consider to be the poem's hallmarks, first, those of its heroes, then, the hallmarks of worlds parallel to theirs. Engagement with them does not require a knowledge of ancient Greek. Most of my readers will have little or none, but if they go on to read a translation of the Iliad, they will find that prior awareness of these hallmarks will deepen their sense of what underlies it. I hope they will proceed to such a reading or even to learning Homeric Greek: it becomes possible within two years to read long stretches of the Iliad in Greek and catch its force and flow.

In my fourth part, I will begin by presenting a hallmark which is central to the heroes' values. Using it as a thread, I will select my top ten of the poem's twenty-four books and give a nuanced appreciation of what they contain. As readers will then have more of a grasp of the Iliad, I will bring out yet more of the heroes' hallmarks by ranging through it as a whole: they include other values which pervade their male world and even the place of those heroic staples, horses, within it. Together they help to characterize the poem's supreme hero, Achilles.

In my fifth part I will address three parallel worlds which Homer sets beside the main action on the battlefield: the world of the gods and goddesses, the world of women and what, to us, is the natural world. Outsiders, new to the poem, may expect it to be directly about the fall of Troy. They may also have heard that it is full of men who are fighting and killing and even that it is a story in which women are never given their own say. Before I proceed, these claims need to be refined.

The Iliad is aware that Troy will fall, but its plot does not extend to tell of it. Indeed, Homer's heroes are at war and their fighting leads to merciless killing, but no death in battle occurs until the fourth of its twenty-four books, about 2400 verses into the poem: only one death, the poignant death of Hector, occurs in its last three. His young wife Andromache has been preparing his bath in their house in Troy. She hears a shout go up from the battlements and without anyone bringing her news, she realizes that her beloved husband is dead.

Homer's women, when captured in war, are enslaved, a standard practice in the Greek world, but until then, they make choices. One has been the cause of the entire war, Helen's elopement with the Trojan prince Paris. At risk to enslavement, women also contribute to the choices men make. Out of shame, partly before Troy's women, Hector chooses to return to battle. If he fails there, those women, he knows, will suffer and be reduced to slavery.

Away from the war, Homer's eye lights on women in quite other settings: he presents them in some of his long similes, or extended comparisons. One of them presents a mother who is caring for her child by brushing away a fly from him while he sleeps; another presents women who go out into the street, angry in a 'consuming quarrel', and denounce one another with insults, 'many true, many not'. Another compares a tautly balanced phase in the fighting to the balance which a woman attains on a pair of scales while weighing wool for her spinning: she is earning 'a pitiable reward for her children', a touching detail which conveys her lowly status.[21] In a dazzling description of the shield which is being made for

8

Achilles, Homer tells how the god Hephaestus, its maker, contrived a scene in which women stand and watch, 'each in her porch', while brides leave their parents' homes and are escorted through the city by the blazing light of torches. The wedding song has been struck up; young men whirl in a dance as pipes and lyres play; the onlooking women marvel, surely also at the brides, younger than their married selves.[22]

These anonymous women show Homer's sharp awareness of everyday life: it extends to children too. In one of his similes, boys beat a stubborn donkey which has strayed into a cornfield. In another, they bait wasps whose nests they stir up 'foolishly' by the side of a road. In the poem's main plot, sons face the starkest future if they lose their fathers.[23] In heart-rending bleakness Hector's wife Andromache imagines what awaits her orphaned little boy after her husband's death. She envisages him begging food and drink from his father's former friends while they dine together. 'Go away, just as you are: no father of yours is dining with us', another little boy, she presumes, will tell him, one whose parents, she adds, are still alive: he will hit her son and shove him away.[24] This scene of callous boyhood was composed some fifty lifetimes before our own, yet like the fly-swatting mother or the street-quarrelling women it is still immediate.

Although women and children are presented in Homer's long similes, they never inspire one themselves. Even so, there is an interplay between the poem's scenes of male heroism and the worlds of women, children and, to us, nature. Much of it relates the heroes' world to the contemporary world of the Iliad's audience, but it also contributes to a particular quality, one which is far more than pervasive sadness. It is the very essence of the Iliad, not matched in other poems which have heroes as protagonists, not even the Odyssey. It is not just a poetic trick: it rests on an entire view of the human predicament. It is the hallmark with which I will conclude.

PART I

*Homer and His Iliad:
Where?*

I

'When first they quarrelled . . .'

The Iliad is more than 15,000 lines long. It is much longer than near-contemporary Greek narrative poems, most of which stopped with 3000–5000 lines and none of which reached more than 7000, but it is not unique among poems about heroic deeds composed in other cultures. In south-west India one such poem, the poem of Siri, is still performed orally by specialized performers in the Tulu language: it is almost exactly as long as the Iliad and has women as its protagonists. In central Asia various heroic poems survive, versions of which extend to half a million verses or more. The Iliad is distinctive for other reasons, prominent among which are the concentrated direction of its plot and the compression of its action's timespan.

I will begin by tracing these features through its first 611 verses. They are what texts now define as the Iliad's first book, identified by the Greek letter 'alpha' and followed by twenty-three more, one for each letter of the Greek alphabet, from alpha to omega. The origin of this division is disputed. In the 520s BC, teams of reciters began to perform the poem in Athens and, on one view, a division into twenty-four parts might have been devised then in order to help them as they recited in sequence, one team taking over from another as each defined part ended. It is not problematic that the name 'Ilias' for the poem is not attested until the historian Herodotus, writing c. 450–425 BC: too little earlier evidence survives for this silence to be significant. It is more telling that he and other authors in the fifth and fourth centuries BC show no knowledge of alphabetic divisions when they quote from it. The likelier view is that the divisions were introduced by scholars of the text in the third or second century BC.[1] Like every modern reader I will continue to use book numbers when referring to verses or episodes: they are a convenience, but not part of Homer's own plan.

'Sing, o goddess,' Homer begins, 'of the wrath of Peleus' son Achilles'. He is invoking a Muse, a goddess, and he repeats the invocation in several other places, usually when the action is about to take a critical turn and he needs to give detailed information. He is not in an ecstatic state, and it is quite wrong to infer that he regards himself as being transported back to envisage the past he is describing.[2] The Muses, he says elsewhere, 'are present' at events both present and past. They witnessed, therefore, what happened long ago at Troy, and they still know it. One of them sings, whereas Homer himself would have had to rely on human hearsay or guesswork. Accordingly, he tells his story fluently in the past tense, narrating what once occurred in heaven and on earth: Achilles 'spoke, and threw to the ground the sceptre studded with gold nails . . .' or on Mount Olympus 'the white-armed goddess Hera smiled and smiling took the cup in her hand from her son . . .'

He starts straight into his story without any introduction of the Trojan war and its nine preceding years. It is the boldest of beginnings, as radical as young Orson Welles's decision to begin his film *Citizen Kane* at the end of its story. By specifying Achilles' wrath, Homer states that his subject is to be an emotion, not just a sequence of actions or a family's deeds across several generations. The wrath, he goes on, was *oulomenē*, a word which stands at the start of his next verse. It is usually translated 'accursed', but no god or man curses it and I prefer to render it as 'damnable' or even 'ruinous': it is a word of strong disapproval and is placed where Homer, per- forming, could emphasize it.

These first verses cleverly set up what will follow. This wrath laid 'countless pains on the Achaeans': suffering and tragedy, we realize, will be prominent in what is to come. The wrath 'sent many mighty heroes on down to Hades', god of the underworld, and 'made them prey for dogs and all the birds'. A death without burial was dreadful for a Greek, especially if birds and animals devoured the corpse: the wrath, then, had consequences of extreme horror. 'And the plan of

Zeus was being fulfilled': importantly, Homer uses the imperfect tense here, meaning 'was being/continued to be'. For the moment Zeus' plan is left undefined. It will unfold with the action, but it is already linked to countless sufferings.

Zeus' plan began from the time, Homer tells us, 'when the two of them first parted in strife, the son of Atreus king of men [Agamemnon] and noble Achilles'. Which of the gods, then, Homer asks, 'brought the two of them to fight in strife?' He replies, 'the son of Zeus and Leto'. After reading on, most of us would give greater weight to Agamemnon's high-handed role in prompting the rift, but Homer goes further back, to the anger of the god Apollo: it was the cue for the events which led to a debate in the Greek camp and thus to the quarrel itself. Homer's answer to his very first question assumes that divine intervention lies behind what happened on earth: it will be a hallmark of the entire poem.

In these opening verses Homer has condensed so much with marvellous skill. Whereas Virgil or even Milton would take tens of lines before engaging fully with their subjects, Homer uses only nine to set the tone and the divine dimension behind what is to follow. He then tells us in the past tense what happened. The next 600 verses, the rest of the first book, use a contrast between past and present tenses and deploy artful changes of pace and place. They, too, bring out the exceptional skill of their composition, so I will survey them before considering how Homer attained it.

Elderly Chryses came to the Greek camp near Troy to offer a ransom for his daughter Chryseis, a girl whom king Agamemnon had been awarded as his slave-concubine when he and the Greeks captured her elsewhere. Chryses was a priest of Apollo and spoke deferentially, but Agamemnon brutally rejected his plea. Chryses departed in fear and 'went in silence by the shore of the booming sea', a superb verse whose concluding words, *polūphloisboio thălassēs*, echo the noise of the sea's breakers. Showing no sympathy with his plight, they boom on regardless, contrasting with his silence and heightening his isolation.[3] Aged fathers are recurring subjects of pathos in the Iliad.

By the sea, Chryses prayed to Apollo, asking him to make the Danaans [Greeks] pay for his tears with his shafts. In reply Apollo came down 'like the night', a terrifying reversal of a god usually linked with light, and sent a plague by shooting his invisible arrows into the Greek camp. First, the mules and swift dogs fell sick, and then the humans. Homer had no idea of infection or viral transmission: each case, he thought, was due to one of Apollo's invisible shafts. 'The fires of the dead were burning densely', he concludes. It is a fine example of his gift for saying much by saying little.

As often in the poem, Apollo was acting apart from the other gods. On the tenth day the Greek army gathered in the meeting place to discuss why he was so angry and how best to appease him. It was Achilles who had called them there, but, again, a divinity guided the action: Hera put the idea into his mind, 'for she cared for the Danaans [Greeks] because she was seeing them die'.[4] At Achilles' suggestion, the prophet Calchas spoke, a seer who knew, thanks to Apollo, 'what is, what will be and what was before': he too owed his role and talent to a god.[5] With cautious tact, he elicited a promise from Achilles that he would protect him, and only then did he cite Agamemnon's rejection of Chryses, Apollo's priest, as the reason for Apollo's anger. A stormy argument began between Agamemnon and Achilles, whose alternating speeches become ever longer: they escalate brilliantly, one taunt leading to another, but important facts underlie them.

When Agamemnon accepted that he must give up his prize Chryseis, he insisted that he must immediately be given another to replace her. Achilles pointed out that there was no store of prizes set aside and that he must wait until another city was captured, whereupon Agamemnon angrily announced he would take somebody else's prize immediately. He then narrowed his choice to Achilles' prize, fair-cheeked Briseis, nobly born but enslaved when her family's city was captured. When a city fell, Homer reveals, a distribution took place, a *dasmos*. Agamemnon did not just take or distribute prizes as he pleased: Achilles and then Nestor refer to the 'sons of the Achaeans' giving prizes, 'dividing them well among themselves' and 'taking out' Chryseis for the son of Atreus, Agam-emnon. By threatening to take Achilles' prize, Agamemnon was not revoking what he himself had bestowed. He was overturning a decision made publicly by others.[6]

There is an important point here about royal authority. Homeric kings have sometimes been interpreted as chieftains, whose pre-eminence was linked to their redistribution of highly valued goods to their followers.[7] In the Trojan war, Agamemnon was no such per-son. He could not always give booty to whomever he chose. If the army, the sons of the Achaeans, had fought to capture it, it was they who distributed it. They did so with due deference to their superiors, the greatest individual warriors and the pre-eminent king, but the decisions were theirs.

From the start, speakers in the Iliad emphasize Agamemnon's kingship, but there was a difference between his rule over his home kingdom of Argos and his relations with the whole Greek army which had assembled as allies for the Trojan war: the distribution of booty was something over which they, as a community, had control. Nor did Agamemnon have a monopoly on physical strength: others had it too, especially Achilles, who had more of it. As old Nestor states, Achilles was the stronger warrior (*karteros*) and the son of a goddess, but Agamemnon was mightier (*pherteros*) because he ruled over more people. It is a crucial point: their quarrel was not a political one about whether to have kings or not. It was rooted in a conflict which occurs often in joint enterprises: like many team captains since, the king who ruled most people was not the best performer.

In anger at the threat to his prize, Achilles began to draw his sword to kill Agamemnon but again divinities intervened. Hera sent Athena to dissuade him, 'because she cared for both of them in her heart': here too Hera is said to care for Greeks, and again Homer does not say why.[8] Visible only to Achilles, Athena told him that if he desisted and withdrew from the battlefield, one day he would receive three times as many gifts because of what these insults had brought about. Achilles agreed, 'as it is better so', and returned to maintain the quarrel. After Athena's assurances, he intensified it just as she had proposed: he combined insults with a solemn oath that henceforward he would indeed withdraw from the war.

Appearances of a god or goddess are another hallmark of the poem. In antiquity, most of its listeners lived with a sense of the gods' presence, but unlike Homer's heroes they did not confront them personally face to face.[9] The elderly hero Nestor had not been aware of Athena's presence, so he tried to calm the two quarrellers, recalling great warriors, 'better men even than you', whom he had once accompanied and advised. He then told Agamemnon:

> 'Noble though you are, do not take away the girl from this man,
> But leave her, as the sons of the Achaeans first gave her to him
>   as his prize.'

As for Achilles:

> 'Do not wish to strive with a king, son of Peleus,
> Force against force, for never has a sceptred king, to whom
>   Zeus gave glory,
> Been allotted honour equal to others.'

Agamemnon states that Nestor's advice is wise, but he and Achilles continue to protest about each other.[10]

On one point Agamemnon had to relent: he surrendered Chryseis and enabled her return to her father. He cited Apollo as the reason why he was giving her back, not anything said by Achilles, whose anger related to a separate matter, the threat about taking Briseis away. Achilles returned to his encampment, but after arranging for a ship to take Chryseis home, Agamemnon sent two heralds to go and remove Achilles' prize. They went reluctantly on their mission, but when they arrived Achilles showed them courtesy and let them take her away: Briseis, still a slave, returned 'unwillingly'.[11] As yet, Homer leaves her reluctance unexplained: he does not always fill in the background to what he tells.

Bemoaning his loss, Achilles wept on the seashore, stretching out his hands in prayer to his mother, the goddess Thetis, who resides below the waves. His prayer emphasizes that she had borne him to live only a short while: it is Homer's first mention of this important fact.[12] Perhaps he assumed that his hearers knew it already from previous tales, but his placing of it in Achilles' prayer, not in his own narrative, is masterly: he lets it emerge where it is relevant, rather than in an introduction where it would have slowed the action. Thetis came up from the sea 'like the mist', a beautiful comparison, and in response to her request Achilles recaps in nearly thirty verses what has happened, although, he begins, 'You know: why should I tell these things to you who knows everything?'[13]

He then tells her to protect him, her son, 'if you can', and to go to Zeus in heaven and entreat him, reminding him of what she had once done to save him. Three of the Olympian gods had been wanting to tie Zeus up, but Thetis had summoned a hundred-handed monster from the underworld to sit beside him, whereupon the gods desisted in fright. Achilles knew of this exploit because, he says, he had often heard her boasting about it in his father Peleus' house: she must remind Zeus of it, he tells her, and take him by the knees, an intense act of supplication, in the hope that he might help the Trojans and allow the Greeks to be penned up and killed beside their ships,

> 'So that they will profit from their king,
> And the son of Atreus, far-ruling Agamemnon, may know
> His own destructive folly, in that he honoured the best of the
>   Greeks not at all.'

Importantly, this wish is Achilles' own, first expressed by him, not Thetis.[14] It is crucial to the plot.

Thetis says she must wait twelve days before visiting Mount Olympus, because Zeus and the gods are far away, feasting with the 'blameless Ethiopians'. They are people with burnt faces, dark-skinned therefore, but they are not the Ethiopians of modern repute: the Odyssey divides them between the eastern and western edges of the world.[15] Being blameless, they are able to entertain the gods to a banquet face to face: for Homer indeed, dark lives matter.

Meanwhile a Greek delegation took Chryseis by ship to her father, Chryses the priest. Odysseus, their leader, 'took her to the altar', Apollo's, and 'placed her in the arms of her dear father' and he 'rejoicing received his dear daughter': again Homer says so much by saying little, that each was dear to the other.[16] As requested, Chryses prayed to Apollo, who duly stopped the plague while the Greeks burnt sacrifices, poured wine and sang hymns in his honour. They then returned in their dark ship, but back in the camp

> He was enraged sitting by the swift-travelling ships
> The noble son of Peleus, swift-footed Achilles,
> And never would he go to the meeting place which wins
>   glory for men
> Nor ever to war, but he would waste away his dear heart,
> Remaining there, and yet he was longing for the battle cry
>   and fighting.

In this book the action on earth ends with these dramatic verses on Achilles' anger and yearning.[17] He will remain away from the battle-field for another eighteen books.

At dawn, after twelve days, Thetis went up from the sea to Mount Olympus. Zeus was sitting apart from the other gods on the highest ridge there, so she sat before him and begged him as an abject suppli-ant, just as Achilles had told her, one hand on his knees, the other on his chin. Among Greeks this position was one adopted by mortal suppliants: holding tightly on to Zeus, Thetis entreated him to help her 'if ever I helped you among the immortals by word or deed'.[18] She gave no details, though Achilles had urged her to do so. So far from being inconsistent here, Homer is beautifully subtle, as Arist-otle, a close reader of the poem, well realized many centuries later. 'A great-hearted man', he wrote in one of his works on ethics, 'will happily remember benefits he has conferred, but not those he has received', as at the time they made him inferior to the giver: 'he hears the one with pleasure, the other not, and that is why Thetis does not tell her past good services to Zeus'.[19] It is proof in the Iliad's very first book that Homer, by clever variation and omission, knows how to imply much more than he states.

Zeus was far superior to Thetis and would not wish to be reminded in detail of a time when he was not. Instead she alluded in a general way to her past benefits to him, with the implication that they should be reciprocated. Here, Homer projects onto the gods a pattern of prayer that mortals use when addressing a god: if we ever did this or that for you, so may you do this now for us. Thetis even aimed to influence Zeus by reminding him that her son was destined to be the 'swiftest of all other men to die'.[20]

Her request was brutally precise, that Zeus should honour him and put might into the Trojans until the Greeks, hard-pressed, would enhance him with honour and persuade him to rejoin the battle. Zeus 'sat for a long while in silence', and so Thetis repeated the request. It is a pivotal moment in the story. Fourteen books later, Homer in his own person will call Thetis' prayer *exaisios*, or immoderate, a crucial insight into the poem's rights and wrongs.[21]

When she repeats her request, wryly she tells Zeus to refuse if he so wishes, 'so that I may know how far I am the least honoured, *a-timotē*, among all the gods'. Honour is her ultimate claim to favour. Zeus then marked his assent by nodding with his dark eyebrows, 'and the ambrosial locks streamed forward from the king's immortal head and Olympus shook mightily'.[22] Supplicated like an aristocrat, he is nonetheless the god who can send elemental storms and tremors through the world by a simple movement of his brow. I imagine Homer lingering over these superb verses in performance, doing justice to the stateliness of their diction and their importance for the plot. Zeus does not reveal that his promise will lead to a fatal sequel, one which Homer surely already had in mind.

The two of them parted, Thetis springing down into the sea, Zeus going to his palace on Olympus, where the other gods rose to their feet in deference to him, their father. However, as Zeus had feared, a quarrel began between himself and his wife Hera. She suspected, correctly, that he had privately agreed to a request by Achilles' divine mother and that he had indicated with his head that he would honour her son and cause many of the Greeks to die by their ships: her care for the Greeks has already been stated twice in the narrative. Zeus told her to be silent and obey him or else he would turn his 'untouchable hands' against her.

Hera sat down in fear and the other Olympians were troubled too. Thereupon, her son Hephaestus, the god of crafts, tried to calm her. He began by telling her that it would be intolerable if she and Zeus were to quarrel in this way for the sake of mere mortals. He did not want to see her being battered, he said, and he reminded her how he had tried to protect her once before, but had been thrown by Zeus out of heaven. On earth, Agamemnon, speaking in public, had just compared his absent wife Clytaemnestra's looks and abilities unfavourably to those of his slave-concubine Chryseis.[23] In heaven, Zeus then threatened his wife with the violence he had used on her in the past. As on earth, so yet again in heaven: the first husbands in the poem are not exactly sensitive about their wives' feelings and persons.

Hera smiled at her son, surely for his past and present attempts to intervene on her behalf, whereupon Hephaestus, lame though he was, busied himself as a butler to the gods, serving them in orderly fashion from left to right and diverting them into unquenchable laughter. For the remains of the day, feasting prevailed, that social unifier, while Apollo played his beauteous lyre and the Muses sang antiphonally with their fair voices. Eventually,

> When the bright light of the sun went down,
> They went each to their own house to lie down,
> Where the famed god Hephaestus, lame in both legs, had made a
>   home for each of them,
> And Zeus, lord of lightning, went to his own bed,
> Where before, he used to take his rest when sweet sleep came to him.
> There, he went up and slept, and beside him, Hera of the golden
>   throne.

The quarrel in heaven had been patched up, but the quarrel on earth remained unreconciled.

2.

Doing Things with Words

This marvellous beginning is rich in implications for what will follow in the poem. It gives a sense of the art and intricacy with which Homer composed. Details like Briseis departing unwillingly or Thetis alluding only in general terms to her past favours were not the work of a poet who was being guided in a traditional direction by nothing but traditional phrases. Nonetheless, he presents individuals and items with recurring phrases or adjectives, 'swift-footed Achilles', 'white-armed Hera' or the 'wine-dark sea'. This blend of recurrent phrasing and individual art will be a valuable clue to his method of composition.

Important points about the poet and his listeners follow from it. Evidently, Homer knew he was addressing people who were familiar with general tales of Troy and their heroes: he introduces Agamemnon by calling him only the 'son of Atreus' and refers to Achilles' beloved Patroclus only as the 'son of Menoitios' when he is first mentioned.[1] His narrative never even mentions Troy or the Trojans, taking them for granted. They are mentioned, rather, in speeches. No less than 60 per cent of this first book is presented as direct speech, a remarkably high proportion. Chryses the priest, five of the Greek heroes and five of the divinities speak, but Chryseis and Briseis remain silent, not because Homer belittles women but because they are enslaved girls and have no agency in what happens. The clear line of the action would be delayed if they spoke while unable to influence it. Three goddesses, by contrast, deliver speeches, because their words can, and do, shape the plot.

Why does this opening have such vitality and beautifully controlled vividness? Major reasons are the even flow of its metre and poetic language, aspects which require a good knowledge of Homeric Greek. Others are accessible even in translation. One is that emotion runs high in many of the speakers, as the narrative states, emphasizing their fear or anger, distress or wrath. Weeping too is explicitly presented. It is not a shameful or unmanly response: when Achilles loses lovely Briseis, he does not lose heroic status when he sits by the wine-dark sea and sheds tears.[2]

Another reason is that speeches implicitly reveal their speakers' character, whether the haughty inconsiderateness of Agamemnon, causing the sending of a plague and then the quarrel, or Achilles' swift temper, becoming violently enraged, or Nestor, dwelling on his past with the habitual discursiveness of an old man. Speakers also characterize one another, using the word 'always' to enlarge our sense of them beyond the moment. Strife and battles, Agamemnon says, are 'always' dear to Achilles. Hera, Zeus says, is 'always' thinking what he is planning secretly and Zeus, Hera says, is 'always' glad to make secret decisions apart from her.[3] We know more of them as a result.

In this first book there are no long similes, though they are hallmarks of the next book and beyond. There is, however, a brilliant use of words in action. Homer narrates events in the past tense, but makes his speakers give speeches in the present, a variation which brings the speeches to life and makes the poem's world, though far in the past, immediate for his listeners. Speaking in the present, his speakers allude to the past, 'if ever', and to the future, 'some day', widening the scope of the poem's timescale.

Words, when spoken, announce what will come to pass, as a neat exchange between Achilles and his mother Thetis shows. 'I will speak out', Achilles tells her, 'and I think this will be fulfilled', that Agamemnon 'may soon lose his life through his insolences'. In reply Athena tells him, 'So I will speak out and it will be fulfilled for sure', that one day he will receive three times as many glorious gifts because of this insolence. She does not enact the future by what she says here: as a goddess she predicts it with emphatic certainty. Unlike Achilles, she does not 'think': she knows, and so Achilles promptly speaks to Agamemnon in accordance with what she has said.[4] 'Insult him with words', Athena has told him, 'as to what will come to fulfilment', and so he insults Agamemnon with renewed vigour, using compound adjectives which never recur in the poem. Knowing what will happen, he also issues threats, stating what he will do.[5]

Simply by being spoken, words bring threats and insults into being. Words also enact oaths: they are sworn by being uttered, nothing else. Achilles takes up a sceptre, studded with gold nails, and swears by it, adding solemnity to his oath, but what makes his oath exist are the words he speaks. The same is true of hymns and prayers. By being uttered, words from elderly Chryses constitute prayers, just as words from the Greek delegates or from the Muses constitute hymns by being sung. Words also engender promises, like Zeus' words to Thetis when he tells her that she must go away but 'these things will be my care, how I shall bring them about'. He then says he will nod with his head, the greatest sign, and that 'my [word] is not revocable, deceitful nor unfulfilled, whatever I nod to with my head'. His words constitute a promise, which is confirmed by his movement.[6]

To an extent which has not been recognized, the first book of the Iliad teems with instances of how to do things with words. The subject is much studied by modern philosophers, but they have not turned to the Iliad for examples. In its beginning Homer deploys a wide range of what they call speech-acts, making it exceptionally vivid and fast moving. He also attends to how words are received, specifying their effects on their recipients. What is done with words adds force to its opposite: silence. Old Chryses is silent, walking by the sea, and so too are the heralds when they come unwillingly to reclaim Briseis from Achilles. The supreme silence is Zeus', as he thinks through the implications of Thetis' request.

Significant speech and significant silence are not the only contrast which this book deploys. Throughout, it has brilliant variations of pace. Homer uses brief speeches to help him present the back-story which leads to the quarrel. The speeches that express it then increase in length and strike off one another as they escalate. Old Nestor then slows the pace with fifteen verses in which he recalls 'better men than you', past heroes who fought the centaurs, with whom 'mortal men now on earth would never fight'.[7] His speech aims to settle the quarrel, but fails, whereupon a flurry of angry words resumes and the story regains pace.

Speeches are preceded by movement, as each speaker takes up a place and only then begins to speak. The entire book is alive with it, yet the actions that accompany it proceed at times in a prolonged sequence. Agamemnon launches a ship; he chooses twenty rowers; he puts animals on board to be sacrificed to Apollo; he brings fair-cheeked Chryseis and sets her on board too; many-wiled Odysseus embarks as leader. They 'sail over the watery ways', while Agamemnon orders the Greeks back in the camp to purify themselves; they throw the washed-off filth into the sea; they sacrifice many bulls and goats on the shore to Apollo: 'the savour went up to heaven coiling in the smoke'. In only ten verses Homer narrates so much on two fronts, but never with breathless haste. The metre of his verse moves smoothly and swiftly, helped by the adjectives which repeatedly attach to particular nouns and persons, 'fair-cheeked Briseis', 'resourceful Odysseus', 'watery ways', 'the unharvested sea'. As so often, it is worth visualizing the range of what he presents, even if listeners could not pause and dwell on it in that way. In the time taken to recite these ten verses, not even a film could show so much in a sequence of shots. Homer's words convey more, more swiftly, than pictures.

Actions then unfold more steadily. Twenty verses, nine of them spoken by Achilles, present the heralds' unwilling visit to take away Briseis. Thirty verses, also from Achilles, recap events in answer to Thetis, followed by twelve days of delay while the gods are feasting with the Ethiopians. Meanwhile, the ship carrying Chryseis comes to its anchorage and the details of its mooring are given one by one. Prayers and offerings are paid to Apollo, each detail being given here too, first the roasting of meat, then the pouring of libations of wine, then the singing to appease the god. Night falls, but when rosy-fingered dawn appears, the ship returns to the Greeks' camp and Homer lingers on details of its billowing sail and again on details of its mooring when it arrives.

In his fine appraisal of the Iliad the poet Matthew Arnold singled out rapidity as one of its essential qualities.[8] However, it also has sequences of action slowed across several verses, especially rituals or recurring actions like preparing and eating food. These slowed episodes were not Homer's devices to give himself time to remember or recover while he was performing: he was capable of hundreds of verses without using them. Rather, they are there for his listeners, allowing them to keep up with his performance.[9] After about 240 verses of wonderfully condensed narrative and fast-moving speech, they are well-judged changes of pace. They run throughout the poem and are relevant to the question of how he composed.

So is Homer's use of space. Most of the action on earth is in the Greeks' camp, while actions among the gods are on Mount Olympus. In the rest of the poem, the fighting occurs in one small area, between the camp of the Greeks, whose ships are made of wood, the river Scamander, which divides the battle-plain, and the city of Troy, whose high walls and towers are made of solid stone. Most of the action is not a siege of Troy. The main assault on a fortified site is conducted by the Trojans on the Greeks' wall around their ships into which they break at the end of book 12. Otherwise the action is a battle waged in open space. When Homer refers to the right and the left of it, a close reading has shown that he presents it consistently as if from the centre of the Greeks' camp looking out onto the Trojan plain.[10] It is as if he has a precise mental setting for the action, one with consequences, again, for how he composed. There are scenes of debate, prayer and lamentation inside Troy itself and there are two brief visits to forests on the mountain of Ida, but otherwise only the gods move elsewhere from time to time.

Despite this concentrated setting, the Iliad's scope extends far further, because Homer persistently evokes a wider Greek world. When he refers to religious cult, he names shrines which are very far from Troy, particularly in his protagonists' prayers. When he presents lesser-known people on or off the battlefield, he animates them with details of their families and homelands, widening his poem's range. He never refers to Hellenes, whom we, adapting their Latin name, *graeci*, call Greeks. He refers only to Argives, Danaans or Achaeans, names, however, with a long prehistory. Occasionally he refers to Pan-achaeans, but only to mean 'all the Achaean army', not all Achaeans everywhere.[11] In two of the poem's books he mentions Hellas, the name used by Greeks for their land, but for him Hellas is only a small part of Thessaly adjoining Achilles' homeland.[12] Like every modern commentator, I have already referred to 'the Greek camp' and 'the Greeks', departing from Homer's wording. This usage is not anachronistic as Homer's near contemporary, the poet Hesiod, refers to the big army which the Achaeans gathered from 'holy Hellas' to go against Troy, using Hellas in a wider sense, what we would call Greece.[13]

The range of cult-places in the poem is exemplified at a vital moment, when Achilles sends Patroclus out to fight in book 16. He prays solemnly to 'lord Zeus of Dodona', far away in north-west Greece, site of the famous oracle in Epirus near modern Ioannina.[14] 'Pelasgian, dwelling far off', Achilles continues, 'ruling over Dodona with its harsh winters: around, dwell the Selloi, your interpreters, with unwashed feet, sleeping on the ground.' This precise invocation of Zeus at distant Dodona is not fantasy, although its details continued to puzzle the ancients, just as they still puzzle us.

When gods fly to and from Troy, their travels, too, widen the poem's horizons. In book 14, as Hera flies across to Mount Ida in the Troad, Homer refers to her passing lovely Emathia, the plain just to the north of Mount Olympus which later became the Greek kingdom of Macedon.[15] In book 21, he refers to Achilles' duel with a warrior from non-Greek Paeonia whose back-story names two major Paeonian rivers in the land which adjoined Emathia to the north-east.[16] In book 15 he refers in a similar back-story to the island of Cythera just off the southern coast of the Peloponnese, the very tip of Greece. In book 9 he has already made Agamemnon refer to seven settlements around that coast, all locatable round the Gulf of Messenia, including Kardamyle, still famous in the Mani.[17] He was offering to give them to Achilles.

In the poem's first book the place names are much more limited. The gods are located on Mount Olympus, debating, quarrelling, dining and sleeping there: Homer felt no need to specify its location in, to us, northern Greece. It was known as a seat of the gods long before he referred to it, but perhaps he had not seen it because he says once in the Odyssey that its peaks are not covered in snow.[18] On earth the main heroes are also linked to particular homes, Agamemnon to Argos, Achilles to Thessaly, old Nestor to Pylos, but these locations too were embedded in tradition. They were not Homer's inventions. In his two prayers to Apollo, old Chryses refers to Tenedos, holy Cilla and Chryse, each of which is a place particularly linked to the god.[19] They are the first examples in the Iliad of a wider horizon evoked through religious worship: they have an exactness which readers often miss.

Tenedos is an island just off the coast of the Troad in north-west Asia. Cilla is not otherwise mentioned in the poem, but it was surely in or near the Troad too, perhaps already on its southern coast, where later Greek authors placed it.[20] Homer might have learned from previous poets that these two places were not very far from Troy, but his presentation of the third one, Chryse, is more specific. When Chryses was rebuffed by Agamemnon, he walked back along the seashore: he was returning to Chryse, we can infer, and was going south from Troy along the coast of the Aegean, the sea, therefore, whose breakers boomed beside him.[21] He would have passed the island of Tenedos, just out at sea to the right of him, and then at Chryse reached the shrine of Apollo at which he was a priest.

The place Chryse was the origin of his name and also the name of his daughter Chryseis. These people are quite likely to be Homer's inventions: did he invent the place Chryse too? Later Greek sources site a real Chryse to the south of Tenedos and close to the south-west tip of the Troad, on a rocky height above the sea. It has been located at Göz Tepe, a promontory on which pottery and tiles dating to *c.* 100 BC have been discovered: an inscription of similar date, found nearby, refers to a garrison at Chryse, an apt use of this site.[22] If it was Chryse in Homer's time, it fits very well with old Chryses' walk home down the coast. It also fits well with the day's journey of the ship which brought his daughter back from the Greek camp. This ship was big enough to carry cattle for sacrifice as well as twenty Greek rowers, who brought it, Homer tells us, to Chryse and moored it in a harbour bay with 'much depth'. Just north of Chryse's promontory is a bay which served as a harbour for yet another settlement nearby: Homer's 'much depth' is a poetic flourish, but this bay is otherwise apt for the mooring he describes.

After landing, the envoys took dear Chryseis to that altar, evidently one for Apollo, and put her in her dear father's arms. Near the start of the poem Chryses had used the name Smintheus when praying to Apollo, a name which the ancients later explained as meaning 'mouse god': they accounted for it by various stories, including one of the god's intervention in a plague of mice, indeed a locally plausible event.[23] By the village of Gülpınar, less than two miles south-east of the bay, marble fragments of a temple were found in 1853 by Commander T. A. B. Spratt, a shrewd researcher, who identified it as the temple of Apollo Smintheus. In autumn 1866, it was partly excavated by Richard Pullan with the backing of the patrician Dilettanti Society in London. Since 1980, the temple has been more fully excavated by Turkish archaeologists and found to be datable to *c.* 150 BC.

Its identity as a Smintheion, or temple of Apollo Smintheus, is supported by coins struck in the second century BC at the nearby settlement above the bay: they were engraved with images of Apollo's statue and inscribed with his name, Smintheus. Fragmentary inscriptions of a similar date were found nearby and also refer to the name Smintheus.[24] No evidence of a temple from Homer's time has yet been found, but in his prayer to Apollo old Chryses refers to roofing over a pleasing temple for him, surely at Chryse, where he served as priest. If this temple was of wood, perhaps thatched, it would have disappeared without trace.

Modern criticism of the Iliad often prefers to explain its names for places and items around Troy as inventions by Homer or as a legacy to him from earlier poems: if later texts fix them to particular places, that fixing, some believe, is the work of admirers of his Iliad, wanting to claim possession of places named in it. Chryse became a site of particular interest in the cultural and political landscape of the third and second centuries BC, but I do not believe it was fixed to Homer's poem only then. The temple of Apollo Smintheus has not yet produced evidence from Homer's time, but its surrounds have yet to be excavated and archaic and prehistoric items have already been identified there. Chryse's site on a promontory, the bay just to the north of it, the temple as currently known all interrelate on the ground. They were not imaginary locations, floating freely in Homer's verse. He or an informant had seen them, enhancing a hallmark of the poem, its vividness, what ancient critics labelled *enargeia*.

Homer is widely considered to be entirely elusive as a person. If he merely inherited traditional material or even, as some have thought, short poems which he or his followers then stitched together, their place names and landmarks are unlikely to be evidence of his own travels and observations. Chryse and the Smintheion imply the opposite, that place names may say something about Homer himself.

3.

Tracking Homer

At the centre of the Iliad stand the city of Troy and its towers. Back in the second millennium BC, at least 600 years before any plausible date for the Iliad, western Asia had been largely ruled by the Hittites, whose kings were based in central Anatolia. Some of their official texts have survived on clay tablets, mostly broken, among which are fragments mentioning a site in western Asia called Wilusa. In 1924, the Swiss scholar Emil Forrer proposed that Wilusa was the Hittites' name for what the Greeks called [W]ilion, Troy. A fierce controversy ensued, but his proposal was supported by close study of other place names then known in Hittite texts. Since 1998, more such evidence has established that Forrer's theory is indeed correct.[1] Whether or not a Trojan war took place, Ilion–Troy was a real city long before the Iliad existed. A Hittite text also refers to Taruisa in a similar region: the exact scope of these place names is still disputed, many considering that Taruisa referred to Troy and Wilusa more generally to territory around it.[2]

In this case, too, Homer and his predecessors had not invented a legendary place called Ilion which admirers of his poem later located in the world. The place pre-existed the poem. In the Iliad it is clear that Homer located Ilion/Troy in the north-west corner of Asia, close to the sea which he knew as the Hellespont, the modern Dardanelles. A city called Ilion certainly existed there later and persisted for many centuries. Most, but not all, of those who wrote about it assumed that it was still on the site of the Ilion of Homer's poem: it was to this Ilion that the young Alexander the Great came before winning his first battle in Asia, fought in the Troad in 334 BC.[3] It disappeared after antiquity, but scholars and visitors, as we will

32

see, strove to re-identify its site, championing various candidates. In the 1870s excavation established that the city of Troy, many-layered over time, lay under a mound called Hissarlik ('fortress' in Turkish) and that old and new Ilion were one and the same. Troy's site is now certain.

Homer was not the first Greek to compose verses about Troy. He refers to it as 'well towered' and high up, or 'beetling', and to the Trojans collectively as 'horse-taming', epithets which he uses for no other city or people: their metrical range and apt content show that they originated with poets many centuries before his own time.[4] They do not derive from his own research. The city was a layer of ruins, largely buried, by the time he could have visited it.

Its surrounds were another matter. Long after antiquity, hopeful visitors came to them and convinced themselves that Homer had preceded them and that his eye for the terrain had been exact. In 1718, the adventurous Lady Mary Wortley Montagu was one of the most articulate. She went up to inspect the Trojan plain and coast-line while her husband was travelling back from service as an ambassador in Istanbul: 'While I viewed these celebrated fields and rivers', she wrote, 'I admired the exact geography of Homer, whom I had in my hand. Almost every epithet he gives to a mountain or plain is still just for it'.[5]

In 1810, after swimming across the Hellespont, the young Lord Byron spent about a month on the Trojan plain and wittily declared it a fine field for conjecture and snipe shooting.[6] Visitors keen to find exact Homeric details still assumed, wrongly, that the terrain and coastline had not changed and that their preferred site for Troy, as yet unexcavated, was the right one. Believing, too often, was seeing. It also minimized Homer's poetic licence. In book 7 he describes the construction of a defensive wall and ditch which the Greeks built to protect their camp and ships, but he ignores it as an obstacle in some of the action thereafter. As ancient commentators remarked, the wall comes and goes when he chooses, a poetic construction indeed.[7] For many modern readers and critics, therefore, Homer invented not just this wall, but most of the spaces and minor landmarks he needed, so that his own travels are irrelevant to what he presents. As in the case of Chryse, I disagree, believing that his memories of what he saw are a component in the Iliad's use of place and space. They are relevant not just to his own whereabouts but to the process by which he composed.

The strongest evidence that he indeed stood at Troy would be some exact, but not obvious, details in a passage where he is most unlikely to have been following previous poets. One is especially pertinent: it occurs in the Iliad's thirteenth book when he describes the god Poseidon

> As marvelling at the war and the fighting, he sat
> on the highest peak of wooded Samothrace,
> For from there all Ida was plain to see
> And plain to see, too, were Priam's city [Troy] and
> the ships of the Achaeans.

Homer himself has chosen this location for the god, fitting it to an episode in which he wants Poseidon to be looking along the same sightline as Zeus, who is sitting opposite him on a peak in Mount Ida far away to the south-east.[8]

In the 1830s Alexander Kinglake, an Old Etonian, went up to Troy with the Iliad much in mind. In his subsequent book, *Eothen*, he recalled how his mother had taught him life's cardinal lessons as a boy, 'to find a home in his saddle, and to love old Homer and all that old Homer sang', albeit in an English translation.[9] With him went Methley, a horse-taming Yorkshireman thoroughly steeped in Homer too, who collected seeds off plants along the Scamander's banks. In a fine passage Kinglake describes how they had assumed that the long island of Imbros would block any view from Samothrace as far as Troy. At the time, they may have mistaken Troy's exact site and gone to a widely credited alternative about six miles further south, but their error does not affect what they discovered: distant Samothrace indeed rises high above Imbros and from it Troy and Mount Ida can be seen, just as Homer had known when positioning Poseidon.

34

'Nobody whose mind had not been reduced to the most deplorable logical condition', Kinglake wrote later, 'could look upon this beautiful congruity betwixt the Iliad and the material world and yet bear to suppose that the poet may have learned the features of the coast from mere hearsay; now then, I believed; now I knew that Homer had passed along here, that this vision of Samothrace over-towering the nearer island was common to him and me.'

His point can be extended and strengthened by following the details of Poseidon's journey to Troy, one which is alive with verbs of movement. From Samothrace's wooded mountains Poseidon descended, making the trees tremble, and in only four divine strides, reached Aigai, where a golden, gleaming palace had been built for him in the depths of a lake. Again, despite modern puzzlement, Homer's topography is exact. In antiquity, several places were called Aigai, but one of them, though little known to historians, was located on the Gallipoli peninsula: Poseidon, I infer, strode across to this Aigai on Gallipoli's north-west coast, probably to the very Suvla Bay at which British troops were to make their fateful landing in 1915.[10] Just behind it lies a big salt lake, surely the lake to which Homer made Poseidon go in order to harness two of his horses in his golden palace beneath its waters. They were gold-maned, as horses of the gods usually are: he put gold on himself too and picked up a whip, also of gold. He then drove his horse-drawn chariot over the waves without so much as wetting its bronze axle. In a marvellous scene, dolphins frolicked on all sides beneath it and the sea parted in delight.[11] He stopped it at a broad cave between the islands of Tenedos and Imbros, just off the entrance, therefore, to the Hellespont, the modern Dardanelles. In it he unharnessed his horses, gave them ambrosia to eat and shackled them with fetters, yet again of gold. Then he went on alone to the bay in which the Greek fleet was beached: here too his behaviour fits local knowledge. In antiquity Tenedos was a recognized waiting point for boats wanting to travel on up through the difficult sea current into the Hellespont: Poseidon abandoned his sea chariot just where sailors stopped and waited for favourable conditions.

Like the view from Samothrace to Troy, Poseidon's detailed progress rests on personal knowledge of the area. Sailors might perhaps
have told Homer about the exact stops which he then worked into
the god's journey, but they were most unlikely to have climbed the
highest mountain on Samothrace, Mount Fengari (5250 feet high),
and discovered from there that there was a view to far-off Troy and
beyond. That view was most readily grasped at Troy itself by looking
back to the peak of Samothrace, as Kinglake discovered. Homer's
placing of Poseidon on Mount Fengari is fitted to his need of the
moment, to match him with Zeus, his rival, who is also sitting on a
mountain peak, one on Ida. The placing was not traditional, and to
contrive it Homer used a detail which was not a fantasy: it had been
grasped at Troy, surely by Homer, who needed it.

While there, he would have seen ruins of an earlier Troy town,
and in the plain beyond it he would have seen some prehistoric
mounds, cues, perhaps, for mounds which he named and placed
there in his poem. He refers to landmarks like the 'tomb of Ilos',
mentioned on three occasions, or the 'tomb of old Aisyetes' on
which a Trojan watched for the first advance of the Greek army.
They have been identified quite plausibly with mounds still visible
near Troy which conform to other topographic clues in the poem.[12]
They are highly relevant to where and how he composed, but I will
limit my discussion to major features, the siting of the Greeks' camp
and ships, the major rivers in the plain and three important vantage
points for divine spectators.

Homer presents the Greek ships as beached and the Greeks as
encamped not far from Troy. He locates their camp by the Hellespont, whose water, to the north of Troy, is indeed still visible from
the hill on which Troy's citadel stands. The modern view to it from
Troy is flat and dispiriting, but there is a reason: the intervening plain
is the result of silting by nearby rivers. In antiquity Troy was much
nearer the Hellespont's shore: this important point was already
made *c.* 200 BC by an authoress, Hestiaea, though nothing more is
known about her, except that she drew mistaken conclusions from
it.[13] Nineteenth-century travellers to the Troad recognized it too,

exemplified in 1867 by the detailed book of George Nicolaides, a cosmopolitan Cretan, who estimated from the ancient geographer Strabo's text that the silt must have advanced a metre each year: he even calculated that it had added 3000 metres since the Trojan war, supposedly 3000 years earlier.[14] In August 1868, his book guided a visitor with a future, Heinrich Schliemann, who was soon to excavate Troy itself: he remarked in his personal diary that the sea had once come far inland, as was obvious from the 'many marshes' and 'many pools of stagnant water' on the plain.[15]

Since 1980, modern scientific study, passing over these predecessors, has established that the sea came far closer in to Troy in antiquity and that what is now flat plainland between two promontories was once its water, flanked by two narrow promontories jutting into it. After renewed debate it is clear that this reconstruction of the coast is correct.[16] It throws important light on the Iliad's underlying topography. In Homer's mind, the place where he presented the Greek fleet lay just below the more westerly of the two promontories, the Sigeum promontory. In 1998 a life-long scholar and student of the terrain, John Luce, proposed convincingly that the Greeks' camp should be imagined on the slope of this promontory where it runs down to what came to be known in modern times as the Lisgar marsh. The marsh was drained in the 1960s, but in antiquity it was probably a lagoon just off the main sea, a suitable harbour for a fleet.[17]

This location for the Greeks has a major consequence for the fighting which follows. Traditionally it has been envisaged as occurring from north to south, from the main shore of the bay where the Greeks were beached towards Troy and its walls on its hill. On the contrary, it ran from west, the Greek position by the Sigeum promontory, to east, Troy and its plain. This location also explains how the Greek army could be imagined as coming out to fight on part of a flat killing field divided in two by the major river Scamander.[18] To the east of the river lay another part of the plain, the one in front of Troy. From book 20 onwards, Achilles, fighting furiously, forces his way across the resistant Scamander and then pursues the Trojans as they run in terror towards their city. The Scamander indeed flowed across the Greeks' line of advance, a point which other theories of their camp's location have failed to accommodate.

Of course, Homer was exaggerating poetically when he numbered the Greek ships as more than a thousand: the bay beside the Sigeum promontory could never have held so many. He has been imagined as 'pacing along the beach' to calculate how many ships could have been drawn up there in rows, but I do not believe that he conducted such prosaic research when on site.[19] He looked and no doubt listened to any local Greek-speakers whose stories accounted for specific features in their landscape. He did not see, draw or imagine a map: maps did not exist in his lifetime. He did not even take notes: I do not believe he could write. He made his poem, blending poetic licence with an underlying sense of the terrain as he remembered it.

The major river in his poem is the Scamander. Homer names it correctly, but remarks that the gods call it Xanthus. Divine second names in the Iliad seem to refer to alternative names applied, admittedly by humans, to one and the same feature: Xanthus means 'tawny yellow', suiting a river whose water flows swiftly in places through sandy banks.[20] From the 1780s onwards, many travellers' maps misidentified it while trying to fit it to their mistaken location for Troy. The Scamander is plainly the modern Karamenderes Çayı, which flows from Mount Ida in the south, on through sandy banks during its lower course and then to the sea just beyond Troy's true site.[21]

In book 21 the god Hephaestus begins a blazing fire to force the flooding Scamander river back off the plain and into its banks:

> The elms were burning and the willows and the tamarisks,
> Burning too was the lotus and reeds and *kypeiros*,
> All of which grew profusely round the fair streams of the river.

Elm bushes, willows and tamarisks have often been sighted by delighted modern visitors to the Scamander, who take them to show

38

that Homer preceded them, but they also grow by other rivers locally, let alone by rivers in Greece.[22] The lotus was probably a type of clover and the *kypeiros* probably galingale, a type of sedge, but neither is conspicuous along the Menderes. They recur elsewhere in Homer's verse and are surely poetic choices, ones fit for a damp place.[23]

Scamander's rapid flooding of the plain is more pertinent: it was given a plausible context by the first Anglo-Irishman to go to Troy with a copy of the Iliad as a companion. In 1750, Robert Wood, classicist and tutor, travelled observantly in the area thanks to the sponsorship, again, of London's patrician Dilettanti Society, of which he eventually became a member. During his visit he correctly inferred from the course which the upper river had cut through a deep gorge that it had sometimes run with great force: he also learned that it still flooded the plain lower down its course when it rose very high in late spring.[24] The river has indeed had a long history of rising rapidly there by three or four metres and all but drowning those in its way: in 14 BC it nearly disposed of Julia, the daughter of the Roman emperor Augustus, when she and her slaves were trying to cross it on a January night.[25]

In August 1868, Schliemann, on site, remarked in his diary on the presence 'of so many storks here due to the floods of the Skamander and the Simois which create large areas of marshland crawling with frogs and snakes'.[26] Homer was certainly aware that the depth and force of the Scamander vary. In book 24, during Priam's journey to intercede with Achilles, he and his driver stop to allow their mules and horses to drink in it.[27] The Scamander's water, therefore, was low again after its sudden flood: in summer it indeed flows at a level from which animals can easily drink.

Scamander's flooding and shrinking are only one example of Homer's information about local rivers. Once, in book 12, he names eight of them in the Troad, most of which are readily matchable to later evidence.[28] They might perhaps have been known to him through previous poets, but he also makes special mention of the river Simoeis, evidently the modern Dümrek Su. In book 5 he presents the goddess

Hera as driving her horses and chariot to Troy and unharnessing them where the rivers Simoeis and Scamander meet, whereupon the Simoeis sends up ambrosia for her horses to graze on.[29] The passage is a charming blend of the poetic and the real. Heavenly ambrosia never grew along the real Simoeis, but the river indeed merged with the Scamander. At present it does so just beyond the northern flank of Troy, at a point which would be too close to the city for the anti-Trojan goddesses to have readily parked their horses. The rivers have changed course since antiquity, but they never met at a greater distance from Troy. It seems that Homer remembered their confluence and specified it because it was a suitably lush place for Hera's divine horses to be left to graze, but transposed it to suit his context. Here, poetic need overrode exactness.

In a famous passage in book 22, exact topography also gives way to poetic effect. Achilles pursues Hector beyond the walls of Troy and during their run they reach 'two fair flowing springs' which 'spurt up from the eddying Scamander', either as its sources or as water fed from it below: Homer tells us that

> One flows with warm water and round it smoke
> Comes into being from it as if from burning fire,
> But the other in summer flows like hail or cold snow
> or ice on water.[30]

About six miles south of Troy, near the base of a hill beside the modern village of Pinarbaşhi, Robert Wood was the first modern traveller to discover that there were hot springs up in the hills: indeed they bubble up, being known in Turkish as 'forty eyes'.[31] Two pools, fed by them, were especially conspicuous. In the 1780s Count Choiseul-Gouffier, the French ambassador to Istanbul, followed up his secretary's identification of these springs with Homer's and had the temperature of two of them measured: he claimed that one was found to be hot, the other to be 30°F colder. Subsequent testers have never confirmed this measurement.[32] Much has been written on the problem, as if Homer knew one deep spring-fed pool

which was cold in summer and another shallower one which sometimes gave off vapour in winter. Perhaps he intensified the contrast
of their temperatures, possibly through a misunderstanding, certainly to make them more vivid in his narrative.

Their siting is more problematic. At such a distance from Troy
they are hard to reconcile with Homer's account of Achilles' pursuit
of Hector and its relation to the city itself, as if the two of them
began by running out for about six miles to Pinarbaşhi and then
looped back as if on a racecourse to approach the walls on the east
side of Troy after another six-mile run.[33] A more plausible answer is
that he knew of the springs, which were indeed a striking feature,
and transposed them nearer to Troy so as to include them in Achilles' pursuit and use them for poetic effect. Brilliantly, he linked them
to two fine washing troughs of stone nearby

> Where the wives and fair daughters of the Trojans used to
>   wash their shining clothes
> In the days of peace, before the sons of the Achaeans came.

This exquisite reference to the past added pathos to the present. In
the late 1960s, the present was still adding pathos to the past: 'the
temperature of the water is convenient for washing clothes', a
meticulous topographer of the Troad, John Cook, observed, 'and
women still flock in great numbers both for that purpose and to
rinse their grain before grinding'.[34]

Although Homer has moved and enhanced these two springs,
they show an underlying knowledge of real features in the terrain,
ingredients in his poetic mix. Two cardinal landmarks exemplify it.
They give shape to book 20 when the gods come down to the battle
in the plain before Troy. As their engagement begins, Ares, god of
war, loudly shouts in order to urge on the Trojans from the top of
Troy's citadel and 'then shouted too, as he ran along the Simoeis
river to Kallikolone'.[35] Soon after, Ares, Apollo and the pro-Trojan
gods are sitting on Kallikolone's brow: 'clearly', remarks the major
English commentary on book 20 and its mentions of Kallikolone,

'his invention (?) stayed in the poet's mind'.[36] There was no such invention. The name means Fair Hill, and later Greek topographers identified it with a steep hill, the modern Kara Tepe, which exists about five miles east of Troy. It rises uniquely there above the course of the Simoeis river, which Poseidon followed to reach it from Troy, and it fits Homer's verses very well. 'Rising to a height of 676 feet, the summit stands out from its surroundings and forms an easily recognizable landmark in its immediate neighbourhood', observes John Luce, who also answers the objection that Troy's citadel is not visible from its summit: Kara Tepe's 'pine-clad slopes', he writes, 'merge into the dark background of the higher . . . range behind. But . . . I can testify from personal observation that the flat summit ridge . . . provides an excellent platform from which to view . . . Troy and the surrounding flood plains of the Scamander and the Simoeis.'[37]

Meanwhile on the other side of the battlefield pro-Greek Athena shouted loudly too, sometimes beside the ditch in front of the Greek camp, at other times on the 'loudly sounding headlands'. Then Zeus thundered on Mount Ida, and Poseidon, also on earth, started an earthquake which shook Troy and caused Hades, god of the underworld, to fear that his subterranean kingdom would be revealed. This tremendous scene has an awesome grandeur which the ancient critic Longinus well appreciated, as did Alexander Pope in his stately translation of the Iliad, published in 1716:

> Above, the Sire of Gods his Thunder rolls
> And Peals on Peals redoubled rend the Poles.
> Beneath, stern Neptune shakes the solid Ground,
> The Forests wave, the Mountains nod around;
> Thro' all their Summits tremble Ida's Woods,
> And from their Sources boil her hundred Floods

and so on, Pope continues, down to the 'dismal Regions of the Dead'.[38]

Soon after this earthquake, Poseidon took the pro-Greek gods uphill to sit on a mounded wall or fort which had been built in the past, says Homer, to protect Heracles from a sea-monster. In the 1780s Choiseul-Gouffier identified this refuge with Kesik Tepe, a natural mound about forty feet high on the once-narrow Sigeum promontory, where it looks down on the likeliest siting of the Greek fleet.[39] It also looks out westwards onto the Aegean Sea beyond the promontory's edge, matching the 'loudly sounding headlands' above which Athena was already sitting. Homer may have invented the explanatory story about Heracles, but I suspect it was already being told locally and he heard it.

On this fort, the pro-Greek gods 'wreathed an unbroken cloud around their shoulders' and watched the battlefield below, while on the other side, Ares and the pro-Trojan gods sat and watched on Kallikolone. It is not just that Homer framed the battle with individual locations which relate to real landmarks on site. One such relation might be a coincidence, but two are less likely to be so: the important point is that he interrelated them correctly, one to the west, the other to the east of the battlefield, presenting their distances from it correctly too.

When he refers to Troy's hinterland to the south of the city, he is aware of its rich fertility along the Scamander's middle course. He places old Dardania, Troy's forerunner, there, and credits Aeneas' ancestors in Dardania with 2000 horses, pastured in marshy grassland: this well-watered land was indeed a haven for horses and horse-breeding and remained so throughout antiquity.[40] It lies where the foothills of Ida's mountain range begin and here too Homer is aware of aspects of the terrain. He makes Trojan Agenor consider whether to run off there and hide in its thickets in order to escape Achilles: the lower slopes of the north face of Ida's range are indeed well covered with bushes. He refers to Aeneas herding flocks there when Achilles formerly came upon him and chased him, nearly to death: Ida's lower slopes are still an apt terrain for flocks and herdsmen. Correctly he refers to Ida's 'many springs' and calls it the 'mother of wild beasts', as indeed its forests still are, with a long history of leopards, jackals and bears.[41]

When Homer refers to the Idaean mountains, he sometimes means the entire range which marks the southern boundary of the

Trojan plain and then runs up to the north-east, but he is specific about a peak on its western end, Gargaron.[42] In book 8 Zeus came from Olympus to sit there, the site of a 'sanctuary and fragrant altar to him': he 'poured much mist around' and sat there to watch events at Troy. Gargaron was to be his main vantage point during the next nine books, broken only by two brief visits to the other gods on Olympus.

The highest peak in the Idaean mountains is Ida, about 5800 feet high, above Dardania, but Zeus did not station himself there. Instead, he sat near the western edge of the range, where later Greek authors locate Gargaron and modern topography identifies it with the Grey Rock, Koca Kaya, 2546 feet high and readily credited with a mountain-top sanctuary to Zeus. On a clear day it has a fine view back across the Trojan plain to Troy and the Hellespont.[43]

Among the trees and flora of Ida's north-facing slope and the plain across to Troy are distinctive varieties of oak and fir and some impressive pines and beech trees. Homer has been credited with noticing these differences, after coming up over Ida's heights from the warmer zone further south along the Aegean coast.[44] There are indeed no olive trees in his Troad, but his references to trees are too general to have required his own close observation: he places an oak tree near Troy but gives nothing to identify it as the distinctive Trojan type of oak. More suggestive, but less realized, is the flora he evokes on Gargaron.

In a marvellous episode in book 14, Zeus is seduced by his artful wife Hera there:

> He clasped his wife in his arms
> And beneath them the earth grew newly flourishing grass
> And dewy lotus and crocus and hyacinth
> Thick and soft which kept them above the ground.

In order to hide them while they made love, Zeus clothed himself and Hera in an impenetrable cloud of gold, from which fell drops of dew, evidently the encouragement for this carpet.[45] At the end of book 7 he had sent thunder and lightning, but not rain. These drops are the first moisture in the poem which Zeus sends onto the earth.

On the slopes leading up to Gargaron, carpets of a superb yellow crocus, the true *Crocus gargaricus*, still appear in spring, specific to this one site. They are followed by blue grape hyacinths and scillas, hyacinths for the ancient Greeks. Nowhere else does Homer mention crocuses or hyacinths in the Iliad: they are not a recurring traditional phrase for him. A post-Homeric poet credits Aphrodite, goddess of love, with 'crocus and hyacinth' among the flowers she wears, but he has imitated the phrase from Homer's verse.[46] In Homer's pre-coital carpet dewy lotus also appeared from the ground, probably a form of clover and certainly a plant suited to damp soil watered by heavenly dewdrops: it is not now present on the dry limestone plateau near Gargaron, the home, rather, to swathes of purple-flowered vetch and a yellow flax and a pink woodruff, both endemic to it.[47] The carpet which kept the heavenly lovers from the ground was a miraculous one, but I still think that Homer included crocuses in it because he had heard of, even seen, Gargaron's carpet of golden crocuses, a heavenly sight indeed.

In the Odyssey, Odysseus recounted his momentous journey among hazards and monsters, the Cyclops, the sirens and so forth. In antiquity, later admirers then tried to locate them at points in Sicily and along the Italian coast: they were mistaken, because the journey was a journey into neverland. There is fiction in the Iliad's topography too: it presents Achilles as the leader of warrior Myrmidons, but no place or land of Myrmidons has ever been located in the real world. Wary of mistaking fiction for fact, translations of the Iliad tend not to provide a map of the Troad and its surrounds: for many years, I admit, I read the poem's beginning and considered Chryse to be an island. In its subsequent books I had a vague idea of Mount Ida, Zeus' vantage point, as somewhere to the south-east of Troy. However, at the centre of the action stands a real city, attested long before Homer, and it is implausible to regard the other landmarks around it as inventions, only later fixed on the terrain by people who had been fascinated by the poem. It was set in a real landscape which grounded it. These landmarks and their interrelations are present because Homer had seen or heard about them, not just from previous poems, but from a personal visit. They fed into his sense of the space which he presented, though poetic licence sometimes reduced distances or enhanced the size of fleets and armies.

In book 20 Trojan Aeneas advances to do battle with rampaging Achilles and answers his fearsome opponent's taunts. He gives a long account of his own ancestry but is about to be set on and killed until the god Poseidon intervenes. It is fated, Poseidon says, for the line of Aeneas' ancestors not to perish and so

> 'the might of Aeneas will indeed rule over Trojans
> And his sons' sons whoever are born hereafter.'

This prophecy of future rule for a family is unique in the poem.[48] It is much discussed, and scholars have often read it as evidence that it was Homer's way of honouring a family who claimed descent from Aeneas and ruled in the Troad in his own lifetime. They were not the patrons who inspired the whole poem and its first performance: they had to wait until five-sixths of it was finished before they received this one oblique compliment. They may have patronized Homer on an earlier occasion: we happen to know from a later local author that self-styled descendants of Aeneas lived and ruled at Scepsis in the Troad, at least *c.* 170 BC.[49] In earlier times an earlier Scepsis, 'old Scepsis', had been sited on a high hill on the edge of Mount Ida's north-facing slopes, overlooking, therefore, the middle Scamander, the site of the Dardania of Aeneas' ancestors. The very hill has been firmly located at İkizce, about 800 metres high, where evidence of occupation in the Bronze Age *c.* 1300 BC has also been found.[50] If Homer once stayed and sang for Greek-speaking members of the ruling family there, his grasp of features of the mountain behind and the horse-pasturing grass in front are readily explicable.

Throughout antiquity, Greek poetry and cult show a strong connection to particular sites and landscapes in the real world. The Iliad already exemplifies it. Homer had visited windy Troy on a clear day when distant Samothrace was visible. He had identified vantage points for the gods and visited them too on either side of the bay on whose shore he placed the Greek ships. I like to think he had walked south, like Chryses, beside the shore of the booming sea and come to the promontory called Chryse and to the sanctuary a little way inland where, for him, Chryses was the priest of Apollo. From there, I take him in my mind's eye on an uphill walk for several hours on a crisp day in early spring, up through the crocuses which were carpeting the slopes with gold below Gargaron and on to the foot of its grey peak, where he stopped, checked the view back to Troy and made an offering to Zeus.

These details went into the poetic mix which resulted in his poem. When he composed he was not just manipulating traditional phrases and episodes. He worked with an underlying sense of place which related to his own life. It runs through what we now read, affecting judgements of the poem's unity.

4.

Homer's Heartland

Throughout antiquity, from the early Near East to Christian Egypt, poets were not tied to one place.[1] They travelled and wandered, a pattern to which Homer was no exception. He went to Troy and looked and listened, but the visit does not fix his whereabouts when he composed and performed his masterpiece.

Wherever he was born, the most obvious clue to his intended audience might seem to be the dialect he used. Of course, he knew that his Achaeans spoke a common language, Greek. Long before he composed, it had split into various mutually intelligible dialects, Ionic, Doric and so forth. Most of the Iliad's language combines the Greek of two dialects, Ionic and Aeolic. Ionic's users included some of the islands of the east Aegean and some of the Greek settlements on the adjoining coast of modern Turkey. Aeolic's users included the east Aegean island of Lesbos and Asia's north-west corner, the Troad. This mixture of dialects is compatible with a Homer who composed and performed in western Asia or on a nearby island or in the Troad itself, but it does not fix him at work there. It was a traditional mixture for heroic poetry and might have been used by an epic poet who was composing and performing elsewhere.[2]

Traces of a particular type of Ionic would be more revealing. Examples of what some call west Ionic have been detected in the Iliad and sometimes taken to imply that the poem crystallized in a west Ionian context, perhaps even on Euboea, the long island off the coast of Attica, west indeed of Asia's Ionian coastline.[3] Euboeans were certainly very prominent in the ninth and eighth centuries BC, when they travelled north, east and west across the Aegean and

Adriatic seas. A coastal settlement on Euboea might seem an attractive place for Homer to have composed and performed, among the
well-connected families whose wide-ranging contacts continue to
be revealed by archaeology.[4]

There is a suggestive detail in a simile. As the Greek army begins
to march out to battle for the first time, Homer compares the sound
of the ground, resonating beneath its feet, to the sound of the earth
on faraway Arima, where, 'they say', is the bed of monstrous Typhon,
tossing and turning when lashed by Zeus. Arima is the early name
for the volcanic island of Ischia, just off the Bay of Naples. As the
Greeks who settled there were Euboeans, the force of 'they say' is
relevant: does it convey authority or uncertainty? It tends to apply
to people other than its poet's immediate audience and if it does
so here, it implies that the poet was not himself from Euboea and
was not composing among Euboeans, some of whom would have
known this detail directly.[5]

There are other strong arguments against a Euboean venue. A
contingent from seven Euboean towns is mentioned in the Iliad's
catalogue of the Greek ships which travelled to Troy, but it is only
one contingent among many and Euboeans play no important role
in the poem. On the contrary, the first Greek warrior to die in it is
Elephenor, leader of the Euboean troops: he is killed while trying to
drag off a dead Trojan, one whom another Greek hero has just
speared.[6] If the poem was composed for Euboean listeners, their
heroes would have made a more glorious showing. Only three west
Ionic forms have been convincingly diagnosed in the entire Iliad, a
very small haul in a poem of such length, and they can be explained
in a different way.[7] Migrants from Euboea settled far and wide,
including on the island of Chios.[8] West Ionic forms might derive
from Euboean settlers abroad: they do not imply that the Iliad is a
poem composed on Euboea itself. Among all the places which
claimed in antiquity to be Homer's home, Euboea, tellingly, never
featured.

Stronger evidence for the location of Homer and his audience
lies in some of the Iliad's similes, or extended comparisons. 'As

when . . .' they begin: they were not intended to evoke faraway fantasy places. They were comparing items or qualities in the poem with items known to Homer and to many of his first listeners. At the beginning of book 9, he says in a simile that the north-and-west wind blows suddenly down from Thrace (modern Bulgaria), stirring the waves into crests and causing them to wash seaweed onto the shore. They only blow to this effect for someone to the south-east of Thrace on the coast of Asia. While there, Robert Wood noticed the particular force of the north-west wind at Smyrna and found its effects were well known to the inhabitants, some of whom had built their houses with balconies to take advantage of it.[9] As he later remarked in his book of 1770, he inferred that Homer knew this wind and its force because he knew this coastline personally and even, Wood thought, the very bay at Smyrna itself.

Homer locates several other similes explicitly on or near Asia's Aegean coast, three of which repay a closer look. They are well-known evidence, but their full value lies in their detail, more so than is sometimes realized. In book 2, Agamemnon tests the assembled Greek soldiers' morale by proposing a return home, which promptly stirs their hearts:

> The meeting was moved like long waves of the sea,
> The Icarian sea, waves which the south-east wind
> Rouses, rushing onto them from the clouds of father Zeus.

This simile is the second long one in the poem.[10] After Homer, the next evidence we have for the Icarian sea and its extent is from Herodotus, composing his *Histories* c. 450–425 BC. When he describes the progress of the Persian invaders' fleet across the Aegean in 490 BC, culminating in the battle of Marathon, he locates the Icarian sea to the south and south-west of the island of Samos, off Asia's western coast, running past the island of Icaria there and on to Naxos, Delos and other islands of the Cyclades. To the south and west of Icaria the sea is indeed deep and often turbulent.[11] The south-east wind in Homer's simile is not the *meltemi* of the summer months which blows down only from the north. It is the wind most prevalent in winter, a rough time for anyone at sea here. The simile is localized and exact: Homer knew this sea and the winter wind either from personal experience or from sailors who were familiar with them and he assumed that many of his listeners would know of them too. They were readily accessible to people in the east Aegean, on or off the coast of Asia from, say, Ephesus down to Miletus.

In book 20, rampaging Achilles spears a Trojan warrior through the back, making him

> gasp out his life and bellow, as when a bull
> Bellows as it is dragged around the Heliconian king,
> Young men dragging it, and the Shaker of the Earth delights
> in them [or 'in these things'].

The Heliconian king here is the god Poseidon, shaker of the earth, and although Homer gives no further indication, the historian Herodotus states in another context that Heliconian Poseidon was worshipped collectively by the Ionians on Mount Mycale, also in western Asia.[12] The west end of its range runs to the Aegean coast just opposite Samos: Homer is most likely to refer to a bull being offered there by Ionian worshippers. The Icarian sea beyond Samos is visible too from Mount Mycale's higher peaks.

About 300 verses after his simile of the wind and sea, Homer compares the sound and numbers of the advancing Greek army to the clatter of hordes of geese and swans as they alight in the Asian meadow near the mouth of the river Cayster. The clatter made by these birds is exactly observed and this Asian meadow was famous. It lay by a rivermouth on the coast just west of ancient Ephesus, also in Ionia, just up the coast from Mount Mycale. Greeks who landed there extended the name for it to the entire continent of Asia.[13]

Even from a cursory reading of these similes, almost every modern scholar agrees that Homer was most at home on or near the Aegean coast of this part of western Asia: the details I have specified make it all but certain. Two further allusions support the inference. In the poem's last book, in a fine speech to old Priam, Achilles refers to Niobe grieving for her children, slain by Apollo and the goddess Artemis:

> 'And now somewhere among the rocks and among the lonely
>   mountains,
> On Sipylos, where they say are the couches of the goddesses,
> Of the nymphs who dance nimbly round the river Achelēsios,
> There, though stone, she broods on cares sent from the gods.'

This location for Niobe and her myth was prompted by awareness of an ancient Hittite rock sculpture, visible above the road from coastal Smyrna which runs inland past Mount Sipylos near modern Manisa.[14] By a creative misunderstanding, Greeks interpreted the sculpture as their legendary heroine Niobe, turned to stone. In these beautiful verses Homer makes Achilles qualify some of his allusion to it by 'they say', but the reference is ultimately the poet's own, to an item just north-east of Smyrna and no more than twenty-five miles from the Aegean coast. He even knows the name of the nearby river, the Achelesios, an exact little detail which most of the later manuscripts of his text failed to transmit correctly.[15]

Four books earlier, he had made Achilles refer to two rivers inland while he addressed a Trojan whose head he had split in two by a cast of his huge spear: sarcastically he told him, as he lay dead before him: 'here is your death, but your lineage is by the Gygaean lake where your ancestral estate is too, by the fishy Hyllos and the eddying Hermos'.[16] Indeed, fish still abound in the Hyllos, the modern Çam Çayı and the Hermos is still turbulent, the modern Gedez, both flowing near gloomy Lake Marmara Gölü, the ancients' Gygaea, just north of Sardis in ancient Lydia.[17] They are the most easterly places mentioned in the Iliad but they are hardly sixty miles inland from the Aegean coast.

Taken together, these exact details imply that Homer composed and performed for listeners in or very near Ionia on the Aegean coast of what is now Turkey. After visiting Troy further north, he returned to what his similes imply to be a heartland for himself and his first listeners. As the poem's fame spread and others further afield heard it, they enjoyed it without the same local knowledge, but these detailed examples had been Homer's choices, aimed at first audiences for whom they were familiar.

One group of protagonists suggests a contact even further down the coast. Two of the most memorable allies, fighting with the Trojans, are Glaucus and Sarpedon, leaders of troops from Lycia, down in the south-west corner of Asia. On his first appearance in the poem, Sarpedon tells Hector:

> 'Indeed being an ally I have come from very far away –
> For far off is Lycia by the eddying Xanthus,
> Where I left my dear wife and infant son . . .'

Twice in these verses, he stresses Lycia's faraway location: why are he and his Lycians prominent in several books of the poem?[18]

One reason is their very distance from Troy and the perspective it gives. Like Achilles, also from faraway Thessaly, their leaders, outsiders at Troy, reflect on life and heroism and threaten to abandon the war they have joined.[19] Yet, more than poetic potential was involved. One attempt at an explanation looks to the far-distant Bronze Age, *c.* 1450 BC, when texts of the Hittites seem to show that Lycians, men from what the Hittites called Lukka land, had fought together with Trojans in a grand alliance, not against Greeks, however, but against a Hittite army, the ruling power in western Asia.[20] Their prominence in the Iliad has sometimes been explained by this distant past and also by supposing that Lycians had a secondary homeland up near Troy. However, this second home is a modern misunderstanding and Homer is extremely unlikely to have heard from anyone at Troy in his lifetime that Lycians had once fought beside Trojans up to 700 years earlier.[21] Their role in the Iliad is due to contacts made many centuries later, much nearer Homer's own time.

LYCIANS

53

In book 6, Glaucus, a Lycian, speaks memorably about his ancestry and its noble links with the land ruled by Greek Argos. His tale becomes highly allusive and seems to presuppose a more detailed story known to Homer and perhaps to some of his hearers. It is quite likely to relate to a tale told in detail in Lycia itself. So may another Lycian exploit, narrated just before. In book 5 the other main Lycian hero, Sarpedon, wins a duel with an enemy from the island of Rhodes. It was a contest of super-heroes indeed, Sarpedon being the son of Zeus and his Rhodian opponent Tlepolemus a son of Heracles: Sarpedon duly killed Tlepolemus, but was wounded and taken out of the battle.[22]

This episode explains why Sarpedon does not feature for another ten books in the Iliad, but it sits rather oddly in a part of the poem which is mostly given to exploits of the Greek hero Diomede. It can be detached and removed without damaging the main action's flow and it too can be related to important concerns of the Lycians.[23] The island of Rhodes lies just to the south-west of Lycia and was frequently a hostile neighbour in later history. A tale of a Lycian's victory over a Rhodian super-hero would have been much to the liking of a Lycian audience. Rhodians also claimed a special relation to Greek Argos but Glaucus' claim to this relation was even older: it too would be much to the liking of Lycians, as would other interconnections now in our Iliad.

In book 16 Sarpedon dies, distressing his father Zeus, who rains tears of blood, his only rain in the poem's main plot. Zeus then specifies a series of rites for the dead Lycian which are unique in the poem: Apollo is to take him far away, bathe him in the streams of a river, anoint him with ambrosia, clothe him in immortal robes and then give him to two escorts, Sleep and Death, who will take him away to Lycia, where his brothers and kin will bury him with a tomb and pillar, 'for that is the privilege of the dead'.[24] It is as if Homer knows about a tomb of Sarpedon in Lycia near the Xanthus river and has fitted it into his poem.

Like the compressed tale of Glaucus' ancestry and Sarpedon's heroic victory over the Rhodian super-hero, Homer may have heard these details down in Lycia during a visit to one or other settlement in the river Xanthus' valley. I do not think that language was a barrier. In that valley people spoke Lycian, but as the thrust of the Iliad's tale of Glaucus implies, there were probably already those who could also speak Greek, the language used on their local coins when they first began to strike them in the early fifth century BC. I like to imagine Homer looking out from the acropolis of Tlos, the 'rock of the Titan', as it was later called. With its sweeping view across the plain beside the river Xanthus, Tlos, or Tlawa in Lycian, would have given him a prospect of Sarpedon's eventual resting place and the land which had once been his estate. A Lycian family was not the patron of the entire Iliad, as Lycians feature memorably in only four of its books, but in honour of his visit Homer may have worked Lycians and tales he had heard from them into his poem.[25]

Their presence in it then inspired the Iliad's heirs. In the late sixth century BC, the Athenian painter and potter Euphronios, one of the pioneers of his age, put a scene of the dying Sarpedon, attended by Sleep and Death, on one face of his masterpiece, a huge Attic vase, exported to Etruscan Italy.[26] In the river Xanthus' valley, Lycians, inspired by Homer, claimed close kinship with his heroes and even with the poet himself. There may have been another reason for Homer to have dwelt on them. According to Herodotus, writing *c.* 450–425 BC, some of the first kings in the Ionian cities along Asia's Aegean coastline were descendants of Lycian Glaucus.[27] People from these Ionian cities were likely to have been the Iliad's first listeners, and if their sense of kinship with Glaucus pre-existed the Iliad, rather than being derived from it, the poem's memorable role for him may well relate to it.

From the Troad to Lycia, Homer's travels, I believe, have left an imprint on his poem. References in its similes imply he composed and performed it somewhere between, say, Ephesus and Miletus, for hearers familiar with the details they presented. To narrow down the occasion and place yet further, the length of Homer's poem, its continuity and its coherence are our best guides. So I will turn from hills and rivers to basic features which pervade it.

5.

Unstitching the Iliad

Before assessing the poem's coherence, the action in it needs to be summarized. After quarrelling with Agamemnon and losing his prize Briseis, Achilles withdraws from the fighting. Eventually the Greeks begin to be hard pressed by the Trojans in battle and Agamemnon relays to Achilles an offer of gifts, including Briseis. Achilles, still furious, refuses them. The Trojans, led by their best warrior, Hector, then break into the Greeks' camp and wound the Greek champions. Achilles, still aloof, sends his beloved companion Patroclus to find out who has been wounded. Patroclus is moved by his fellow Greeks' plight, returns and as Hector begins to burn some of the Greek ships begs to be allowed to go into battle. Achilles allows him to go, dressed in his own armour, but tells him not to attempt to take Troy itself. Patroclus goes too far and is killed by Hector. Achilles then returns in a rage to the battle, seeking revenge, and eventually kills Hector outside Troy. He refuses to give back the body and drags it day after day behind his chariot along the seashore. Eventually the gods intervene and Zeus sends an order to him to desist and give back the corpse in return for a ransom. When aged father, king Priam, dares to come out from Troy to Achilles' encampment and ask for it, Achilles obliges him. During a brief truce, Hector is then given a proper funeral, the last episode in the poem. After it the fighting is set to continue.

This brutally minimal summary omits the pervasive role of the gods and all the accompanying scenes, speeches and refinements which give the Iliad its special power. It is simply a means of showing that the plot has a clearly shaped beginning, middle and end. That fact is important, because other long heroic poems, including some composed in Greek, are very different. They are made up of a succession of episodes set loosely one after another: Homer's lesser followers were referred to as the 'and then's by a later Greek poet.[1] The Iliad is not a long 'and then' poem at all.

Even so it has peaks, troughs and inconsistencies. The last three books, from 22 to 24, sustain a masterly variety across some 2000 verses, the finest such run in poetry, but other equally fine books are followed by ones which leave less of an effect. The wondrous book 1 is followed by book 2, in which the action begins by moving in a contorted direction. The sublime return of Hector to Troy and his family in book 6 is followed by book 7, which contains an inconclusive duel, fought in the hope of ending the war, although book 3 had already contained an inconclusive duel fought earlier in the same day for exactly the same purpose.

Up to this point, there has been a prolonged digression from the course of the plan which Zeus had stated in book 1 in response to Thetis: contrary to what he promised her, the Greeks have continued to press the Trojans very hard. Not until the beginning of book 8 do the Trojans begin to drive back the Greeks and kill many of them: only then does Zeus put two lots of death in his golden scales, one for the Trojans, one for the Greeks, and hold the balance until 'down sank the day of doom for the Achaeans'.[2] Until then, the young Argive hero Diomede has been winning glory on the battlefield, guided by the goddess Athena and killing so many Trojans that Hector has had to return to Troy and urge the Trojan women to pray for help. In book 11, Diomede is eventually wounded by Paris with an arrow and then falls out of the battle-scenes, as if all his previous prowess had belonged to a separate storyline.[3]

After the fine scenes in book 9 and the failed attempt to persuade Achilles, books 11–13 may seem to dwell too long on the Trojans' successes and their assault on the Greeks' camp. Book 18 gives an entrancing account of the making of a new shield for Achilles, but is followed by book 19, much of which is widely considered to be rather flat.

Within the main plot there are also inconsistencies, quite apart from the odd course taken by book 2, in which Agamemnon was assured in a deceptive dream sent by Zeus that he would promptly take Troy. As a result he summoned an assembly in order to test the Greeks, in which he proposed exactly the opposite, that they should go home, whereupon they began to try to do so and had to be restrained. In book 9 there is a significant detail, much discussed by scholars.[4] The arrival of the embassy to Achilles is described by a Greek form of the verb, the dual, which requires two subjects. This form is used seven times in seventeen verses, but its subjects, the main ambassadors, are three, not two: it looks as if one of them, Achilles' old tutor Phoenix, has been added later to an original twosome. Achilles refuses their requests, but in books 11 and 16 he appears unaware that the embassy has ever been sent.

These and other difficulties are important for hypotheses about how and where Homer composed. A long line of scholarship has regarded them as evidence of piecemeal composition over many generations. This explanation has implications for the Iliad's first context, as it assumes several stages in its formation, each of which might have addressed different types of occasion. Proponents of it are known as analysts, some of whom regard the Iliad as a patchwork stitched together from separate short songs of which only some were by Homer. Others regard it as a rolling snowball, whose nucleus was composed by Homer, but which grew when others added bits to it over time. Snowballers have sometimes wondered if there was originally an Achilleid by Homer, which others expanded later into an Iliad, with the implication that these additions spoiled the original core. In fact, the two themes cannot be separated so neatly, because Achilles is a constant, brooding presence in the poem, even in physical absence, and the rest of it is not just a poem about Ilion, Troy.

What did readers in antiquity think of this question, being nearer to Homer than we are? Some of them indeed proposed that it was a patchwork. They had no external contemporary evidence, but the most influential exponent of this view was a Greek-speaking Jew, Josephus.[5] Writing polemically *c.* AD 90, he contrasted illiterate

Josephus

Homer, who, 'they say', did not leave his songs in writing, with the literate authors of the Jewish scriptures who had lived far earlier, the earliest such author, he wrongly thought, being Moses. Homer's songs were transmitted by memory, Josephus stated, and only later was a poem put together from them: as a result it 'has many inconsistencies in it'.

Josephus' partisan view was to become very influential because it referred to the Jews' scriptures and therefore impressed later European scholars, to whom those scriptures were extremely important. Their discussions of it began even earlier than modern readers sometimes realize. In the 1560s, a great scholar, Joseph Justus Scaliger, addressed it when he was in Holland.[6] He endorsed Josephus' view, that the poem was a patchwork of orally composed songs. His scholarly equal, Isaac Casaubon, addressed it again in the 1580s and drew an important conclusion: 'if what Josephus says is true, that Homer did not leave his poems in written form, but that they were preserved by memorization and written down much later, then I do not see how we can ever have them in a correct form even if we have the oldest manuscripts. For it is likely that they were written down in a form quite different from that in which they were first composed.'[7] That inference, too, has continued to haunt Homeric studies.

A stitched-up Iliad and a long-evolving Iliad continued to attract scholars, alert to its digressions and inconsistencies. Even in 1907, a variation of the patchwork theory was argued with wonderful force by the impassioned Hellenist Gilbert Murray: he claimed that the Iliad was basically a traditional book, going back to traditions of a remote era, like a book of the Hebrew scriptures, his underlying model. Over many centuries literate poets, he considered, had humanized and expurgated its grosser elements: they had even cut out 'sexual irregularity', including, Murray believed, the practices of 'Sodom and Gomorrah'.[8] Poet after poet worked over its stories and sanitized them, until one of the later ones, 'how great or small a poet matters little', pieced together the old poetry which he had memorized or acquired on scrolls: he 'arranged his scheme to make room for all'.⁹ There had never, therefore, been 'one man of genius' called Homer, a name which poets invented. Instead, there had been short written poems, or lays, including one on Achilles' wrath and another on his refusal of the embassy sent to placate him. The last poet in a long chain simply pieced together what he inherited and produced, in Murray's memorable phrase, 'a Lay with encrusted additions'.

Encrusted or not, the poem has a quality which challenges views of its piecemeal origins and Homer's irrelevancy: it begins in the tenth year of the Trojan war and, in all, its action spans only fifty days.¹⁰ Of them, the first nine cover the opening plague, told in only forty-six verses; another ten are days of truce, quickly told; near the end, nine more contain Achilles' angry mutilation of Hector's corpse, told in nine verses; the last two days contain Hector's funeral and burial, described in a mere twenty verses. Readers can easily miss that the poem focusses intently on no more than twenty days, of which fighting is told in detail on only four. These four account for four-fifths of the poem. They are a structure even more impressive than the delays and ups and downs in the narrative as it moves through them.

The first of these days is the most varied and remarkable day in all poetry. It dawns in book 2, when Agamemnon calls an assembly of the Greek army, and it continues far into book 7. Among much else it includes an inconclusive duel between Menelaus and Paris, a meeting of the gods in their golden hall on Olympus, Agamemnon's review of his commanders and troops, the first fighting and then the prowess of the young Greek hero Diomede while some of the gods participate in the battle. Hector, hard-pressed, leaves to go back to Troy and organize prayers to the goddess Athena, whereupon many readers feel that days, not hours, of fighting have already passed. Yet, they are still in the same day, not because Homer has forgotten to mark time's passing but because he has envisaged the action throughout this one day as a tight sequence. It is not yet near its end.

When Hector arrives in Troy, the women come running to him, to ask for news of their 'sons and brothers and kinsmen and husbands', a harrowing scene narrated with Homer's consummate, eloquent brevity: Hector 'commanded them all, one by one, to go and pray to the gods' but 'for many of them', Homer adds, 'grief had already been sealed'.[11] Hector's visit takes him to his mother Hecuba and then to Helen and ends with an overwhelming scene of parting from his wife Andromache, and their baby son. Back on the battle-field, another duel is then arranged to decide the war, this time one between Hector and Ajax, but it too ends without a winner. The contestants agree to part and afterwards the Greeks and the Trojans each hold meetings to decide what to do next. The Trojans agree on an offer for peace to be sent to the Greeks. Only then does night fall, leaving us to wait to learn if the Greeks will accept it on the following morning.

This one day spans enough in lesser hands for an entire poem. Whenever I read it, I have to keep reminding myself to envisage its remarkably compressed timing. Even so, another day accounts for even more, the action of eight books, a third of the poem: it is the Iliad's own longest day before modern war films made the phrase famous. It runs from book 11 to the end of book 18. Among the twists and turns of its many battles, Homer cuts to and fro from one fight to the next, interrelating them with the utmost skill, like a maestro of film-making before films or cameras existed. This longest day delays the plot but preserves what Aristotle called its almost 'divine' com-pression, a quality which makes the Iliad quite different from long heroic poems elsewhere in the world and their detachable episodes set one after another: some of them begin with their hero's birth and con-tinue with the exploits of his children and then his grandchildren.[12]

Into a very few days Homer compressed what he chose to tell from the story of a ten-year war which had involved countless battles and hundreds of heroes. Artfully, he used two devices, flashbacks into the past and anticipations of the future. He may even have invented them. He deployed them in his protagonists' speeches. From book 2 onwards we know that Troy will fall in the tenth year because a speech by Calchas the prophet flashes us back to an omen which had inti-mated as much when the Greek expedition was waiting to set out.[13]

As a result we know what Trojans in the poem do not. We also know Achilles' brief future: anticipating it, he states in the very first book that he is destined to live only for a short while.[14] These facts about the future are not used to make the rest of the plot a race against time. What they tell us is kept out of its scope. They add pathos to what then unfolds in a sequence, prepared and pre-announced.

In the narrative there are next to no gaps in each of the days on which Homer focusses. Almost always we know what was happening. The main exception is the twenty-third day, when each side, in book 7, collects its dead, beginning at dawn, but twelve verses later the Greeks are building a wall and gates while another dawn is about to break. The reason is that this day is a truce, lacking heroic individual action, and so it is rapidly covered.[15] Everywhere else in the poem, dawns and nightfalls, eating and sleeping mark the regular passage of time. Smaller marks of time within each day are few: when Helen and Paris re-meet in his bedroom in book 3, how much of the day has passed? They make love, but are they having prime-time sex, in the afternoon?

This mixture of compression and fullness with a strictly controlled use of past and future is not easy to reconcile with theories of the poem as a patchwork. Theories that it grew like a snowball from one poet to the next can cope with it, but only by assuming that each poet respected the tight timescale already present in what he inherited. They have more difficulty with other elements in the poem which are strikingly consistent, its language, its characterization of gods and heroes and, as we will see, its social customs and values. If poets were adding to the poem during many centuries in an ever-changing world, such consistency is very hard to credit. The poem's sense of landmarks and terrain round Troy is also very telling. Not only does it view the battlefield from one direction, the Greeks' camp, and work with a coherent view of its distribution, but where it points to personal knowledge on site, poets adding to an older nucleus would have had to have visited the Troad in order to weave their additions so smoothly into it. Such a sequence of Iliadic visitors to Troy is decidedly implausible.

There is also, as Homer announces, a guiding plan, revealed bit by bit. At the very beginning of the poem, Homer tells us 'the plan of Zeus continued to be fulfilled', but he leaves it undefined there. This plan is his own, ascribed poetically to Zeus, and is gradually revealed during the poem, usually when Zeus is speaking to his wife, the goddess Hera, and thus to us. These gradual revelations are essential evidence for the poem's unity, so I will follow them through.

In the first book Zeus makes that promise to Achilles' mother Thetis that he will honour her son, dishonoured by king Agamemnon, and will help the Trojans, but only until the hard-pressed Greeks honour Achilles. As book 2 begins, Zeus is in bed with Hera, but 'sweet sleep was not taking hold of him': he was pondering how best to honour Achilles and kill many of the Greeks and 'this plan seemed best to him', to mislead Agamemnon with a ruinous dream. In due course many Greeks die in battle as a result. Near the end of book 8 he tells Hera rather more of his plan: he will destroy a great many Greek warriors and Hector will do battle against them until Patroclus, Achilles's beloved companion, is killed.[16] For the first time we learn that Zeus' plan includes a terrible twist for Achilles: the loss of the man he loves most in the world. About 3500 verses later, near the beginning of book 15, Zeus reveals yet more to Hera, that Hector will be roused by the god Apollo to kill many Greeks by their ships, that Achilles will send Patroclus out to fight, that Patroclus will kill many Trojans, including their ally Sarpedon, a son of Zeus, and that Hector will kill Patroclus before the walls of Troy. Thereupon an enraged Achilles will return and kill Hector. Thereafter, Zeus adds, the Greeks will capture Troy 'thanks to the counsels of the goddess Athena'.[17] The poem stops before this capture happens. It never mentions the Wooden Horse.

The poem's story is sufficiently signposted and directed to be called a plot. Book 1 anticipates the main plot until book 9. Book 8 anticipates it until book 19. Book 15 anticipates it until book 22. Together, they imply the guiding hand of a single poet at work, knowing very well where he is heading.

6.

Plotting an Epic

The existence of a plot, gradually unfolding, should not be taken for granted as a natural way for a long poem to proceed. So far as we know, it is one of Homer's great inventions. In a deep investigation of plots in works of fiction, Nick Lowe has recently compared them to 'chess problems revealed a bit at a time . . . the gradual revelation of actual moves, and hints about moves, allows the text to manipulate the reader's developing model of the game as a whole in the linear process of reading.'[1] He considers the Iliad, and the reactions to it of the Odyssey and then Greek tragedy, to be three seminal moments in the emergence and fixing of the entire Western sense of plotting. Without the Iliad, he concludes, that sense might never have developed as it has.[2]

In the Iliad Homer does not set up Achilles against Hector early in the poem, though the two of them will be its ultimate combatants. He presents old Priam in book 3 but gives no hint that he will leave Troy and bring the poem towards its fine conclusion. However, there are many anticipations, not all given directly by Zeus, and they counter any worry that in the middle of the poem Homer was losing his way. In book 9, words by Achilles anticipate the breaking of the wall around the Greeks' camp, which occurs in book 12, and the burning of their ships, which occurs in book 15.[3] Bit by bit, the main deaths in the plot are revealed in advance too. In book 8 the poet makes Zeus reveal to Hera that Patroclus will be killed. In book 11 he anticipates trouble for Patroclus, the next mention we have of it: it is duly realized by his death 3000 verses later. During book 16, as Patroclus asks and prepares to leave for battle, four more comments by the poet anticipate his death: when it occurs at the end of this long book, it is no surprise to listeners.[4] In book 18 Achilles realizes it must have happened, before anyone brings him the news. His mother, he says, once told him that the 'best of the Myrmidons', his followers, would die at the hands of the Trojans while he himself was still alive.[5] It is the first we have heard of this forewarning, but he and we now realize who was 'the best'.

As for Trojan Hector, the superb book 6 in which he returns to Troy and its women leaves us in little doubt that he is going out from the city to his death and will never see his wife and baby son again. We then learn in book 15 from Zeus that he will be killed by Achilles.[6] Later in the same book the poet repeats and amplifies that fact: Hector will not live long now, 'for the goddess Athena was hurrying on for him his day of doom at the might of Peleus' son [Achilles]'.[7] Shortly before Patroclus dies, he loses his helmet, formerly Achilles' own, whereupon Hector is given it by Zeus 'but', we are reminded, 'Hector's death was near'. The dying Patroclus then warns Hector it is near too, at Achilles' hands. Zeus then watches Hector put on the dead Patroclus' armour, but we are reminded again that Zeus knows he is soon to die.[8] Five books later he does so.

Achilles' death is even more artfully signposted. In the first book his mother Thetis observes that he is destined to die young. In book 9 we learn from Achilles himself that he has had the choice of a long life, but without glory, and that he has chosen the very opposite.[9] We still do not know how young he will be. Seven more passages refer to his coming death, giving ever more details as they occur.[10] In book 19 one of Achilles' horses is briefly enabled to speak and tells him he will be killed by a god and man together, but does not say who they will be. In book 21 Achilles remarks that his mother Thetis has told him he will be killed by the weapons of Apollo: the divine agent is now known to us. In book 22 dying Hector then tells him he will be killed by Trojan Paris and the god Apollo by the Scaean gate of Troy. In a gradual sequence, therefore, across thirteen books we have learned when, by whom, with what and, finally, where Achilles will be killed, culminating in details given by Hector as he dies, a climactic moment in Achilles' own wrath and revenge.

I have spelt out these signposts because they imply a single poet at work: readers will find many others, even in translation. They also relate to a general quality of the poem. Sir Ronald Syme, the great Roman historian, used to say that it was the mark of good historians not to be surprised: one event, in context, should enable them to understand another. Long before histories began to be written, the Iliad had eschewed surprise and suspense, except in the games in Patroclus' honour, presented in book 23. Nor does chance play a part, though Balzac once called chance 'the greatest novelist in all the world'.[11] Sometimes, Homer tantalizes us by saying that this or that 'would have happened', but he adds promptly, 'had this or that participant not intervened'. Alternatives are pre-announced, but come to nothing: neither they nor the action are fortuitous. Until book 22 we would never imagine that old Priam would go out on his great mission to Achilles, but when the time for it draws near Homer prepares us for it in advance and, through Zeus, anticipates the outcome before he narrates it.

Throughout the poem there are many smaller connections and patterns, sometimes spanning long sweeps of verse. In book 12 Glaucus, the Lycian, is wounded in his arm by an arrow and then, some 2400 verses later, resumes in book 16 by referring again to this same wound.[12] Even more impressively, Agamemnon is badly wounded in book 11 and after nearly 5500 verses comes with other wounded Greek heroes to a meeting called by Achilles, arriving last of all, hampered by the wound whose giver Homer names exactly.[13] Even smaller sections of battle maintain conspicuous continuity. Early in book 12 Trojan Asios foolishly presses beyond the Greeks' defensive ditch together with several followers, individually named. His death is then narrated nearly 700 verses later, to be followed by the deaths of the remaining three of his followers after yet more verses have passed.[14]

In speeches and in small episodes patterns can be even more intricate. Homer sometimes composes in an encircling ring, ending a speech with the point with which he or the speaker began. In reply a second speaker may take up a previous speaker's points in reverse order.[15] The entire poem, indeed, has been read in this way. The pattern of action in the very first book has similarities to the pattern in the last book. In the first one the goddess Thetis goes up to heaven to plead with Zeus for her son. In the last book she is sent down by Zeus to give her son instructions. Both books contain a twelve-day interval. Both narrate the return of a child to an aged father, though the first child is a captive daughter and the second a dead son. Modern scholars have looked for more such patterns and claimed that the Iliad itself is an example of ring-composition, circling back to end with echoes of how it began. Similarities exist, but I do not think they amount to a ring.[16]

These patterns and anticipations bind most of the Iliad into a unity, but there are two obvious exceptions. Only one book of the poem, the tenth, can be detached without damage to the whole. It tells the story of a raid on the Trojan camp by Odysseus and Diomede and their encounter with a Trojan spy, Dolon. The raid occurs, uniquely, by night. For various reasons, it is rightly regarded as a later addition, not least because the spoils of the raid, the famous horses of Rhesus, never feature again in the poem. Its author has been shown to be familiar with the detailed techniques and vocabulary of the rest of the poem but to depart, significantly, from them.[17] I too will omit this book from my discussions of the Iliad's values, material context and so forth, accepting that it is the work of a later poet, composing, however, by *c.* 600 BC. That date can be deduced from the presence of its otherwise obscure figure, Dolon, in heroic company on a big decorated Greek amphora, or storage vessel, made *c.* 580 BC: he is captioned and shown in a crouching pose which suits his presentation in the Homeric book. The image seems to presuppose Dolon's role in what has become our Iliad.[18]

One other long passage is likely to have been added, the list of Greek ships and commanders who have come to Troy. In our book 2, it follows four fine similes, beginning with one about that perennial hazard, a forest fire, which build up the Greek army's first advance to battle and help us to envisage it. It runs for nearly 270 verses, itemizing the contingents, their homes and leaders. Catalogues sometimes feature in, or as, early Greek poems and this one has its admirers because it does yet more to build up the beginning of the great battle. However, its point of view and its topography point to a different poet at work and I accept the widely held view that it is not by Homer himself and was not in his own poem.[19] It is followed by a brief list of some of the horses on the Greek side and then by a brief list of the Trojans' allies, both likely to be additions too. The catalogue of the Greek ships has sometimes been argued to trace back to distant Mycenaean times, *c.* 1250 BC, five centuries before Homer, but I am one of those who doubt this bold view and prefer to take it as the composition of a poet soon after him, working *c.* 700 BC with traditions about the past from a base in Boeotia, the point from which the catalogue radiates.[20]

In general terms it is a fallacy to assume that unity of design entails a single author, but the rest of the Iliad's plot is so pervasively signposted that a single author is evidently guiding its course. This author is certainly an individual, a 'he', not a long impersonal tradition, an 'it', nor a female 'she': no long Greek heroic poem is ever credited in antiquity to a woman. Topics like Achilles' future death are too artfully revealed to have been added piecemeal by later poets to an ever-growing poem, stitched together over a long time. Each signpost is integral to its surrounding context and cannot be cut without further damage: they are fatal to patchwork theories. Except for the intrusive book 10 and the catalogues in book 2, bits of the poem have not begun life as separate 'and then' episodes. The important point here is that almost any imaginable ones, 'Hector Returns to His Family', 'The Embassy to Achilles', 'The Funeral Games for Patroclus', presuppose knowledge of the main poem. They did not originate as free-standing episodes. They only make sense in the light of the whole. Until audiences had heard it they would not ask for bits to be performed on their own.

Homer's composition is indeed remarkable, about 15,000 verses even without what is now book 10 of the Iliad and the catalogues in what is now book 2. The result is universally classed as an epic, a term which has become very widely applied, ranging from the ancient tales of Gilgamesh, which had been current in Mesopotamia from the second millennium BC onwards, to lengthy narrative films in the second millennium AD, *Lawrence of Arabia* being a prime example. In modern usage epics are narratives of length and scale, telling about great deeds of action and tending to focus on a particular hero or heroine: they tend to be 'of' someone. If they are poems they tend to be told in an elevated style and involve the relations of gods to mortals.

The label 'epic poetry' is a Greek one, first attested long after Homer, but examples might have existed elsewhere before the exact label existed.[21] Many consider the surviving poems about Gilgamesh to be an 'epic of Gilgamesh' and indeed they tell of his great deeds in response to great challenges, classic material for an epic, and end with a quest, a fine element in a narrative plot: Gilgamesh sets off to discover the means of immortality. Grand narrative poems of this type continue to be performed in many cultures, from central Asia to India, from Sri Lanka to west Africa. Even so, I restrict the term 'epic'.[22]

The two Homeric epics, the Iliad and Odyssey, are distinctive. They have plots which move in one direction, Achilles' wrath in the Iliad and Odysseus' return home in the Odyssey, and they are exceptionally compressed in time, fifty days for one, forty-two for the other: the tales about Gilgamesh differ on these cardinal points. I regard a single, directing plot as the hallmark of an epic. Rather than looking for epics in other languages and cultures, I prefer to decolonize the category and not to ask if African societies had an epic, as if they somehow should. They and many others, including the ancient Babylonians, have long heroic poems, which I define as poems about heroes or heroines and their deeds. So far as we know their contents, the poems of Homer's Greek near contemporaries were 'and then' heroic poems too, and not his type of epic at all. Homer, I believe, invented not just the device of a plot, but also a new genre, epic.

Modern definitions of an epic sometimes specify that it must 'centre on deeds of significance to the community'.[23] Conspicuously,

the Iliad, our first surviving epic, does not centre on deeds of significance to the community in any strong sense at all. Its primary
subject, Achilles' wrath and its consequences, is no such thing. The
poem predicts, but does not describe, the fall of Troy, and even that
event was not of fundamental significance in founding a Greek
'community'. After it the Greek heroes simply went back to their
pre-existing homes and confronted what separately awaited them.
The Iliad was not composed to be a formative poem for a Greek
nation. It differs fundamentally here from Virgil's *Aeneid* and its
relation to the Romans. Homer's listeners, unlike many of Virgil's,
were not conscious of a mission to rule others.

Homer chose to make it so: he had a very long poem in mind
without any formative message for a community, so what sort of
context for it did he envisage? Certainly, he addressed it to an audience of listeners, not readers: '*Sing, o goddess*', he begins. In the
Odyssey, one of the poets in the plot sings at a feast for the assembled guests of a king. That setting for poetry is well known in later
historical societies, from Europe's early German tribes to the halls
of Anglo-Saxon chiefs.[24] However, the Odyssey is presenting a
legendary feast in the distant past: a feast in the poem does not indicate that the Odyssey and the Iliad were poems performed in a
similar setting. The Greek style of dining also changed over time.
Homer's heroes sit upright on chairs and eat meat and drink wine at
one and the same feast, but by *c.* 800 BC, at least in Athens, and by
c. 750 elsewhere in the Greek world, party-goers developed a distinctive new style in which they drank wine quite separately after
their dinner.[25] In due course, by *c.* 630 BC, they reclined on carefully
arranged couches for these separate drinking sessions, or symposia.
Symposiac parties were much smaller than feasts in a hall and
became impossible to conduct if the reclining guests numbered
more than thirty.

On one recent view the Odyssey was composed for thirty-nine
nights of performance at such symposiac parties, but considerable
licence is needed to cut the Odyssey into thirty-nine symposium-
sized chunks.[26] The guests would have had to come back night after

night for nearly six weeks in order to follow the plot to its essential *!!*
conclusion. As for the Iliad, its subject was quite unsuited to such a
context: to judge from later examples, a symposium was a setting
for the singing of short lyrics and intimate poems of wit and love.
An old-style feast at which food and drink were served together
would be a more apt occasion and even in the age of symposia,
noble families, before *c.* 650, might perhaps have continued to entertain their social equals and retainers to such meals. Yet, the Iliad
does not address such patrons, as their role as hosts would surely
have demanded. Performance of it at a feast would have needed the
same audience to attend several very long dinners night after night
if the poem was to be completed and make sense. Each occasion
would involve several hours of sitting on a stool or one of those
upright chairs.

Long heroic poems in other cultures suggest other options.[27]
Some of them have been performed at wedding feasts, but the Iliad's bleak plot is quite unsuitable for such an occasion. A harvest
festival is another venue, but the Iliad's theme does not fit one,
either. The most attractive guess is that it was performed at a religious festival.[28]

For many hundreds of years before Homer, in the many different
societies and cultures of the Near East, poets had been performing
at festivals which were held at a temple, often on fixed days in the
year, for one or other god. Some of the later Greek hymns assume
such a context: one, addressing Apollo *c.* 525 BC, refers to boxing and
dancing and poetic song during a gathering in honour of him on
the island of Delos.[29] From *c.* 520 BC onwards the Iliad was certainly
performed by teams of reciters at the Athenians' Panathenaic festival, a grand occasion in honour of the goddess Athena which
extended over several days.

A recently found Greek inscription has given fascinating details
of what a local Greek festival's programme could include. In AD 124
a donor, Demosthenes, gave a festival of the arts to little Oenoanda,
a Greek-speaking city in Lycia in south-west Asia. It was to extend
over three weeks in July of which five of the first nine active days

were to be devoted to poetic performances.[30] At Oenoanda these days were days of competition, including competitions for comic and tragic poets: poetic competitions were a long-standing Greek practice but not a Near Eastern one. Back in Homer's time, they cannot have been the occasion for his Iliad: if his poem was to be understood, it had to be performed in one full sweep, leaving little or no time for other poets to compete against it. From this fact two compelling inferences can be made. A poem as long as Homer's required a free run for several days, and as he was granted one, he was evidently well known to the occasion's organizers as someone capable of an exceptional poem, one worth hearing without any rivals. If so, he had presumably performed a version of it already in another context.

We can only guess, but my preferred guess has novel elements, one of which is that he first performed a version of the Iliad for troops who were out at war. In the poem itself, no poets are present in the Greek heroes' camp, but their absence in this distant past need not reflect facts of Homer's own lifetime. In 334 BC, Alexander the Great, a passionate admirer of the Iliad, took epic poets with him on his long march into Asia and even in India staged poetic dramas to entertain his troops.[31] Admittedly these epic poets were to celebrate Alexander's own deeds, but commanders in Homer's lifetime may have been less egocentric. During several nights, I suggest, during or after a long raid or a siege of a city in western Asia, Homer performed a first version of his great poem about heroes at war to fascinated listeners, all of them, therefore, men. Its fame then spread and earned it a free run at a religious festival, this time for men and women, perhaps in a longer version.

The poem does not honour one particular god, nor does it honour any city or presiding family. These features suggest it was composed for a more general festival, one not limited to a particular city. In the heartland of Homer's first listeners one such festival was the Panionian festival, founded by the Ionian cities which had been settled down the west coast of Asia. It is the likely setting for the dragging of that bull for sacrifice to Poseidon in one of Homer's similes, and up on Mount Mycale a site for it has recently been located at Çatallar Tepe. The festival has sometimes been connected to the commemoration of a victory by Ionians over a settlement called Meliē, which seems to have been non-Greek and Carian. The finds at Çatallar Tepe fit that theory quite well, but Greek occupation of the site proposed to be Meliē seems to have begun only *c.* 650 BC.[32] There is no reason to see this victory as the origin of the Panionian festival itself. Ionians may have been meeting and holding a religious festival which expressed and confirmed their common identity long before such a battle. We do not know where these earlier festivals were held, but presumably on or near Mount Mycale, a seat of worship for Poseidon. Wherever they took place, Homer may have performed at one of them, perhaps on Mycale's lower slopes, looking out towards the Icarian sea. Afterwards, he may have travelled across the Aegean and performed his masterpiece at other Greek festivals, refining it and adding yet more to it.

>> These contexts are guesses, but they are not totally uncontrolled. The poem's unity, necessary length and subject make many other venues highly unlikely: a festival is a widely favoured option among current scholars. It rounds off what can be inferred about where Homer lived, moved and performed. We do not know where he was born, let alone where he died, but he travelled up to Troy and the Troad and possibly down to Lycia and the valley of its river Xanthus on the coast of south-west Asia. He was at home, like his listeners, with aspects of Asia's western coast and its adjoining sea, evidently in a zone from Ephesus to, say, Miletus. The arguments for these locations have already thrown light on elements of his poem and its making: they take us, next, into contested scholarly territory, not just where he may have composed, but how he did so.

PART II

Composing the Iliad:
How?

7.

'Sing, o goddess . . .'

The Iliad begins with a much-discussed clue to its manner of performance. 'Sing, o goddess . . .', it commands, but after its first verse it never refers again to the poet or the Muse as singing. Elsewhere, Homer calls on the Muse to 'tell'. By comparing other early Greek poems' use of the words 'sing' and 'tell', Martin West, life-long expert in early Greek poetry, argued in 1981 that they refer to one and the same type of delivery, one which was 'truly "singing" . . . based on definite notes and intervals, but that it was a stylized form of speech, the rise and fall of the voice being governed by the melodic accent of the words'.[1]

In the ninth book of the Iliad, when three ambassadors come from Agamemnon to Achilles' encampment to plead with him to re-enter the war, they find him singing the 'famous deeds of men', heroes like himself, while his beloved Patroclus sits opposite him, alone, in silence, waiting until he stops. The scene is readily visualized and its detail is precise. Achilles is performing as a poet, the only hero in the Iliad who ever does so. He is accompanying his song, 'delighting himself on a clear-toned lyre with its bridge of silver', one which he took when he sacked the city of Eetion. Three books earlier, Homer has told us that Eetion was the father of Andromache, Trojan Hector's wife, and that he and his seven sons were killed there by Achilles. He may not have intended these further facts to resonate behind Achilles' playing: he may simply have wished to give the lyre an origin, explaining how something so fine was with Achilles during a war. Achilles is singing a song of heroic deeds, much as Homer's predecessors sang in real life.[2]

The Odyssey, too, presents poets who sing with a lyre, also in the far distant past, and perform for listeners at dinner. Lyres indeed had a long history in Greek hands, being attested (*la-ra-ta*) in the Greek which was used in palaces in what is now known as the Mycenaean age (*c.* 1300 BC). In one such palace, at Pylos, a fresco painting, *c.* 1250 BC, showed a musician holding a five-stringed lyre: he is seated on a rock with pairs of diners shown in a much smaller scale below and beyond him. He was a poet and singer on the wall of what probably served as a dining hall. He was surely shown there because players performed there too.[3]

Martin West argued that Homer too played a lyre, one with four strings, but concluded that he did not stop them with his fingers and adjust their lengths. The four strings gave him four notes only. West projected back into Homer's lifetime what later Greek authors call the 'Ionian scale' and allotted one note to each of the four strings, approximately our E, B, G and F. He then distributed them to each word in the Iliad's opening two verses according to their likely pitch-accent and gave an example of how Homer might have sung them.[4]

Two experts in Vienna, Georg Danek and Stefan Hagel, have refined his argument and taken it further. To exemplify it Hagel has performed various passages from Homer's epics, including the very song in the Odyssey which one of the poets in the story is presented as singing: at www.oeaw.ac.at/kal/sh he can be heard performing it. Homer's voice, he assumes, would rise at the start of a verse and tend to fall at the end. Exceptions would sometimes occur, to judge from the accentuation of words at the end of some of the verses, but they enhance the singing's general effect by varying it. The reconstruction sounds unfamiliar to our ears, but not perhaps to Homer's experienced listeners.

Did Homer really sing the Iliad throughout in this way, or did he sing the very beginning before slipping into an unaccompanied chant, returning to song only when someone in the story was himself singing? In West's view his singing often paused at the end of a verse, but regular pausing throughout the poem would have greatly prolonged its performance. I believe, therefore, that Homer sang only for a small part of his performance, but, even so, that hypothesis opens up yet more skills which he commanded: melodic phrasing and musical invention. They make his achievement even more remarkable. They also mean that what we admire as a classic has survived with only a part of its original glory. Ancient Greek statues are admired for their whiteness, but originally their stone was painted in bright colours. The choruses of Greek drama are read without their original music and singing and accompanying dance. What classicists justly admire has often been amputated.

In prose translations of the Iliad the mutilation is extreme. In our Greek texts, Homer's performance has vanished, but at least the metre of it survives, giving the rhythm which his performance projected. It is lost in prose translation, but remains essential to appreciating his art. Throughout, he used the hexameter, a combination of long and short syllables into six measures or 'feet' ('hex' = six, 'metron' = measure). It was certainly not his own creation. Linguistically, some of the Iliad's phrases which are convenient for hexameters are likely go back to the distant Mycenaean past, c. 1300 BC ('silver-studded sword' or *xĭphŏs ārgŭrŏēlŏn* has been a favourite example). In Greek palace-tablets surviving from that era, most of the names of places and persons would fit into a hexameter, implying that the Greek used in everyday speech, from which the names were constructed, was also quite readily usable by hexameter-poets. It is possible, then, that hexameters were already used by poets in the Mycenaean age, though no verse from that era survives.[5]

The hexameter is an amazing metre, far more complex than any known in long heroic poems elsewhere in the world. The words in it break midway, and modern scholars prefer to analyse it into two *cola*, or limbs, separating in the third foot. Even so, it was not made up from two parts, originally separate: the verse is fixed firmly together as one. Here is an example, with each long quantity marked by ¯, each short by ˘, each foot by | and the break in the line, or the caesura, by / /: if recited it gives the rhythm:

Ēū găr ĕ | gō tŏdĕ | oīdă / / kă | tā phrĕnă | kaī kătă | thūmŏn |
Ēssĕtaĭ | ēmăr (h)ŏt | ān / / pŏt' ŏ | lōleī | Īlĭŏs | (h)īrē |

These verses occur in two separate places in the poem but are best known in the second, the magnificent speech of Hector to his wife Andromache, as they meet for the last time inside Troy: 'well I know this in my heart and mind / There will be a day when holy Troy will perish'. These poignant words were to be repeated many centuries later by the Roman general Scipio Aemilianus as he looked over the great city of Carthage which his army had just destroyed.[6] He wept as he spoke them: one day, Rome too, he sensed, would fall. Empires, ultimately, do.

As these verses show, the hexameter rests on two basic metrical units: one is the dactyl, a long syllable and two shorts ($-\,\smile\,\smile$), and the other is the spondee, two long syllables ($-\,-$). Both are easily contrived in Greek, a language which abounds in vowels, sometimes long, sometimes short: unlike English, it even developed separate letters for its long 'o's and 'e's and its short ones. Dactyls or spondees can stand in the first five feet of the line, but the sixth foot, the last one, must be either a spondee or a trochee, $-\,\smile$. A run of dactyls gives the verse more speed, a good example being Homer's artful use of them for Poseidon's rapid journey from that mountain peak on Samothrace.

Spondees, with two long vowels in sequence, are slower and more solemn. They might seem harder to contrive, but Homeric verse almost always treats the combination of a short vowel before two consonants as a long, or heavy, syllable ('Hēktor' begins with a long syllable because the short 'e' becomes heavy before the 'kt'). A long vowel was also required in the first syllable of every single verse. This requirement was more awkward and in order to satisfy it the poets sometimes artificially lengthened a vowel in that position. Priămĭdēs, son of Priam, is an example, because Priămos, Priam, begins with a short ĭ everywhere else. Even a word as brief as the preposition diă, 'on account of', might be lengthened into dīa if it was in the first place in the verse. Here and elsewhere, poets sometimes stretched vowels in order to fit the hexameter's demands.

If each of its six feet had ended with a word's end, the effect would have been flat and monotonous, but Greek words vary greatly in length. This variation gives a fine rhythm, words and feet ending separately. The first long syllable of each dactyl ($^-$ $^\smile$ $^\smile$) was also emphasized, driving the rhythm along. In English poetry, hexameters rely on the stress of the words, not, as in Greek, on the quantities of each vowel. They have been used seldom, and usually without much success. The exception is A. H. Clough's excellent *Amours de Voyage*, which he composed in 1849 as a sequence of letters exchanged between English correspondents in that year of rebellion, mostly during its turbulent fighting in Rome. When one young lady writes breathlessly to another, she uses the rhythm of the hexameter verse very well:

> George has just seen Garibaldi, dressed up in a long white cloak, on
> Horseback, riding by, with his mounted negro behind him:
> This is a man, you know, who came from America with him,
> Out of the woods, I suppose, and uses a lassŏ in fighting,
> Which is, I don't quite know, but a sort of noose, I imagine.

Clough's hexameters convey his characters' differing tones and emotions, from the supercilious to the amorous and, eventually, wistful.[7]

His poem is long, but the Iliad is very much longer and poses a much greater challenge to translators. In Russian, Nikolai Gnedich's translation, finished in 1829, used hexameters throughout, a tour de force which took him some twenty years. In German, a hexameter translation has worked well, the achievement of Johann Voss in the 1790s. Renderings of it into English hexameters have been attempted, but the most successful vary the metrical template. In 1940, Cecil Day Lewis translated the hexameters of Virgil's *Georgics* into lines with either five or six stresses. The result read well on the radio and was used as a starting point by Richmond Lattimore in his admired translation of the Iliad, published in 1951. It has been adopted by the classicist Peter Green for his fine translation, published in 2015, which also aims to be easy to declaim. Green too varied lines with six stresses and lines with only five and made concessions to the natural rhythm of English, especially the prevalence of iambics ($^\smile$ $^-$) and anapaests ($^\smile$ $^\smile$ $^-$) in it:

Thus he spoke in prayer, and Phoebus Apollo heard him.
Down from the peak of Olympos he hastened, enraged at heart,
carrying on his shoulders his bow and lidded quiver,
arrows rattling loud on his shoulders as in his rage
he strode on his way: he came as nightfall comes.

In performance, Homer began by singing to his own musical playing. He then performed for hours in a complex, brilliantly flexible metre with a lyre beside him, I believe, using it only when persons sometimes sing in his poem. It is essential to realize that what his listeners heard was not close to the language of everyday speech. On the contrary, Homer's Greek combined very old and more recent forms and also mixed different Greek dialects.

Its ancient elements include respect for the digamma, a Greek letter which had been largely superseded in Homer's own time. By 1713 the brilliant classical scholar Richard Bentley had deduced, by scrupulous study, that phrases used in Homeric verse very often presuppose the presence of a missing digamma, but at other times proceed as if it did not exist.[8] He inferred, correctly, that the digamma had prevailed when the phrases presupposing it were coined, but that it was disappearing at the date when Homer himself composed. Here is a clear example. When Helen addresses Priam respectfully in book 3, she calls him 'phĭlĕ hĕkŭrĕ dēinē tĕ', which does not scan at all for a hexameter, not least with its run of five short vowels. If we restore the missing digammas and change the initial 'h' to an 's', another valid change, we have 'phĭlĕ sFe'kŭrĕ dēFēinē tĕ' which is a metrically regular ending to a hexameter.[9] Words of address are obvious candidates for the use of old, inherited phrases.

Since Bentley, philologists have gone even further back in time to explain apparent irregularities. Homer quite often separates the prepositional prefix of a verb from the verb itself: *pros muthon eeipe*, 'he addressed a word', instead of joined-up *proseipe* as in later Greek prose. This separation makes a verb and its prefix metrically much more flexible. It was already rare in what we now know of Greek in the Mycenaean era and possibly goes back even earlier: Homer and

his contemporaries inherited it as a metrical convenience and continued to deploy it.[10]

As for the mixture of dialects, Aeolic, Ionic and so forth, it was
already recognized by eighteenth-century admirers. In 1756 Lady Mary
Wortley Montagu, that incomparable wit, wrote to her beloved Fran-
cesco Algarotti, 'imitating Homer', she said, by combining three
'dialects' in her letter, English, French and Italian.[11] She knew no Greek
but had been a close friend of Homer's translator, Alexander Pope.
Translations into readable prose miss this dimension of the Iliad entirely.

To eighteenth-century critics, this amalgam of dialects and the
presence and absence of the digamma seemed to fit well with views
that the Iliad had been stitched as a patchwork from shorter poems
composed at varying times. In 1713 Bentley remarked, famously,
Homer 'wrote a sequel of songs and rhapsodies, to be sung by himself for small earnings and good cheer at festivals and other days of
merriment; the *Ilias* he made for the men, and the *Odysseïs* for the
other sex. These loose songs were not collected together into the
form of an epic poem till . . . above 500 years after.'[12] Bentley's words
can be pressed here, showing that he differed from Josephus and his
heirs on a crucial point: Homer, he considered, wrote.

In 1788, the analysts and their theories seemed to receive unexpected support. A major manuscript of Homer was published from
Venice, where it had been part of the great library which Cardinal
Bessarion gave in 1468 to the Venetian Republic.[13] It had originated
in Constantinople in the tenth century AD but it contained notes by
ancient critics, including the learned Alexandrian Aristarchus of
Samothrace, 'best of the grammarians', and his discussions of interpolated verses and alternative readings. These additions and variants
showed that the text of the Iliad and Odyssey had not been entirely
fixed at an early date.

Impressed by this textual discovery, a German scholar, Friedrich
Wolf, published in 1795 results of his own careful analysis, conducted over some twenty years. He argued that the Iliad, and also
the Odyssey, had arisen in at least three stages. The first had been a
variety of short, separate oral poems, Wolf believed, composed by

Wolf Homer himself *c.* 900 BC. At that time, Wolf stated, Homer and his fellow Greeks were illiterate. Homer's short poems, he inferred, were preserved orally and meanwhile some of his followers composed yet more oral poems of their own. When alphabetic writing became current among the Greeks, perhaps as much as three centuries later so Wolf believed, all these short poems were written down. Even then, he assumed, they remained separate texts. Only in the 520s BC, in Athens, were they amalgamated and sorted into one long Iliad and one long Odyssey, as later ancient sources seemed to recall, attributing some such action to the then-rulers of Athens, Peisistratus and his sons.[14]

Wolf's views were to shape analytic scholarship on the Iliad for the next 150 years. As he himself emphasized, his general view was very much the view of Josephus and the majority of scholars in Europe who had written on the topic since 1560. His originality lay elsewhere, in the systematic detail with which he supported it. Though ignored at first in England, he convinced analytic scholars in Europe that the challenge when reading the Iliad was to identify the short original poems which underlay it. Inconsistencies in it, they assumed, were pointers to such poems' existence.

In the 1840s, fifty years after Wolf, the view that the Iliad had grown like a snowball was also alive. The poem was still being compared by highly literate scholars to a building which had evolved gradually. A fine Greek historian, the London banker George Grote, likened it to a 'house built upon a plan comparatively narrow and subsequently enlarged by successive additions'. It then became compared to a church, especially to a medieval cathedral, to which side chapels, side aisles and alterations continued to be added.[15]

Whether Homer sang or chanted, wrote or composed in performance, one point still remained to be recognized: this special mix of dialects was a finely worked convenience.[16] As forms from different Greek dialects scan in different ways, a blend of them was an asset for anyone composing complex hexameters. The verb 'to be' could be *ēmmĕnai, ĕmĕnāi* or *ĕmĕn* from Aeolic or *eīnāi* from Ionic, each of which has a different metrical value. Almost always, an Aeolic form in Homer's language offers a metrical alternative to an Ionic one: it is for that functional reason that it has been retained. Aeolic *pĭsŭres* occurs as well as Ionic *tēssăres*, both meaning 'four', or Aeolic *pāntēssĭ* as well as Ionic *pāsĭ*, both meaning 'to' or 'for' all. There are two telling points about this blend of dialects. It does not duplicate word forms of equal metrical value: in that sense, it has economy. Yet it also has scope: the words which its blend retains cover a range of different placings in a hexameter verse. A language with these slimmed-down functional qualities certainly did not evolve with Homer himself, as if he travelled round speakers of the various Greek dialects and cherry-picked forms which he felt would suit his verse. It was a tool which had evolved and been sharpened for many decades before he inherited it and began to use it.

Many such features of Homeric language were observed by nineteenth-century German scholars who were trying to analyse the poems into early and late constituents. Homeric style, they then realized, has a similar feature. It is not just that it is famous for recurrent combinations of a noun or name with an adjective or epithet, 'swift-footed Achilles', 'hoofed horses' and 'cloud-gathering Zeus' being examples. Every reader and scholar notices them, but in 1872 Heinrich Düntzer realized that such phrases worked similarly to the blend of dialects. The poet, he observed, had several ways of describing wine, but none, he believed, overlapped metrically with another.[17] Their use was not primarily determined by their sense, he inferred, but by the place in the hexameter which they had to fit. They too show scope and economy. The hero Menelaos is an example. He can be 'tawny Menelaos' (*xānthōs Mĕnĕlāŏs*), 'Menelaos dear to the war god' (*ărēïphĭlōs Mĕnĕlāŏs*), 'Menelaos good at the war cry' (*bŏēn ăgăthōs Mĕnĕlāŏs*, beginning with a consonant 'b', influencing the quantity of a vowel at the end of the previous word), and, in the genitive case, 'of glorious Menelaos' (*Mĕnĕlāŏu kŭdălĭmōĭŏ*), which uses two genitive case endings from different dialects, each with a different metrical value, thereby fitting the phrase for the final feet of a hexameter verse.

Why had poets elaborated this artificial language? There is a real clue here to the Iliad's origins. It is not enough to say that Homer was a traditional poet: what was the tradition and why did it exist? In antiquity Josephus had already drawn on the view that Homer composed without writing, a notion which Scaliger followed in the 1560s. In the mid eighteenth century Robert Wood gave the topic a new twist. He did not simply take over the contention that Homer composed short songs orally: he compared him to 'Italian and Eastern poets when they recite in the open air', performers whom he had seen on his travels, especially in Syria, where he visited the ruined city of Palmyra in the 1740s and heard songs by the illiterate Bedouin. He referred to these 'Italian and Eastern poets' as pointing out 'imaginary scenery of their own extempore creation' while they performed.[18] He did not elaborate, but his implication was that Homer too, without writing, had extemporized some of what he sang. Wood's remarks then impressed the scholarly Friedrich Wolf, who also opted for a Homer who composed short songs without writing.

Here, comparative studies of oral poetry in other cultures become important. What Wood encountered in Syria, others were encountering in Europe and interpreting in the light, or mirage, of their view of Homer. In the Ottoman empire, heroic poems in Serbia and Bosnia had been known to outsiders since *c.* 1200 and a collection of Serbian songs had been printed as early as 1568.[19] Already in the eighteenth century the singers and their songs were being compared with Homer. They seemed to offer living evidence of how he had composed, evidence which study of his text could never match. It rested on fieldwork by admirable travellers, people who set off to hear oral poetry in languages which were very difficult for outsiders to understand. Comparison with living cultures elsewhere in the world is a resource which Homeric scholars still apply to the poem's values, social practices and styles of fighting. In the next two chapters I will dwell on its pioneers and their contribution to the study of Homer's way of composing, because it transforms our ideas of the possibilities and brings them to life. Through it Homer's poetry has come to play a founding role in yet another branch of study, not just classical studies, but the comparative study of world literature.

8.

Homeric Fieldwork

In the early nineteenth century interest in oral poems became related to an impassioned topic, national consciousness and its roots. The topic was nowhere more impassioned than in the Balkans. In Serbia, songs which were being performed orally were considered to be folk poetry and were used to support arguments for a local national consciousness ('Illyrianism'). They became compared with Homer's poetry, thanks to a series of chance encounters which modern students of Homer tend to foreshorten.

Shortly after a Serbian revolt against Ottoman Turkish rule, songs by Serbian rural poets, some of them about recent battles, were collected first hand by a fine researcher who is still revered as a hero of the Serbian language and its culture: Vuk Karadžić.[1] He had been born into a peasant family but, as he was lame, was disqualified from full military service and agricultural work. He was educated, partly in a monastery, and then set off to collect songs, mostly from lowly singers, three of whom were women and some of whom had taken to singing because they were blind and unfit for other work.

In 1814, when Karadžić came to Vienna, his detailed range of songs caught the interest of an important cultural figure, Jernej Kopitar, who happened to have recently met the Homeric scholar Friedrich Wolf.[2] He had engaged with Wolf's theory of an illiterate Homer, the composer of short songs. As Karadžić's collected songs were also quite short, never more than a thousand verses, Kopitar sent four of the battle songs to Friedrich Wolf in 1819 and presented their poet as a 'rhapsode', the name for a singer of Homeric poetry: it is the first written testimony to the idea of there being Homers in Serbia. In due course Karadžić too was called 'Serbian Homer' and the comparison caught on. His first book, a small songbook, became enlarged into four volumes and went on to be translated into French and German: it also attracted the attention of Jacob Grimm, editor of *Grimm's Fairy Tales*. One of Karadžić's main singers, Filip Višnjić, was compared with Homer and by the late 1830s 'Serbian Homer' was even being used as a caption for a popular image of a Serbian singer-poet.[3]

Karadžić went on to study songs in Bosnia in his later years, but in the 1850s yet more evidence for oral poetry and its link to Homer came from an unexpected quarter: singers active in central Asia. As Russian power expanded in that region, military officers and envoys began to become more interested in the peoples and languages it contained. In the mid 1850s, in what is now Kyrgyzstan, a nobly born Kazakh, Chokan Valikhanov, encountered performances of a long and compendious poem about the warrior-hero Manas and his descendants. None of its performers could read or write. In 1856, he described this poem as a 'kind of Iliad of the steppe'.[4] In the version he heard, Manas was a Muslim, fighting against many enemies, especially invaders from China. As a Kazakh he could understand Kyrgyz and so he even transcribed one episode, about 3400 verses long, making its poet repeat it twice while he took down the words in his own disorderly handwriting. His discovery was ignored by scholars in western Europe, but in the 1860s a remarkable scholar, Wilhelm Radloff, took it further.

Born in Berlin, but resident in St Petersburg, Radloff was one of a generation of talented Russian-speakers who were to classify so much in central Asia, its flora, language, archaeology and even its wildlife: Nikolai Przewalski's find of small wild horses is a famous example which still bears his name. In what is now Kyrgyzstan, Radloff transcribed a long performance of the Manas poem, dictated to him by an expert local singer. Radloff had learned other Turkic dialects, but as yet knew less of the 'Kara-Kirgiz' which the poem used. Rapid transcription, therefore, posed problems for him, but even so, he realized a cardinal fact: an expert Manas singer, or *manaschi*, 'always improvises according to the inspiration of the moment so that he is incapable of reciting his poem twice in an absolutely identical manner'.[5] He even compared him to 'an improvising piano-player who creates a mood by putting together various sequences, transitions and themes with which he is familiar and thus he creates the new from the old'. Radloff was writing long before the invention of jazz, but his analogy was well chosen. As it related to poetry very far from the classical world, classical scholars ignored it.

In the thirteenth book of the Iliad, Homer describes how Zeus looked away from the Trojan war to people of the steppes, 'justest of men' and 'mare-milkers', as indeed they still are, drawing milk from their mares and churning it into cream for themselves and visitors to their yurts.[6] The mares-milkers now turned out to be poem-churners, composers of a vast heroic poem at least twenty times as long as the Iliad, not a word of which they had ever written. Its core goes back many centuries before 1800, though the date of the first reference to anything in it by an external author is still uncertain.[7] The very long poem of the deeds of Manas, his son and grandson is a classic 'and then' poem in which one episode follows another, each able to be performed separately. Its performers still chant it and vary their intonation, but they do not sing melodically or accompany themselves on an instrument. In 1995 the poem's thousandth anniversary was declared in Kyrgyzstan, a national rallying point, though the calculation of the date was optimistic. A huge statue of Manas on horseback stands in the centre of Bishkek, Kyrgyzstan's capital, and the airport bears his name.

Radloff continued to transcribe the Manas poem and others in central Asia, but in 1872 he returned and became Inspector of Turkic Schools among another mare-milking public, the Tatars around the fine city of Kazan: they still eat horsemeat. In 1884–5 he published the central Asian poems he had transcribed and gave a translation into German. He had had a good classical education and in his preface to the Manas poem he had the Homeric poems very much in mind. Perceptively, he considered its episodes to be comparable to the 'same phase which the Greeks experienced when the epic poetry of the Trojan cycle of legends was still alive in the

people's minds as unrecorded genuine folk poetry'.[8] He even identified the poet Demodocus in Homer's Odyssey 'as precisely the
singer of the Kirgiz songs. He never sings others' songs, he always
composes them himself.'

In the Odyssey, Demodocus is a poet active in fairy-tale Phaeacia.
At a feast in the palace, he sings of a quarrel between Achilles and
Odysseus, beginning the story on the spur of the moment and composing as he goes along. Later, he goes outdoors and during athletic
sports, followed by a performance by dancers, he sings a more ris-
qué song about the adultery of Aphrodite with Ares, god of war,
and their entrapment, naked, in bed, a sight which fascinated the
gods and goddesses who promptly came to look.[9] At another feast
he sings of the Wooden Horse at Troy. He begins each of his songs
set at Troy as episodes from a larger whole, just as Manas singers
perform short episodes from the vast Manas story. There is never a
hint that Demodocus could read or write.

In the Odyssey another of the oral poets in the story, Phemius,
describes himself as 'self-taught, but the god has planted all sorts of
paths [of song] in my heart'. In Kyrgyzstan one of the singers, quite
independently, told Radloff, 'I can in general sing every poem because
God has laid the gift of singing in my heart . . . I have learned none
of my poems: everything flows from my inner being.'[10] Despite this
analogy, Radloff did not call the Manas poem itself the 'Iliad of the
steppe'. The Iliad's building blocks were oral songs, he believed, but
Homer himself might still have used writing, he considered, or if
not, somebody near him used it very soon. He insisted on one very
important point. From his findings in the field he ruled out oral
transmission of 'very long songs, like for instance the length of several books by Homer . . . According to my experience, then, I hold it
impossible that so enormous a work as Homer's poetry could have
survived a decade had it not been written down.' A poem performed
orally, he considered, is 'always in a fluid state and becomes something completely new in ten years'.[11]

His acute insights anticipate much which was to follow in Homeric
studies. In 1903–4 Russian fieldworkers, ignored by classicists and

anthropologists further west, recorded episodes of the Manas poem directly from Kyrgyz poets by using early phonographic equipment.[12] Other oral poems, whether in Arabic or Sanskrit or central-European languages, were indeed known to scholars in literate Europe, but the striking fact about the Manas poem was that although it was extraordinarily long, none of its singers, listeners or contemporaries could read or write. They had never even heard readings from a book. In the 1920s a masterly Manas-poet dictated his long improvised version of one episode to scribes, one of whom took it down in Arabic script. A Kyrgyz written language did not exist until 1924.

In 1864, while Radloff was with the Kyrgyz, a Croatian researcher, Luka Marjanović, travelled into north-west Bosnia and during the next twenty years collected no fewer than 255,000 verses of oral heroic poetry, thitherto unknown. He edited them in the versions he published, but even so, he emphasized two cardinal points, the variations between an oral poet's performances on the same subject, especially the verses with which he opened it, and the mixture of dialects in his language, a precious observation as he was hearing the poems while this mix was still prominent.[13] Both of these features can be matched to Homeric poetry, but Marjanović was not much concerned with Homer. Nor were classical scholars concerned with Marjanović. They could not read his language.

In 1884–5, the date of Radloff's great book, another cluster of Bosnian poets was interviewed and their verses were transcribed, this time by a researcher well grounded in ancient Greek. Friedrich Krauss was a Croatian Jew who had been educated in Vienna, where he translated the books of dream interpretation composed in Greek by Artemidorus in the second or early third century AD.[14] It was through his German translation, made in 1881, that Artemidorus' remarkable text began to interest Freud and his early research into dreams. Three years after publishing it, Krauss was funded by Prince Rudolph of Austria to go to Bosnia and Montenegro and study their oral poets first hand. He met no fewer than 127 of them, *guslars* as they were known from the one-stringed instrument, the *gusle*, which they played with a bow while performing. Although they were illiterate, he collected some 170,000 verses, also unknown to outsiders. He heard from them that they had begun to learn their craft in childhood and that they repeated their songs over and over again so as not to forget them. They were all humbly born and prone, he wrote, to *dolce far niente*, doing sweet nothing, while they imagined their verses, he presumed, and went over their songs. Outsiders told him that nonetheless they could compose poems of a length of 30,000, even 70,000 or 100,000 verses.[15] They were probably exaggerating, but some of the poems Krauss found were indeed impressively long. One of them, a long song about a wedding and its consequences, was to have an unexpected scholarly future.

These Bosnian researches were conducted separately from the study of Homer: Krauss was a classicist, but his book never mentioned the Iliad. His interests lay elsewhere, in the social realities and the history, if any, in the *guslars'* songs. After his return, he took up sexology, a newly fashionable subject in Vienna, and argued that sex was very important for the understanding of heroic poems. Perhaps it is, but nobody has yet explained exactly how. When translating Artemidorus' dream-book Krauss had omitted all the references to sexual practices which he, and sometimes Artemidorus, considered unnatural.

Krauss's book of his researches did not appear until 1908, but it had a swift and important effect. Among anthropologists, at least in Paris, its Bosnian poets were promptly related to Homer's way of working. In 1909, one of them, the gifted Arnold van Gennep, soon to be famous for the phrase 'rites of passage', published a book on the 'question of Homer', relating the poems to archaeology and popular poetry, and remarked in it that a good Bosnian poet 'plays with his clichés as we play with cards'.[16] In 1925 another anthropologist, the Jesuit Marcel Jousse, adopted this same phrase in his study of oral style and rhythm, a topic which classicists had not explored at all.[17]

Jousse had grown up in the rural Sarthe region south-west of Paris and had been greatly impressed by the skills of the illiterate peasants.

His own mother, he remarks, was also a fine storyteller, although she never read books. He was most interested in the relation between oral style and its underlying psychology and neurology, especially its accompanying body language, an aspect which he had observed among native Indians during a year's visit to America.

Jousse went on to argue that parts of the Bible had been orally composed but that there was no difficulty in assuming that Jesus's disciples had remembered the exact words of his parables, because much greater feats of memory were attested among oral composers. He cited a recent oral performer in Afghanistan but also referred to Bosnian poets' playing with clichés and to Homer as an oral poet.[18] Without any systematic study of the matter, van Gennep and Jousse had grasped a way of understanding Homer. Neither, however, showed any awareness in their writings of the 'Iliad of the steppe', the Manas poem and its enormous scale.

Since the 1850s fieldwork in central Asia had established a crucial point which analytic scholars, including Friedrich Wolf, had never realized, that very long poems, not just short songs, could be composed without writing. By the 1920s analysts' failure to agree on the extent of the Iliad's first, short constituent parts had led to a re-emergence of unitarians, scholars who believed that the Iliad was essentially the work of one poet. However, even they assumed that he had composed it all in writing. Fieldwork could have changed their views, but the two types of study had yet to meet. Their meeting was to be unplanned, a crucial accident in Homeric studies.

9

Singers of Tales

Serbian Homers and an Iliad in the steppes were not just the fancies of song-collectors: they related to the prevailing view of analytic scholars, that if Homer existed, he had been the composer, without writing, of shortish songs, later enlarged or stitched by others into long composite poems. That view still needed to be tested by detailed linguistic research into Homeric technique and diction. Such research was to be the distinction of a young Californian, Milman Parry, whose meticulous studies remain landmarks in the understanding of Homeric verse. Orally composed narrative poems are a truly global genre, and Parry's work has shaped and encouraged outsiders' comparisons of them across different cultures. It has done most to foster study of world literature as a category.

I will follow the growth of his understanding in some detail because it is an instructive blend of chance and dedication, growing, as he himself would acknowledge, from roots which others had already established. In 1923, as an undergraduate in California, Parry wrote a short thesis at Berkeley on the 'traditional, almost formulaic quality' of early Greek epic diction: 'there is no other poetry in the world as smooth and rapid as this epic poetry', he declared, qualities which he attributed to the use of traditional diction. Experiment over the centuries, he concluded, had fitted it 'perfectly' to the hexameter. He also emphasized the effect of its use of what he called ornamental words, 'swift-footed' for Achilles or 'white-armed' for Hera: they 'eliminated even more completely any discrepancy in the pattern'. The effect was one of 'extraordinary beauty'.[1]

In 1924 Parry, his wife and their baby daughter left California and settled in Paris. After learning French for a year, in the next three he wrote a detailed French doctorate on traditional epithets in Homer. He showed the 'great extension and ... great simplicity' of the noun and adjectival phrases in the Homeric poems, what he later defined, crucially, as their economy and scope.[2] Again, he stressed their traditional nature, but nowhere considered that they might have been used in oral composition. One of his advisers in Paris was Antoine Meillet, a fine linguistic scholar who also believed the Homeric poems to be traditional: he had even written in 1923 that they were 'entirely composed of formulae handed down from poet to poet', an extreme view which an able English reviewer promptly described as 'enough to make one stare in disbelief'.[3]

Oral poetry, Parry's most famous field of study, came to his notice at the last minute and even then, he passed it by. A week or so before he defended his doctoral thesis, he happened to see a poster for lectures on popular epic poetry in Yugoslavia, to be given by Professor Murko at the Sorbonne, not, however, at the invitation of classicists. He ignored them, but Murko, an Austrian professor, was an important authority. He was to change the scope of Parry's thinking.

From 1909 onwards Matija Murko had studied Bosnian poets in the field and had published important articles on them between 1912 and 1919. By a fine coincidence he had met Radloff during a visit to St Petersburg in 1887-9.[4] For his work in Bosnia, he had taken something Radloff had lacked: a primitive phonographic machine, acquired from Vienna, on which he could record a singer, albeit for only thirty verses at a time. Like his predecessors, he had encountered poets who could compose in performance at considerable length. He had also learned that in 1887, between January and mid February, a Bosnian singer had performed on demand ninety songs, more than 80,000 verses in all, each improvised, an output more than five times as long as the Iliad. There was still a difference: none of these songs was even a tenth as long as the Iliad or Odyssey. Frequent venues for prolonged poetic performance, he discovered, were weddings. At one, three members of the same family had been married off, one after another, and the celebrations lasted for thirty-four days. Throughout them, singers attached to the brides' and the bridegrooms' families competed by composing songs in performance. Poetic weddings have gone out of fashion, but this one makes performance by Homer for several days at a festival seem eminently possible.[5]

After giving his lectures, Murko attended Parry's defence of his doctoral thesis, probably with the encouragement of Meillet, a member of the jury. During the debate Meillet pointed out for the first time that Parry had ignored the question of oral composition. His thesis was accepted nonetheless, but after the defence, Parry promptly met Murko: he later remarked that it was Murko who 'led me to the study of oral poetry in itself and to the heroic poems of the South Slavs'.[6]

Parry returned to America in summer 1928 and took a job as professor of Latin in Iowa. In 1929 he moved to Harvard to teach Greek on a temporary contract. In that autumn he published a well-founded article on verses in the Homeric poems which run on beyond the end of one hexameter into the start of the next and add words and ideas to what the former verse already contains: he explained this feature, 'enjambement', by 'oral versemaking' which 'by its speed must chiefly be carried on in an adding style'. In 1930 and 1931 he published two further articles in which he stressed the crucial role of the fixed phrase, or formula, in Homeric language, what he defined as 'an expression regularly used, under the same metrical conditions, to express an essential idea'.[7] He now saw no way of explaining these formulas' pervasive role except by oral poetry and 'the necessity of making verses by the spoken word': oral poets have to compose very quickly, he remarked, and so they use metrically apt phrases which are already rooted in their minds. Among others, he cited Radloff's and Krauss's books on the Kyrgyz and Bosnian poets and insisted that 'the failure to see the difference between written and oral verse was the greatest single obstacle to our understanding of Homer'. By recognizing it 'we shall no longer look for much that Homer would never have thought of saying, and above all, we shall find that many, if not most of the questions we

Parry -

were asking were not the right ones to ask.'[8] Initially in classical
studies his detailed articles were largely ignored, although they
were the first to unite a systematic study of Homer's language with
an awareness that orally composed poems were still being collected
from performers. They have since become milestones on the path
of understanding.

By spring 1931 Parry had read the short book which Murko had
published in 1929, based on his lectures in the Sorbonne. In it Murko
discussed the history of first-hand study of oral epic poetry in Yugoslavia and remarked on the long history of its comparison with
Homer's poetry: he also included photographs, still fascinating, of
many of the singers whom he had met during his five journeys
among their villages.[9] Parry had also begun to try to learn the Serbian language, remarking that after 'two years or so' he would apply
to 'spend a year in Jugoslavia to find the explanation of the Iliad and
the Odyssey'.[10] In summer 1933, he set off to do so. Although he was
aware of Radloff's work in central Asia, the 1930s were no time to
revisit it in the wake of the Russian Revolution and its aftermath
under Stalin. It would have taught him so much, adjusting some of
his conclusions. Instead he went to the other hotspot. There was
nothing brilliant about this choice. As he himself well knew, Yugoslavia was the obvious place, already sampled by previous researchers,
even if he did not know about those Serbian Homers who had been
hailed more than a hundred years earlier.

For an English-speaker the enterprise was a major challenge, but
Parry based himself and his family in Dubrovnik, and promptly
made two important friends in a café.[11] One was a Russian, Ilya Kutu-
zov, who also had a doctorate from the Sorbonne and could help
Parry with lessons in Serbo-Croat. The other was a local poet, Nikola
Vujnović, a Catholic and a stonemason by trade. As he was literate,
he was not a suitable poet for Parry to record, but he became an
invaluable negotiator with the singers found through that fundamental method, time spent courteously in local coffee houses.

These singers still sang to the *gusle*, their traditional instrument
resembling a mandolin. *Gusles* were usually made of maple wood,

on which a single string of horsehair was stretched and struck with a bow: often their narrow end was carved to resemble a horse's head. At first Parry used his helpers to transcribe what was being sung, but in early August he left for Belgrade and bought a heavy recording instrument, a Parlograph. As its wax cylinders could run only for a few minutes, and as it did not clearly distinguish the singer's voice from the *gusle*, it was little help. Nonetheless he and a helper went up into some of the mountain villages north of Dubrovnik, pressing on as far as Herzegovina. He persuaded most of the singers he encountered that they should dictate while Vujnović transcribed their words, and in a few weeks amassed about 55,000 verses, most of them previously unknown.

None of these poems was of a quality to compete with Homer's. Even so, after returning to Harvard in the autumn, Parry wrote that 'when [some]one hears the Southern Slavs sing their tales he has the overwhelming feeling that, in some way, he is hearing Homer'.[12] It is not clear if he knew that others before him had long made the same connection, but he insisted that the analogy was not just sentimental: like Homer, these poets used repeated verses to introduce and end speeches in their poems and to mark changes of time, just as Homer used phrases about dawn and night. They also used 'formulaic phrases' fitted to their metre, much as Parry had already demonstrated for Homeric poetry before he set out. Yet his findings lacked one crucial dimension. Muslim singers composed at greater length than Christian ones, because of the longer holidays in their calendar, but so far, the few Muslim songs presented to Parry were much shorter than Homer's epics.

In June 1934 Parry returned for a second visit, taking with him a fellow American, Albert Lord, who was to return to northern Bosnia in 1937 and then to Albania in 1950. Lord's lucid books and essays, *The Singer of Tales*, in 1960, and *The Singer Resumes the Tale*, published in 1995, four years after his death, were to do most to publicize and advance Parry's findings and lines of thought. With them Parry took an improved recording machine, equipped with two turntables, designed for him in Connecticut. He also shipped out his black Ford car whose battery could eventually help the machine to run. From their base, again in Dubrovnik, the group travelled off for weeks at a time, penetrating further into the mountain villages. One singer whom he and Lord encountered was especially adept at performing a song in Bosnian and then all over again in Albanian, a virtuoso feat.

In early 1935 he was amazed to hear a poet, twenty-five years old, compose a poem of about 1300 verses in two continuous hours of singing. Even so, it was barely a twelfth as long as the Iliad. It was not that Parry was finding and recording too little. In summer 1933 and on his second visit from 1934 to summer 1935, he found, elicited and transcribed or recorded mechanically some 12,500 oral songs from Yugoslav singers, mostly Muslims. No fewer than 11,000 were 'women's songs', short ones, however, and often laments.[13]

On 27 June 1935, he was introduced to a great find, Avdo Mededović, son of a village butcher and, at times in life, a butcher himself.[14] This exceptional man had spent seven years of his youth in the army and had seen a wider world, but was living, a devout Muslim, in the little village of Obrov in east Montenegro. Aged at least sixty, with a swollen goitre on one side of his neck, he was homeless: he and his family had just lost their house in a fire. He was a man of strict principle but as Parry was offering to pay handsomely, he was particularly willing to perform for him at length. During forty-five days, until 11 August, he composed in performance a total of about 78,000 verses, thirteen poems in all, nine being recorded, four being dictated to Parry and his assistants for simultaneous transcription. It was a very taxing business. Mededović considered that he was already past his best, which he had attained some twenty years earlier. He could perform only in stretches of up to half an hour before needing a break for coffee or alcohol. He could do two hours in the morning and two hours in the afternoon, but no more. Dictation was no easier: it made him sweat and it too required half-hourly breaks.

Between performances, Parry put detailed questions to him about his life and craft and recorded them and the answers: they survive on dozens of twelve-inch discs, still preserved at Harvard.

Mededović explained that his father too had been a singer and had known well a master performer, now dead, whom other poets had also acknowledged, the great Blind Huso. When in action, he himself could perform up to twenty verses a minute, but dictation reduced him to about sixteen: Murko, too, had found the same average rate in poets about twenty years earlier.[15] Mededović began each poem by playing his *gusle* with a bow and singing, but then fell into an unaccompanied chant, much, I believe, as Homer did himself. He was completely unable to read or write.

Mededović turned out to have a rich repertoire of long heroic songs. On being asked to perform at the greatest length he could, he began with one of about 7500 verses, vastly longer than any Parry had heard before. It was a surprise but he then performed another which extended to 13,331 verses, nearly the length of the Odyssey. He then performed another one of 12,323 verses, based on the very wedding song which Krauss, from Vienna, had recorded some fifty years before. In 1925 Mededović had heard it five or six times when a friend read it to him from a bad edition of Krauss's text. In 1935 he performed it for Parry in a form nearly six times as long as Krauss's written one, ornamenting it in his own distinct style: the 12,323 verses took him a week. It was a revelation. Parry referred to their poet as the 'Homer of Obrov'. Fifteen years later Albert Lord recorded him again and named him the 'Homer of Jugoslavia'.[16]

Remarkably, 'Homer' was not the only transformative find to be recorded in these years. Back in America, also between 1933 and 1935, the collector John Lomax, known to Parry, was recording on a heavy, wired machine the songs of Huddie Ledbetter (Lead Belly), whom he had found doing time in a tough prison in the South. Lead Belly's genius as a guitar-player and singer already rested on nearly thirty years of oral performing and composing: his performances were to transform knowledge of American oral folk songs, work songs, blues and their history.

In the wake of the Russian Revolution, meanwhile, Russians present in central Asia continued to collect the pre-Soviet epics they discovered. In 1898 one of the singers had been taken off to Kazan and made to dictate: a text of his song was published in Moscow in 1925. In 1936 another Manas singer was taken to Moscow and recorded on a disc, copies of which still survive.[17] In that same year, Chinese transcribers set to work with Kyrgyz singers who had emigrated to Xinjiang, especially after the Russian Revolution.[18] Transcriptions were already being made by the singers' friends, one of whom was the older brother of Jusup Mamay, eventually the most famous of Manas singers, who performed the poem in eight sections, more than 230,000 verses in all: he had begun to learn his craft at the age of eight and became praised as a modern Homer.[19] Transcripts of the poem's many versions had a precarious life during China's political turbulence, but forty versions of it have been preserved in the Institute of Ethnic Literature in Beijing.[20] Parry was to base his understanding of oral poetry on his field research in Yugoslavia. Lord, patiently and clearly, was to base his studies on his own further research there and on Parry's heaps of transcribed texts and discs, preserved in Harvard. Neither knew that the Manas poem, the 'Iliad of the steppe', was piling up in notes and transcriptions in China, exemplifying at great length what they were laboriously rediscovering in Yugoslavia.

By such twists and turns, oral poets in Yugoslavia became central to arguments about the making of Homeric verse. It was not that Parry first made the connection, as classicists sometimes assume: a hundred years of fieldwork had preceded him, as he would surely wish to point out. Rather, he was the first to put systematic questions to the singers and to have studied Homer's verse and phrasing in great scholarly detail before making comparisons. One ill-advised reaction by library-based scholars has been to dismiss his poets as 'backwoods' and consider them to be illiterate irrelevancies: Homer, surely, had not been a village butcher. In fact we do not know his social class. The Odyssey includes travelling poets among what it calls 'public workers', people who were paid for what they did for a wider public.[21] As they depended on a craft for their livelihood, they were certainly not members of the upper class, though that class may have patronized them. However, neither they nor the Yugoslav poets were simple as a result. As Marcel Jousse knew from his early experience in the Sarthe region in France, people are not to be classed as simple or ignorant just because they cannot read or write. They are often adept and practical in ways that their self-styled superiors are not. Mededović and his contemporaries belonged near the end of a once-grand tradition, in which oral poets had performed for local notables and princes in Bosnia, much as Homer's Demodocus performed at the Phaeacian court in the Odyssey. In the 1930s the full-time exponents of orally composed poetry were beggars, but in Bosnia their craft had not always been socially so humble.[22]

Oral poets, active in cultures far from Homer's, are analogies for Homer's composition, not proofs that he composed as they did. In Homeric studies, Bosnian and Kyrgyz poets retain their primacy because it was they who opened up an entirely new level of study of the Iliad, one which Parry joined and took forward, but which library-based scholars would never have pursued. Their leading researchers fared less well. Radloff, a man of genius, was to extend his travels and researches ever wider, to runic inscriptions in Mongolia and the language and monuments of the Uighurs and of peoples in Siberia. He became director of St Petersburg's huge Museum of Anthropology and Ethnography and served until the revolutionary year, 1917, but died in 1918, aged eighty-one. In 1937, his portrait and all mentions of his name were obliterated by order of Stalin on the ludicrous charge that he had been a German spy while carrying out his fieldwork.

Back at Harvard in autumn 1935, Parry began to consider the uses of themes, or set-piece episodes, by his orally recorded poets. In 1885 Radloff had already highlighted them as crucial items in the Kyrgyz poets' oral technique: Parry's interest was encouraged, rather, by a book on Homer's use of 'typical scenes' which had just appeared in traditional Homeric scholarship.[23] He began work on a comparison between Homer and the style of the past master Blind Huso, so far as interviews with poets of the younger generation in

Bosnia allowed him to reconstruct it. He also began to consider his emphasis on Homeric poetry as the outcome of a determining tradition, as if it owed only a very small debt to one poet's genius. However, on 3 December 1935, aged thirty-three, he died in a hotel room in Los Angeles. He was keeping a pistol in his suitcase, as often during his Yugoslavian adventures, and it went off, shooting him through the heart while he was in the bedroom. There are three possibilities: suicide, which seems the least likely, an accident, which requires the pistol to have been loaded with the safety catch off and to have been directed by chance at his heart, or even murder, by his wife, the only other person present. She was, however, exonerated by police officers who promptly attended the case. Nobody knows the truth.[24]

Avdo Mededović, the Homer of Obrov, was to be recorded again many years later by Albert Lord. By then he was in his eighties and no longer in good health. Sixteen years had passed since he last performed the wedding song but he sang it once again, this time in a version only two-thirds as long as the one he had performed for Parry in 1935. Nonetheless, in about a week he composed more than 14,000 verses in performance, including a song in which one Bećiragić Meho tells assembled listeners about the wanderings and adventures which have brought him to a wretched state. In 1935 Mededović had performed a song on this theme for Parry, alternating between dictation and a recorded performance. In 1951 his performance was only half as long, but Lord concluded, extravagantly, 'To those who have ears to hear, Homer is singing of Odysseus in the court of Alcinous, recounting his wanderings and the misfortunes which had brought him to the shores of Phaeacia', our Odyssey books 9–12.[25]

Mededović was to live until 1955, whereupon Lord paid him a fine tribute, honouring his humanity and principled Muslim values. Oral poetry continued to be composed in Bosnia and as late as the 1980s some of its maestros could still be recorded at length. However, the art was dwindling and the civil war of the 1990s did it no favours. One of its best-known recent exponents is the warlord Radovan Karadžić, the 'butcher of Bosnia' in a very different sense.

Once a prize-winning poet, he was an adept reciter and bower of the *gusle*. When he was arrested in summer 2008 on the charge of war crimes, he had just been playing a *gusle* and performing poems orally.

In Kyrgyzstan meanwhile, the collapse of Russian rule reopened study of the Manas poem to Western scholars. Though in retreat, it was found to have some famous recent singers, several of whom were both literate and capable of fresh oral composition. Their skills were unexpected. Ranked in three grades, the top performers, or *manaschi*, are esteemed for the new versions of episodes which they add to their performances. They are both transmitters and composers, therefore, categories which Homeric scholars had usually kept separate. They also correct one of Parry's most striking emphases. He found in Bosnia that a poet who became literate and began to write new poems could no longer compose orally. Literacy, he concluded, destroys oral technique. In Kyrgyzstan and elsewhere it does no such thing.[26]

10.

The Uses of Analogy

During the eighty years and more since Parry's researches, field-work across the world has continued to widen outsiders' awareness of orally composed narrative poetry. Quite independently of Parry and his work, Chinese researchers recorded some 350 long heroic songs from Mongolia. Closer attention has been paid to the huge narrative poems long known in India and to oral poets still active among Greeks. Modern Greek poets who compose in performance remain notably skilled, especially those on Crete and Cyprus, but their poems are brief, seldom more than two or three hundred verses. As for the best-known modern Greek heroic poem, the deeds of Digenes Akritas, it was a deliberate concoction by literate scholarship in the mid nineteenth century in order to give the recently recognized Greek nation a national poem.[1]

Elsewhere, oral poets have been found performing in west, but not east, Africa, Korea, Sri Lanka and the musical culture of Sindh in south Pakistan. In Arabic, the songs of Bedouin migrants into north Africa were studied before their performances became limited to Egypt. In India the Story of Hamza, father-in-law of the Prophet, grew to enormous length before the last reciter who could perform the entire tale, a marathon of seven days, died in 1928. Heroic poems by oral composers among the Khanty tribe in west Siberia were taken down in dictation in 1844–5. Renewed study has claimed they have a structure worthy of Aristotle's notion of an epic, but their content is far inferior to the Iliad's.[2]

In the 2000s, we stand near the end of this type of composition, even in its oldest venues. Television and films, available on discs, have undermined audiences' willingness to sit and listen to poems for hours on end now that they can view and hear their stories abridged on a screen. However, these orally composed poems remain important for scholars of Homer.

Whether Homer sang, wrote or composed in performance, they give new depth to a neglected question: his lost early years. In Bosnia or in central Asia, oral poets begin to learn and practise from a very early age, from five, even, in Kyrgyzstan or from ten onwards in Mongolia. In antiquity, Homer's fictitious biographies ignored the fact altogether. One of them imagined him going to school, but not to learn his poetic craft there: in due course he succeeded his teacher and taught the same subjects as his predecessor and only then began to aspire to composing poetry.[3] Ancient admirers never realized that he had learned his poetic diction from years of listening to others, members, perhaps, of his own family, as often in central Asia, and very possibly his own father, as Mededović and others exemplify. Behind Homer's teachers stretched generations of yet more oral poets, makers of the finely honed poetic diction that they and he used. Not one of them is known by name, but they had been experts during the Greek 'dark age', from c. 1050 BC to c. 850 BC, years dark to us, but not to them. These centuries teemed with song, but it is significant for Homer's dating that none of its maestros was remembered later by name. At least from the 720s BC onwards, Greek poets were remembered by their names and home cities. Homer's teachers were not. Their anonymity is a powerful argument against attempts to date the poet of the Iliad as late as c. 650 BC.

Comparative study adds life and range to two other important subjects: Homer's relation to his audience and theirs to him. When Kyrgyz *manaschi* compose in performance, they vary the speed of their voice; they strike one hand onto another or extend an expressive arm and so forth. There are conventional patterns to these gestures, but they should make classicists think of a neglected dimension to Homer's own oral performance. The Iliad abounds in words for movement, as heroes leap from chariots or speed like Achilles across the killing field. At other times they stand firm, resolute and immobile. In performance Homer could adapt the speed of his voice to bring out these varying paces. There was also scope for differing intonation. Heroes, about to speak, are often said to be scowling or groaning; Achilles is frequently furious; speakers range in tone from the drowsy god Sleep to woeful Helen: surely Homer brought out these various tones of voice in performance. If he set aside his lyre after performing his poem's first verses, he had ample scope for gestures with his hands, whether for the rough rejection of a suppliant or the magnanimous offering of hospitality, the movement of Achilles' hand when about to draw his silver-studded sword in anger or Hector's extending of his arms to receive his baby son. When composing in performance, Homer may have been a fledgling actor, not masked like the tragic actors who later performed at festivals of the god Dionysus, but bare-faced, directly addressing listeners.

When dictating to only two or three listeners, oral poets need encouragement and approving responses in order to maintain momentum. Before a bigger audience they can expect even more. Here, central Asian listeners extend our sense of the possible. In 1864 during a heroic poem's performance among the Uzbeks, 'young nomads uttered deep groans . . . hurled their cups to the ground and dashed their hands in a passion through the curls of their hair'.[4] They even began a fight. In India listeners still engage robustly with great poems which are being recited to them. Ancient Greeks were certainly emotional listeners, whether to Aristophanes' hilarious comedies or speeches delivered in the law courts in Athens. We know that these comedies were received with gales of laughter and that the jurors in an Athenian court would barrack the speeches which we now read quietly as texts. Homer's listeners may have anticipated them. Plato, writing *c.* 380 BC, credited an accomplished transmitter of the Iliad with making his audience weep and even with weeping himself so as to bring about the effect.[5] Plato disapproved of this emotionalism, but Homer himself may have done much the same.

The Kyrgyz *manaschi* are especially instructive examples. In the 1860s Radloff noted how 'the excited approval of the audience keeps spurring the bard to new efforts, and at the same time he knows how to adapt the song completely to the circumstances of the listeners . . . I myself saw how one sultan leapt up suddenly in the middle of a song, tore the silk robe from his shoulders and with a cheer threw it to the bard as a gift'.[6] After 1990 and the end of Soviet Russian rule, the most famous *manaschi* began to travel to Europe and perform on demand, breaking the Manas poem into smaller pieces. Since then, the internet has made their performances available to a global public. The short verses of the Manas poem have none of the length and variety of the Greek hexameter, but I find performances of them the most seductive analogies for a performance of Homeric epic. In the fourth and fifth parts of this book, therefore, I will sometimes cite from the Manas poem as a foil for what the Iliad contains. A black-and-white film of a great Manas poet, Sayakbay Karalaev, can be found online under Karalaev Kyrgyzfilm.m4v: despite being commissioned, it gives a very evocative sense of an oral poet, his rhythm and energy and his audience in all weathers. He chants in a compelling fashion, varying his tone but ending each verse with a cadence of three descending notes. As the subtitles emphasize, he is not transmitting what he has memorized. He is composing as he goes along.

Whether or not the Iliad was orally composed, it was certainly composed to be recited, not read. Comparative study helps to refine our views of how Homer's first listeners may have appreciated it. As a practised maestro, he would not try to be cryptic. He was addressing people whose attention he had to retain: they could not discover half-hidden subtleties afterwards by reading a text, because no text of the performance existed. There is no knowing what passed through individual minds in a gathering to hear him, even allowing for those who were thirsty or hungry or needing to go out to relieve themselves during a performance which might have been many hours long. Listeners vary and it is quite wrong to narrow an entire audience down to one high level of response.

Scholars can cross-check the Iliad's text with modern computers and find a wide range of repeated themes and phrases in it, but two questions need to be kept distinct. One is what Homer himself may have intended, an opaque question, especially given our lack of knowledge of Homer himself, and one which many, but not I, consider to be critically naïve. The other is what we, his heirs, can find in the text during our own reception of it as readers. In quick succession, replies to a speech in the Iliad certainly address points made by the previous speaker, sometimes in reverse order: this pattern may have helped the poet but it may also have helped listeners to follow the altercation. Across longer intervals, repetitions were much harder, surely, for them to pick up. The first time the verses 'well I know this in my heart and mind / Holy Troy will perish' occur, they are given to Agamemnon as he consoles his brother Menelaus after his wounding by a treacherous Trojan archer. Some 1750 verses later exactly the same words are given to Hector, a Trojan, in a very different context.[7] He is conversing with his wife Andromache as he prepares to return from Troy to the battlefront. This second use is far more powerful, as it is a recognition by the leading Trojan warrior of his city's imminent ruin just as he leaves his wife and baby son, but I do not think Homer meant it to be understood here in the light of Agamemnon's earlier, very different use of the same words. It is not an example of allusive art.

When Patroclus dies in book 16, his 'soul flew from his limbs and went to Hades lamenting his manhood and youth'. Some 3600 verses later, and only there, these verses recur for the death of Hector, killer of Patroclus.[8] Most scholars think that their earlier use adds depth and poignancy to this later one, but again I doubt that Homer deliberately contrived this effect. It is present in our reception, but not, I believe, in his intention. When he reuses verses after a long intervening stretch of the poem, their reuse may simply be a consequence of his need to compose fluently in performance: the same theme, when addressed, came out in words already used earlier in the poem. We need to read the Iliad for its forward movement, just as its first hearers received it and he composed it. Comparative evidence implies that even the most practised hearers were unlikely to relate one use of a verse to another made long before.

His listeners brought a different capacity, their familiarity with episodes in other oral poems. Parry and Lord never found that the poems performed for them alluded to other poems beyond themselves. However, oral poems are not necessarily self-contained. Parry never recorded Serbian oral poets, but they certainly allude to stories outside their poem of the moment, and even in Bosnia counter-examples have now been established.[9] Listeners to the Manas poem are a helpful analogy. The poem is so long that only pieces of it are usually performed, but audiences know many other episodes, a knowledge which the poets themselves exploit.

Homer's listeners were similarly aware. Oral poems, now lost to us, had familiarized them with tales of other heroes and their ancestors and with other episodes of the Trojan war. In this wider context, passages of the Iliad become easier to appreciate. In the course of the main plot, usually in speeches, Homer alludes briefly to mighty Heracles' labours and his service for a previous king of Troy. In book 11 he makes elderly Nestor tell stories of past deeds in his kingdom of Pylos, presenting them in the 'and then' style of a typical heroic poem. In book 6 he gives the Lycian hero Glaucus a fine speech in which he condenses tales of the young hero Bellerophon and his Lycian kin. In book 9 Phoenix tells a tale of the wrath of the hero Meleager as a warning to wrathful Achilles, but abbreviates it so much that it becomes hard for modern readers to follow.[10] Their first listeners may have had less difficulty as these shortened stories probably related to fuller poems about their subjects which they already knew. Before the Iliad, such tales had flourished like episodes of modern serials, the soaps of the illiterate dark ages.

Homer might even have alluded to such stories without being explicit. Some scholars of the Iliad believe they can detect such implicit allusions, applying what they call neo-analysis, an old approach with a new aim.[11] One favourite candidate is a passage at the start of book 18. In it, Achilles begins to lament beside the dead body of Patroclus, whereupon his captive slave girls join in the lamentation and beat their breasts. His mother Thetis the sea goddess hears his grief, even though she is beneath the waves, and laments too while her sea nymphs join in, also beating their breasts. Thetis then comes up from the sea with them and begins to lament beside Achilles while she cradles his head. Some scholars have argued that this scene would fit better with Achilles' own death, an event which was surely narrated in poems beyond the Iliad.[12] Did Homer fall here into using an episode suited to a later point in tales of the Trojan war: did he even expect experienced listeners to pick up this undertone in what he was performing? I am sceptical, not just because I have admired these wonderful verses for many decades without any sense of an incongruity in them or an implicit reference to poems now lost. Thetis' first two speeches dwell on Achilles' sorrowing, not on her future loss of him, but Achilles then introduces the theme of his own death. Next, he elaborates it in a speech which opens with a brilliant twist to Thetis' tearful response. The theme of his imminent death emerges cleverly from his sorrow and then enters into hers.[13]

From later summaries of their contents and from brief quotations by later authors, something is known of other Greek narrative poems, close to Homer's likely date, which attach to tales about the Trojan war. In my view they are all later than Homer, but even so they might have been drawing on stories already known to him and his listeners. Much ingenuity has been applied to arguing that, say, the tales about Memnon, who arrived at Troy with an army after the end of the Iliad, are also evoked by Homer in parts of his poem: Memnon kills Achilles' close companion Antilochus, Nestor's son, and is then killed in revenge by Achilles, whose own death, however, is near. In later books of the Iliad, Antilochus makes several appearances: Achilles' revenge-killing of Hector is indeed broadly comparable to his subsequent revenge-killing of Memnon.[14] I am one of those who remain wary of specific attempts to pin such allusions down, as none of our sources of these stories is earlier than Homer and attempts to postulate their pre-existence are fragile.

Poetic fieldwork has a negative implication too, relevant to our appreciation of Homer. Even in central Asia or Yugoslavia no long poem has ever been discovered which comes close to Homer's in style and quality. This judgement is not the biased prejudice of a classicist. It is obvious to anyone who can read Homer in Greek. The Manas poem is composed in stressed verses of only seven or eight syllables which Kyrgyz poets and listeners compare, engagingly, to the various paces of a horse, trotting, pacing or galloping according to the speed of delivery. The Bosnian ones usually used verses of ten syllables, breaking invariably after the fourth. None of their poets used a metre as complex as Homer's hexameter. They used rhymes, refrains and alliterative patterns, items he never used in the same way.

There are also clear differences in conception and style. Some of Mededović's poems had a unified plot and a relatively compressed timespan, but none had the artful direction of the Iliad. They centred on the doings of one central figure, whereas the Iliad's use of Achilles is more subtle and its human empathy and range are far wider. The Manas poem exists in many dictated versions, several of its parts being known in versions from the 1850s to the 1920s. On a first encounter they seem bewilderingly fond of catalogues and proper names, until re-engagement gives a sense of the underlying oral performance, driving the poem onwards.

Like the protagonists in many of the Bosnian poems, Manas, when heard by Radloff, was a Muslim: there was no scope, therefore, for Homer's many gods and their quarrels, their deceptions and assistance to mortals and their artful guidance to his listeners about events to come. Whereas the Bosnian and Manas poems indulge in listing and amplification, Homer has that supreme art of saying much by saying little. Noble reticence is one of the qualities that mark him out.

If there is such a gap in quality, might it be due to a gap in technique? Might Homer have composed his poems with an awareness of writing, whereas the heroic poets in other cultures, from Kyrgyzstan to Siberia, did not?

Poetic fieldwork with oral composers around the world has demonstrated one point, at least: Homer's poetry arose from a heritage in which oral composition had prevailed. Modern scholars agree, therefore, in calling it 'orally derived'. Previous Greek poets, composers of the soaps of the dark ages, had not used writing, but for Homer himself there are three main possibilities. One is that he was illiterate and composed the Iliad in performance, whereupon others, also illiterate, learned it by listening to it and then transmitted it orally until eventually it was written down. That possibility has obvious consequences for what we now read, as the poem would have evolved and altered, probably quite extensively, during post-Homeric transmission.

A second possibility is that Homer was illiterate, but dictated a version of the Iliad to someone who was not, and from that copy our poem ultimately derives. Dictation had been practised by Sumerian poets, some 1500 years before Homer, and had a long history in the many poetic cultures of the Near East.[15] However, composition at great length while dictating is so far unattested there. Unlike Greeks, writers in Babylonia and western Asia Minor did not use an accessible alphabet: reading and writing were confined to a small scribal class.

A third possibility is that Homer himself was literate. The simplest version of it is that he could read and write and that he composed the Iliad himself by writing it down. He then recited it after memorizing his own copy. However, literacy is not a simple option. It is a matter of degree, ranging from an ability to read a few simple words to actual writing of a long complex text. Most importantly, people may learn to read, but not bother to learn to write, as abundant evidence, ancient and modern, establishes. In antiquity it explains how someone recognized as an official reader in the early Christian Church was also described as 'unlettered', unable, that is, to write.[16] This fact of life has not been applied to Homer: might he have been able to read someone's copy of his Iliad without being able to use writing himself to compose it? If so, he might have composed it orally in performance while dictating it to a literate helper, and then have read the resulting copy himself and dictated changes and additions to it.

We do not know the answer, any more than the ancients did, but once again the likelihood can be narrowed down. It is difficult to accept the first possibility, though some do, that Homer and all those around him were illiterate, and yet his poem was able to survive through the centuries with its overall coherence and persistently signposted direction intact. As Radloff remarked after years of experience among illiterate poets in central Asia, a long poem transmitted without writing would become a different poem within about ten years. In India, there are counter-examples, long poems, orally transmitted, which have remained relatively fixed, but there is a crucial difference: they have a religious content, whether the Mahabharata or the heroic tale of Pabuji, performed in Rajasthan. In 1990 William Dalrymple gave a fine account of a travelling singer's oral performance of the Pabuji poem which he himself witnessed and discussed with the performer.[17] He emphasizes how its words, its context and the images which accompanied it on a long length of unfurled textile were strongly associated by its hearers and performers with religion and even with healing. Performances of Homer's poem lacked this religious glue and surely never worked miraculous cures. Without them, so far from becoming more fixed as it was transmitted, his poem would have become ever more disparate if its only transmission was oral.

There is a strong argument here from the relation of the Iliad to the Odyssey. The Iliad was certainly composed before the Odyssey and the Odyssey is aware of it.[18] The Iliad, by contrast, shows no awareness of the Odyssey even though Odysseus is an important hero in both poems. If the two of them had been circulating only in oral versions, the influence would not have been one way, from the Iliad to the Odyssey: they would have influenced one another. There is an obvious explanation of why they did not: by the time the Odyssey was being composed, the Iliad was a text, one whose performances could influence the Odyssey, whereas the Odyssey could not influence the Iliad because the Iliad's form was essentially fixed.[19] Then most of the Odyssey became a text too. The poems did not float orally side by side, open to mutual influence.

Despite this argument, some of the Iliad's modern scholars accept the possibility that it evolved orally for a long time. However, another feature, its language, points in the opposite direction. In 1982 detailed study by the expert Homeric scholar Richard Janko showed that, whatever its date, the Iliad's language is earlier than the language firstly of the Odyssey and then of Hesiod. His argument still holds good.[20] If the Iliad were evolving orally over as many as two centuries, its language would have evolved too and would not yield this clear conclusion, that it is consistently earlier than the language of these other hexameter-poems. Its allusions to social practices and material culture would also have evolved. Among them the poem's ubiquitous similes are particularly important evidence. They draw comparisons, as we will see, with items in their hearers' own world, but they show no trace of any of the innovations which occurred after *c.* 680 BC, neither military nor political nor even the use of a particular type of coinage which also spread, we now realize, among cities in western Asia, Homer's likeliest sphere of activity, by *c.* 650 BC.[21] Some scholars believe, nonetheless, that the poem evolved during an even longer phase of oral transmission, down to *c.* 530 BC, a date when, in their view, it first became a written text. By 530 BC there had been even more pronounced changes in social and material culture, but none has left any trace, not even in a simile.

Many classicists have accepted, therefore, that Homer himself was literate, writing with the Greek alphabet so as to fix or even compose his poem: the Iliad's 'scale and organic structure' surely 'demanded this new device'.[22] However, other heroic poems, composed later than Homer's, have none of these same qualities, although writing was available to their poets: the skill of writing is not the key which necessarily unlocks them. Inconsistencies in bits of the poem suggest strongly that Homer did not write every word nor reread his own or someone's copy of it: if he had been able to, he would have revised the text and removed them.[23]

The most famous inconsistency involves those three ambassadors who are sent to Achilles in book 9. Repeatedly Homer relates them to the form of the verb, the dual, which requires only two subjects. If he was writing as he composed, he would surely have corrected this obtrusive slip. If he was (re-)reading what he had dictated to a scribe, he would also have corrected it.[24] There is a further problem in this notion: if he wrote the entire poem and then went over it, revising it and expanding it in his own hand, how would he have reworked it? He has been imagined to have cut bits of papyrus or animal skin out of each scroll and pasted in a new bit in order to insert each of his written corrections, a procedure which scholars have also proposed for the historian Thucydides, writing complex prose many centuries later, *c.* 400 BC.[25] Thucydides' long text indeed contains early and late passages, but for an early epic poet this sort of papyrus-processing is hard to credit.

If Homer did not write every word or correct it once it was written, his use of literacy might, some think, have been more modest, enabling him to make notes, at least, to help him keep the story straight before he composed orally in performance. Certainly, writing's full potential would have needed a while to be fully exploited, hard though that is for us to appreciate after so many centuries at ease with literate versifying. The change from expert oral technique to sophisticated literary composition, Parry's assistant, Albert Lord, justly concluded, could not have occurred in the lifetime of one individual.[26] Might preliminary notes, jotted down, be a first stage, one which Homer used? Classicists have been attracted to this possibility, as it might account, they feel, for the sustained direction of the Iliad's plot and the remarkable compression of its timescale. However, it is not compelling. The many patterns in shorter stretches of the poem, the way that one speaker picks up and answers in sequence points made by a previous one, the flexible variations of phrases and recurring scenes, arming, welcoming, wounding being examples, show the poet's brilliant dexterity and control at a level which no written synopsis would have set out and predetermined for him. If he could work so coherently at this small-scale level without writing, he could surely do so at the general level of his plot. The theory that he wrote notes, then composed orally with their help, rests on a refusal to believe what oral composers can do without any notes at all: the fieldwork in Bosnia and central Asia is the crucial corrective to it. Like a stabilizer on the bicycle of a child, which reassures parents when the child has learned to ride, notes as an aid for Homer are a comforting presence to literate scholars, but are superfluous.

The remaining possibility, oral composition while dictating to a literate helper, is one that scholars would probably never have credited for Homer without the fieldwork of Radloff in central Asia or Parry in Bosnia. It is, however, one with analogies in the ancient world. Long after Homer, composition by dictation is well attested, at least for works in prose. In AD 397 Christian Augustine composed his *Confessions* as an oral prayer to God, delivering it in his room while it was taken down by a scribe. He was composing in fine Latin prose, not in demanding Greek hexameters, but he too drew on a reservoir of phrasing, the Latin Bible, interwoven with the many tricks of style and echoes of pagan literature which his lifelong training as a public speaker had drilled into him.[27] He could also proceed more quickly as his scribes had a technique which scribes around Homer did not: shorthand, an invention of the first century BC.

If dictation was the procedure which Homer followed, does it fit aspects of the text we have? How indeed should we think of him composing? Here, too, studies in the field suggest, but do not entail, answers which scholars might not otherwise formulate.

II

A Great Dictator

Dictation might have been from written notes or a largely written text, but it is far more likely to have been dictation of a poem being orally composed as the poet went along. There are clear signs of oral composition in the poem itself. When messages are sent, their speakers set them out in hexameter verse, but when they reach their recipients and are passed on, the poet makes the messenger repeat them word for word all over again. He also uses recurrent blocks of verses for actions like eating, drinking and so forth. These features strongly suggest oral composition in performance: later Greek heroic poems, composed in writing, abandoned them.

Homer also uses ring-composition, by which he rounds off a speech or an episode, but not perhaps the entire poem, by returning to the point from which he started and then restating it. Rings of this type take ever more intricate forms in the poem, not for reasons of symmetry or elegance but as patterns, perhaps often intuitive, which guided the poet's progress. Ring-composition has been identified in orally composed heroic poems, including those in central Asia and Bosnia, and although it can also be deployed by literate composers, the scale and, at times, intricacy of it in the Iliad fit particularly well with a Homer composing orally.[1]

He also expresses himself paratactically, setting one point after another and avoiding complex subordination. This style is crucial to his poem's exceptional élan and its marvellous combination of rapid movement and retardation. An example will make it clearer. In our book 1 Homer says of Apollo as he sends the plague:

> For nine days the shafts of the god went through the army
> But on the tenth Achilles called the troops to the meeting place,
> For the goddess white-armed Hera put it in his heart,
> For she cared for the Danaans because she saw them dying.

One point flows after another, whereas a subordinated version might have said, 'When the shafts of the god had gone through the army for nine days, on the tenth Achilles called the troops to the meeting place because the white-armed goddess Hera, who cared for the Danaans because she saw them dying, had put it in his mind.' Homer's style carries listeners along. It does not prove that he composed orally in performance: centuries later, the historian Herodotus also tended to use such a style but although he performed extracts of his work in public, he composed it all by writing. Homer's unsubordinated style is highly compatible with oral composition nonetheless.

So is a related feature of it: enjambment, when an adjective or participle sometimes follows a completed hexameter and qualifies it, taking up the beginning of the next verse. This feature has been much discussed, but in one of his first scholarly articles, even before visiting Yugoslavia, Parry connected it convincingly with oral composition.[2] It can also have a fine poetic effect as it can add to the force, even pathos, of what the held-over word expresses. To enhance it, Homer, I believe, would dwell on the word as he performed.

> Sing, o goddess, of the wrath of Achilles son of Peleus,
> *Ruinous*, it was . . .

is an example at the poem's very beginning, in which I have italicized the run-over word:

> and his dear wife went back to their house,
> *Turning and turning around* as she went, and shedding heavy tears

is another example, one of exceptional pathos. In the Greek a single word, qualifying the subject of the previous verse, runs over into the start of the next verse, *entropalizomenē*, 'turning and turning around', and fills the first half of the hexameter.[3] Homer surely slowed on it in performance to add emphasis: my translation struggles to catch its force.

On a bigger scale, oral composition sits well with underlying patterns in the poem's plot, ones which are particularly evident in the fighting on its longest day. Like a film-maker, Homer usually narrates simultaneous episodes sequentially, finishing with one before moving back to the other, punctuating the change, meanwhile, by verses on the general din of battle: this practice, too, fits well with composition in performance. In book 5 the dominant fighter is Diomede, in book 11 king Agamemnon and in book 16 Patroclus. In each of their series of exploits, similar guiding themes are detectable: a combat with two brothers is a favourite device, one of whom is killed, whereas the other then wounds the dominant hero before being killed himself.[4]

Diomede's prowess is particularly telling. It matches major themes in what will later be Achilles' prowess. Like Achilles, Diomede is guarded in battle by Athena. Like Achilles he carries a shield made for him by the god Hephaestus. Like Achilles he confronts Aeneas in a duel but fails to kill him because a god spirits Aeneas away. He too fights with divinities, wounding one, as Achilles never will, although his victim is only a goddess, Aphrodite. Like Achilles he fights with Hector and though he does not kill him, he wounds him heavily. Eventually he is wounded in the foot by an arrow shot by Paris, just as Achilles was to be wounded in the encounter which kills him after the Iliad ends.

Diomede never overlaps in the action with Achilles. Homer, I presume, inherited tales about his prowess and used them before he allowed Zeus' plan to help the Trojans to come into effect. This delay to the main plot had a poetically helpful consequence: Diomede's victories cause Hector to return to Troy, allowing Homer to set up the scenes there with Troy's women, culminating in the great encounter with Andromache, one whose themes he will pick up sixteen books later. I do not think Homer had in mind a different story, in which Diomede, not Achilles, led the capture of Troy.[5]

I think he worked with a pattern in mind, which plays out first with Diomede and then, even more powerfully, with Achilles as the poem draws nearer its end.

Major patterns recur there across what, to us, are several books. In book 21 a lesser Trojan, Agenor, stands alone to confront Achilles, soliloquizes about his course of action and is then pursued by his swift-footed attacker. This pattern recurs in the next book, 22, in the far more powerful episode of Achilles' final confrontation with Hector. Scholarly study has found many more such patterns, one scene mirroring another or varying it. Homer's adept shuffling of his cards has become ever more evident: it is particularly apt for a game played without a text.

Why, though, should Homer be thought of as dictating? Notably, digressions, amplifications and zigzags remain in the plot. I find it easiest to explain the confusing direction of book 2, the testing of the army by Agamemnon, if the poet was straining to combine two earlier versions of this part of the poem, one in which Agamemnon simply tested the army and they opted to leave, and another in which he urged them, under guidance from Zeus, to renew the fighting in the belief that Troy was about to fall.[6] When dictating, as Parry found, a poet composing orally will often strain to produce a longer and finer poem, the very best he can contrive: our Iliad book 2, blending two different stories, may be an example. Another may be the deliberate delaying of the Trojan advance to burn the Greek ships in books 13–15, a part of the poem which readers may at first find to be the most slow-moving. Amplification is not a universal consequence of dictation: that women's poem in the Tulu language in India came out shorter when dictated than when first performed. However, in the 1920s a version of a fine episode in the Manas poem, the funeral feast for a chief, spread to about 13,500 verses when dictated, far longer than the version Radloff had transcribed about sixty years before.[7] Homer, too, when dictating, may have strained to leave the best possible version to posterity and, in places, slightly overdone the result.

I hypothesize that his dictated version had immediate authority: as he could not read or write he did not personally go over it and revise or correct it. The zigzags and amplifications passed, then, to his followers in authoritative written form. If he was composing in performance, the error of the three, not two, ambassadors in book 9 is more readily explicable. In previous performances, now lost to us, he may have sung of only two ambassadors and then increased them to three in the special version he dictated for posterity: the obvious addition is elderly Phoenix, whose presence and long speech are the only role he has in the poem. As other embassies in it involved only two people and, correctly, attract dual forms of the verb, there was a pattern which Homer, composing orally, might have followed even when adding Phoenix to the plot. He went onwards without putting the error right: an oral composer, working in performance, would not ever think of returning and correcting. A scribe took the error down and so it was preserved in writing.

If not a pen, what were Homer's resources when he began? He confronts us, in most people's view, as the first ancient Greek poet and indeed the ancients themselves considered he had composed when the 'meadow was still unshorn'.[8] Nothing could be further from the truth. Since boyhood, he had acquired and worked with an ever-increasing store of phrases compatible with the hexameter. He had learned them from Greek oral poets and he was certainly not the first to compose hexameters about heroes or even about events in a Trojan war. Some of the metrically compatible phrases he used have been claimed to go back not just to *c.* 1200 BC but even to the early Mycenaean period, *c.* 1400 BC.[9] For years, certainly, he had composed and practised with the poetic vocabulary he inherited, one which had already evolved to fit the complex hexameter. He then had his big idea, to focus his poem on an emotion, Achilles' wrath, and to compress its action into an epic of a few days.

To help him organize the battle action, he had his own memories of the Troad, its coast, rivers and mountain range, the results of a personal visit. He was not trying to give a spatially accurate account, as if constructing a map: maps had not been invented. Rather, his memories gave him a mental space onto which he could project the main action. He also had a view of gods and mortals whose central emphasis, I believe, had never been expressed so powerfully before.

So he began to turn his big idea into epic verse. As Radloff realized, poets who compose in performance are not reciting a text which they have memorized. Memorization presupposes a written text, but they have no such thing. They are not like actors who perform a long part in a play. Since boyhood, they have learned themes and a vocabulary from other singers, much as a pianist picks up phrases and runs from another pianist, the analogy which Radloff already used in 1885. They recall them and draw on them in performance, but not because they have memorized them like passwords or numbers.

If Homer too composed in performance, he was not straining to repeat what he had committed to memory.[10] He was using what he had often rehearsed. His underlying use of space and place has been suggested to be a memory strategy, like the memory games which are prescribed in later rhetorical theory.[11] However, he was not reciting or composing from memory. Spatial markers helped to keep his narrative orderly, but they were not binding: distances could enlarge or contract and the Greeks' wall could come and go.[12]

At the level of words, not themes, there is a fundamental question: if his Iliad was orally composed, even while being dictated, must we be wary of admiring individual words in it for specially chosen beauty? A modern poet works hard and long to find the *mot juste* with pen or screen in hand, but an oral poet, composing as he goes along, cannot pause to make such a search. However, comparative studies establish that an oral poet can rehearse and practise before a performance, making the choice of a *phrase juste* possible: the more the Iliad's diction is studied, the more such phrases can be found. Usually the goddess Hera is called 'ox-eyed', *boōpis*, a conventional epithet which probably refers to her round eyes. However, once, in book 18, her son, the god Hephaestus, calls her 'bitch-eyed' or 'bitch-faced', *kunōpis*, a rude word never applied to a goddess elsewhere.[13] As Hephaestus is recalling how his mother threw him out of heaven for being lame and disabled, Homer's use of this slur for her here, and here only, is apt and surely chosen to be so.

In book 3, there is a more famous example. When Helen's brothers are dead, Homer says she did not know it 'but the "life-giving earth" already contained them'. The phrase was prized by John Ruskin for its pathos, based on a contrast between the life-giving earth and the twins' death. In more recent scholarship the word 'life-giving' has been argued to mean 'wheat-growing', but even if it does, Homer may have used it for the effect Ruskin admired.[14] Its use was not mechanical, simply to meet the hexameter's needs. Homer could have said 'Sparta's earth', *Lăkĕdāimŏnŏs aia*, to fit the same place in the verse.

Throughout, his formulaic phrases and his vocabulary are far more flexible than Parry implied. Parry began his Homeric studies by accepting and emphasizing a view favoured by students of linguistics, that 'tradition' drove Homer's diction. When he heard Avdo Mededović, he regarded him in the same light, a judgement that still stands despite a recent claim that Mededović arose within a tradition, but was not determined by it.[15] It is not, however, a judgement that readily fits Homer. Close study has shown that about 2000 of the words in the Iliad occur once only. It is hardly convincing to argue, as Parry did, that they must have occurred in other poems by Homer which we do not have.[16] The obvious inference is that Homer could indeed choose a word carefully, not least by rehearsing to himself before performing publicly.

Is prolonged dictation really compatible with Homer's exquisite use of words and phrases, sustained for hundreds of verses in sequence? It is a process which can be slow and laborious. Radloff admits that he kept on interrupting the singer and asking him to repeat or explain. Parry found that Mededović would sweat under the pressure of dictation and need a rest after only half an hour. In other examples, especially before oral poetry became a formalized study, a transcribed poem could owe much to its transcriber's own tidying and cutting.[17] However, Radloff was transcribing a language he only partly understood and Mededović was elderly and past his best. Elsewhere, younger poets have been found to dictate with greater ease and for longer periods, particularly if they are dictating to someone who knows their themes and is a native speaker of their language. Homer was not dictating to suit an outsider's wishes: the decision, I believe, was his own. He was doing it with great authority, to scribes who wanted to catch their maestro's every word. They revered him. He had no reason to become disengaged from the process as it was one, with good reason, he had inflicted on himself.

In Bosnia, Murko and then Parry each found that poets, composing in performance, could dictate about eighteen verses a minute, but they were verses of only ten syllables.[18] The Iliad's hexameter is at least half as long again. Five hexameters could perhaps be dictated in a minute and if we allow for pauses, maybe 250 could be dictated in an hour. Leaving time for interludes, a dictating poet and scribe could perhaps manage 1000 verses in a day. If so, the Iliad might have been dictated in just over a fortnight, assuming that the scribes were thoroughly at ease with the technique of writing longhand.

The bigger question is why an orally competent Homer would ever have wished to dictate. He could perform perfectly well without writing and so he had no apparent need to resort to it. Each version of his poem, composed in performance, was as authentic to him as another, and he had no previous conception of a fixed text motivating him to create one.[19] Special arrangements would have to be made to enable it. A scribe could not possibly take down the poem from one of its public performances: there would be no scope for pauses or questioning when needed. Day after day there had to be a separate performance in which verses could be dictated slowly to one or more writers. To account for it, two explanations have been offered, one imitative, one ideological.

The imitative one is that Homer or his patrons were aware of written poems in the Near East and therefore copied the idea for their poem in Greek. Such poems certainly existed, above all the ancient poem of Gilgamesh, which had evolved in various ways in Mesopotamia since *c.* 2000 BC.[20] Texts of it had also travelled and been translated. It had reached western Asia in the Bronze Age and had been translated there into Hittite. Texts of it in the cuneiform script had also travelled to north Syria. They were used as writing exercises by scribes and schoolchildren and on one widespread view, which I share, that use was the reason for their existence far from home. There is no firm evidence yet that the poem was performed to audiences in these places.[21]

Contacts between Greeks and non-Greeks certainly occurred in western Asia in the Bronze Age and later, as also in north Syria and the Levant, but despite large claims to the contrary it is far from obvious that Homer or his immediate poetic predecessors knew any of the Gilgamesh poem.[22] He shows no sign of knowing a non-Greek language, let alone a non-Greek script. Even if he or one of his patrons had once gone to, say, Aleppo and heard someone reciting stories about Gilgamesh they would not have understood them.

At the Assyrian court in Mesopotamia, poems of victory and so forth were performed live for kings who were Homer's contemporaries. There is no compelling evidence for a hotline from them to his poetry: he would not have understood a word of their poems, either.[23] Even if he or his patrons knew in very general terms that poems in these distant rulers' libraries were preserved as texts, they had no reason to imitate this foreign practice for its own sake. They had to have another motive for doing so.

The ideological explanation is that Homer's patrons wished to preserve the Iliad in writing because it was a support for rule by kings and princes like themselves, at a time when it was beginning to come under attack.[24] This explanation is not credible, either. All the main speakers in the Iliad are aristocrats, but its presentation of the leading king, Agamemnon, is far from laudatory. He is a poor advertisement for kingship in action, let alone for it in the face of growing opposition in the real world. The very notion of a poem to explore or justify kingship in the eighth or even early seventh century BC is anachronistic. Homer lived in a society without political theory, a Greek invention of the mid fifth century BC. In its absence people did not think in abstract political terms.[25] Challenges to aristocratic rule would arise from specific grievances thrown up by it, not from a theoretical belief that 'kingship' was unjust. If Homer composed in the mid to late eighth century, no such challenge to kingship is attested then or even likely. Socially and politically, aristocratic rule had a further safety valve, at least from the mid eighth century onwards: the practice of despatching Greeks from their home settlement to a new one, to be founded overseas.[26] Ruling aristocrats could send potential troublemakers abroad before a challenge to their dominance at home intensified.

There was quite another reason for wanting to create a dictated text: there was profit for Homer's heirs in having one. These heirs did not have to be his patrons: they may have been his own family. Other crafts in archaic Greece were transmitted from father to son, medicine being a clearly attested example, scribal literacy another.[27] Homer, I suggest, wished to leave his son or sons with a precious inheritance, the only copy of his poem, one which they could memorize and perform for a fee or lease out to others on payment of a worthwhile sum. A written copy was a major family asset. In the early fifth century BC the poet Pindar refers to *Homeridai* ('sons of Homer') who are 'singers of songs stitched together'. Prose authors, at a similar date, located these *Homeridai* on Chios, where a later fourth-century BC inscription has recently been found to attest them.[28] They became regarded as special authorities on his life and work, although their claim to descent from Homer himself has been much debated. If they indeed trace back to his own kin, their authority is readily intelligible. In the younger generation of his family during his lifetime, there might have been newly competent writers, trained on a tablet like the dexterous children of undigital fathers in the current millennium. We do not know, of course, that Homer married or had children, but even if not, he had other family members for whom he might wish to leave his great legacy. I like the idea of him in older age dictating the Iliad to his daughter: there is even evidence in a classical author that a daughter of his was thought to be the recipient of a long poem by him. Pindar, c. 470 BC, claims that when Homer needed to marry her off, he gave her the Cypria poem as a dowry.[29] Unfortunately the Cypria is not by Homer and the story is probably a fiction.

Of the various possibilities, oral composition in performance is my answer to how the Iliad was composed. In general, Homer moves from theme to theme with amazing skill and varies even the most closely recurring episodes to suit their context: they include arming, hospitality, combat between second-rank figures, scenes of supplication and so forth. The intricacy of his patterning seems ever more remarkable the more it is brought out by computer-assisted study. Could he really have done it while illiterate?

I believe he did so *because* he was illiterate. Composition in performance in no way excludes repeated practising, improving and enhancing, as Friedrich Krauss already discovered from the Bosnian poets he heard in the 1880s.[30] For years and years, since early boyhood, Homer had listened to his elders performing poems and had learned from what he heard. Every day and night he performed his own versions, working for an ever finer effect. What we now read was the product of years of dedicated practice and performance. It is not a 'Lay with encrusted additions'. It goes back to Homer's own version, which he dictated while he composed: the only additions, book 10 and the catalogues in book 2, are readily identifiable and detachable.

We cannot match it because we are steeped in literacy without any such reservoir, orally learned, of poetic themes and phrases. As Radloff hinted, pianists are indeed an apt comparison. Humdrum sight-reading pianists, playing only in their spare time, find it almost impossible to credit what an Erroll Garner, master of swing, or a Donald Lambert, master of stride, could compose and accomplish in performance without the ability to read music. From boyhood these masters had played and listened, making music their dedicated way of life. Homer, too, had learned by listening and practising since boyhood, like a piano prodigy who begins to play at the age of three or four. For him, too, poetry was a craft to exercise every single day of his life. Eventually he dictated the version of the Iliad which is, substantially, ours. I like to think of him as epic poetry's Erroll Garner, one whose masterpiece was eventually transcribed from a performance which he specially slowed for that purpose. We are still buying the sheet music.

PART III

Composing the Iliad: When?

12.

Problems of Literacy

My argument for Homer's method of composition has depended on evidence within his poems and on analogies with fieldwork, conducted among poets in cultures far from his place and time. My argument for his date will relate items in his poem to external evidence for Greeks and their culture, much of it found by archaeologists at ancient sites. Such evidence is disparate, never intended by origin to answer questions about Homer's date and technique. It has required sharp-eyed selection and interpretation by many minds to make it relevant: ingenuity, and its limits, are part of the process.

If Homer, still illiterate, dictated, somebody close to him, the person who transcribed each verse, could write. That skill has immediate implications for his date. Writing had not been an uninterrupted skill among the Greeks: if somebody wrote what Homer dictated, there are dates before which he cannot have been active.

In the Mycenaean era of palaces in Greece, scribes had used a syllabic script for lists and bureaucratic records in Greek, what scholars know as Linear B (*c.* 1400–1200 BC). It is most unlikely that anyone used such a cumbersome script to write down a long poem. When the Mycenaean era ended and the palace societies broke up, this arcane script disappeared. Greeks became illiterate, except on Cyprus, where a syllabic script persisted. Outside Cyprus, Greeks' illiteracy lasted for many centuries, but eventually a new type of writing was invented. It is known as an alphabet, from the Greek names for its first two letters, alpha and beta. Conceptually it was very different from its Mycenaean predecessor: it tried to convey the sound of human speech. It therefore showed vowels as well as consonants, making it much easier to read. Whereas syllabic writing had been confined to trained scribes, the new alphabetic writing could be learned by anyone inclined to do so. It is one of the Greeks' transformative inventions, the reason, ultimately, why alphabets are still in widespread use throughout the world.

In the Iliad, Homer does not ascribe literacy to the heroes at Troy. They cannot even read. In the poem's seventh book, nine Greek heroes each put a 'mark' on a lot and cast them into Agamemnon's helmet, hoping to be the one to be chosen to fight a duel with Hector. One lot jumps out of the helmet and is taken round the nine for identification. None of them recognizes it until it comes to Ajax, who confirms it as his.[1] If the marks had been written names, the other heroes, writing theirs, would have been literate and able to read Ajax's as soon as they were shown it.

In the sixth book, marks or signs are mentioned again, but they are quite different. In their strange meeting on the battlefield, the Lycian hero Glaucus tells Diomede about his ancestor, the hero Bellerophon, whom the king of Argos had obliged to carry a message to his father-in-law in Lycia: it told him to kill its bearer, young Bellerophon. The Argive king had scratched this message as 'grim signs' on a folded tablet which Bellerophon duly took to the recipient.[2] They were not a picture, as there were many of them. They were scratched in a script, but Bellerophon did not read them, perhaps because he was illiterate or at least because he did not wish to open the sealed tablet before delivering it.

These 'grim signs' are the one reference to writing in the Iliad. Their nature has been endlessly discussed, whether they were syllabic like the script used in the former Mycenaean palaces or the script used on Cyprus, whether they were in a Semitic script used in the Levant or in the alphabetic script which Greeks eventually devised. Their context has had less emphasis. Homer set this writing two generations before the main plot of his poem, in the time of Glaucus' grandfather. A Greek king sent it to a recipient in Lycia who was able to talk to Bellerophon in Greek: the signs, presumably, were imagined as being Greek too. The passage shows that

Homer knew about Greek writing, but does not prove that he himself could write Greek or even that he had full understanding of any script for it, syllabic or not. His word for the folded tablet is no more helpful. It is a *pinax*, a folded tablet, but not a *delton*, the latter being the word for a tablet which Greeks derived directly from Phoenicians, as they called them, people from the coast of what is now Lebanon and Syria. Folded tablets, made of two wooden or ivory boards, were used by Phoenicians, but not exclusively so. They are attested from *c.* 1320 BC to the seventh century BC and beyond.[3] The mention of a *pinax* does not require the writing inside it to have been in, or based on, Phoenician or another Semitic script. Homer could have envisaged it as syllabic: he projected it into the very distant past, without revealing anything about his own literacy or lack of it.

The Greeks themselves later recalled that their alphabet had been adapted from letters in the script used by Phoenicians. They did not remember where this innovation happened, and so its time and place remain much discussed. At the very least it required one Greek to talk and attend to one Phoenician, but opinions vary on how protracted their contact needed to be. Perhaps a list of letters, adapted into Greek, was the first result and then, later, actual writing of words using them, the result of continuing careful thought and practice. There was plenty of scope for such a contact. Phoenicians travelled far and wide by sea into the Aegean Greek world and then beyond, north to the island of Thasos and westwards as far as the coast of south-west Spain. They settled on Cyprus and also on Rhodes. On the south coast of Crete, at Kommos, they made use of a small sanctuary and by *c.* 850 BC were in contact there with local Greeks and then by *c.* 700 BC with travelling Greeks from further afield, some of whom left graffiti there on local Cretan cups. The site is neat evidence for Greek and Phoenician interaction.[4]

Wherever the site, it remains likely that the alphabet resulted from one single contact and was then diffused to other Greek settlements, where later it took on local characteristics: its diffusion in the Greek world remained patchy for some while. Our earliest direct evidence for it has emerged quite recently from two far-apart locations, the island of Euboea and the Latin site of Gabii in Italy, eleven miles east of Rome. Indirect evidence has also emerged from ancient Gordion, seat of the kings of Phrygia in western Asia, modern Turkey. More evidence may appear, but these pieces' implications for Homeric poetry are important and need closer examination.

In the ninth to mid eighth centuries BC, Greeks from the island of Euboea travelled widely by sea, first to the north and east, then to the west at least as far as Sardinia, and had ample occasion to meet Phoenicians while they did so, whether in the Levant or on travels across the Mediterranean.[5] In the eighth century BC, the most celebrated towns on Euboea were Chalcis and Eretria, both on its western coast, as later Greek texts attest. Sixty-six inscribed items from that century have been excavated in an area formerly identified as Eretria's sanctuary of Apollo, and among them are two broken bits of pottery with lettering scratched on them, each datable to before 750 BC.[6] One of them had been broken off a pottery storage jar and then, on its inside face, scratched with recognizably Greek letters, probably to be interpreted as *theoi*, 'to a god'. As the context in which this piece was found is soundly dated by archaeologists to *c.* 770–760 BC, the inscription should belong then too: it is certainly not as late as 750 nor as early as 800.[7] The other inscription is on a decorated cup, below whose rim were scratched the Phoenician letters *kpls*. One interpretation is that they represent the Phoenician word for 'double', attested elsewhere. Another possibility is that Phoenician letters were being used to spell a Greek word or name, perhaps *kapēlos*, a trader. If so, the writer was a Greek-speaker, but used Phoenician letters because he did not have knowledge of a Greek alphabet. The cup is datable to as early as *c.* 800 BC and the inscription was scratched on it while it was still in one piece. It is still controversial whether these Phoenician letters are representing a Greek word, but if they are, they may well belong just before the invention of Greek alphabetic writing.[8] The Greek letters scratched on the other piece, the bit of the storage jar, attest the existence of that writing a little later, *c.* 770–760 BC.

At another important Euboean site, modern Lefkandi, three pieces of pottery inscribed with Greek lettering had already been found and dated to *c.* 770 BC by their excavator.[9] Then, at Gabii in Italy, a small flask, found in a tomb, was published in 1992: it had been scratched with five letters in alphabetic script, including the vowels, E, I and, on one view, that distinctive Greek invention, a capital U or *ypsilon*. Whether the word to which these letters belonged was itself Greek is disputed, but the flask belongs to *c.* 775 BC, perhaps even a decade or so earlier. Just to complicate matters, the letters do not all face in the same direction.[10]

Euboean Eretria and Gabii may seem far apart, but Euboeans had settled on the island of Ischia just off the Bay of Naples, at a date of *c.* 775 BC as archaeological finds there imply: their presence is also attested by well-based later literary texts. They had contacts with people on the Italian mainland, including Etruscans, whose system of numerals, parent of our Roman numerals, has recently been argued to derive from the Euboeans' own.[11] The Greek lettering found at Gabii resulted from another such contact. Whether or not a Euboean was the first Greek to devise a Greek alphabet, Euboeans are prominent in our evidence for early use of it. They took it with them along their trade routes as far as western Italy.

Further evidence has come from western Asia. Inscribed bits of pottery have been found in a destruction level on the citadel of Gordion, the inland seat of the kings of Phrygia, one of whom was Midas, famous in legend for his golden touch. These pieces are inscribed with alphabetic lettering, Phrygian, however, not Greek. The letters for vowels used by Phrygians match those used by Greeks but rather than derive them from a shared time of contact with Phoenicians, I accept the view that this Phrygian alphabet derived from a Greek one. The level in which these pieces at Gordion were found is dated by radiocarbon evidence to *c.* 800–750.[12] Again, they imply that a Greek alphabet existed in the early decades of that era.

So far, it looks as if the new Greek script was devised *c.* 790–780 BC, causing these traces of it to occur within a generation. There is an important proviso: the evidence is all from inscriptions on durable material, the only survivors through the centuries.[13] The inference that one of the inscribers at Eretria was using Phoenician letters (*kpls*) to write a Greek word (*kapēlos*) implies that he, at least, was writing on the very threshold of Greek alphabetic writing, but whether or not that inference is correct, other people might have been writing some while earlier on perishable, more easily inscribed materials. It seems safe to say that Homer could not have composed while dictating, before, say, 850 BC: nobody then would have been able to take down his dictation, whatever the surface used.

Almost no scholar wishes to date Homer so early, but what if he composed *c.* 780–750? In 1952 the eminent Greek historian in Oxford, Theodore Wade-Gery, came up with a remarkable hypothesis, that the Greek alphabet was devised in order to write down Homer's poems. In 1991 the same hypothesis was advanced independently and with greater force by Barry Powell, a classical professor in Wisconsin.[14] In Powell's view, the deviser of the alphabet was a Euboean: he invented alphabetic script specifically in order to take down what Homer dictated to him. He decided on its most novel feature, the representation of all vowels as well as consonants, because vowel sounds are crucial to hexameter verse and its scansion. 'Homer', Powell concludes, 'is the *fons et origo* [the source and origin] of classical Greek civilization in a way not clearly understood before; his poems . . . established alphabetic literacy for Greece and for mankind.'[15]

This exciting proposal was made before the inscriptions from Gabii and Eretria were published. Like the inscribed pieces of pottery from Lefkandi, they challenge it: alphabetic writing was being used for simple purposes of identification or marking ownership before it is known to have been used for recording hexameter verse. No doubt it was also being used by traders and shippers and other record-keepers on perishable materials which have not survived. However, soon afterwards, some of our subsequent examples are indeed related to poetry. Four of the Greek inscriptions on pottery which date from *c.* 750 to 730 are certainly in verse, and three of

them use the hexameter.[16] The one which does not was recently
found at coastal Methone up in the north Aegean, the gateway to a
major settlement in lowland Macedon which was only a morning's
walk away: Euboeans from Eretria settled at Methone in 733/2 BC.
Once again, this inscription is in lettering matched at Eretria. It was
partly in iambic verse, a metre used for lyric and satiric poetry but
never for epic.[17] It is a reminder that heroic hexameter poetry was
not the only type of poetry being composed in Greek in the mid to
later eighth century.

The earliest known inscriptions which use the hexameter are
justly famous. One is on a small jug for pouring wine, found in 1871
in a cemetery in Athens. Dating to *c.* 750–740 BC, it begins with a
hexameter verse, some of whose individual words are also known
in Homeric epic: 'whoever of the dancers sports most gaily' and
adds the start of a second verse: 'His is this [jug]'. A second hand has
then added six uneven letters, perhaps as decoration: they have no
meaning.[18] The verses marked the jug as a prize for the best dancer
in a competition, although a modest pottery jug is not much of a
reward.

The other inscription is truly remarkable, as it relates, many
believe, to an item mentioned in the Iliad. It was found on a cap-
acious cup deposed in a cemetery on the island of Ischia, settled by
Euboean Greeks. Again its lettering is best matched at Eretria.
Recent studies have changed our understanding of it. The cup was
found in a complicated context which was not the grave of one person, let alone of a young boy, who was previously considered the
grave's only occupant.[19] It was found with four big pottery mixing
bowls for wine, the only ones known so far in an Ischian grave, and
three small jugs for pouring it. The items are suitable for use at a
grown-up drinking party, or symposium, and a widely agreed date
for the cup is *c.* 725–720 BC.

The inscription on it is set out in three lines of Greek alphabetic
lettering, in which vertical dots mark breaks in the text, a practice
known in Aramaic texts from the Near East. They say, 'I am the cup
of Nestor, good to drink from', the reading I prefer, or 'Nestor had a

cup, good to drink from', a possible alternative: some of the Greek letters are missing or illegible, so the text is disputed. 'Whoever drinks from this [cup], desire from fair-crowned Aphrodite will at once seize him.' The latter two lines are in hexameters. The clay of the cup has recently been analysed, leading to an important discovery: it matches the clay of cups made at Teos on the western coast of Asia Minor. An Eretrian from Euboea acquired it, surely at Teos, and then scratched verses referring to his use of it.[20] Writing and partying were early companions.

As I and others read it, the first line alludes to the cup whose owner is Nestor, not to a cup which someone called Nestor once had.[21] The two hexameter verses might seem to say only that a drinker from this particular cup will be seized by sexual desire. However, in Iliad book II Homer describes a 'very beautiful' cup which the elderly hero Nestor had brought from Pylos, his home: it was 'studded with golden nails', he says, 'with four handles and two doves of gold feeding around each of them'.[22] The inscription on the Ischia cup is best understood as a playful allusion to this other Nestor's cup. It explains the effect of drinking from the owner Nestor's cup ('this cup') as one of sexual desire, not the effect of drinking from the cup which the famous hero Nestor once had: 'drink for love', it is saying, but not for war. If so, it alludes, I and many others believe, to an item known from heroic poetry. The first hexameter verse has the Greek *de* as its second word, which in many contexts has the force of 'but', but not in other early inscriptions now known on pottery, not even in a sentence which follows the owner's name. On the Ischia cup the contrast with heroic Nestor and his cup is implicit, not explicit.

The inscription on the Ischia cup uses the word 'fair-crowned', which occurs nowhere in the Homeric poems: it is not a pastiche of Homeric verse. Modern scholars have tried to detach the reference to Nestor's cup from Homer too: they have considered the one in the Iliad to be based on a cup of distant Mycenaean date, one which would have existed long before Homer and which might have been mentioned already in pre-Homeric poems. This explanation is no longer convincing. The most careful discussion of Homer's cup for

Nestor has concluded that his 'elaborate description . . . could as easily be understood to imply that the cup was invented for this episode'. I agree that the allusion is indeed to the cup described in the Iliad, and known in no other surviving verses of a heroic poem. The cup's origin at Teos fits excitingly with this inference. Teos lay in Homer's heartland, on the Asian coast just across from Chios, about thirty miles south-west of Smyrna. A Euboean, probably from Eretria, acquired it from a Teian, surely while visiting Teos: he was within easy reach there of Homer and his heirs, performing the very poem which mentioned old Nestor's heroic cup. He heard it and inscribed a witty contrast to Nestor's cup on his own cup and travelled with it to Ischia, a Euboean settlement in the west. The words on his cup attest knowledge of the Iliad's existence by *c.* 725 BC and the diffusion of that knowledge as far as the Bay of Naples. The Eretrian owner no doubt explained to inquirers there just what he intended his inscription to express.

In the eighth century, as the surviving examples show, those who wrote poetry on pottery could manage only a very few verses. The argument that scribes meanwhile could take down the entire Iliad, some 15,000 verses, while Homer dictated it seems a huge quantum leap. However, lettering scratched on the hard surface of pottery may not be much of a guide. If we only had contemporary graffiti on walls, we would never guess that someone in the late 1650s and 1660s could have written out *Paradise Lost*, dictated by Milton in his blindness, or that a secretary could have taken down Dostoevsky's *The Gambler* in 1866 while he dictated it, composing as he went along: he even went on to marry her.[23]

Inscriptions on pottery were surely only one of the early uses to which alphabetic writing was put. Other materials for it were available, though paper was unknown, a much later invention of the Chinese, who made it from old rags and clothing. In its absence papyrus, in rolls, was a material on which to write, as is very well attested in texts referring to Egypt and the Phoenician cities. In the eighth century BC nothing is known of papyrus as an import in the Greek world, let alone of its cost there, but as it was a highly perishable item in the Greek climate, the silence is not significant. The earliest piece which happens to survive was found in a grave in Attica dated to *c.* 430 BC: in the later fifth century, a reference in an inscription shows that a roll in Athens then cost eight obols, less than two days' pay for a sailor but still a significant sum.[24] No Greek ever looked back and credited, say, the sixth century BC with a papyrus revolution. Papyrus could have been in use among Greeks much earlier, for all we know, which as yet, admittedly, is nothing.

Books, strung together page by page, had not been invented. Instead, readers and writers used tablets or unrolled scrolls. Perhaps Homer's scribes used papyrus rolls, even though we have no trace of them. According to Herodotus, the Ionian Greeks also wrote on the skins of goats or sheep, as was certainly the case in Near Eastern societies. A Spanish scholar, J. M. González, has recently calculated that the Iliad, in a text with margins, would have needed 'eighty-six goats of average size . . . even if one assumes the complete absence of skin defects that would prevent writing'.[25] A major goat cull, specifically to preserve the Iliad, is a fine possibility, but it might not have been needed: Homer and his family could have obtained skins already prepared for other reasons, including the making of shoes and shields. As a pre-eminent performer, Homer might have received valuable prizes from his performances at festivals and been able to acquire the quantity needed without depending on a patron. Goatskins, like papyrus, are perishable, so none has survived, but writing on them could have been at much greater length than was possible on a hard and curving pottery surface.

Tablets coated in wax were also used by writers, who scratched them with a fine writing instrument, a proto-pen. On wax, corrections and even insertions would be far easier to make than on papyrus, but there is an obvious objection to their use by Homer's transcribers. A double waxed tablet would hold about fifty verses at most, so that at least 300 tablets would be required to contain the entire Iliad. Their numbering and ordering would be a major undertaking and their bulk when complete would never have been practical. Eighty-six goatskins would be difficult enough: Homer's poem on wax would have required dozens of hives of bees.

On present evidence, the skill of alphabetic writing had been invented by *c.* 770 BC and was used for short bits of verse at least by *c.* 740 BC: I assume, though other scholars do not, that soon after it had been pioneered, skilled individuals used it at much greater length on materials other than pottery. I do not think it was a gendered skill. Inscriptions are attested on cups and an oil flask belonging to women from the eighth to the later seventh centuries BC, who presumably could read the lettering which identified them as owners. One such inscription ascribes agency to its female owner. As there was profit in being able to write, I assume that slave girls might be made to learn it and also, in families, a competent daughter, perhaps – why not? – one of Homer's own.[26]

By *c.* 725–720 BC, a Euboean could allude wittily to Nestor's famous cup, the one known in Homer's poem, which was already enshrined, I believe, in a text. Others deny that allusion, to my mind unconvincingly, and continue to doubt that a poem of more than 15,000 verses could ever have been written out at such an early date. If this cup on Ischia is set to one side, what are the earliest surviving allusions to bits of the Iliad in art, material culture or poetry?

Our knowledge of post-Homeric poetry is extremely fragmentary and new finds may enhance it at any time. The poet Mimnermus, *c.* 620 BC, seems to know the scene between Diomede and Agamemnon in Iliad book 4. Then, almost every scholar accepts that when the aristocratic poet Alcaeus alludes to Zeus' promise to Thetis he knows this distinctive episode from the Iliad.[27] Alcaeus was active on the island of Lesbos *c.* 610–600 BC.

Mid century, *c.* 650 BC, a poet of martial elegies, Tyrtaeus, composed a poem for the Spartans in Sparta which urged on their warriors and told them not to retreat and leave an old warrior dead in front of their ranks.[28] His verses echo verses which Homer gives to old Priam when he is imploring his son Hector to avoid Achilles and retreat inside Troy: Priam evokes the dreadful plight which will befall himself, an old man, if Hector dies and Troy falls, leaving him to be killed and devoured by his own dogs.[29] His words are integral to his speech and cannot be explained as later insertions into the Iliad:

'When dogs work shame on the grey head and grey beard
And private parts of an old man who has been killed
This is the most piteous thing for wretched mortals.'

Tyrtaeus also represents an old man dying in the dust, his 'head white and his beard grey': a grey head would not have scanned in his verse, but his other words match Homer's. He is 'holding his private parts in his hands' and is a shameful sight. Just as in Homer, the fine death of a fine young man is contrasted with the shaming death of an old man. Other small details of Tyrtaeus' words are explicable in terms of Priam's very words in Homer.[30] It is far-fetched to ascribe them, though some scholars have, to a separately existing prototype in other heroic poetry, lost to us but accessible to Homer and, independently, to Tyrtaeus, both of whom used its very words. The obvious inference is that Tyrtaeus was echoing Homer's Iliad here. The notion that Homer suddenly drew on Tyrtaeus, as nowhere else, is wholly implausible: Tyrtaeus composed primarily for a Spartan public, far from Homer and the eastern Greek world, and was addressing soldiers who had adopted a very different type of warfare from the one Homer presented in his epic. Tyrtaeus' echo of the Iliad is another counter to the extreme contention that Homer composed as late as the 640s.

I believe there is another implicit echo of Homer, even earlier. In his poem on the birth of the gods, his *Theogony*, Hesiod addresses near the beginning the Muses who sing on Olympus, *homēreusai* with their voice, and 'their untiring voice flows sweet'.[31] The word *homēreusai* is only otherwise attested in Homer, where it has a different sense. To judge from its root, it means for Hesiod 'fitted together'. As Hesiod uses puns elsewhere, I think he chose this unusual word because it allowed him a nice pun here too: it sounded like 'Homerizing', a punning tribute to his great predecessor Homer

Hesiod–Homer

who also invoked the Muses and was guided by them. Hesiod's poem dates to the later eighth century BC, *c.* 710, and so his reference to the Muses as Homerizing dates Homer before that decade. I am the first person to cite this passage for this purpose and suggest this pun, but I continue to believe it, though as yet I am in a minority of one.

Allusions in art to the Iliad are even harder to pin down.[32] The main source of them is painted pottery, with the further difficulty that figures on it are never captioned in the eighth century BC. Two much-discussed items exemplify the problems. An Athenian pottery bowl, said to have been found at Thebes, is datable to *c.* 725 BC and is painted on one side with a long warship leaving a shore and, to the left of the ship, two much taller figures of equal height, a man and a woman. She is holding a garland and he is holding her by the wrist. She stands with her feet close together, implying a reluctance to move with him. The couple have been interpreted quite plausibly as Paris abducting Helen, the origin of the Trojan war, though nothing identifies either person specifically.[33] Even if this interpretation is correct, the artist did not necessarily know the scene from Homer's Iliad. It is hardly evoked there, and the painter could have known it from the many other heroic poems about the war. Evidence of such poems' use by a craftsman survives from around 700–680 BC when a big bronze brooch for fastening a robe was made in mainland Boeotia and incised with various scenes of myth, including a horse on wheels, evidently the Trojan horse, an item not in the Iliad.[34]

On a pottery wine jug from Athens, evidently deposed in a grave, a broad frieze with fifteen human figures runs all round the broadest band of the vessel's decoration. Datable to *c.* 730 BC, two of these figures have been identified as Hector and Ajax, engaged in the exchange of weapons which concludes their duel in Iliad book 7. Two more figures have been read as the two heralds who persuaded them to behave in this way. However, the eleven other figures are then unexplained and these four are not obviously engaged in any such business. There is no good reason to accept a Homeric interpretation.[35]

The most compelling case for painters' engagement with Homer rests on several representations of the blinding of the Cyclops, a famous episode in the Odyssey. Four are relevant, the first one dating to *c.* 660 BC, whereupon two others, also on large vessels, follow within twenty years.[36] The most detailed is on a mixing bowl for wine, found in Etruria and painted by a Greek who signs himself as Aristonothos, using lettering which is Euboean: probably, he made it there as a travelling craftsman.[37] Five aggressors, just as in Homer, wield a long instrument, probably modelled on a spit, and drive it into the eye of the Cyclops. Behind him is a stand with a rack for, it seems, cheeses, items mentioned by Homer, and on a pole a milk pail, which Homer also mentions. The Cyclops may have been known in tales outside the Odyssey, but these further details indicate that the artist is overwhelmingly likely to have had Homer's poem in mind. If so, the Odyssey was current by *c.* 670, preceding this cluster of paintings. The Odyssey was certainly later than the Iliad, as internal references prove, and so the Iliad existed earlier.

I have selected these Homeric allusions as the most plausible among those which scholars have proposed. Even so, the full list of suggested candidates is brief, implying that the poems did not immediately inspire patrons and potters to show Homeric scenes in preference to the many other stories known in myth. Of course, if I had lived *c.* 730 BC, I would have commissioned a set of Iliadic pottery, including cups and a big mixing bowl for wine, and used them at my drinking parties to entertain my guests while pointing out how the scenes painted on them showed highlights from the great poem. As yet no such set has been found. In their absence, such poetry and painting as survive from before *c.* 620 BC are reticent but do not require a downdating of the Iliad to *c.* 640. In English painting, scenes from Shakespeare begin only with William Hogarth in the 1730s, a century and a half after their performance. They are not an argument for redating the playwright.

Inscriptions, poetry on papyri and painted scenes on pottery are random survivors, not always preserved with details of where they were discovered. Meanwhile, other archaeological finds continue to offer evidence external to the Iliad. The most suggestive discoveries here were made in the 1960s during careful excavation of royal tombs at Salamis on the east coast of Cyprus, just to the north of modern Famagusta. In the corridors which led up to the tombs' entrances, their excavator, Vassos Karageorghis, found skeletons of horses, a chariot, a silver-studded sword, a big vessel for olive oil and a male skeleton with hands bound and evidence that he had been killed before being deposed. Inside some of the chamber-tombs, he found iron skewers and fire dogs, and, in one, gold blinkers and a gold brow-band for a horse. All these items recalled items in the Iliad, especially those put onto the big funeral pyre which Achilles organized for Patroclus in book 23: he put horses on it and twelve young Trojans with their hands bound. The finds at Salamis were promptly classed as Homeric and in 1977 were even interpreted as 'an attempt to emulate the magnificence of heroic funerals', Patroclus' being the prime example.[38]

The Salamis tombs date to between *c.* 700 and 670 BC. If they were imitating Homeric splendour, the Iliad indeed existed before that era. However, renewed study and ever more finds of comparative evidence have reversed the inference: the Salamis burials were not influenced by Homeric epic, but Homer was influenced by what they represent, upper class burial customs extending from the Levant as far as Italy, of which they are examples. Some of these customs trace back as far as the eleventh and tenth centuries BC.[39]

A different approach needs consideration. Rather than reflecting the influence of an already current Iliad, archaeological finds might enable us to define when items in it became current in the real world. The more clear-cut those dates are, the more relevant they are to the date at which Homer composed a poem mentioning them. Naturally, they involve controversy and complexity, the very essence of ancient history, especially about a time before historians existed.

13.

Trojan Wars

Of all the items in the Iliad, the biggest is the Trojan war. The poem is set near the end of a prolonged siege of the city of Ilion, Troy. The attackers are Achaeans, Greeks to us, led by king Agamemnon, who was 'king of many islands and all Argos', specifically of 'Mycenae with much gold'. Whether there was a Trojan war of this type is a question which arouses much public interest, but enjoyment and understanding of the poem do not depend on its answer. The truth of the Iliad lies in its human insight and understanding, whether or not any of the events in the poem ever happened. The war's historicity, or lack of it, bears on something else, Homer's own relation in time to the world he presented.

Outside the Iliad we have two types of evidence with which to assess the war's reality. One is a random array of texts, mostly on clay tablets, which have survived from the major ruling power in western Asia, the Hittites. The other is an ever-increasing range of archaeological finds, particularly those from ancient Troy.

Hittite texts from between *c.* 1450 and 1250 BC contain references to a people called Ahhiyawa, who are ruled by a king. After much discussion, it is now clear that these Ahhiyawa are not simply a resident people on the Asian mainland. They are based west of it, on or more probably across the Aegean Sea.[1] They have a king who has ships. Evidently, the Ahhiyawa are Greeks, to Homer the Achaioi, in what we call the Mycenaean age after its best-known centre, Mycenae. The Hittites assume they have a central kingdom, but it is not named in any of their tablets, and one modern view is that they were mistaken to suppose that such a centre ever existed: some scholars prefer to interpret the palaces of the Mycenaean age as

146

independent competing centres. Others infer, as I do, that there was indeed a central kingdom: at first it may have been Thebes, a major Bronze Age site, before it became Mycenae, the site we know best, until *c.* 1180 BC. Twenty-nine Hittite tablets refer to Ahhiyawa, and others are surely yet to be discovered among the thousands that survive: do any of them show the Ahhiyawa waging war against Wilusa, a real Trojan War?

They indeed show some interesting things, that by *c.* 1400 BC the king of Ahhiyawa had a claim to islands in the east Aegean and that some of the Ahhiyawans then settled on a promontory of south-west Asia at Milawanda, the site later known in Greek as Miletus. It was a particularly defensible site for settlers from the Greek main-land, given its position and relation to the nearby river Maeander's mouth.[2] Their control of it came and went, but existed in *c.* 1290 BC, a time when the king of Ahhiyawa also extended his influence northwards up the Asian coast. In their letters, it is striking that Hit-tite kings sometimes address the king of Ahhiyawa by the highly respectful term 'brother', otherwise used by them for rulers as grand as Egypt's Pharaohs: Ahhiyawa was not a trivial realm. One king of Ahhiyawa even received a Hittite queen in exile. When the Hittite king Myrsilis II fell ill, *c.* 1310, the statues of two foreign gods, one from Lazpa (the island of Lesbos) and one from Ahhiyawa, were summoned to attend him by his bed: those present with him wondered how best to worship them.

Some of the personal names in the Hittite tablets about Wilusa are tantalizing. Several Greek names have been proposed to underlie them, but they remain contested, except for the mention of an Alak-sandu as king in Wilusa *c.* 1280 BC, a name which strongly suggests the Greek name Alexandros. A king of Wilusa had perhaps married a Greek bride, possibly for diplomatic reasons, and had given their son a name quite likely to be derived from Greek.[3] It has a resonance for admirers of the Iliad, as Alexandros is an alternative name in the poem for Paris of Troy. The Hittite king states that he had helped Alaksandu previously and had killed his enemy, but we do not know who the enemy was. A Hittite force had then, it seems, gone on to attack Wilusa, after which the king made a treaty with Alaksandu, regarding himself as being in control.[4] None of this interaction resembles anything in Homer's Trojan war. Alaksandu is not Homer's Paris, and the only similarity between them is their name.

What is missing in this intermittent evidence of contacts is any reference to a siege of Wilusa and its destruction by Ahhiyawan invaders. The most recently found evidence of a defeat involving Wilusa emerged in 1991 during work on a road into the huge site of the Hittite kings' capital, inland at Hattusa, the modern Boğaz Köy. A bronze sword was unearthed by chance, inscribed with words which declared it to be one of many swords dedicated to the storm god by a Hittite king after a victory over the Assuwa alliance: he ruled *c.* 1450–1420 and this event belonged late in his reign. This alliance was already known from Hittite texts to have included Wilusa–Troy. The sword resembles a type of sword known to be in use only among Mycenaean Greeks, but it puts them on the side of an alliance which included Troy, exactly the opposite to the war in the Iliad.[5]

A fragmentary Hittite tablet, datable to *c.* 1290–1270, is more informative.[6] In it a Hittite king remarks that he and the king of Ahhiyawa had been hostile to one another about Wilusa, but as he does not specify a war, the hostility may only have been a dispute: he regards it anyway as past history. Very few other references to interventions at Wilusa survive, but they are interventions made by Hittites, not Achaeans. The latest in date, *c.* 1220–1210, concerns their king's wish to reinstate one Walmu as king of Wilusa, from which he had been driven out. In this case too his enemies are unspecified.[7]

Hittite tablets, then, show that Achaeans, the Ahhiyawa, had been active in western Asia in the fifteenth to later thirteenth century and that they had intermittent control of Milawanda, a place identifiable as Miletus. They do not show that they had ever besieged and captured Wilusa: here, the ruins at Troy become relevant.

In 1822, Charles Maclaren, founder of the *Scotsman* newspaper, reoriented the modern search for the ancient city. In his book *The Plain of Troy Described*, he argued that it was at Hissarlik, not Bournabashi. Some of the land around the site was acquired by the Calvert family, merchants based in the Troad, one of whom, Frank Calvert, then bought the eastern half of its mound and, in 1863, began to excavate there, impelled by a second edition of Maclaren's book. Five years later, in August 1868, he entertained a newly arrived excavator, none other than the businessman Heinrich Schliemann, fresh from his recent visits to Ithaca and Mycenae in Greece.

Schliemann had had a profound love of Homer since his youth. Before coming to Troy, he had already sat reading from the Odyssey to villagers on Ithaca, Odysseus' home, and on the island's main mountain he had wept profusely while reading to himself its verses about Odysseus' reunion with his wife Penelope. A year later he was to call Sophia, his bride-to-be, his Helen. They then had two children, whom they named Agamemnon and Andromache. Schliemann baptized Agamemnon by holding a copy of the Iliad over his head and reciting a hundred of Homer's hexameters: few of his modern detractors could do as much.[8] As a recent student of his diaries has well remarked, 'unlike most men, Schliemann was gifted, not burdened, with an ability to overcome the weighty constraints of rational thinking and, ignoring the sarcastic asides of his "betters", to give substance to his dreams'.[9]

In 1868 he had already spent the summer making soundings for Troy at the most widely credited site for it, Bournabashi, near those puzzling water springs, supposedly hot and cold. It seems clear, despite his later claims, that it was Calvert who redirected him to consider digging at Hissarlik instead. In 1870 he conducted a brief excavation there for eleven days and in 1871 returned with a large team of local workers. During three years, he and they drove a big trench down through the north side of the mound and found a whole series of ruined settlements, one built on top of another, the second earliest of which he claimed to be king Priam's Troy. It was no such thing, but the settlements indeed stretched back to *c.* 3000 BC. What Maclaren, the newspaper proprietor, had proposed, Schliemann, the global businessman, proved on the ground.

Since the 1870s, years of careful archaeological work, mostly by teams from America and Germany, have refined and extended

Schliemann's impetuous excavation. In the 1890s, Wilhelm Dörpfeld, himself one of Schliemann's great discoveries, identified nine chronologically separate layers on the site and named them Troy I, II and so forth. His classification still stands, though some of his levels have been subdivided: his Troy VII has become Troy VIIA, Troy VIIb 1, Troy VIIb 2 and Troy VIIb 3, increasing the complexity. Archaeology resumed on the site in the 1930s and then began again under Manfred Korfmann in 1988 in a joint venture between Tübingen and Cincinnati universities: it continues under Turkish direction, led by Rüstem Aslan, himself a fervent lover of the Iliad ever since he first encountered it after moving from his rural family in central Turkey to a school in Istanbul.

Troy I, though small, was a walled settlement and is dated *c.* 3000–2550 BC, long before Homer, whereas Troy IX is dated *c.* 85 BC–*c.* AD 550, long after him. Visitors to the site find most of these levels baffling despite the best efforts of signs and information points: Troy, to outsiders, seems a mess. To insiders, nine Troys and their subdivisions raise many intriguing problems, but the crucial one for dating Homer's poem is which of them, if any, shows evidence of destruction in war.

Four Troys are relevant to this question. The first, Troy II, was championed by Schliemann, who even claimed to have found the very treasure of king Priam, supposedly unearthed as a single deposit near a part of the city's wall. The treasure is now widely considered to have been a variety of valuable objects assembled by Schliemann from various locations on this level, but Troy II was indeed quite impressive, as the clusters of precious metal found there, twenty-one in all, imply.[10] It was defended by stone walling and it had two huge gateways: the paved ramp up to one of them is still visible. Its population spread over about twenty-five acres of the plain outside the wall, but, even so, modern estimates of it put it only in the low thousands: by modern standards Troy II was more of a town than a city. A great fire ravaged the site *c.* 2300 BC but as only one human skull has been found in the debris, most of the population may have escaped what was probably an accidental, not a military, destruction.[11] As Schliemann himself came to realize, Troy II ended at a date far too early to be linked to the heroes of Homer. It has produced no evidence at all of a Greek presence or of anyone who could speak Greek.

Troy IV and V are more modest settlements, but very hard to assess because Schliemann's deep trench went straight through the main evidence for them. Troy VI is much more important. Pottery found in it dates it from *c.* 1700 to *c.* 1300 BC, but despite radiating streets and the remains of impressive walls, implying a height of up to thirty-five feet, Schliemann was surprised by its rather modest extent. It is now clear that he was excavating only its citadel. Further excavation and survey in the 1990s has shown, despite much controversy, that this Troy spread further out into the plain below the citadel and covered some 50–85 acres, implying a total population of perhaps 5000–8000: this lower town was protected by two specially dug ditches.[12] Until then, visitors were justifiably surprised that it seemed so small, a teacup for such an epic storm. When Alexander the Great visited Troy in 334 BC, he ran to the tomb of Achilles, as then shown on the site, 'naked', Plutarch says, 'as was the custom'. In 1976, in Alexander's honour, I decided to outdo him by running naked round what I took to be the entire city of Troy VI. It has turned out since that I ran round its citadel only.

Discussion of Troy VI is very complicated because it has been subdivided into nine phases. The later ones certainly flourished while Mycenae in Greece, surely the centre of the Ahhiyawa, was at a peak. The eighth of them, Troy VIh, still had impressive stone walls and towers around its citadel, but when it ended at a date now placed convincingly at *c.* 1300 BC, the big blocks of its wall were scattered apart. There is no sign of burning or casualties and although it is arguable what exactly a destruction of a city has to involve, the collapse of Troy VIh is currently agreed to be best explained by an earthquake, Troy being on an active earthquake belt. It was not sacked after a military siege.[13]

Its successor used to be called Troy VIIA, but as it was a prompt rebuild, showing no cultural break, it is now known as Troy VI i. It was much more modest than its predecessor, but it lasted for at least a hundred years, including the time when Hittite tablets attest Alaksandu as Wilusa's ruler *c.* 1290–1280 BC. It was eventually destroyed, and on this occasion warriors were probably involved: ash and debris became piled up to a depth of several feet and in Troy VI.i's lower part, beyond its citadel, traces of burning were found in a public space, as well as three piles of stones, 157 in all, probably sling stones, and skeletons of people, rapidly buried, one of which, a girl's, showed traces of burning too. However, there is no evidence about the attackers' identity, let alone that they were Greeks, and in all only two bronze spear points, three bronze arrowheads and bits of two bronze knives have been discovered.[14] The total is very small if a full besieging army was involved.

There is a false trail here in later Greek evidence. Greeks long after Homer calculated precise dates for the fall of Troy, of which ones in the 1180s BC became especially authoritative. Archaeologists have sometimes appealed to them, but they are historically worthless: they are the ingenuities of ancient Greek scholars who were working without valid historical evidence.[15] They do not support a link between tales of the Trojan war and the destruction of Troy VI.i. Dates for its destruction are based on associated finds of pottery and vary from *c.* 1230 to 1180 BC, the later decades being ones which many consider to be too late for an expedition to have been mounted from Mycenaean palaces in Greece, some of which were already under stress after earthquakes. They were to collapse by *c.* 1180 BC anyway.

Among this uncertainty, one life-long expert, Sinclair Hood, has championed a bold alternative: Troy VIIb.2, a level which also shows a few signs of burning by fire.[16] It is not a grandiose ruin. Its fall apparently dates to *c.* 1050, long after the fall of the Mycenaean palaces, but some sort of raid by their survivors has been suggested by Hood as a possibility even then. Memories of this raid would indeed be closer to Homer's own time, but this lone proposal has yet to gain supporters.

In the Iliad, Homer refers to two sackings of Troy. One is the imminent sacking by Agamemnon's besieging army, but the other had already occurred under Priam's father, king Laomedon, by implication about 60–80 years earlier. Laomedon had refused to pay Apollo and Poseidon their reward for building walls for his city. When Poseidon sent a sea monster, Heracles killed it, but Laomedon denied him his reward too. So Heracles then 'sacked the city', Homer says, 'and made its streets desolate'.[17] The sack by Heracles was superhuman, to us a myth. It is not a historical event, but might perhaps have arisen from a memory that Troy had once been destroyed by an earthquake, to be followed after two or three generations by another destruction, which involved armed attackers. About 600 years separated Homer from Troy VI h and VI.i's collapses but it is just possible that memories of these two big events survived long enough to inspire a later tale about Heracles, followed by a tale about an Achaean siege, to each of which Homer was eventually an heir. They were tales, however, not history.

Even if it emerges one day from a Hittite tablet that there was once an attack by Ahhiyawa on Wilusa, that attack would not necessarily be the blueprint for Homer's Trojan war. In the Iliad there is a crucial absentee: there is not a single reference to the Hittites or their empire, though they were the great power in Asia while the Mycenaeans' strength was at its height.[18] They would surely have been involved in Troy's defence against a significant siege and a capture of the city. Despite its difficulties, an attractive aspect of Stuart Hood's theory, that the end of Troy VIIb.2 inspired the Greek tale of the Trojan war, is that it occurred when the Hittite empire had already disappeared.

The Hittites' absence in the Iliad extends further. In the final book of the Iliad, in an episode of profound power, Achilles sympathizes with his visitor, king Priam of Troy, and remarks how 'we hear' that 'before, you were fortunate', ruling over 'all that out to sea, Lesbos, seat of Macar, encloses' and Phrygia and the Hellespont: he is referring to features which were not parts of Priam's realm but which bounded it on the west, east and north.[19] His reference to Lesbos as the seat of Macar is revealing. The island is mentioned, Lazpa, in a Hittite king's letter in the early thirteenth century in a context which assumes that it was subordinate to him.

Place names on the island also attest its close relationship with Hittite power, but Homer ignores this past entirely.[20] Instead he refers to Macar, who was a mythical forbear of families who later ruled on the island. Until *c.* 1050 BC it was the home of non-Greeks and only then of Greek immigrants. If Priam's Troy was one or other Troy VI, Lesbos was in the Hittites' sphere of influence at the time, but again, Homer ignores them.

The notion that Homer drew on accurate memories of a Greek siege of Troy is anyway highly implausible. On any reasonable dating of his life, some 400–600 years had passed since any level at Wilusa which might have been destroyed in a siege. For most or all of this intervening period, Greeks had been illiterate, except on Cyprus, and had had no ability to read anything which might have been written about a war when the Ahhiyawa were at their peak. Homer's version of the siege is manifestly fiction: the war at Troy is in its tenth year and involves many tens of thousands of troops, raising obvious questions about supplies and so forth, while not one major hero has died in battle before his poem begins in the war's final months.

The story of a big Greek naval campaign which eventually sacked Troy has no support in the Hittite tablets as currently read and studied. A very few modern scholars consider it to be historical nonetheless, while others consider it unsupported 'as yet'. Proof of it, I believe, will never appear, a belief which is supported by other heroic poems' relation to historical events. They invent or distort a past: they do not preserve it. The great Manas poem tells of Manas and Kyrgyz warriors' battles against hundreds of thousands of Chinese and other infidel non-Muslim troops, but no wars on such a scale are known, though Chinese tribes were near neighbours of the Kyrgyz and in the 1750s conquered some of their chieftains for a while. The medieval *Chanson de Roland* freely distorts a single skirmish, datable to AD 778, between Christians and Saracens: it even changes the participants and the outcome. Homer's heroic Trojan war need not derive from a real assault on Wilusa by Greek warriors, either on their own initiative or as a group in a bigger force. It is natural to suppose there was no poetic smoke without a real

Trojan fire, but as Oliver Dickinson, an expert in the archaeology of the Greek dark ages, *c.* 1100–800 BC, has aptly remarked, even 'assuming that what we see in the Homeric tradition *can* be described as "smoke", it may simply be mist'.[21]

Beneath that mist was an old ruin, not a historical war. From *c.* 1050 BC onwards, Greeks again arrived across the Aegean and this time, in the Hittite empire's absence, settled at sites in the Troad and along the Aegean coast of Asia. From their grandfathers, they could have heard stories of distant times when a king on the Greek mainland intervened in west Asia and was recognized there as a significant contemporary. When they established themselves on Asia's coast, some of them visited the non-Greek site of old Wilusa and its visible remains and as a result stories began to circulate among them that it had once been ruined by Greek heroes, their ancestors: Troy VIIb.2 had indeed been destroyed quite recently. Again, an argument from analogy is helpful. In other cultures, the idea of a heroic age arises in hindsight after the disruption of a grander era, often among people who have migrated and settled anew: heroic ages 'are a looking back after a breakdown, and the past itself moves along with the generations of the present'.[22] There were no historians in the eleventh to eighth centuries BC and in their absence there was no historical consciousness. Instead, poetic storytellers reshaped a past to suit the present. They developed a tale of a great expedition by their ancestors which had sacked a great Asian city, traces of which were still visible. It was a heartening story for listeners who were settled precariously in nearby Asian lands, but I doubt there was any historical truth to it. They imagined a vast expedition with hundreds of ships and masses of bronze armour, giving it the huge scale which is still such a feature of Homer's war.

My answer to the question 'why Troy?' as the site of such a war is simply that Troy's visible ruins greatly impressed later Greek visitors. There is a similar instance on Crete. After the destruction there of the big palace at Cnossos, visitors and settlers explained its winding passages and jumble of rooms as a custom-built labyrinth. Fresco paintings and images of bulls on the site encouraged the tale that the child of a bull and a woman had been concealed in this impenetrable labyrinth. The legendary Minotaur was born.

The Trojan war, I believe, is an invention of the eleventh to ninth centuries BC, originating among east Greeks, forerunners of Homer's audiences. It is one of the distinctions of what is still called a dark age, an era for which we should light a candle on behalf of Homer, its beneficiary. Certainly, he was not the first Greek poet to tell about it. He uses fixed phrases when referring to Troy whose scansion and spelling show that they had developed earlier than his own lifetime.[23] They call Troy steep, with broad streets, a stone wall and stone towers, features which fit old Troy VI rather well, though it ended *c.* 1300 BC. They also call the Trojans tamers of horses: 'there are immense quantities of horse bones from the later phase of Troy VI . . . one must wonder whether Troy served as a market in the horse trade, perhaps even as a breeding and trading centre'.[24] During Troy VI.i, formerly classed as VIIa, the city had been ruled for a while by Alaksandu, someone whose name may be Greek (Alexandros), possibly because his mother may have been Greek herself. Might a visiting Greek poet have sung then about Alaksandu's horse-breeding, towered city, phrases which passed into later Greek poets' repertoire?

Linguistically these phrases have been proposed to go back to the Mycenaean era, although the inference is far from certain. Even if they did, they need not have been deployed then in poems which told of Troy's siege and sack by invading Greeks. Walls, towers and horses were memories which could have survived without any Greek war at Troy and then surfaced in verses about a war long after Troy VI's phases ended. Some of Homer's recurring phrases for Ilion–Troy certainly derive from a later era, '*poti Ilion irēn*', 'to holy Ilion', being a clear example: *poti* and *irēn* are Aeolic forms, deriving from *c.* 1100 BC onwards when speakers of Aeolic Greek entered Lesbos and the Troad.

Wilusa, our Troy VI.i. and the Hittite empire had fallen *c.* 1180 BC. By 1050 BC yet another level on the site, Troy VIIb.2, had ended too. Around that time, there is clear evidence of cult being paid by people at the ruined site. In the remains of a building left empty since *c.* 1180 BC, outside the citadel on the 'West Terrace', they were offering animal sacrifices and burning incense on incense-burners, three of which have been found in fragments.[25] There is no sign that they were Greeks, but below the wall of Troy VI's old citadel a later cluster of cups, a jug and a mixing bowl imply that Greek visitors were paying cult there too.[26] They did not need to talk and learn from non-Greeks on Troy's site in order to devise a tale of a great Greek siege and explain the ruins at which they were worshipping. At various other Bronze Age sites and burial mounds across the Greek world, from the tenth century onwards Greeks were also paying cult to what they interpreted as landmarks from an old heroic past.[27] They could have invented the Trojan war without local help.

Before Homer, Greek poets then made it famous, to judge from the way Homer assumes knowledge of a full story of it among his listeners. In the ninth to eighth century two Greek kings with highly evocative names were active locally, though attested only in later Greek texts. On Chios a king called Hector is said, by a fifth-century Chian author, to have ruled as the great-grandson of the first Greek ruler on the island: his date is best placed *c.* 800 BC.[28] At Kyme, on the west coast of the Troad, a king called Agamemnon ruled, and Aristotle and others tell that he married a daughter to king Midas of Phrygia. From Near Eastern contemporary texts, Midas is known to have been active in what we can calculate as 719 BC: he lived on to the year 694.[29] If he married this daughter *c.* 700 BC, Agamemnon, her father, was born *c.* 735 at the latest.

These two kings bear names well known in the Iliad. An attractive guess is that 'Hektor in the poem *owes* his name to King Hektor of Chios, whereas Agamemnon in the poem *gave* his name to King Agamemnon of Kyme'.[30] I too do not believe these names are coincidences, unrelated to Homer's poem: this guess about their relationship implies that the Iliad existed by *c.* 735, in time to inspire the king of Kyme's name. To test this notion, other items in the Iliad need to be considered, some from its social background, some from its material culture.

14

'Not as mortal men are now . . .'

In the Iliad, there are two distinct social worlds, the world of the heroes and the world of the poem's many similes. As we will see, similes, or extended comparisons, present a world familiar to Homer's listeners, because one of their aims is to illuminate moods or qualities in the main narrative. In the rest of the poem Homer tries to present the heroes in terms which differ from his hearers' world: he is explicit that they are not as mortal men nowadays. As his Agamemnon rules Mycenae 'with much gold', it is apt to consider if what we know of Mycenae and the Mycenaean age, c. 1500–1200 BC, contextualizes Homer's heroes.

Some indeed have thought so. After his remarkable finds at Troy, Schliemann went on to dig at Mycenae with spectacular results. In 1876 he even believed he had found the very death mask of king Agamemnon, ruler in the palace-city. Surely, he and others concluded, his finds there must relate to the Iliad and Odyssey's material world. In 1952, tablets found at Mycenae and other contemporary palaces nearby were shown, brilliantly, to be written in Greek. That discovery renewed discussion of Homer's relevance to the Mycenaean age of splendour. It still haunts interpretation of his poems, but as others promptly argued, it is not quite the key that Schliemann once claimed.

When the main Mycenaean palaces fell c. 1180 BC, they took literacy in Greece with them. What subsequent Greek poets composed about them was based only on hearsay. In his lifetime, some 400 years later, Homer would be even less well informed about them than modern film-makers are about the remote Middle Ages. Without consulting history books, they present them as a time of knights in chain mail, women in veils and wimples, hawking conducted on horseback, clerics, fat or thin, and peasants working with ploughs and axes. The social world with which they interlink these items projects stereotypes from their own time.[1] Valiant peasants prevail with hearts of gold; wicked nobles come to a bad end; women show strength and autonomy and black protagonists excel at court. From these social stereotypes historians could justly infer that the script was not planned in, say, the 1930s.

In such films, material items like chain mail or hawks can indeed trace back to accurate memories of the remote period being presented. Conversely, social items, the strong autonomous woman or the virtuous working peasant, derive from social expectations of the auteur's own time. They are an amalgam, but one to which audiences readily relate: I will assess the Iliad's presentation of its heroes' world with this analogy with film in mind.

The poem tells of a great naval expedition led by Agamemnon, a sceptred king of Mycenae, who also 'ruled over many islands'. Contingents came from all over the mainland and participation was often not voluntary. We happen to hear that a fine was payable by a rich man at Corinth in the north Peloponnese if he tried to evade the call-up: his father, a respected seer, had warned him of it.[2] Agamemnon also controlled enough of the southern Peloponnese to be able to offer Achilles a site as far south as Kardamyle, deep down in the Mani.[3] The scale of this expedition has been related rather vaguely to a growing sense of Greekness, or Panhellenism, in Homer's own lifetime, yet Homer never uses the word Hellene. Such a concerted expedition into Asia, led by the ruler of many people, based at Mycenae, does not relate to history in Homer's own lifetime. Whether or not some sense of Greekness was implicit then, it relates to memories of a distant Mycenaean past when kings of the Ahhiyawa had indeed been involved in western Asia.

Important other kingdoms in the Iliad have a similar derivation. They include Menelaus' Sparta, old Nestor's Pylos and Cadmus' Thebes, each of which was important in the Mycenaean era, including Sparta, where finds of Mycenaean tablets have been made at

Agios Vasileios as recently as 2008.[4] Three much-discussed verses in Iliad book 9 refer to the riches which travel into the cities of Orchomenus and Thebes: they too are related to memories of a Mycenaean past, because Thebes and Orchomenus were impressive then, but not in the ninth or eighth century. They passed to Homer as part of his poetic inheritance, but they are incidental to the poem. Homer or an early reciter revised them, making Greek Thebes into Egyptian Thebes, as Greek Thebes was unimpressive in his own time whereas Egyptian Thebes was rumoured to be extremely rich.[5]

There are also the personal names of at least fifty of his lesser heroes. Soon after the Mycenaean tablets were deciphered as Greek, personal names in them were matched with clusters of names used by Homer in the Iliad: they cluster particularly among people from Pylos around old Nestor and among the Myrmidons whom Homer lists around Achilles.[6] Of course, they are not therefore historical people, but these names seem to have been introduced into heroic poetry by poets before Homer, using names, even then, with a long prehistory: Homer did not invent them.

His awareness of real Mycenae is superficial nonetheless, even when he calls Mycenae a place 'of much gold'. Visitors to the superb Mycenaean items in Athens' archaeological museum readily endorse this description while they admire Mycenaean gold cups, gold face masks and even a little child's gold clothes. However, the gold is cut from hammered-out thin sheets and even the many bits of gold found in Mycenae's famous Grave Circle A amount to hardly half a talent of gold by weight. In the Iliad, Homer presents Agamemnon as offering Achilles ten whole talents of gold, a figure way beyond what we know of Mycenaean reality.[7]

The Mycenaean era's legacy to items in the Iliad is otherwise far from impressive. Two of the most-cited items relating to it are not from Homer's own poem at all: a helmet made of boars' tusks is mentioned in book 10, but that book is a later addition to his work. Traces of Mycenaean topography have been considered to occur in the Catalogue of Ships, but it was added later to what we know as Iliad book 2. The boars' tusk helmet might anyway have been known to a post-Mycenaean poet as an antique, a class of objects well attested in the archaeology of post-Mycenaean times: one such helmet has been found at Elateia in central Greece in a context datable to the tenth century BC, long after the Mycenaean era ended.[8] The origin of information in the catalogue remains a matter of dispute, but even after advances in our knowledge of Mycenaean place names it is highly unlikely that a Mycenaean text underlay it.

In the main poem, prime candidates for a Mycenaean origin are the items of bronze used in battle. When the Greeks teem out with Achilles as he re-enters the war, the 'gleam from the brightly shining helmets and bossed shields . . . and breastplates' went up to heaven and 'all the earth laughed because of the flashing of bronze'.[9] The heroes' bronze weapons include bronze arrowheads and spearheads, the latter being known to us from big mould-made examples in the early Mycenaean age and from small pointed ones found at Cnossos then too. The Mycenaean era was part of the late Bronze Age, whereas iron weapons, requiring a new technology, began to be used in parts of the Greek world only from c. 1020 BC onwards: Homer's heroes never use iron swords. They wear items of bronze armour, including bronze greaves on their legs, bronze breastplates and bronze helmets, and they carry round, bronze-coated shields: an entire bronze panoply has been excavated near Argos, dating to c. 1400 BC.[10] Although a bronze breastplate dating c. 710 BC has also been excavated at Argos itself, it is likely that memories of Mycenaean bronze underlie the equipment of Homer's heroes.

His heroes' shields have been much discussed and studied. Sometimes they are individualized to bring out their status and physique: Nestor has a gold shield and Agamemnon one which is awesomely decorated. Most of the heroes' shields are rounded and are held with a strap which is slung round their neck and shoulders: a base of leather is bossed or coated with bronze. Round shields are attested in late-Mycenaean art, as are bossed shields, but the survival of metal bosses, though few in number, shows that round bossed shields persisted in the subsequent dark ages too. Bronze-coated shields, however, are unknown in Mycenaean art. On present evidence, they did not appear until *c.* 700 BC at the earliest. I believe that the round bossed shields of Homeric heroes are derived from round bossed shields used in the 'dark ages' but that their bronze coating is a poetic invention, matching the general bronzing of other heroic armour and weaponry in the poem.[11]

Sometimes a hero's shield is even bigger and longer, but not without reason. Periphetes, in book 15, is the only warrior to be presented in the entire poem as a man from Mycenae and he is one whose shield is said, uniquely, to extend down to his feet: it is a body-shield, therefore, of a type best known in the early Mycenaean era.[12] As he retreats before rampant Hector, he trips on his shield, worn, therefore, on his back, and falls, exposing himself to a fatal frontal wound. Some scholars consider, though I do not, that it is only a coincidence that Homer equips his one warrior from Mycenae with a Mycenaean type of shield which is the death of him.

When Homer presents such body-length shields in other contexts, he does not sustain them consistently. Early in book 6, Hector leaves the battle with the rim of his shield bumping against his neck and ankles, evidently a long body-shield. It makes his retreat impressive to Homer's listeners, but elsewhere his shield is not a long body-shield at all: he could never have carried one when pursued for miles by Achilles. Stubborn Ajax also carries a shield 'like a tower', one flung behind his back, which emphasizes his obdurate role and behaviour on the battlefield, but elsewhere he is presented as carrying a rounded shield with one strap, a later type.[13] Homer was aware, I believe, that an ancient body-shield was appropriate for a man from Mycenae, but when he mentioned one elsewhere, he was using it to suit a character at a particular moment.

Most importantly, horse-drawn chariots are used by Homer's heroes as their means of transport into battle. They emphasize their high status and bring them to fight on foot in the duels which win them glory. Mycenaean warriors used chariots in battle, but in a very different way, driving them into the enemy and shooting arrows and throwing spears while standing inside them. Homer's heroes are accompanied by a chariot-driver, but although they have their hands free they almost never fight or shoot from the chariot itself. They dismount on reaching the main battlefield and leave their chariot and horses to wait for them and taxi them back to safety.[14]

Chariots are attested in Greek use during the century after the Mycenaean palaces fell: in the eighth century BC too they were still used in battle in kingdoms on Cyprus, as in many parts of the Near East and in western Anatolia by the Lydians who ruled near Homer's own heartland.[15] They are also shown then on big Greek pottery vessels painted in the Geometric style, particularly in Attica: mostly they are shown there in processions, a use for them in real life.[16] Outside Cyprus, however, Greeks no longer used them in battles. Once again Homer and his predecessors have ascribed to their heroes an item dimly remembered from the remote Mycenaean age in order to project an image of warriors 'not as mortal men are nowadays'.

These intermittent items from the Mycenaean past have been adapted to new poetic purposes, but they coexist with significant absentees. Homer presents halls and kings' houses in Troy in the Iliad and at many other places in the Odyssey, but he never alludes to painted frescoes on their rooms' walls, although fresco paintings are one of the glories of the Bronze Age palaces in Crete or Pylos.[17] Details of dress, too, are significant. His heroes wear a simple combination of a tunic and a cloak pinned at their shoulders, but big dress pins are best known archaeologically from the post-Mycenaean world. Women wear a long *peplos*, also pinned, which reaches to the ground, and a head-veil whose two ends extend down to the shoulders. In the Mycenaean era the usual fashion for high-ranking women's dresses was a sewn robe, not a pinned one. They are not shown wearing veils.[18]

As for social and political practices, Homer is unaware of the complex type of kingship, governance and land tenure attested in tablets found at Mycenae and elsewhere. Whereas fifty slaves seem to him to be an impressive number for a hero's property, the masses of dependent workers in Mycenaean kingdoms were of a different magnitude: in all, tablets from Pylos refer to 654 slave-women and

370 slave-girls.[19] His heroes' funerary rites are particularly revealing, as they attach to practices which archaeology can indeed itemize. Hector and Patroclus are cremated in ritual splendour, after which their bones are gathered in a casket and only then interred: cremation was not a funerary rite in the Mycenaean kingdoms, let alone in this distinctive way. In 1981 an impressive parallel for parts of the Homeric rite was found at Lefkandi in Euboea, where a bronze urn contained the cremated body and weapons of a socially eminent male, deposed beneath the floor of an impressive building: it is dated convincingly to *c.* 925 BC. Homeric funerals, we now know, are shaped by practices in the so-called dark ages.[20] They are the era not just for the origins of the tale of a Greek war at Troy, but for the origins of much of the Iliad's material world.

Attempts to interpret tablets from the Mycenaean world by adducing evidence in Homer's poems are misguided. 'Homer is not only not a reliable guide to the Mycenaean tablets,' wrote Moses Finley in a major study, following his ground-breaking book, *The World of Odysseus*, first published in 1954, 'he is no guide at all.' He was writing when it had recently been shown that tablets from the Mycenaean palaces were written in Greek, but he was quite right.[21] The Iliad's bronze weapons, chariots and so forth were items Homer and previous poets considered to belong in a remote past, but their presentations of power and social relations are not Mycenaean at all.

After refuting a Mycenaean date for Homeric society, Finley advanced two reasons for accepting that the Odyssey and even the Iliad drew nonetheless on a historical background. One was that their social relations and practices showed demonstrable consistency. The other was that some of them could be matched by what he regarded as the only other available evidence, modern anthropologists' accounts of simple societies far from Homer's in space or time. He cited very few such anthropological studies in the first edition of his brilliant book, but he dated what he considered to be the coherent social background to the tenth or ninth century BC, long before Homer himself, who composed the Iliad, Finley believed, in the later eighth century. Finley dated the social background to this earlier period because it was embedded, he believed, in the many fixed phrases, or formulas, which run through the Homeric poems. As they were traditional, not Homer's own creation, he considered that they enshrined a largely coherent social world from long before Homer's own day, one which he simply repeated. Finley also emphasized the absence of a *polis*, or citizen-state. *Polis* in Homer, he believed, 'means nothing more than a fortified site, a town'.[22] This limited meaning, he thought, also implied that the term *polis* was being used in an older, traditional way.

There are problems with parts of his argument. Closer definition and analysis of these traditional phrases show that they convey very little about social realities or institutions. Most of them refer to abiding facts of life like the dawn or the sea, cattle or horses. Homer uses a recurring phrase for kings and princes, 'lords nurtured by Zeus', *diotrephees basilēes*, but it had not ossified the social reality of an earlier period: it was used by the poet Hesiod, just after Homer, when referring to princes active as a social reality in his own world.[23]

Homer was certainly helped by the store of phrases he had learned from previous poets. Working with them, he, and no doubt his predecessors, exaggerated their heroes' strength and prowess to emphasize they were 'not as mortal men are nowadays'. A famous example is their diet. Like poets before him, Homer presented the Iliad's heroes as eaters of meat, rather than the regular Greek diet of grain, olives and vegetables. Their meat was roasted, not boiled. Spits, fire irons and so forth are quite frequently found in Greek graves from the tenth to eighth centuries BC, but in the classical age meat was eaten only when animals were killed out hunting or when an animal was offered as a sacrifice to the gods.[24] The heroes' diet of meat was probably not Homer's own invention, but by making it their exclusive diet he gave a sense of epic distance to their world. It was out of the question for a hero to be a vegan.

Epic distancing of this kind was deliberate: it was not just due to the repetition of metrically convenient phrases, inherited from past poets. In order to give their heroes a social context 'not as mortals are nowadays', Homer and his predecessors could not consult past texts: even if they had ever found some Mycenaean tablets they could not have read them. In their absence they would partly repeat what they inherited, but they would also reach back to what they and their audience knew of an earlier world. Comparative studies show that such knowledge would most readily extend as far as their grandparents' generation, as that is the point beyond which oral memories of a social context usually tend to fade.[25]

The Iliad's presentation of political authority is best located there. The poem freely refers to kings. It uses two different words: *anax*, which means lord as well as king, and *basileus*, best translated as prince. The main *anax* in the poem is Agamemnon. He is represented as *skēptouchos*, holding a sceptre, one which had passed to him down the generations of his royal family. He can also be called a *basileus*, but that word applies to lesser leaders too, including Achilles, who is not yet the king in his homeland. It is not that the Iliad lacks a notion of hereditary monarchy, let alone that it presents a society ruled by competing 'big men' or 'paramount chiefs', as some have claimed, reading these items into it from anthropologists' studies of simple societies far from Greece and Homer's era.[26] Homer never applies the word *basileus* to someone who is simply the head of a household. In a definitive study, Pierre Carlier has shown that when used in the singular, in 63 cases out of 67 'basileus . . . designates the hereditary leader of a political community – what we call a king'.[27] However, Homer also uses the word in the plural, *basileis*, for people who are princely nobles. That plural use is attested in Hesiod's poetry, addressing real life in the late eighth century BC.[28]

At that date monarchical kings also ruled in parts of the Greek world, not least in cities on Cyprus. They are attested, too, in places settled by Greeks in western Asia and the nearby islands: king Hector on Chios and king Agamemnon at Kyme are examples.[29] In the eighth century, therefore, Homer had prototypes for royal rule without reaching back to the Mycenaean age, but like Hesiod he would also know of sceptre-holding *basileis* as local notables, ruling as a group. For dating him, a crucial point is that an individual *basileus* or *anax* can be challenged, even denounced, in his poem, but that royal authority in the abstract is never contested. A *basileus* is descended from Zeus. In the mid 680s BC, the hereditary royal line of the Lydian kings in western Asia was boldly and brutally ended by a usurper, Gyges. He did not take the title of king, but from the mid 650s BC onwards his example was followed in several city-states in Greece, leading to the overthrow of rule by Zeus-descended *basileis*. This change was a political shock wave, but Homer gives no sense of it. Quite the opposite: in a simile he describes Zeus as sending storms against a community, a *polis*, whose *basileis* are giving crooked judgements in the meeting place. All are punished for the injustice of the ruling few, a presumption shared by Hesiod, c. 710 BC.[30] There is not a hint that others in the *polis* might right the wrongs by throwing their *basileis* out.

This simile shows that Homer indeed knew of public government in a *polis*, implying more than Finley's 'fortified site': one of the scenes which he set on the famous shield of Achilles has a similar reference. However, a fully fledged *polis* included citizens with political rights. The first known recognition of citizens' political rights is a ruling adopted in Sparta, datable to some point between c. 700 and 670 BC: it gave the citizenry a formal power of confirming or rejecting items put to them in public meetings. Those meetings were to be held at defined times in the year.[31] As Finley correctly insisted, no such rights are visible anywhere in Homer, neither in the narrative, nor in a simile. In the narrative of the Iliad, the troops in the Achaean camp and the Trojans in Troy meet in assemblies, but only when they are called by their leaders: they never vote.[32]

Away from home, a Greek army could indeed resemble a city-state, as participants sometimes remark in later Greek historical texts, but Homer's assemblies of the Greek soldiers at Troy have no formal powers beyond the parcelling out of booty after a joint campaign.[33] The political life of his heroes' army is not in its members' hands. Heroes sometimes resort to use of the lot, whether as competitors or duellers to decide who shall have the first throw, or as sons to decide which one should go to war at Troy or as heirs to divide an inheritance, as even Zeus and his brothers are assumed to have done with the heavens, the earth and the underworld.[34] There is nothing specifically political about use of the lot, let alone democratic, but unlike political aristocracies in later Greek history the heroes never use it to allot fixed public roles among themselves.

These hints of public political government are consistent with relatively simple communities, what some scholars call proto- or pre-*poleis* 'not without some rudiments of a wider political structure'. They fit quite well with what we infer about such communities between, say, 830 and 760 BC, again within two generations of Homer's first listeners. In keeping with them ambassadors go off from one community to another, but relations between heroes from different cities are linked to *xenia*, the personal tie of guest-friendship. In real life, around 710 BC, Greek allies from far and wide were still drawn into a war on the island of Euboea in response to their leaders' ties of *xenia*. Inter-city relations in Homer already fit this pattern, one he readily projected back from an eighth-century world into the heroic past.[35] The personal ties of *xenia* would long persist in Greek societies, but in the seventh century BC they were joined by the formal role of *proxenia*, one which city-states began to bestow on publicly chosen individuals.[36] It was at odds with the heroes' world and Homer never mentions it: it did not exist when he was composing,

Xenia, or guest-friendship, was a personal relationship symbolized by the exchange of gifts. Homer's heroes exchange gifts to mark it but they also bestow and exchange gifts where we would think of sales and priced transactions. In penetrating pages of his book, Finley argued that this pervasive practice is evidence of a historical society because it matched the role of gift-giving in simple societies which modern anthropologists had observed elsewhere in space and time.[37] Social practices like marriage, he well showed, involved gifts, not purchase. Gift-giving is more prominent in the Odyssey, Finley's main subject, whereas the Iliad's main narrative contains only two examples of gift exchange: in book 6 Diomede and Glaucus exchange armour when they realize they are kinsmen, and in book 7 Hector gives Ajax his silver-studded sword and Ajax gives Hector his scarlet belt when they part from their inconclusive duel.[38] Nonetheless, reciprocal giving is presupposed elsewhere in the poem, especially in the relations of gods and mortals: in the Iliad, a gift or vow from a mortal is a strong claim to receipt of a counter-gift from a god.

The role of gift-giving among the heroes is striking, but it can be paralleled without looking as far afield as pre-political societies in Borneo or the Trobriand islands. It has been aptly used by Mediterranean archaeologists to account for impressive items with foreign provenances which are found in rich burials anywhere from Cyprus to Sicily from c. 920 BC onwards and which may have travelled to or from Greeks as gifts. Such items are particularly evident in the eighth and early seventh centuries BC and include bowls of precious metal, like those bestowed in the Homeric poems.[39] However, gift-giving is not specific only to that period. It is also prominent in exchanges in Herodotus' Histories, where it occurs in episodes whose dates range from c. 700 to 500 BC. It has even been interpreted as a peg round which Herodotus' oral information was arranged and structured.[40] It can also be traced in the kingdom of Macedon, whose kings Philip and Alexander still lived in a culture of gift-giving in the fourth century BC, even though coinage was a well-established resource for them.

Gift-giving's prominence in Homeric society does not coexist with coinage: it fits well, but not exclusively, with the ninth to eighth centuries BC, including a phase which I have loosely classed as the lifetimes of grandparents of Homer and his first listeners, within ready oral memory. Even so, gift-giving is not the only type of exchange in the Iliad. At the end of book 7, when boatloads of wine arrive from the king of Lemnos, the Greek troops stock themselves up with it, 'some for bronze, some for gleaming iron, some for hides, some for live cattle, some for slaves'.[41] Intensive barter, it seems, underlay what were surely negotiations with an eye for value. Yet, here too there is the same absentee: coinage, an invention which began to spread in Greek cities in western Asia as early, it is now realized, as c. 650 BC.

800s –700s In the absence of contemporary histories it is notoriously difficult to distinguish social forms and practices in the early to mid
eighth century BC from those of the ninth. By relating Homer to
oral dictation, I have implicitly dated him to no earlier than 800 BC:
our surviving evidence for the Greek alphabet depends on inscriptions on hard surfaces, but even so there would surely not have been
writers in the mid ninth century able to take down his long dictated
poem at speed. The social background of his poem fits this date too.
It is best understood as the projection of a poet composing in 750–740
BC, but trying to convey men 'not as mortals nowadays', both by
equipping them with items remembered vaguely from a distant
Mycenaean world (all that bronze . . .) and with practices mostly current a generation or two before his listeners' time (those feasts . . .),
perhaps *c.* 800–780 BC. The result was an amalgam, but one his listeners could readily follow, much as filmgoers can relate to a combination
of genuinely medieval items with a web of social values from their
own present era.

There is a difference between Homer and a modern historical
film-maker: he tended to link up his items from a distant past with
what he and his listeners ascribed to social and political life some
two generations earlier, projecting what was not like 'mortal men
nowadays'. Film-makers, by contrast, draw on contemporary social
priorities of their audiences' better selves. Unlike Homer, historical
films are limited by presentist criticism.

The amalgam I detect is too general to pin Homer and his Iliad to
a date within several decades. However, there is a further resource:
mentions of individual places and objects. They can be set beside
archaeological evidence which sometimes allows us within relatively close limits to date the beginnings of a practice or object and
the beginnings of Greeks' contact with particular places: the alphabet has already been an example. Such evidence has been used to
date Homer in ways which seem gratifyingly precise, but complexity, as ever, besets them.

15.

Dating Homer

Alone of Greek authors, Homer has given his name to a branch of archaeology. 'Homeric archaeology' was once a label for excavation and study of sites and items from the Greek world between *c.* 1300 and *c.* 680 BC. It is no longer regarded as an apt one. It obscures a wide local diversity whose context was quite other than Homer's epics. If the material world of the poems, 'not as mortal men nowadays', is an amalgam of the old and the near contemporary, it will never emerge from one level of the past. Archaeologists now look on the Iliad as if it is itself a mound built up of layers of widely differing dates.[1]

'Homeric archaeology' has lost its former scope, but a promising approach is still to use archaeological evidence to date when particular objects mentioned in the Iliad became current. A modern example will make the point clearer. If a poem mentions a mobile phone, we can be sure it was not composed in the 1960s. Homer would usually eliminate items and practices which were particular to his own time, but while composing orally he would not be wholly consistent: comparative study of orally composed heroic poems shows that anachronisms intrude nonetheless. A piquant example has been studied on modern Crete.[2] A Cretan oral poet composed a poem whose subject was the heroic deed by Patrick Leigh Fermor and his associates when they ambushed the German general Heinrich Kreipe on the island and abducted him in April 1944. While setting this exploit in a remote heroic context, the poet let contemporary items like aeroplanes or typewriters show through from time to time. With their help a historian would be able to date the poem's composition quite closely.

The most obvious anachronisms in Homer's heroic society are mentions of iron, otherwise minimally present in the heroes' bronze repertoire. In book 4, the arrows of the Trojan Pandarus are said to be tipped with iron when he breaks the truce between Trojans and Greeks. In book 23, at his games for Patroclus, one of the prizes offered by Achilles is a lump of iron which, he says, he had taken as plunder: it had belonged to that recurring source of items, Andromache's father Eetion:[3]

> 'Rise up, those of you who will attempt this contest too.
> If his rich fields are very far off,
> He will have it to meet his needs for five revolving years:
> Not for want of iron
> Will his shepherd or ploughman go to the city, but he will
> provide it himself.'

His announcement assumes that an upper class owner's estate might lie far from a town and that its workers would usually go there to buy metal: the town is not simply parasitic on the country. It also assumes that farm goods will be made of iron, as never in the Mycenaean age. Such a use for iron began only from c. 1020 BC onwards, being customary in the eighth and seventh centuries: Achilles' remarks draw on practices nearer to Homer's own time than to the iron-free Mycenaean past.

There are also some unexpected details of social organization. Occasionally Homer is specific about the organization of the armies or parts of them, the Myrmidons who accompany Achilles or the five units of Trojan troops, each with three leaders, who assault the wall around the Greek camp in book 12. The details then fade from his mind and are forgotten within a few hundred verses. Twice, however, he refers to that basic principle of social organization in many Greek communities, the phratry, or 'brotherhood', each time in words spoken by elderly Nestor.[4] A man who loves war among his own people, Nestor says in book 9, is like a man without a phratry. Earlier in book 2, when the Greeks' army first prepared to go out to battle, Nestor told Agamemnon to draw it up 'by tribes, by phratries so that phratry may help phratry and tribe, tribe'. This manner of organization never reappears in the action: it has been much discussed but it seems most likely that Homer was briefly referring here to phratries as they were known in 'dark age' societies, certainly by the ninth to early eighth centuries BC.

These anachronisms do not slip in for poetic effect, deliberately sought. They occur because Homer is composing orally in performance, running ever onwards at speed. Generally, what an epic poet includes is stronger evidence of his date than what he omits, because he may sometimes have maintained a deliberate silence about an item of his own day. In his main narrative Homer sustains some considerable silences: he never mentions cavalry in battle, nor alphabetic writing nor the distinction between Dorian Greeks and Ionians. He never mentions any of the settlements along the Aegean coast of Asia which existed in his own time, not even Miletus, Milawanda to the Hittite kings, which had been settled by Greeks by c. 1420 BC and held intermittently by them thereafter.

There is another pervasive silence. During the eighth century BC, that new style of partying, the all-male symposium or drinking party, was becoming fashionable in parts of the Greek world, as we can infer from surviving sets of the pottery vessels used for it. Homeric heroes ignore it. Unlike symposiasts they eat their meat and drink their wine at a single meal, held at any time in the day. They sit on upright chairs and are served by male attendants, whereas symposiasts were served by slaves, especially slave girls. Homer sustained the older type of eating and drinking, without anachronistic hints of a symposium showing through.[5]

These silences are not clues to the date when he composed. They were deliberate. The alphabet had been in use since at least c. 780 BC and if Homer dictated his poem he was well aware of its existence. Historical anecdotes and even, within limits, painted pottery show that cavalry warfare was also known to Greeks by the later eighth century BC. It was fought by mounted warriors whose horses were not just their means of transport before they dismounted and fought on foot.[6] As for Ionians and their settlements in Asia, a mention of them would have clashed with the poem's theme of a great

173

Greek invasion without Greek bases already in Asia. As for symposia, it was out of the question for heroes 'not as mortals nowadays' to lounge at a drinking party on a low couch.

Our knowledge of important social changes is decidedly patchy between *c.* 750 and 650, the timespan within which Homer is usually dated, but two major ones are securely known: they affect warfare and political authority. Homer excludes both, but they were so transformative for such central aspects of his poem that I think they would have shown through it, if only in a simile, if he was composing when they had already come about.

One is the overthrow of that long line of kings, carried out in Lydia in the mid 680s BC: neither in his narrative nor in similes does Homer show any awareness of such a response to high-handed actions by a *basileus*. The other is the change from warfare waged by heavily armoured champions, often accompanied by groups of armed followers. Instead, battle began to be conducted by fully armoured infantry, or hoplites, arranged in long lines and protected by big shields held on one arm and by spears and swords, wielded with the other: as they marched in step into battle, they were sometimes kept in time by pipe-players.[7]

In the Iliad the exact nature of the general battle is not entirely clear, perhaps not even to Homer. At times, he refers to concerted action by one and all together and illustrates it with similes which imply a mass engagement of troops who clash like waves on the seashore.[8] His main focus is on individual heroes who engage in single combat, supported by groups of companions. The hero throws a spear and sometimes follows up with another spear for thrusting: less often, nineteen times in all, he goes on to engage with a drawn sword. Heroes fight in what Homer calls the *stadiē*, the space in front of a general mass of lesser infantry into whom they sometimes retreat, a withdrawal which Homer presents in a recurring phrase. That mass, too, throws spears and engages in combat, following up when the enemy ranks break, whereupon its members sometimes need to be told not to plunder the dead on the ground in front of them.[9]

Whatever the pattern we impose on these phases of combat, it is certain that the battles are never waged between heavily armoured lines of hoplite infantry, shields held on one arm, spears in the other, each man sheltering his unshielded right side with his close neighbour's shielded left.[10] Crucial innovations for this formation were the two gripping points of a shield, the *porpax* in the centre and the *antilabē* at its further edge, positioned for the arm in the shield's inner surface: Homer never uses either word. This fundamental change to Greek warfare had come in by *c.* 675 BC, probably beginning among Greeks in western Asia, the main audience for whom Homer performed.[11] If he was composing *c.* 660 BC, it is hard to believe he systematically eliminated every trace of infantry warfare as he and his audience knew it and ignored the shift in individual warriors' mentality which began to come with it.

Specific datable items included in the poem are also indicative. Absences can only imply a date before which the Iliad might have come into existence; they might, after all, be deliberate silences by the poet. Objects, however, if datable, fix a date after which it was composed. Homeric Troy has temples and at the very start of the poem Chryses prays to Apollo, 'if ever I have roofed over a *temple* to you . . .': cult in the Mycenaean age was paid at shrines inside the palaces, not at temples outdoors. Homer's mentions of temples and of statues of gods or goddesses have been considered to count against a date as early as the eighth century BC, but temples are now known in that century and could anyway be made of wood, a material too perishable to survive for archaeologists.[12] So could statues of a god. Homer locates a temple of Apollo inside Troy and also one of Athena which has an image of her big enough to receive a robe. He might have been influenced here by reports of big stone statues and temples in Asian cities, known to Greek visitors in the eighth century BC. If so, he imagined them in non-Greek Troy too.

More specific items are the goddess Hera's earrings. Before going off to her planned seduction of Zeus, Hera dresses in an ambrosial robe worked for her by Athena and 'put in her pierced ears earrings, triple eyeballs, like mulberries'. This jewellery already puzzled ancient scholars of the text, but it has at last been understood.[13] The earrings were eyeballs because they were set with three dangling rounded balls, and these balls were like mulberries because each of them was granulated, like the lumpy outside layer of a mulberry's fruit. The words are not formulaic, nor are they based on some remote Mycenaean memory: Mycenaeans are not known to have worn earrings.

Granulation was a complex technique which originated in the Near East and had to be learned directly from a practising craftsman. Examples of it in the mid ninth century are known from items deposed in graves at Athens and at Lefkandi on Euboea: probably they were imports from Cypriote jewellers.[14] Earrings with three drops like eyeballs were another Near Eastern invention, first attested in Assyrian court circles, also in the ninth century. At that time they are also attested on Cyprus. Homer has not decorated Hera with fantasy jewellery or with half-remembered items from a remote heroic era. She wears relatively recent fashion, known to Homer, who seems to have devised the particular wording which describes it. He had evidently seen such earrings, imports into the east Aegean from Cyprus. They may have retained an oriental aura for his listeners, heightening Hera's exotic dressing.

These earrings are consistent with a Homer composing in the late ninth or mid eighth century. The shield he presents for Agamemnon poses different problems.[15] In book 11, when Agamemnon is arming himself for his brief bout of prowess in battle, he picks up his 'fine, much-worked shield which surrounded a man'. It had ten circles of bronze, Homer tells us, probably on top of a leather frame, and twenty-one bosses on it, all of tin except for their central one, which was made of blue paste. It was fixed to a belt of silver. Unlike Hera's earrings it is plainly a fantasy item, combining a wide span of precious metals. It was crowned with a Gorgon, grinning terribly, and round her were the figures of Fear and Rout.

This shield resembles the awesome aegis which the goddess Athena had cast round her shoulders when arming herself in book 5: on it were figures of Strife, Might, chilling Assault and the 'Gorgon head of the dreadful monster'.[16] The Gorgon was an orientally derived monster, appropriate to the orientalizing phase of Greek art which began

176

in the seventh century BC, but gorgons are known from other Greek objects of eighth-century date and the Greek story that the Gorgon's gaze turned men to stone derived from representations encountered by Greeks in coastal Asia well before 700 BC.[17] As yet, shields emblazoned with figures are not attested before the mid seventh century, when one with the Gorgon's head is indeed known to us. However, Athena's aegis was an imaginary item, and Homer may have imagined the trio of a Gorgon, Fear and Rout on it without seeing an emblazoned example and then modelled Agamemnon's shield on Athena's awesome aegis. A gorgon's presence on Agamemnon's shield is not a good reason for dating the entire Iliad down to *c.* 650 BC.

There is another possibility: the verses about these figures may have been added as an elaboration by a later poet. As others have observed, they sit most awkwardly on a shield whose face had so many protruding metal bosses. They can be deleted without damaging the verses which stand immediately before and after them.[18] The likelihood of additions by later reciters is a constant risk in pinning a date for the poem on any single item in the text we have.

Mentions of places and peoples may seem more revealing. The most indicative would be mentions of a people who did not exist where Homer locates them until a relatively defined date. The cardinal examples here are the Phrygians.[19] In the Iliad, Priam's wife Hecuba is from Phrygia and in book 3 Priam tells Helen how once, he

> '. . . came to Phrygia with its vines
> Where I saw very many Phrygian men with their
>   glistening horses . . .
> Who were encamped then along the banks of the Sangarios . . .'

Priam explains that he had gone to help them long ago when they were confronted by the Amazons, 'equals of men'. Homer regards Phrygia as a land beyond the borders of Priam's kingdom to which many treasures from Troy had had to be sold to raise funds during the war.[20]

Phrygia here is an anachronism, as it only existed long after the heroes' age of bronze. Phrygians settled at Gordion, archaeology attests, *c.* 900–850 BC, and so mentions of them exclude a Homer composing, say, in the mid tenth century.[21]

Phoenicians, travelling in the Aegean, are a different matter. They were people at home in cities of the Levant, 'purple people' as the Greeks' name for them meant, referring to their skills of making purple dye. They were once thought to fix Homer to a seventh-century date because Greeks were considered to have met them only then. That notion has collapsed: Phoenicians, as Greeks called them, are now firmly attested in the Aegean in the tenth and ninth centuries BC.[22]

Arguments from dates when Greeks became aware of particular countries or seas are extremely perilous. Their knowledge of the Black Sea or Egypt has sometimes been considered to be a seventh-century innovation, but Hesiod was already aware of Black Sea rivers in a poem composed *c.* 710 BC and it is risky to date Greeks' presence only by random finds, or not, of pieces of Greek pottery in a region.[23] In important studies, Assyriologists have recently presented a text from the Assyrian empire which refers to a man with a name translatable into Greek as Antikritos, evidently from Cyprus: he had been active east of the river Tigris in the 670s BC. In another Assyrian text, dated about twenty years earlier, they have endorsed the presence of Ionians, Greeks from the Mediterranean coast, who had been brought to serve in the Assyrian king Sennacherib's navy in the 690s and had been active on the Euphrates and Tigris rivers and on the Persian gulf.[24] From Greek texts alone we would never have assumed a Greek presence so far inland in Asia at that date. News spread rapidly in the harbour cities of the east Greek world: Greeks' oral reports of eastern lands, including Egypt, may have extended far further in the previous century than surviving Greek texts attest.

There is a specific sign of as much in a fine simile at the start of Iliad book 3. It compares the advancing Trojan army to cranes flying south and bringing death and destruction to the Pygmy men, *andrasi pugmaioisi*. The likeliest location for these people in the south is beyond Egypt, in what Greeks later knew as Nubia.[25] No evidence survives of any Greek visitor there in the eighth or seventh century BC, and yet, from hearsay at least, pygmies were already presented by Homer as living there.

Names of cities or sanctuaries, being specific, might seem more solid evidence. In the Iliad five are particularly relevant. Homer never refers to the great Phoenician city of Tyre on the Levantine coast, whose splendour was well known to prophets in the Hebrew scriptures. He refers instead to Sidonians, people from the city of Sidon, about twenty miles north of Tyre: in the Iliad, Sidonians are expert craftsmen who work fine textiles and objects of silver. As the great city of Sidon was destroyed by Assyrians in 677/6 BC, these mentions of Sidonian experts, not Tyrian ones, are unlikely if Homer was composing c. 650 when Sidon was a wreck. In the eighth century, however, Sidon controlled a significant hinterland and was a major presence: his mentions of Sidonians do not hark back to a distant Mycenaean past.[26]

Achilles' great speech to the envoys in book 9 contains two particularly arresting place names. Rejecting Agamemnon's offer of gifts, Achilles states that he would refuse even if Agamemnon offered as much as 'goes into Orchomenus or into Thebes', but the next verse in the text is the one which qualifies Thebes as 'Egyptian Thebes', which had 'very many treasures in men's houses' and a hundred gates 'from each of which 200 men drive out with chariots and horses'.[27] Orchomenus and Thebes in central Greece were rich in the Mycenaean era, but not in Homer's own time. Thebes has therefore been qualified in the following verse as Egyptian, an allusion to the city we know as Luxor. It was once suggested that the riches of Luxor would not have been known to Greeks until the Assyrians sacked it in 663 BC and carted its treasures away, but that suggestion is not at all convincing: rumours of those riches could have circulated long before this sack.[28] As the 'hundred gates' show, Homer's allusion is based on hearsay. Patently in this passage, the verses referring to Egyptian Thebes have been added to the older phrasing about Greek Thebes.

The constant risk in dating the entire poem by one or two place names in it is that they may have been added by a later singer, not Homer himself. Scholars whose primary interest is not the poem's date have proposed that solution for the verses about Egyptian Thebes, and although cutting verses from the text may seem a drastic one, it may well be correct in this case. If not and the verses are indeed Homer's, he could have composed them in the mid eighth century BC when Greek visitors to the Nile delta could already have heard about a fabulously rich city upriver.[29]

Achilles goes on to state that a man's life is not worth all the riches that Troy had had 'in the days of peace before the sons of the Achaeans came' nor even all that the 'stone threshold of the archer god Apollo contains in rocky Pytho'.[30] Pytho is the site of Delphi. This allusion to great riches and a stone-based temple or store at Delphi is most striking. It would not have been made in the early to mid ninth century, when Delphi had no oracular cult of Apollo, nor even in the early eighth century BC, when the cult was still of local interest and not a source of great riches. It has been considered to be most unlikely before *c.* 680 BC, thereby dating the entire poem after that point, but neither our knowledge of the site nor of its contents is sufficient to prove as much: considerable riches could already have come to Delphi from *c.* 750 BC onwards, not least from recent Greek settlers in western Italy who considered that Apollo, Delphi's god, had guided them to their settlement at Cumae. By the later 730s BC Greek settlers in eastern Sicily surely sent treasures in gratitude to Apollo their guide. Such gifts had to be stored somewhere: even if not found by archaeologists, a shrine or store of Apollo with a stone threshold may have existed already.

Again there is another possibility, because the reference to Delphi, the only one in the Iliad, is not necessary to Achilles' argument. Here, too, scholars not primarily concerned with the poem's dating have observed that the verses can easily be cut without disrupting the flow of his speech.[31] A later reciter of the poem may have included verses about Delphi, famous in his own time, and they may have been taken into the text.

In book II old Nestor mentions another significant site when he delivers a long speech to Patroclus, and harks back, as usual, to feats of his youth. At that time, he says, he raided Elis and took away many herds of animals, including 150 mares. They were regarded, he tells us, as a reprisal for an earlier theft by the people at Elis, who had stolen 'four prize-winning horses with their chariots' which Neleus, Nestor's father, had sent to compete for prizes there.[32] In the eighth century BC Elis was the host of the games at Olympia, but later sources state that races with four-horsed chariots were included in the Olympic games' programme only in 680 BC. However, Homer speaks of the four horses as travelling to Elis with chariots in the plural. As a competitor could enter several teams in one and the same race, Neleus might have sent two teams, each with two horses. Homer goes on to refer to their driver in the singular, but the plural, *elatēras*, would not have scanned. He was anyway making Nestor refer to games in the past, set long before the war at Troy. He could perfectly well have imagined four-horsed or two-horsed chariot races at Elis before either became fixed events in the Olympics' regular programme. He was not transposing into the distant past what could only have been known to him at Olympia after 680 BC.

The mention of the riches of Egyptian Thebes, treasures inside a stone threshold at Delphi and four horses racing with chariots at Elis are precise and important. They do not suffice to date the entire poem even if, which I doubt, the first two of them stood in Homer's dictated version of his poem. I would counter them with another specific reference, given in a simile in book 2. As the Greek troops begin to march across the killing field for the poem's first battle, the ground gives off that sound which Homer compares to the sound 'when Zeus is lashing the ground around Typhon in Arima, where they say is the bed of Typhon'. Arima is a reference to faraway Ischia off the Bay of Naples: it is the name by which Greeks first knew it through Etruscan informants. Greeks from Euboea first settled on Ischia *c.* 775 BC, but the island is volcanic and on the coastline where they settled the rumbles of its underground volcano can still be heard. Homer is alluding to such rumbling, a continuing sound, he believes, while Zeus 'is lashing' the buried monster Typhon underneath. In *c*. 700 BC the rumbling became a massive eruption which split Ischia apart and showered it with clouds of volcanic dust. Homer refers to hearsay, 'they say', about continuing rumbling, but not an eruption: he said nothing about this cataclysmic event surely because it was yet to come when he composed.[33] The simile occurs in the middle of the catalogues which intrude in book 2, works, I believe, of a later poet, but if these catalogues are cut out, it picks up neatly from the similes which precede them. On poetic grounds there is no reason to dismiss it as a later poet's addition. It implies a date for Homer before 700 BC.

These place names illustrate problems in using topography to date the entire poem. Arima, I believe, is original to it, but others may prefer to contest the significance I have given to it. I hold, nonetheless, to six arguments for an eighth-century Homer.

Our surviving evidence, admittedly far from complete, tells very strongly against use of the Greek alphabet before 800 BC in order to take down Homer's dictated poem, one of the occasions for its composition in performance, the type of composition which I support. A linguistic argument is particularly important, that significant details in the language of Homer's Iliad, statistically studied, precede those in Hesiod's poetry: Hesiod's *Theogony* is datable *c*. 710 BC. The argument from Homer's teachers is important too: they were highly skilled poets, as his debt to their language and phrasing proves, but nothing is known of their names or origins or poems. From the later eighth century onwards, poets' names and origins were transmitted: if Homer composed *c*. 680, his teachers, active from *c*. 700 onwards, would have been remembered by name or place in our evidence.

I also believe, like many others, that Nestor's cup on Ischia, deposed in a grave *c*. 725–720 BC, alludes to the very cup of Nestor in the Iliad. Two further arguments are my own. I consider that Homer's simile about rumbling Arima in book 2 belongs before 700 BC. I also consider that the Muses in Hesiod's *Theogony*, composed *c*. 710 BC, are said to be 'Homerizing' as a tribute to the Iliad's poet.

The Iliad certainly preceded the Odyssey with its tales of travel west of Greece and into a neverland far away. Such tales fit well in an incipient age of Greek settlement in the west Mediterranean. I would date the Odyssey *c.* 735–725 BC, therefore, within a generation of the first Greek settlement on the western coast of Italy and at a time when the main thrust of Greek settlement in east Sicily and south Italy was occurring: the Iliad, composed before it, dates to *c.* 750–740 BC, though precision to a single decade can only be indicative.

A seventh argument emerges from the historian Herodotus. He refers to Homer as living 'not more than 400 years' before his own time, implicitly answering others who wanted to date him even earlier. These 400 years are not chosen, as sometimes claimed, merely because they were the half-way point in the timespan which Herodotus believed to have elapsed between his own lifetime and the Trojan war: he considered that war to have been about 800 years earlier, as he himself tells us.[34] As he wrote this comment about Homer in *c.* 450 BC, he might seem to be dating the poet to an upper limit of *c.* 850. However, complexity applies even here. He may have reckoned his 400 years as ten generations, a more usual way of measuring past stretches of time in a society without numbered records. He has two different notions of a generation, either one of forty years or one of three generations to 100 years: if we opt for the latter, ten generations become *c.* 333 years, bringing his upper limit for Homer down to *c.* 783 BC.[35] Whatever underlies his figure, 400 years certainly do not put Homer in the early seventh century: for that date, either six or seven generations were needed, giving a span of about 240 years before Herodotus himself. He attests a belief in an eighth- or even late-ninth-century Homer. Ancient history would not be ancient history if the reference was simple and straightforward.

The social background to the Iliad fits well, but not only, with a poet composing *c.* 750–740 BC and trying to present a world not as mortals are nowadays, linking it up by what he and his hearers might assume about society two generations before their own, *c.* 800–780 BC. The considered dating by Herodotus fits this hypothesis. Neither suggests we should prefer a date in the seventh century, not even one as early as *c.* 680 BC.

16

In Transmission

All we have of Homer's Iliad is a text, not a recording, but it is not a reason for assuming it was all that ever existed. 'Sing, o goddess . . .', the poem begins. The great Greek tragedies and comedies survive only as texts, but we know they were acted and performed and we need to try, though many have not, to relate their words to acting, gestures and groupings on stage. Behind the Iliad's text as I read, I hear a poet beginning by singing his first verses to a lyre, then composing orally as he goes along, modulating his voice and pace as his characters and action require and trying to match his speed to the writer, or writers, men or women, who were valiantly taking down what he performed.

If Homer dictated his Iliad c. 750–740 BC, how was it transmitted after his lifetime? In due course we can infer from the meagre surviving evidence that poets knew it, Tyrtaeus in the 650s, Mimnermus c. 620, Alcaeus c. 610–600, but what had happened to it in the intervening years?

The ancient Gilgamesh poem was copied and recopied as a text over nearly 2000 years, but it has become clear from ever more evidence of it that versions varied and that whole speeches, even, could be transposed and given to other speakers.[1] Unlike the Iliad it was being widely translated during this time and although it was a text, it was not ascribed to one named poet. Some scholars believe that it was being recited orally during festivals and so forth, but the evidence for continuing oral recitation has yet to be conclusive.[2]

Some scholars believe that the Iliad, too, emerged gradually over a long period of oral transmission, but even so they accept that dictation occurred in the process. Their major modern representative, Gregory Nagy, has insisted that 'in principle, my own model explicitly allows for a variety of historical contexts in which dictation could indeed have taken place, resulting in a transcript, or a variety of transcripts, at various possible stages of the transmission'. In Nagy's view, transcripts 'existed long before they became definitive scripts'.[3] Performers, he remarks, may have had a transcript which they consulted as a starting point, but, he believes, they added or deviated in their own performance. I do not accept this model of the poem's gradual evolution: the consistency of its language and the absence of anything later than, say, 650 BC in the social background it implies are among the arguments which tell strongly against it. There was indeed dictation but it occurred, I consider, at the very beginning, with illiterate Homer's own dictated text. I believe this text to have been controlled after his death by his family, the reason why he made it, but then the problems in our scanty evidence begin.

Homeridai, or sons of Homer, certainly existed: they are attested on Chios, but not, as it happens, until *c.* 480 BC.[4] I consider them good grounds for linking Homer in his lifetime with Chios, whether or not he was actually born there. I assume these Homerids performed the text of his Iliad after memorizing it and that they also made it available for paying clients to copy and for others to memorize and perform. I assume that Homerids persisted for several hundred years because they allowed outside students of the poem to call themselves Homerids too: performance required great skill and would never have been assured from one generation to the next if the performers were selected only by narrow heredity.[5] They and other reciters who imitated them became known as rhapsodes, stitchers together of song. They differed from Homer in one crucial particular: they memorized what they sang. Nonetheless, they also added bits of their own. One rhapsode composed a long catalogue-poem about the Greek and Trojan forces who fought at Troy: it became part of his and others' versions of the Iliad quite early in its transmission and is still in our book 2. Another rhapsode, active in the seventh century BC, composed the night-time adventures of Diomede, Odysseus and Dolon which are now in our Iliad as book 10. These parts of the Iliad are widely accepted by modern scholars to be later additions, but nobody knows how or where they became embedded in versions of the poem. I find it hard to believe that the Homerids promptly included them in the dictated text which Homer had left with them, but there is no ancient evidence to resolve the question. I assume they became embedded in others' texts and performances and persisted because many enjoyed hearing them. As a result the Homerids could not exclude them for ever.

We know that recitations of all or part of the poem spread far and wide, not least because thinkers and philosophers reacted strongly against its ethics and its presentation of the gods: by *c.* 480, they even proposed, long before Plato, that it should not be allowed to corrupt the young or be performed at festivals.[6] Plainly such performances were widespread and popular. By the later seventh century they were occurring regularly, we happen to know, in the city of Sicyon in the Peloponnese, because its ruling autocrat banned them: they contained too much that was favourable to neighbouring Argos, his enemy.[7] The Iliad is the first poem in history to have been no-platformed.

The next surviving evidence concerns the arrival of the Iliad and Odyssey in Athens. In a fourth-century work of philosophy, falsely ascribed to Plato, Hipparchus, one of the autocrats who ruled there, is said to have been the first to bring Homer's poems to Attica and to have compelled the rhapsodes to go right through them, one taking over from another in turns at the city's big festival, the Panathenaea.[8] Cultural competition with other Greek autocrats indeed typified Hipparchus and his family's years of rule over the Athenians from 528 to 514 BC. The story implies, surely rightly, that the poems were already being performed elsewhere as extracts, not as continuous wholes, and so Hipparchus tried to patronize full performance. In later antiquity performers of extracts from Homer even had a special name, Homerists, and were eligible for special prizes at festivals where they performed as competitors.[9] Hipparchus is not said to have acquired a text from Chios and its Homerids for the rhapsodes who were to perform the poems as a whole at Athens. Perhaps he did, but at Athens a version of the

Iliad was promptly known and performed which included the Catalogue of Ships: I doubt whether the Homerids' text yet included
this addition.

In the fifth century BC, performers could be widely heard at festivals in the Greek world, but their versions varied, not at the level of
plot or character but in details of wording and the arrangement of
verses, extra verses being included if Homer's seemed too brief or
obscure.[10] There was also ignorance of which poems Homer had
or had not composed. A medical text, *On Joints*, contains a neat
example. It seems from its language to be a fifth-century text, one
which was later ascribed to the great doctor Hippocrates, and it
refers to Homer to support its view that cattle are at their thinnest
after winter: Homer, it says, states that of all flocks cattle suffer
most at that season, particularly oxen for ploughing.[11] No such
statement is known in either of the Homeric epics. The author may
be citing some extra verse he had heard in performance or he may,
like others, be citing some other poem which he wrongly regarded
as Homer's work.

Most adults in antiquity heard the Iliad, rather than reading it,
but texts of it became a resource for schoolteachers, certainly by the
later fifth century BC. In Athens at that date, the flamboyant Alcibi-
ades was said to have asked a schoolteacher for a 'book' of Homer
and to have hit the man with his fist when he said he did not have
one: whether the story was true or not, it assumed that a school-
master should have a text of Homer.[12] At a similar date, Niceratus,
a rich and upper class Athenian, was able to recite both the Iliad and
Odyssey from memory, a skill imposed on him by his famous father
Nicias. He and his father were politically conservative, people who
never did a populist thing in their lives, but they were not members
of the old Athenian aristocracy.[13] Proficiency in the Iliad was a way
of burnishing their social credentials: what, though, was the Iliad
which Niceratus had learned?

His memorization of it is known from an artful text, the *Symposium*, composed by Xenophon, also no natural democrat, in the
early fourth century BC. He set it in 421 BC and devised it so as to

present Socrates and members of his upper class circle in a beguiling light. In it, Niceratus, or Xenophon, quotes several lines from the Iliad, but one of his quotations differs slightly from the wording in our texts and another, a half-verse, is not attested there at all. Nonetheless Niceratus is made to say that he listens to rhapsodes' reciting 'almost every day'.[14]

Later in the fourth century, another Athenian, the political orator Aeschines, quoted Homer and shows similar variation. In 345/4 BC he was a prosecutor of the elderly Timarchus in a politically motivated trial, centring on Timarchus' sex life. In his fascinating, but highly tendentious, speech, he quotes the Iliad twice. One quotation is made at some length, but does not quite match the text as we now know it: verses are omitted or moved around and little details of the wording differ.[15] A few of the changes suit Aeschines' case and were probably his own, especially when he was reciting from memory. However, they cannot all be put down to faulty recall in the heat of the moment. Not only was Aeschines a trained actor but he states explicitly that the longer of the quotations is to be read out by the clerk of the court from a text.[16] He had given the clerk this text, which was perhaps one he wrote out from memory, but I believe that most of the variations between its wording and ours reflect a pre-existing text, not simply Aeschines' version of the moment.

This continuing variety helps to explain how two even more famous minds, within three years of Aeschines' speech, were engaging closely with the Iliad. Up in Macedon, the world's most intelligent man, Aristotle, came to teach young Alexander, soon to be the world's greatest conqueror. The Iliad fascinated young Alexander, a self-styled rival to Achilles. One of his officers, Onesicritus, later wrote a history, now lost, of Alexander's youth and career and is cited for the view that Alexander used to keep under his pillow a dagger and the text of the Iliad, 'which Aristotle had corrected'.[17] I take the formal word 'corrected' to be Onesicritus' own word, one which he used with its usual sense, meaning that Aristotle had indeed corrected words in a text of the Iliad which he had had in his possession: other stories attach to Alexander and the Iliad and are worth reconsidering in this light.

Aged twenty-three, Alexander defeated the Persian king Darius at the battle of Issus and captured a beautiful bejewelled casket among the king's possessions. Famously, he arranged for the Iliad to be stored inside it. It became known as 'the Iliad from the casket' and Alexander is even said to have made marks on this text while in the company of Greek scholars in his entourage.[18] These testimonies to textual work on it have been doubted, not just because their sources are late in date but on the grounds that subsequent scholars of the Iliad's text never refer to any corrections by Aristotle himself and no such text of Homer is present in ancient lists of his works.[19] Neither point is convincing. As Aristotle's work was a personal work for Alexander, it was not something to include in lists of Aristotle's published works. It was not a commentary, and so the author, strictly, was Homer, not Aristotle. It made no impact on future scholars simply because it disappeared in the turmoil after Alexander's death. The text which was supposedly kept under Alexander's pillow and the 'Iliad of the casket' were surely one and the same. If Alexander really slept at times on his Iliad, it can only have been a scroll or two from the bulkier whole. That bigger whole could indeed be the Iliad 'of the casket', stored in the precious box on all its rolls. I wish it could be relocated, but fear it never will be.

As Aristotle corrected this text for Alexander's use only, it left no impact on the general tradition. After his death Greeks continued to settle in Egypt, a natural home of papyrus, and from the early third century BC bits of the Iliad have survived there on that material. They still vary from our texts, having extra verses and small differences of wording, and there is no sign yet of one standardized Iliad.[20] Scholars in Alexandria's Museum and Library then went to work on the problem, culminating in the 'best of the grammarians', Aristarchus from the island of Samothrace, who lived from 216 to 144 BC. His work is crucial for the Iliad we now read.

Aristarchus worked on Homer throughout his adult life. He began by issuing a preliminary text which omitted many lines he considered to have intruded. In this first work he did not give *argumenta* for these exclusions, but he went on later to issue a text with a commentary in which he discussed alternative readings.[21] After his work, texts of the Iliad which survive on papyrus become noticeably less wayward: they agree on the number of lines and differ mainly on details of spelling and so forth. The most compelling explanation of this change is that the book trade and its copyists adopted Aristarchus' first publication, his corrected text without commentary. They ignored his later work, the one which gave variant readings and discussed them.[22]

After Aristarchus, a tireless scholar, Didymus, began in the late first century BC to work in Alexandria on Aristarchus' preliminary text. He cited many other commentators on Homer whom Aristarchus appears to have ignored and he also cited texts of Homer 'from' particular cities, extending from Marseilles to Sinope on the Black Sea. He had had access to these texts in the great Library in Alexandria, but they were not texts officially recognized and championed by each city: they were simply scrolls which had been acquired for the Library from each city and tagged as being 'from' it.[23] Didymus' work, so far as we know it, attests a range of Homeric texts and scholarship even wider than Aristarchus' fundamental contribution.

The poem retained the length which Aristarchus' work had defined, though copy after copy continued to be studied and admired throughout the Roman empire. In the AD 360s, in north Africa, it encountered its most articulate pupil: in little Thagaste, schoolmasters required young Augustine to engage with it in Greek. However, he made no headway: Augustine is the patron saint of Homeric dropouts. His difficulty lay in the Greek language, he recalled, as it was not, like Latin, his spoken tongue.[24] Nonetheless, papyrus texts of Homer are known uninterruptedly into the early Byzantine period: a fragment of four pages from a previously missing era, the seventh to ninth centuries AD, turned up in the library of St Catherine's monastery on Sinai as recently as 1975. Texts of the Byzantine period, then, underlie our modern printed texts, spearheaded by that finely produced text from Venice of tenth-century date, the one acquired by Cardinal Bessarion from Constantinople, donated by him to the city's library and made known to Western scholars in the 1780s.

Varied though words and spelling in such manuscripts still were, after Aristarchus there was general agreement on the Iliad's length. Modern editors' efforts to correct and purify its text continue to advance it and to crystallize awareness of the many problems of detail in its transmission, but in the expert opinion of a major editor, Martin West, uncertainties about its exact wording and intrusive verses affect only about 1.1 per cent of the whole, excluding book 10.[25]

About 750–740 BC, in my view, Homer in the Greek east began to compose in performance versions of his great epic. In one extended performance he dictated a version and it is from that copy, long since lost, that our knowledge of it ultimately derives. We are literate, without the resources of a special poetic dialect and its phrases, assets which evolved over many centuries: there is no way we could compose such a poem. It remains to see why its contents are both so immediate to us but quite beyond our abilities.

PART IV

Heroic Hallmarks

17.

Heroism: the Highlights

A Homer at home on the west coast of Asia who composed in performance and dictated a version of his poem *c.* 750–740 BC is not a new proposal, but I have argued for it with a combination of details and observations which gives a distinctive emphasis and is not all familiar, even to the poem's experts. I have also made it in reasoned preference to the many alternatives which have been postulated by other scholars and close readers. My arguments for preferring it have ranged from the Icarian sea to the western slopes of Ida, from Bosnia to Kyrgyzstan. Many of them were unknown to analytic scholars at work between the 1560s and the earlier twentieth century. Understanding of Troy and the Greeks' 'dark ages' has also advanced beyond anything those scholars could possibly have known. Future advances in our knowledge may transform arguments for the Homer I favour.

Those arguments have already invoked the poem's plot, its time frame, its sense of space and the amalgam of its material world. I will now turn to the male heroes who contribute to its profound power. Much of that power survives translation, which has to be imposed on the poem even by those who know Homeric Greek. I will address the areas in which it most affects me, in the hope that it will also affect those who engage or re-engage with it as a result.

So far, I have given only a flat summary of the poem. Before discussing its heroes and their hallmarks, I will broaden and deepen readers' grasp of it by selecting my top ten of its twenty-four books. In this chapter and the following two, I will give an appreciation of them, emphasizing the presence of a particular ideal whose implications for life and death run right through to the Iliad's end.

At the centre of the poem stand the male heroes, watched, helped and at times impeded by the Olympian gods. In these heroes' lives, as in ours, there is only one certainty: death. Every one of them knows that it is his allotted destiny and that he will not escape whenever his time comes. At death, a hero's *psychē*, or life force, flies away squeaking from his limbs: 'the only recorded function of the *psyche* in relation to the living man is to leave him'.[1] It goes off to be contained and hidden in Hades, an invisible region beneath the earth where it exists in the gloom like a bat hanging in a cave. As there is no meaningful afterlife, nothing done on earth will be punished or rewarded there. This fact is brought out especially clearly in Achilles' final encounter with the ghost of Patroclus. Since his death, Patroclus' body had been lying unburnt and unburied. His *psychē* was in limbo, therefore, at the gates of Hades, from which the other ghosts of the dead were keeping it away. It comes to Achilles by night as if in a dream and addresses him while he sleeps, evoking how they used to make plans together: it even recalls significant details of Patroclus' boyhood which Homer has not mentioned before. It then asks for due funerary rites so that it can enter Hades. In a fine scene Achilles reaches out to try to hold it, but it disappears 'like smoke, squeaking' and Achilles states that now he realizes there is no physicality, as we would say, in Hades.[2] After Patroclus' funeral, his *psychē* will never appear on earth again.

Once a hero is dead, he is gone for ever. This total cut-off is essential for the power of Homer's poem. He may not have invented it, but he certainly sustained it in the face of alternative views. In real life, there were Greeks in the eighth century BC who are known from archaeological evidence to have thought otherwise: they were making offerings in and around great burial mounds from the distant past, believing, therefore, that their unnamed occupants were still able to intervene in aspects of their lives. They were not worshipping them as ancestors: ancestor cult was not a Greek practice.[3] Probably they looked on them as semi-divine heroes from long ago. They needed to be honoured because they could still help the living and they needed to be appeased because, locally, their anger could still work great harm.[4] Offerings to them were not inspired or fostered by an awareness of Homeric epic. The poem's message was quite the opposite, that the dead make no further impact on the lives of the living, not even on those once closest to them. Very occasionally, Homer shows awareness of a different view. Twice, in relation to breaches of an oath, he remarks that perjurers will pay recompense after their death. This notion remained entirely marginal to his poem and did not impinge on its central presentation.[5]

Life and death in the Iliad exemplify two modern phrases, both still valid: 'all or nothing', for life, and 'when it comes, it comes', for death. Death's finality relates to aims in life, as heroes in the poem forcefully and often poignantly observe. For them, a major aim is personal glory, *kūdos*. It is accorded only to the living and is almost always the glory of a victory in battle. Heroes are not concerned to make a social difference, the aim of worthy people in the modern world. They are concerned to leave a personal mark, one which will be prolonged by fame, *kleos*.[6] After a hero's death, his fame is kept alive only by others' spoken words. He is not remembered in their prayers: there was no need to pray for him as he had become little more than a bat squeak. Talk of him might, however, be prompted by someone else's monument: Hector imagines how people will remember his fame whenever they see the burial mound of an enemy he has killed. Above all, fame might live on in heroic poetry, as Homer makes his protagonists say.[7] His Iliad has indeed granted what it made them anticipate.

The phrase 'imperishable fame' occurs once in the poem, in a speech by the impassioned Achilles. It has a fine ring to it and is attested in old Vedic poems in India.[8] It may, therefore, trace back long before Homer to a shared past, conventionally known as 'Indo-European', far back in man's history *c.* 2000 BC. However, even if this ideal was an ancient part of Homer's heritage, its origin explains nothing about his use of it: as ever, he transforms it, bringing out the pathos and cost of this old ideal. When Achilles sets out to take revenge for the killing of Patroclus, Homer still presents his killing of Trojans as a winning of *kudos*, glory. When he eventually kills

Hector, Achilles declares, 'We have won great *glory*, and killed noble Hector', as if striking up a song of victory.[9]

Guided by these crucial facts of heroic life, I will now give my selection from the Iliad's books. Once again, selection involves important losses, especially of the poetry's exquisite rhythm and language. Of my top ten, nine give important roles to the gods, and five to women, but I will discuss the poem's gods and women in more detail in the fifth part of this book. Here, I aim to give a sense of the plot's development, its supreme episodes and honour and glory's place in them.

Book 1, as we have seen, is a masterpiece of changing scenes and action which begin with the fatal quarrel between Achilles and Agamemnon. At the heart of it is the matter of *timē*, usually translated as honour but sometimes better rendered as value. By taking Briseis, Achilles' prize, Agamemnon publicly belittles Achilles' own value, or *timē*: when she is taken away, Achilles is left to sit and weep by the seashore, calling on his mother, the goddess Thetis, in five verses which refer to his honour, or *timē*, three times. When Thetis then goes up, as requested, to Zeus on Olympus to entreat him as an abject suppliant, she refers to honour, or *timē*, four times, each in relation to Achilles, in her first request, eight verses long. When she repeats her request in three more verses, she again refers to *timē*, but only once, in relation to herself. Wryly, she tells Zeus to refuse if he so wishes, 'so that I may know how far I am the least honoured [*a-timotatē*], among all the gods'.[10] Honour is her ultimate claim to favour.

Honour, or *timē*, is not the honour of one's country: no hero fights for that ideal. It is an individual's honour, just as it was later to be for *hidalgos* in early modern Spain or landowners in the American South before the civil war of the 1860s. While Achilles is absent, resenting the slight to him, book 3, my next choice, shows the Greek and Trojan armies marching out to do battle, whereupon Trojan Paris, abductor of Helen, challenges the best of the Greeks to fight him. His challenge becomes a duel between himself and Menelaus, Helen's former husband, to decide to whom

Helen, the cause of the war, should be returned, whether to Menelaus, from whom she had absconded, or her current husband, Paris,
with whom she had eloped.

Inside Troy, Helen appears for the first time, in an episode of
marvellous pathos and delicacy: she goes out, her head veiled, onto
the city walls to converse with king Priam, her elderly father-in-law.
Unlike most of the people in Troy, he shows kindness to her, and
she in turn addresses him with courtesy. The Greek leaders, except
Achilles, are visible in the plain below and deftly Homer lets us
learn more about them through Helen's answers to Priam's questions and the comments of others around him: Odysseus' impressive
way of speaking is recalled, a reminder that fighting is not the only
accomplishment for which heroes win praise.[11] Helen then returns
to her room while her husbands, past and present, fight their duel.
Menelaus prevails and 'would have won glory beyond telling', but
Paris is saved from death by his protectress, the goddess Aphrodite,
who whisks him away. She then brings Helen to him in his bedroom. With typical insouciance he evades the truth of the duel,
blaming his defeat on the gods: in fact a goddess had saved his life.
Set up by Aphrodite, they go to bed in broad daylight and make love
while those on the battlefield are still searching for Paris, 'hating
him like black death'.[12]

By book 6, my next selection, the Greeks are temporarily pressing hard on the Trojans. After a long sequence of deaths, Homer
dwells on an encounter with a very different outcome. Two heroes,
Diomede on the Greek side and Glaucus the Lycian on the Trojan,
meet to fight a duel, but discover they are linked by old ties of
guest-friendship, once formed by their grandfathers. They agree,
therefore, to avoid each other in battle: Diomede points out that
there are many other Greeks and Trojans for them each to
kill. They clasp hands, a sign of good faith, and they exchange
armour: others whom they encounter in the battle will then know
that they claim to be ancestral guest-friends. They show a noble
disregard for quantifiable worth. Glaucus gives Diomede gold
armour, whereas Diomede gives Glaucus bronze, 'a hundred

cattle's value for nine', Homer cannily points out, remarking that Zeus took Glaucus' wits away.[13] This memorable example of upper class ties in action, across two generations and in a context of war, is worth comparing with the ties explored in Jean Renoir's great film *La Grande Illusion*. There, too, shared values lead to a sympathy and link between two class allies, also on opposite sides of a war. The film, however, presents these values as almost obsolete, except for the upper class individuals involved. In Homer's poem these values are unchallenged. This strange meeting interrupts nearly a thousand verses of death and combat and emphasizes one of the Iliad's cardinal insights, that noble warriors on opposite sides can have more in common than keeps them apart.

During Priam's questioning of Helen, Hector was never mentioned. He now comes into the foreground. In book 5 he has just had his first burst of prowess on the killing field, interrupting young Diomede's feats but only for about 120 verses. While Diomede and Glaucus converse, he returns to Troy, allowing Homer a brilliant change of tone and setting. He has gone to encourage the Trojan women to pray to the goddess Athena and make offerings to her in the hope that she will help. Through hard irony, Homer intensifies the pathos of this appeal: we know, though Hector does not, that the prayers and offerings will be pointless, as Athena is implacably opposed to Troy.

In superb scenes inside the city, Hector goes to meet his mother Hecuba, his sister-in-law Helen, still with Paris, and finally, on the city walls, his wife Andromache and their baby son. These encounters, each with a different scope, set off Hector's own heroism and what he has to resist in order to sustain it. The most powerful plea is Andromache's. She begs him to remain inside Troy, but he tells her he feels shame before the Trojan men and women for whom he must therefore go out and fight: shame, as we will see, is a crucial sanction on a hero's conduct. The details of their meeting and parting are overwhelming, leaving us and Andromache with the sense that Hector will never return alive to her again.

By book 9, my next choice, it is the Greeks who are being pressed very hard, just as Zeus had promised to Thetis. Before the assembled troops, Agamemnon, in tears, states that destructive folly had seized him, impelling him to believe an apparent promise by Zeus that he would take Troy, whereas Zeus deceived him and is now bidding him to return in infamy, without *kleos*, to Argos. He is disabused by young Diomede and old Nestor, whereupon a small group of elders goes to his tent to devise a better plan. Nestor, with due tact, proposes an approach to Achilles, telling Agamemnon he had been in the wrong. Agamemnon agrees, again admitting his destructive folly. In book 2 he had already stated that he began the quarrel, but now he admits his folly in doing so and 'obeying grievous passion'.[14] He declares he will give recompense beyond counting. He names an enormous array of gifts he will give Achilles, including Briseis, and on elderly Nestor's advice sends three envoys to offer them. The plan is kept away from a general assembly, presumably in case it fails and damages the army's morale.

Achilles receives the envoys, offers them food and wine and in a spellbinding speech, unmatched in the poem, rejects the offer. Material goods are not in themselves enough, he states: 'hateful to me are his gifts, I value them no more than a hair'. He then elaborates, in verses which were among the first I chose as a boy to learn by heart:

> 'Cattle and goodly sheep can be taken as spoils,
> Tripods and tawny horses can be gained,
> But for the life of a man to return, that cannot be taken
> as spoil nor gained
> When once it has passed the barrier of his teeth.'

He had had a choice of destiny, he states, either to stay and fight at Troy and win imperishable fame, *kleos*, but die young, or else to lose fine fame, and live a long and unremarkable life.[15] He has hitherto chosen the former, putting fame first, but now he threatens to choose the latter and return home. The envoys 'all fell silent, marvelling at his words, for he had spoken forcefully indeed'. Well they might, after such a speech: Homer, I assume, paused briefly in performance here, while his listeners, too, marvelled at what they had just heard.

Achilles' refusal in book 9 is a turning point in the poem's plot. I believe it was Homer's innovation, altering previous tales of the hero's anger: it amazed its listeners, therefore, as they realized the poem would now be prolonged in a way they had not expected. Achilles would not accept the offer and promptly re-enter the war. Much more would need to happen before he would relent, and then his anger would move in quite another direction.

One of the envoys to him, his old tutor Phoenix, is reduced to tears by what his pupil has just said and tries to sway him with a long, intricate speech about his fatherly role for him and his own earlier life. He then appeals to Achilles to bend and not to have an unpitying heart: 'even the gods themselves are flexible'.[16] He begs him to accept the gifts and lay aside his anger, citing an old tale of the hero Meleager and his eventual relenting from anger during a military crisis for his city. 'Come to battle', old Phoenix finally says, 'while gifts are on offer: the Greeks will honour you like a god.' If Achilles enters the battle without gifts, Phoenix says, he will not be similarly honoured 'even though he keeps the war at bay'.[17] These final words refer twice to the *timē*, honour, which Achilles will gain, especially as manifested in material gifts. However, that sort of *timē* has just been rejected by him.

Phoenix has been added to an embassy whose earlier version had involved only two envoys: why did Homer include him in the version he dictated? The embassy, he may have felt, was too short with only two speakers. By adding Phoenix as another one, he could include an appeal to a past story, a myth to us: myths are used in this way in other such appeals in the poem. Phoenix's speech could also be a cue for themes exploited elsewhere in the poem, fatherly care for a young protégé, appeals to pity, examples of anger, human and divine, and the importance, ultimately, of relenting and entering battle.

Another envoy, blunt, stolid Ajax, then makes a short but powerful speech, strongly deploring Achilles' pitiless heart. At first, in his great speech, Achilles had talked of departing from Troy on the very next morning but, in reply to Phoenix and then Ajax, he shifts his ground: he ends by saying he will fight, but only when Hector begins to burn the Greek ships and reaches his own. He has relented, but minimally so.

I include book 14 in my selected ten because of the wonderful scenes it presents among the gods. Zeus has continued to favour the Trojans, just as he promised to Thetis, but his wife Hera hates Troy and wants it ruined, so she plans to activate successes for the Greeks. She sees Zeus sitting on the top of Mount Gargaron, 'and he was hateful to her heart': Homer has no illusions about a marriage made in heaven.[18] She decides to seduce him nonetheless and to send him into a post-coital sleep so that she and others can help the Greeks without his intervention. Her plan involves persistently saying one thing while we, the listeners, know she intends another: Homer is a master of speech which hides a speaker's real purpose. Hera dresses and scents herself to be supremely sexy, puts on those earrings like mulberried eyeballs and then deceives her fellow goddess Aphrodite with a clever lie so that she can borrow her precious breast strap, a wonderbra which contains 'love, desire and seductive love talk'.[19]

Next, she visits the god Sleep, whose help she will also need post-coitally, but instead of telling lies to him too, she bribes him outright to help her plan: she promises him one of the younger Graces for sex 'and to be called your wife'. Sleep agrees, specifying the very Grace he has long desired, and returns with Hera to Mount Gargaron. There, she causes Zeus to make love to her on that carpet of crocus and hyacinth, hidden from view in the cloud of gold which drips with dew. Sleep then fulfils his side of the bargain: he makes Zeus slumber in Hera's arms, and hastens to alert the pro-Greek god Poseidon, who rallies the Greeks for battle, holding in his big hand a terrible 'long-edged sword, like lightning'. He and they re-engage with Hector and the Trojans.

In book 15 Zeus awakes and angrily reverses Hera's help for the Greeks. Poseidon withdraws, but Apollo helps Hector to reach the Greek ships and is ready to set fire to them, while, one after another, major Greek heroes are wounded. However, the next book, 16, is the one I select, not only because its action is critical for the plot. As it begins, Patroclus deplores Achilles' anger and, yet again, his pitiless heart: he pleads with him to allow him to enter the battle with his warriors, the Myrmidons. Achilles should loan him his armour, he proposes, so that the Greeks will think he is Achilles himself: this crucial request is a major turn in the poem, but it had already been anticipated in a speech. In book 11 old Nestor had urged Patroclus to do this very thing.[20] Homer's listeners, as often, had been prepared for what would eventually happen.

In reply, Achilles says he will indeed set aside his anger just as he intended when the battle came to his ships: in book 9 he had said he would relent when Hector reached them, killing Greeks and burning ships with fire, something which begins only after this speech.[21] He does not agree to fight in person, but he agrees, nonetheless, that Patroclus should promptly go into the battle, 'in order', significantly, 'that you may win great honour and glory from all the Greeks for *me*': he even says that they will give him back lovely Briseis and will give glorious gifts too, the very same offers he had refused in book 9.[22] However, he orders Patroclus to return when he has driven the Greeks from the ships and not to go further, 'for you will make *me* less honoured if you do'. Again he is concerned for his own *timē*, his honour and value: he even prays to Zeus that none of the Trojans and none of the other Greeks may escape death, but that he and Patroclus may alone survive, so that the two of them can then 'loose the holy diadem of Troy' and bring it down.[23]

Meanwhile Hector and the Trojans press on and set fire to one of the Greek ships. Seeing it, Achilles urges Patroclus to put on his own armour and hurry: he himself will not go out to fight in person, but his armour will, implying to observers that he is indeed back in the fray. When Patroclus and the Myrmidons enter the battle, powerful verses follow on the relative roles of Zeus and a hero's destined day of death, culminating in the deaths of Sarpedon, Zeus's son, and then Patroclus himself. After winning many duels, Patroclus is led on in his folly by Zeus. He goes too far, a persistent

pattern in the poem's plot which applies to Agamemnon, then to
Hector and finally to Achilles himself. Ignoring Achilles' warning,
Patroclus has to be thrust away three times from Troy's battlements
by the pro-Trojan god Apollo. When he tries for the fourth time,
Apollo warns him with a 'terrible call' that it is not to be that he will
take the city and sack it.

The fighting in this book rests on Homer's oral direction of a
complex sequence and his skill of cutting from one scene to the next
while allowing the necessary outcome to develop. It exemplifies how
composition in performance did not make him lose the plot, but,
rather, helped him to move from one habitual pattern to another
and thereby to develop a narrative. After another foray in late afternoon, Patroclus again rushes three times into the Trojans, killing
nine with each onslaught, twenty-seven in all. Kindness is repeatedly
ascribed to him when he is off the battlefield, but on it he shows
none whatsoever, planning to mutilate Sarpedon's body if he kills
him, exulting over those he spears to death and 'exacting requital for
many' by killing many in return.[24] Despite the warnings, he advances
for another onslaught, but Apollo, concealed in mist, stands behind
him and swipes off his helmet, breaks his spear and undoes his
armour. Another Trojan, Euphorbus, wounds him and finally Hector too comes after him and kills him with a thrust of his spear. This
sequence is significant: Homer gives Hector the final thrust, but not
the full credit for killing so great a hero.[25] Dying Patroclus underlines
the point by stating that it was a god who overcame him, and that
Hector merely delivered the last blow: unlike Paris in book 3, he correctly refers his defeat to the gods. He then predicts that Hector will
soon die too: 'death is standing near you and mighty destiny also, as
you will be laid low by the hands of Achilles'.[26] Once again, a speaker
anticipates a major turn in the plot.

18

'Not ingloriously may I die . . .'

In book 17 Hector strips Achilles' armour off Patroclus and sends it back to Troy to be a great source of fame, *kleos*, for him, a heroic hallmark indeed. Battles persist, fought for Patroclus' dead body, which Hector strives to drag away while one Greek hero after another prevents him. Instead, I select book 18, one with powerfully contrasting tones.

At the start of it Achilles learns of Patroclus' death and is visited by his divine mother Thetis, who comes up once again from the sea, grieving at his grief. In a fine scene he expresses his heart's command, to kill Hector in revenge even though it will mean he will die and Thetis will never receive him returning home. His choice is made, one which will shape and colour the rest of the poem: 'as for now, may I win fine fame', *kleos*, that significant aim, and 'may I cause one of the deep-bosomed Trojan women with both her hands to wipe the tears from her soft cheeks and lament aloud'.[1] Again, a speech anticipates the plot. Four books later, one of these women, Andromache, will do that very thing.

As Hector has stripped from the dead Patroclus the armour which Achilles had lent him, Achilles needs a replacement. Thetis leaves to fetch one, divinely made, and in her absence Iris, messenger of the gods, comes down at Hera's bidding, 'in secret, without knowledge of Zeus and the other gods': she urges Achilles, still prostrate on the ground, to rescue Patroclus' body from the battlefield, where the two armies are still fighting for it and Hector and the Trojans are having the upper hand.[2] He stands up, and the goddess Athena sets a golden cloud around his head and lights a gleaming flame from his body. He then goes out and shouts three times at the

Trojans, a 'shouting in the trenches' which, many centuries later, was to earn the awed admiration of the poet John Keats.[3] Each time he shouts, the Trojans are thrown into panic and their horses turn their chariots back 'because in their hearts they foresee grievous pain'. Twelve of the Trojans die in the confusion.

In the Aegean, in another Great War, a supreme classical scholar, pre-eminent at school and university in an age when such scholars were titans, was waiting briefly at leisure on the island of Imbros 'speaking the Greek of Demosthenes', he wrote, to the inhabitants, 'who are really quite clever at taking my meaning'.[4] On 13 July 1916, Patrick Shaw Stewart was about to leave again for battle at Gallipoli on the Hellespont, and, as a past master of verse composition in Homeric Greek, wrote a memorable English poem with a Homeric dimension: here are the first and last verses:

> I saw a man this morning
> Who did not wish to die.
> I ask, and cannot answer,
> If otherwise wish I.
>
> . . .
>
> I will go back this morning
> From Imbros, o'er the sea.
> Stand in the trench, Achilles,
> Flame-capped and shout for me.

He survived, but a year and a half later, he was killed in France, ten months before the war ended.

Out on the battlefield, after the effects of Achilles' shouting, the Greeks are able to recover Patroclus' corpse. They bring it back to Achilles' encampment, whereupon he begins to weep beside it, continuing as night falls: meanwhile the Trojans hold an assembly to decide what to do now that the hero they most fear is about to return to battle. Hector, in anger, answers a wise proposal that they should withdraw from the plain and shelter inside Troy, and convinces the assembled Trojans to do the opposite: it is an outcome which Homer judges forcefully in his own person, calling it bad counsel, foolish, and the result of the goddess Athena taking away their wits.[5] Two crucial decisions are now in place, Achilles' to rejoin the battle and Hector's and the Trojans' to remain in the plain nonetheless. From them the poem's last four books will follow.

Meanwhile, Thetis is away soliciting fresh armour for Achilles from the god Hephaestus. Before he begins work on it, he guarantees to make 'fine armour such as anyone from the mass of men will marvel at when he sees it'.[6] A divine craftsman, he lives up to his word by making a metal shield and decorating it with superb scenes of peace and war. Homer allows us to watch them as they are being made, but he elaborates them beyond what even Hephaestus could have shown in solid metals. Sustained for some 150 verses, they are one of the supreme wonders of the Iliad and of all poetry since.

In book 19, as dawn breaks, Thetis brings this new armour to Achilles, who is still lying beside Patroclus and weeping loudly. She allays his fears that flies will enter the wounds on Patroclus' body, breed worms and cause it to rot: she infuses ambrosia and nectar through its nostrils and keeps the flesh firm, an essential provision, because four more books of the poem will have to pass before Achilles gives it its funeral. Then, shouting fearsomely, Achilles summons the other Greeks to an assembly.

Book 19 is not in my selection but its contents are important for the next ones I will include. When the Greeks gather, Achilles tells Agamemnon in their presence that he will end his anger: 'out of necessity', they must both leave alone what has happened. Agamemnon replies, blaming his taking of Briseis on Zeus, Destiny and a Fury; destructive folly, he again says, came upon him, but she has afflicted even Zeus in the past.[7] He offers to give Achilles all the gifts he offered in book 9, though Achilles, in reply, does not insist on his doing so: Agamemnon even agrees to swear an oath in public that he has never had sex with Briseis. After various preparatory scenes, including Briseis' return, Achilles drives his chariot and horses into battle.

Book 20 is also not a book I select, but I will pause briefly on it and its sequel because they too bear on the exceptional power of my next choice, book 22. First, the gods come down to join in the fighting but while they wait to do so, Achilles confronts Trojan Aeneas. He charges at him after an exciting preliminary encounter, but the god Poseidon transports Aeneas away to safety. Achilles then kills four named warriors on the Trojan side, whereupon Homer leads his hearers to expect a climax: Achilles encounters none other than Hector, who throws his spear after a fierce exchange of words. The goddess Hera, ever hostile to the Trojans, causes the spear to fly back and fall uselessly before Hector's feet, whereupon Achilles rushes at him, 'eager to kill him, shouting terrifyingly', but . . . Homer, I think, paused here in performance, 'Apollo snatched Hector away, easily indeed, as a god can'.[8] After charging vainly at him three times, Achilles can only exclaim that he will meet him again and 'put an end, utterly, to him' if this time a god is helping him, not Hector. Their duel is a prequel to the duel which will conclude the poem's fighting.

Achilles fights on, killing another ten Trojan warriors and driving his chariot over so many dead bodies that its axle is spattered with blood: he keeps pressing on 'to win glory, and his invincible hands were spattered with blood' too.[9] As book 21 begins, he kills yet more of the Trojans who are scrambling in the river Scamander and also beside it, so much so that the river god is roused against him and nearly overwhelms him. He escapes, and continues to rout the Trojans, whereupon old Priam plays a crucial role: he orders Troy's great gate to be opened to receive them. 'Then high-gated Troy would have been taken by the sons of the Achaeans', Homer continues, again holding his listeners in suspense, 'if . . .' Apollo had not emboldened the Trojan hero, Agenor, and hidden himself in mist beside him.[10] Agenor debates with himself whether to run to the hills of Ida, hide there, wash off his sweat and return at evening to Troy, but decides instead to confront Achilles, who, he tells himself, is not immortal. He taunts him but when his spear fails to pierce Achilles' armour, Achilles rushes at him, ready to kill. However,

Apollo does not allow him 'yet' to win glory, the recurrent phrase for his killings during this foray: he whisks Agenor away and then, taking on his likeness, makes Achilles pursue him on foot towards the river Scamander. Meanwhile the Trojans can pour safely inside Troy.

Agenor had been the first Trojan to kill a Greek in the poem: now, eighteen books later, he rounds off the fighting, leaving only Hector to confront Achilles. I have given these episodes space because they anticipate themes and scenes which Homer is about to deploy. Three times in books 20 and 21, a god intervenes to whisk away an imperilled hero, each time confounding Homer's listeners' expectations. The final one of the three, Agenor, even has a soliloquy on how best to respond to Achilles' advance: in Agenor's likeness, Apollo then causes Achilles to pursue him away from Troy's walls. In book 22, these themes come together again, resulting in another soliloquy by a hero at risk to Achilles, another pursuit, another confrontation between Achilles and Hector and then another deception by a divinity in disguise. Homer has already made his listeners familiar with these themes before rearranging them to even greater effect in what follows. They are an insight into the way in which patterns underlie his oral composition, contrived without a memorized text. They facilitate it for him and also for his listeners.

Book 22, a masterpiece, begins with Achilles protesting at Apollo's diversion of him. He returns to confront Hector, who has remained, alone of the Trojans, outside Troy's walls. The poem has reached a critical point, but even after so many hours of composition in performance, Homer rises to an amazing run of 2,200 verses which sustain the highest control and effect. My selection includes them all, our books 22, 23 and 24.

In a superb scene, old Priam on Troy's walls is the first to see Achilles shining like the deadly Dog Star in summer and speeding towards Hector. So he 'raises his hands on high and beats his head with them' and in a compelling speech pleads with his son to come inside for safety. Hector's mother, exposing her bosom, implores

. A poet, long before Homer, playing a lyre and singing: a modern reconstruction from ragments of fresco in the Throne Room at Pylos, *c.* 1350–1200 BC. The bird symbolizes the vinged words of his song.

3. Silver two-drachma coin from Ios, with the earliest known representation of Homer, modelled on portraits of Zeus, *c.* 350 BC.

.. Red-figure storage jar depicting
 rhapsode reciting a verse of heroic
 oetry: 'Once upon a time in Tiryns ...',
 oo–480 BC.

4. *Crocus gargaricus* on Mount Gargaron, where Zeus made love to Hera in Iliad book 14 on a carpet of crocus and hyacinth.

5. Hellenistic temple of Apollo the mouse god, *c.* 150 BC, recently restored with model mice on its steps, at Chryse, where Chryses was priest in Iliad book 1.

. Red-figure mixing bowl showing the dead Sarpedon, son of Zeus, being carried away by
leep and Death, as in Iliad book 16; painted by the Athenian master-artist Euphronios,
. 515 BC.

. Suvla Bay, near ancient Aigai, to which Poseidon strode in Iliad book 13, and the lake
nder which he kept his horses.

8. Milman Parry (1902–35), the scholar of Homeric verse and oral poets in Yugoslavia.

9. Wilhelm Radloff (1837–1918), the great Russian scholar of Central Asian languages and heroic poetry.

10. Avdo Mededović (*c.* 1875–1955), the 'Homer of Obrov' with his *gusle*.

11. Sayakley Karalaev (1894–1971), a great performer of the Manas poems, a 'Homer of the twentieth century', born near Lake Issik Kul, Kyrgyzstan.

12. Red-figure vase representing the embassy to Achilles, derived from Iliad book 9. Elderly Phoenix is on the left, Odysseus is kneeling, Achilles is seated and Patroclus is on the right; *c.* 490 BC.

13. A fragment of a black-figure cauldron showing the chariot race at the funeral games for Patroclus, described in Iliad book 23; the spectators are imagined in a race-stand. *c.* 580 BC.

14. Red-figure drinking cup showing Menelaus lowering his sword while confronting Helen, her beauty unveiled by Aphrodite, during the sack of Troy; *c.* 490 BC.

15. Black-figure vase depicting Thetis bringing new armour to Achilles, as in Iliad book 19, and also a wreath; *c.* 570–550 BC.

6. Silver cup found in Denmark. The front shows Priam kissing the hands of Achilles, who had killed his son Hector. The reverse side of the same cup shows Idaios the Trojan guarding Priam's chariot, while a Greek sleeps in the foreground. The decoration is based on Iliad book 24; c. 30 BC–AD 40.

7. Divine honours for Homer, on the left in the bottom row, as he is crowned by Time and the Inhabited World on a throne supported by figures of the Iliad and Odyssey; a cast of a marble dedication, sculpted in 225–205 BC.

18. G. B. Tiepolo depicts Briseis being brought from Achilles to Agamemnon by the two heralds, based on Iliad book 1; *c.* 1757.

19. Peter Paul Rubens' painting of Achilles killing Hector, watched by the goddess Athena, based ultimately on Iliad book 22; *c.* 1630–35.

him too, but to no avail. It is Hector, now, who has a soliloquy, also one which turns this way and that: he reflects on the disgrace which other Trojans will heap on him if he comes into the city, as he had refused to withdraw with the army at the earlier assembly and had caused many lives to be lost. He would feel shame, therefore, if he withdrew now, and so he remains outside, either to kill Achilles in a duel, he still hopes, or else to die 'famously' before the city. Then, at the sight of Achilles' fearsome approach, he loses his nerve and it is he who runs away from the city's gate. Achilles pursues him round Troy, and Homer brilliantly compares Achilles to a pursuer in a dream who is unable to overtake the person he seems to chase.[11] All the while, the gods watch them from heaven, spectators of what is no spectator sport:

> It was not for an animal for sacrifice nor for an oxhide
> > that they competed
> Nor for what are men's prizes in races on foot,
> But it was for the life of Hector tamer of horses that they ran.[12]

They stop to fight, but this time there is a goddess, Athena, taking Achilles' side. During a harrowing confrontation, accentuated by her presence, Hector believes that a helper has come out from Troy to assist him, but then Athena vanishes and he realizes the awful truth, that he is alone before Achilles and 'indeed the gods have called me to my death'. Nonetheless, Hector declares that he wishes he 'may die not without keenness nor without fame, but after doing something great for future men to learn of'.[13] Even when his death is imminent, fame and glory are still his concerns. Of all the Iliad's heroes, Hector is the one who most often refers to what other people, present and future, may say of him.

Achilles kills him, whereupon other Greeks come to join him, a brilliant vignette, and stab Hector, now safely dead. Achilles exhorts them to take the body with him back to the ships and raise a song of victory, uttering those verses which Homer, I believe, also sang, with the emphasis on glory I have already cited:

'We have won great glory, we have slain noble Hector,
To whom the Trojans throughout their city used to
    pray as if to a god.'

'We', Achilles says, not 'I': he relates his lone exploit to his fellow warriors and, yet again, glory is the ideal of heroes in battle.[14]

Despite Hector's previous offer of an oath that each would return the other's body if he won, Achilles takes Hector's corpse, runs leather straps through the tendons of its feet (whence our Achilles tendons) ties it to his chariot and drives it off, dragging the body behind. Its head trails in the dust, 'and around it his dark hair fell'.[15] For the first time Homer specifies the colour of Hector's hair. He presents it here because it adds to the pathos of the scene: elsewhere in the poem dark hair is mentioned only for gods and god-like persons.

Watchers on the walls of Troy lament at the sight, 'as if all of high-browed Troy were being consumed by fire from its very top'.[16] Old Priam is distraught. He grovels in dung and calls on each Trojan by name to keep away from him even though they care for him: he wants to go out alone, he says, to the Greek ships and beg shameless Achilles to see 'if somehow he may respect my years and pity old age; he too has a father like that, Peleus who fathered him and brought him to be a pain to the Trojans'.[17] Once again a major turn in the plot is signposted in a speech, preparing the audience. It is combined with the theme of pity, a major element in what is still to come.

Inside their house in Troy, Hector's wife Andromache hears and fears the worst: she has been supervising a bath for her husband's return from battle, but now she goes out to learn the dire truth of his death and maltreatment and what they mean for her and their baby son. Her response, and then her speech, are heart-breaking. In the absence of Hector's body all she can do is to bring out his fine clothes and have them burnt on a blazing fire. They will not be any use to him, she says, but they will be *kleos* from the Trojan men and women, a glorious tribute, rather than lasting fame.

These scenes, which I will dwell on later, overpower all who engage with them, but book 23 maintains the momentum with a sequence of episodes, each with a contrasting tone, which show Homer at his most intuitively filmic. It is worth trying to visualize them, one after another. First, Achilles orders his Myrmidons to begin the formal mourning for Patroclus, the first stage in due funerary rites: they drive their horse-drawn chariots three times round his dead body and then Achilles leads the lament, laying his hands on the corpse itself. Next, he arranges a funerary feast, killing bulls and sheep, goats and pigs, in such quantities that 'all round the body, blood ran, flowing enough to be taken up in cups'.[18] Like his revenge, his funerary rites are characterized by impassioned excess. It is on that very night, while he has been lamenting on the seashore, that Patroclus' ghost makes its final appearance.

Nightfall and dawn are significant markers which intensify the poem's contrasts from now on. Previously, 'Iliadic nights are . . . times of reflection and deliberation rather than action', but now Homer extends action and description artfully into the night, using it in a way which a subsequent poet, author of book 10, was to carry further, making night the setting for a daring raid on the Trojans' camp.[19]

When dawn breaks, Homer duly changes the tone of the action: men go off to fell high-branched oaks on Mount Ida and use them to make a funeral pyre for Patroclus. Achilles' warriors, the Myrmidons, a crowd beyond counting, carry his body to it, cutting off their hair and casting it onto the corpse. Achilles himself cuts a lock of his own hair, a symbolic gift which he places in dead Patroclus' hands. He had vowed to give it to the river god in his homeland in Thessaly when he came back, the god to whom his father Peleus had also vowed offerings in the event of his son's return. In later Greek practice the vowing, and then cutting, of a lock of hair is attested as a rite of passage for boys entering manhood.[20] Here, it is the exact opposite, an acceptance of imminent death. By cutting it for Patroclus, Achilles expresses his acceptance that he will never return from Troy.

Under this furry layer Patroclus burns when the pyre eventually catches, but Achilles remains all night beside it, drawing wine into his two-handled cup from a golden bowl and pouring it onto the ground while calling on the '*psychē* of poor Patroclus' and pacing round and round the fire. Only after dawn does he fall asleep, a reversal of normality. He awakes in daylight and arranges for Patroclus' bones to be buried beneath a temporary mound.

When the mound has been piled up, Achilles presides over games in Patroclus' honour, bringing out the gifts he will offer as prizes to the competitors. The games, as we will see, are memorably presented. Unlike other outcomes in the plot, the results of each event are never anticipated, and so, in almost every case, they keep us in suspense. Achilles, their host, shows magnanimity and conciliation, a sign of his return to good relations with his fellow Greek heroes. Thereupon night falls and book 24 begins, transfixing all who attend to its interconnections. Such are their power and construction that they are a hallmark of the entire poem as well as of Achilles, its supreme hero.

19

'If it must be so . . .'

During the night after the games, Achilles continues to lament Patroclus, turning sleeplessly this way and that, 'remembering wistfully all the grievous things he had endured with him, passing through wars and waves'.[1] With the break of dawn, action again replaces lamentation. Three days have passed since Hector's death, but Achilles still takes his body and drags it in revenge behind his chariot, circling three times round Patroclus' grave-mound. As the games have shown, he has reconciled himself to his fellow Greeks, but in no way is he reconciled to Patroclus' killer. He continues to drag Hector for the next eight mornings, but, all the while, Apollo keeps unseemliness from Hector's flesh, 'pitying him, though dead'. Just as Thetis preserved Patroclus, so Apollo preserves dead Hector: the gods keep both of them fresh, despite their wounds and mutilation, for that ultimate honour, a fine cremation.

Most of the gods, too, take pity on dead Hector. They even urge Hermes to go down and steal the body, but the anti-Trojans in heaven disagree. On the ninth day of dragging on earth and disagreement in heaven, Zeus speaks out and summons Achilles' mother Thetis to Olympus. She has not been there since her supplication in the poem's first book. She arrives, wearing the darkest of veils, a mark of her continuing grief for her son's loss, and in the presence of all the gods the anti-Trojan goddesses welcome her, Athena making way for her, Hera giving her a cup of wine. Thereupon Zeus tells her that he will not let Hector's body be stolen, but will 'attach this glory', *kudos*, to Achilles. It is not, as sometimes misunderstood, the glory of finally showing pity and relenting. Just as old Phoenix had emphasized in book 9, it is glory linked to the receipt of glorious gifts: this time, they are to be the gifts Achilles will receive in return for surrendering Hector's corpse.[2]

To that end, Zeus sends two goddesses down from Olympus with messages for two separate recipients. Thetis is to go to Achilles and tell him that the gods, especially Zeus, are angry at what he is doing in the 'madness of his mind', in the 'hope that he may fear me and ransom Hector'. Meanwhile Iris is to go down to Priam in Troy and tell him to go to the Greeks' ships and ransom his son, bringing gifts for Achilles 'which may soothe his heart'. Once again, a dramatic turn in the action is anticipated by a speaker, guiding the audience's expectations. The outcomes are not wholly determined, as these moves are made 'in the hope that' Achilles may ransom Hector and that the gifts 'may' soothe him.[3] So we wait, fascinated, to hear.

Thetis flies down from Olympus and finds Achilles groaning and lamenting while his companions are preparing a meal early in the day, a shaggy ram slaughtered for the purpose. She strokes him and asks him how long he will go on grieving, forgetting food and also sex, 'for it is good to make love with a woman'.[4] 'Come now, ransom him,' she tells him: he accepts immediately, assuming, he says, that Olympian Zeus indeed commands it. 'Let whoever brings a ransom take away the body', he agrees, but unlike Homer's audience he has no idea who that person is to be.

Meanwhile, Homer is about to play his ultimate card, touched on already in Priam's distraught words at the end of book 22: old Priam will go out by night from the city and dare to visit Achilles' encampment with a ransom for his son's body. There could be no more fraught and hazardous undertaking.

Meanwhile Iris, sent by Zeus, arrives in Troy and finds Priam and his household weeping. Homer presents a fine family triptych, one which gains from being visualized with the sounds he specifies. Indoors in the household, Priam's daughters and daughters-in-law are lamenting the many fine warriors whom the Greeks have laid low, including their own brothers and husbands. Outside in the courtyard Priam's sons are sitting around their father and are 'soaking their robes with tears' while Priam, in the middle, is 'covered in his cloak so as to show the outline of his body', a particularly graphic scene.[5] Signs of his extreme grief are visible nonetheless, as 'there was dung in plenty around the head and neck of the old man': he had continued to roll in it and smear it on himself with his hands. Iris stands by him and tells him quietly, for his hearing only, that Zeus cares greatly for him and pities him: pity, divine and human, is emerging as a recurring element in this final book.

For our ears too, Iris tells Priam what Zeus has mapped out: he is not to be afraid, because Hermes will guide him and Achilles is not 'foolish, careless nor malicious', an emphatic triple assertion. Rather, 'with kindly care indeed he will spare a man who is a suppliant'. In the poem so far, suppliants have never been spared on the battlefield, least of all by Achilles in his recent foray. Off it, he will now show 'kindly care', a word which has just been used for his father's care for Patroclus when he first arrived as a fugitive in their household.[6] Yet again, Homer makes his audience aware in advance of what will happen, a crucial aid for following his oral performance. As usual he does not exploit surprise. He magnetizes his hearers and readers, not with uncertainty about the story's outcome, but with foreknowledge of its outline. It makes us attend on tenterhooks to learn how each particular move will come about.

In response, Priam, presumably still covered in dung, goes to his inner chamber 'fragrant with cedar wood'. He summons his wife Hecuba in order to share with her his intense desire to go to the ships of the Greeks, but frantically she tries to dissuade him. 'Of iron surely is your heart', but the old man replies that he has seen and heard a goddess. Iris has already told him that Achilles will not kill him, but nonetheless he insists, to emphasize his purpose, that 'even if it is my due destiny to die by the Greek ships, I want to'. His desire is not to pay due funerary rites to his son: it is more personal. 'There and then let Achilles kill me, once I have taken my son in my arms, when I will have set aside my intense desire to lament . . .'[7]

In chests inside the chamber Priam finds fine robes and blankets for the ransom and adds gold, two tripods, four cauldrons and a very beautiful cup, given to him by the Thracians when he went to them once on an embassy. He goes out, using his stick to chivvy onlookers away from the palace colonnade: 'Be gone, you shameful harmers, disgraces . . .' He then calls for the nine sons who remain to him and reproaches them too for being disgraces, 'liars, dancers, best at beating the ground in dance', four words in Greek, each of which resonates with a contemptuous 's' and 't'. 'Robbers of lambs and young goats in your own land', they must hurry up and make a waggon ready for his journey.[8] Petulant old age has never expostulated more forcefully: in 1742 Joseph Spence learned from Alexander Pope, translator of the Iliad, that he was unable to read these verses 'without weeping for the distress of that unfortunate old prince'. Pope read them then and there, Spence recalls, 'and was interrupted by his tears'.[9]

'In fear at their father's rebuke', the sons prepare a horse-drawn chariot for him and a mule-drawn waggon for the ransom and for Hector's body if it returns. In his translation Pope makes them act out of pity, but it is not in the text.[10] However, there will be ample occasions for pity and tears in what follows, as for another 500 verses Homer sustains a sequence of speech and action which, even by the standards he has already set, remains supreme for vivid detail, emotion and empathy. Priam is about to cross the killing field alone, scene of the ebb and flow of the previous battles. He will go where no Trojan has ever gone before, inside the encampment of Achilles, the man who has killed his son.

With a herald, Idaios, who drives the mule waggon, Priam sets out, driving his horse-drawn carriage himself. His sons and sons-in-law follow him, lamenting as if he is going to his death, but this time a lamentation will turn out to be ill-founded. The family followers turn back in the plain, but Zeus is watching and 'has pity' seeing the old man: he has already sent an eagle, a favourable and most conclusive omen, in answer to Priam's prayer. Now he sends Hermes as a guide, the god 'for whom it is especially dear to accompany a man', a role which continued to be credited to him in subsequent antiquity.[11]

Out on the killing field, encounters have almost all been aggressive, fatal for one or other party. Now, Homer exploits a different tone. The setting is night, uniquely for a meeting outside Troy, and the register is one of gentle irony. By the grave-mound of Ilos, Troy's ancestor, Idaios the herald notices a stranger and proposes supplication to him in the hope, again, that he may show pity: it is an anticipation of what will soon happen in Achilles' presence. The stranger is Hermes in disguise. He has the look of someone the exact opposite to Priam, 'a young man with the first signs of a beard, which is the most pleasing time of youth', but neither old Priam nor the herald realizes who he is.[12] Priam is scared, but when the stranger takes him kindly by the hand and speaks to him, Priam, still unaware, considers him to be heaven-sent, a divinely guided friend, but not a god himself. They share a conversation whose irony, still gentle, is marvellously rich.

Hermes says he would gladly protect Priam from anyone else as 'I liken you to my dear father': love and respect between fathers and sons will play a crucial role in the sequel. He hides his knowledge of Priam's purpose and even asks if he is taking his treasure away to safety now that the best of men, his son, Hector, has been killed. He pretends to be one of Achilles' Myrmidons, but he also remarks that Hector's body is still dewy-fresh although it is being dragged each morning round Patroclus' grave. One of Priam's concerns is thereby laid to rest: his son, he learns, has not been mangled. Hermes then guides him to Achilles' encampment, whereupon he reveals his identity and departs, telling Priam to go in and clasp Achilles by the knees and to entreat him on behalf of his father and mother and his son. These moves are the moves, once again, of a formal supplication, an act already presumed in what Zeus had announced.

Priam enters Achilles' room, to Achilles' utter amazement. In a scene of transcendental power, he indeed falls before him as an abject suppliant and grasps his knees, but he also does something else: he kisses Achilles' hands, those 'terrible manslaying hands which had killed his many sons'. Hermes had not proposed this ultimate reversal, one which is unmatched in other known supplications but exactly suited to this unique context. At the end of book 22 Priam had already talked of Achilles having a father, elderly like himself, as if he would be a reason for Achilles to pity him. Now, he begs him to remember just that, a father as old as myself, he says, who is still at home without anyone to ward off maltreatment, but at least alive and hoping daily to see his son returning from Troy. He never names Peleus, but his mention of a father aims to engage Achilles' sympathy. It also brings out that Priam is even more pitiable: unlike Achilles' father, he has lost his sons in the war, he says, all fifty of them, culminating in Hector, the best. He has come nonetheless with a huge ransom, so 'respect the gods, take pity on me, remembering your own father'. He does not mention Achilles' mother or son, though Hermes had told him to do so. He has one further claim, unique to him. 'But I am more pitiable still, as I have dared to do what no other mortal on earth has ever dared, to stretch to my lips the hand of the man who has killed my son.'[13]

At the end of Shakespeare's *King Lear*, old Lear carries his daughter's body out on stage and talks intermittently as if she may still be alive: 'Ha? / What is't thou sayst? Her voice was ever soft, Gentle and low, an excellent thing in woman . . .' We already know what Lear cannot fully accept, that she is dead. It is the one scene in literature whose intensity approaches Priam's appeal, but unlike Shakespeare Homer does not deploy irony: Priam has chosen to humble himself to the utmost degree, and so he shares the pathos of the scene as knowingly as we do. Anything might have happened next within the framework outlined by Zeus, but Homer excels all expectations: Priam, he says, 'stirred in Achilles the desire to weep for his own father' and so he pushes Priam away 'gently' and the two of them weep together, Priam for Hector, slayer of men, Achilles 'now for his own father, and then again for Patroclus'.[14]

Rising to the occasion, Achilles begins by saying that 'indeed your heart is of iron' for daring to come out alone to confront the man who has killed your sons: the same words about Priam's iron-heartedness had been uttered by his wife on learning of his plan. He then invites Priam to sit and 'though we sorrow, let our distresses lie at rest in our hearts'. A jar of good and a jar of evil, he says, stand in the halls of Zeus, who either mixes their contents before distributing them to an individual mortal or else distributes from one jar only. To Peleus and to Priam, first good, then evil have been divinely given. These words are spoken by a special hero in a very special context, but what they say runs, I believe, through the entire poem.[15]

It is not for me to summarize the rest of this supreme encounter, as it transfixes all who follow it, its alternating speeches, the awareness of danger just below the surface of Achilles' pity, Priam's unwillingness at first to sit when asked, then his doing so in fear. Tact and forethought coexist with volatile emotion. Asking for a swift return of Hector's body, Priam ends by wishing Achilles enjoyment of the ransom and a return to his own land. There is irony here, unexpressed: Priam does not know, though we do, that Achilles knows he will never return home. In reply Achilles, scowling, tells him not to provoke him and not to 'rouse him further among his sorrows'.[16] In all innocence Priam has said the wrong thing, and hence Achilles' scowl and sense of provocation, though Homer leaves us to pick up the connection. It is yet another clear example of his implying more than he states.

With two of his aides Achilles springs from the house 'like a lion'. It is the last simile in the poem and it compares him, as often, with the lord of the beasts and evokes his potential ferocity. Yet, he and his aides take the ransom from the waggon and thoughtfully leave two robes there: Hector's body, they consider, can be wrapped in them when Achilles gives it to Priam to be taken home. Achilles then orders his maids to wash and anoint it, but here too he thinks ahead: he commands them to do so apart from Priam so that the old man may not be moved to anger at the sight and he himself may not be moved too and kill him contrary to Zeus' commands. He then lifts the body, washed, anointed and wrapped, onto a funerary couch and with his helpers sets it in the waggon on which it arrived. He and his aides have begun the preparation of Hector for his ceremonial funeral: there could be no greater reversal of his previous behaviour to him. He then addresses dead Patroclus and asks him not to be annoyed with him if he hears, even in Hades, that he has ransomed Hector, as the ransom, he says, is aptly big and he will set aside an appropriate share for him.

Thereupon, he returns to sit on the far side of the room, but now for the first time Priam is sitting too, opposite and apart. After a fine speech on the need to eat even when grieving, Achilles kills a lamb and roasts it so that they can eat together, Priam not having eaten since Hector's death. The food's preparation is described, as usual, in conventional phrasing, but the meal is followed by unprecedented empathy. 'Then indeed Priam was marvelling at Achilles, how big he was and what he was like, for he looked just like the gods', and Achilles was marvelling at Priam, 'looking at his noble appearance and hearing his speech'.[17] Once more, noble heroes on opposite sides of the war relate to each other in shared humanity and wonder.

Achilles orders bedding to be prepared for Priam and his herald under the colonnade, but his mood is still volatile: speaking brusquely, he tells Priam to sleep there so that none of the Greek entourage may see him and go to tell Agamemnon, thereby delaying the body's ransom. Nonetheless, he asks if Priam would like a truce in order to attend to a funeral for Hector. Priam concurs, asking for eleven days, including a day for a funeral feast and a day to raise a mound over Hector's burial: on the twelfth day, 'we will go to battle, if it must be so'.[18] *Ei per anankē*: in those three simple Greek words Priam wishes poignantly that it could be otherwise. Achilles agrees to the request and his brusqueness fades: he takes 'the old man's hand by the wrist, in case he might be afraid in his heart'. It is their final interaction, Achilles' last deed in the poem. It is exquisitely eloquent.

Priam sleeps outside, Achilles inside, 'and beside him slept fair-cheeked Briseis': Homer needs to say no more about her presence with him and what it concludes.[19] During the night, however, Hermes returns to Priam and tells him to leave at once: if Agamemnon or the Greek army learn of his presence, he will be taken prisoner and ransomed for three times the sum being given for Hector. So back Priam goes to Troy, Hermes departing at dawn, and as the old man goes on his way, he laments and wails: Homer does not give his words, though Priam's urge to lament his son Hector had been central to his mission to recover him.

When Priam arrives with Hector's body, he touches off collective grief in the entire city. Again, the process is told in a sequence which can readily be visualized, one of Homer's sustained series of precise moving pictures. Cassandra, Priam's prophetic daughter, is the first to see him coming: he is standing in his chariot, she announces with a shrill cry which travels through the city. Widowed in book 13, she delivers her one speech in the poem. 'Not a man or woman was left in the city', Andromache and elderly Hecuba being the first to rush upon the waggon as it came near the gates, and then holding Hector's head and tearing their hair. All the Trojans would have lamented by it while it was still outside, but Priam tells them to make way for the mules to pass. They part and let them through: only when Hector is inside his palace is he laid on a couch while the lament begins.

It is the most formalized lament in the poem. Expert singers begin it as leaders of a 'song of grief', a dirge to which women lament too, surely in answer as was customary in the Greek way of death.[20] The preparation for Hector's funeral had begun with actions by Achilles and his household: it ends with women's words. Hector's wife Andromache then utters a solo speech of lament, followed by his mother Hecuba and, finally, Helen, one after another, in magnificent speeches, none uttering vengeful words or curses. Helen has the last word, one which prompts the assembled Trojans to lament too.

Could Homer really have composed this matchless sequence of action, movement, speech and reaction without a prepared text? Again, I believe he was able to do so *because* he had none: he had rehearsed it orally beforehand so that its episodes would run in a tight sequence, one from another, the major ones signposted in advance, riveting their audience and adding to the emotional impact of what he performed. What we read is not exactly what he had composed in previous public performances of his poem, each of which varied: it is what came out in a subsequent composition, one dictated in performance to a literate aide. I find it hard to credit that any previous performance could have been better than this one, the one he wished to preserve. It is perfect.

During the truce, Hector's funeral is at last carried out. First, the Trojans go out for nine days to gather wood and make a pyre before the city. On the tenth, at dawn they carry Hector out and lay him on the pyre and set fire to it. Homer is hastening through the days of the truce, no longer filling each day with all its actions in sequence. At dawn again, on the eleventh day, Hector's brothers and companions gather the white bones, 'lamenting all the while with warm tears rolling down their cheeks'. They cover them with soft purple robes and place them in a golden chest and lay it in a hollow grave, setting big stones and a mound on top of it.[21] All the while, watchmen are placed in each direction in case the Greeks descend upon them: the war is certainly not ended. Then they go to Priam's palace and hold a glorious banquet, the last action in the poem. It is, however, a poignant one, as the fighting, we know, will resume and Troy will soon fall.

'So they attended to the burial of Hector, tamer of horses': the poem ends quietly, matched, I like to think, by an awed silence from Homer's listeners. We know that Achilles will die and that Troy will fall: the Iliad does not need to continue.

Over three days at the very least, Homer's audience entered into this profoundly affecting, all-absorbing world: behind the final scenes with Priam and Achilles I hear their tears too. One reason why this world absorbs us is that, throughout, the plot implies, and its gods and heroes exemplify, values which modern readers can reflect on, pausing over passages which seem at odds with values they most readily understand. When it was first performed, the values in the poem were not a straightforward illumination of its listeners' own. They too had to make an imaginative effort, because Homer emphasizes repeatedly that the heroes are not as mortal men nowadays. Heroes can pick up rocks ten times heavier than two men could move with the help of a waggon. They are stronger, bigger and, as he himself once calls them, demi-gods.[22] They belong to an era quite separate from Homer's and his listeners', but their choices and priorities are not like those of fantasy heroes in modern action films: we can infer from other post-Homeric poetry that they magnify values shared by real aristocrats in Homer's own time.

They are hallmarks of the poem but they were not to be the values of all Greeks ever after. Their political and social context changed, and in many city-states aristocratic rule ended. Already Plato could present Socrates in the late fifth century BC as a severe critic of ethics and conduct in the Iliad, especially those of Achilles, criticism which later Greek philosophers advanced too.

In 20 BC the Latin poet Horace addressed an urbane verse-epistle to young Lollius, who was studying rhetoric as a final part of his education.[23] Horace begins by telling him how he himself had been rereading Homer at Praeneste, modern Palestrina, about twenty miles south-east of Rome. Homer, he says, states 'what is fine and foul, useful and not' more clearly than ethical Greek philosophers. He goes on to specify the 'seething passions of stupid kings and peoples' in the Iliad, in which 'whatever madness the kings exhibit, the Greeks are wracked for it . . . With sedition, deceits, crime and lust and anger, bad behaviour occurs inside the walls of Troy, and outside too.'

Reading the Iliad for its ethical values has a long history, but they are more instructive than those to which Horace wittily reduced them.

20

Heroic Ethics

The values of Homer's heroes continue to engage philosophers because of the assumptions which underlie them and the questions which they raise. Some are problems of translation: do words in Homeric Greek have the same range as the words which we often use to render them? What does a Homeric hero mean by saying he is 'responsible': is he to blame and does he ever feel guilt? Others are problems of coherence. Is there a frequent conflict between a hero's ultimate goal, victory for his own side, and his immediate concern, his own honour and glory? Does a hero win honour, *timē*, only at the expense of another hero's *timē*? Others are problems of scope: is a hero liable to make amends because of his intentions or only because of the outcome of his actions? What are the values of women in the poem and how far are their ethics at odds with those of the men? No reader of the heroic poems about Beowulf or Manas confronts such ethical questions: their heroes are far more straightforward. The Iliad teems with them, through what its heroes say as well as do.

One basic hallmark sets the Iliad's protagonists apart from most of their modern readers: they are all upper class. The heroes seldom spell out long family pedigrees, but it is fair nonetheless to call them aristocrats.[1] The word *agathos*, meaning good, is frequently applied to an individual hero, but is not used simply to mean virtuous. It refers to 'a good man', or 'one of us', we being the upper class.

The only non-aristocratic speakers in the poem are Hector's housekeeper, a slave who utters eight respectful verses to help her master on his way, and Thersites, a speaker from the Greek ranks who delivers eighteen verses in book 2.[2] However, Thersites is viewed through a decidedly upper class lens. Significantly, Homer says nothing about his father or family. He was known, he tells us, for his habit of speaking up in public. Elsewhere in the poem, such speaking is an aristocratic monopoly, but Thersites spoke ignobly and regularly provoked laughter from the assembled troops. Homer is more explicit about his appearance than about anyone else's in the poem: he is hunch-backed, lame, with patchy hair on his head and so forth. Later Greek authors refer to upper class males as 'the fine and good', fine having the sense of handsome. Aristocrats looked aristocratic, unlike their social inferiors, those whom the philosopher Nietzsche once called the bungled and botched.

This insistence on Thersites' misshapen physique sets him apart from the nobles, though later Greek authors tried to invent a noble family for him. He was certainly not 'one of us'. He habitually insulted his betters, as Homer calls them, the upper class, and on this occasion he voiced criticism of Agamemnon both for having insulted Achilles and for wanting ever more prizes from Troy when he had so many already: 'it is not proper for a leader to launch the sons of the Achaeans onto woes and troubles', he says, and so the Greeks should go off with their ships, leave Agamemnon alone at Troy and teach him what he owed to them. He had a point, but Odysseus replied to him, calling him the basest person in the Greek army, and then thumped him across his back with 'the staff', surely the sceptre he had just borrowed from king Agamemnon and had been using on other malingerers. On its first appearance, back in book 1, Homer explained that Agamemnon's sceptre was studded with gold nails. No wonder it produced a bloody stripe on Thersites' back and reduced him to tears.

Homer chose to present Thersites in unusual detail and to set this scene near the start of the poem: it is the last we hear in it from a non-aristocrat. The response of the troops needs to be weighed too. They were all 'terribly angry and resentful' at Thersites when he began to insult Agamemnon. When he is thumped, they say that the best of all the many good things Odysseus has ever done is to silence him: he will not be keen to speak so insolently to kings again. They laugh at him, as he wipes away a tear 'with a helpless look'. They share their nobles' view of the social order, but they do so 'even as they are vexed'.[3] The word 'vexed' here is often taken to refer to their exasperation at the general situation, as they have been wanting to return home from Troy, have just tried to do so and Thersites has indeed spoken up for such a course. However, I take it closely with the preceding verse about Thersites' distress and read it as their being vexed to see one of their number, even the ugly, rude Thersites, in such a condition. They also laugh at him and side with Odysseus for teaching him a good lesson, but Homer, as elsewhere, is aware that emotions surrounding laughter can be complex.

In the Iliad, the one non-aristocrat to speak in an assembly is thumped for speaking too frankly. Odysseus had already shown form here when, shortly before, he set off to rally the troops who had reacted too literally to Agamemnon's speech about returning home.[4] Whenever he met a 'king or a highly eminent man' he stood by him and addressed him with 'gentle words', saying it was not 'seemly for him to frighten him like a bad man', 'bad' referring here to someone of a low social class. Instead he asked him to sit down, please, and make other people sit too. However, whenever he 'saw a man of the ordinary people and found him bawling', he drove him, a noisy oik, along with the sceptre (the one with those gold nails in it) and rebuked him, saying 'Sit still, man, and listen to what others say who are more prestigious than you, whereas you are unwarlike and feeble, not to be counted in war or counsel.'

This class-based way of behaving and regarding others is accepted by the troops and never challenged by the poet. A 'good' man is good by birth and social status and is therefore expected to be courageous. It is disgraceful if he falters, but he can regain his credit if he resumes being brave: he loses all or most of his goodness only if his status changes and he becomes enslaved.[5] If Homer performed at religious festivals, many of his listeners were not upper class, but they surely accepted this close connection between values and the social hierarchy. They lived long before aristocratic rule risked being overthrown and they accepted, as near-contemporary poets affirmed, that their rulers were descended from Zeus. In Homer's eighth-century world, there was no middle class. In the Iliad there are no middle-class values.

At the bottom of its social pyramid there are slaves. When a city is captured the men are killed and the women enslaved, but Homer assumes slavery as a fact in other contexts too. It is taken for granted in the households of Achilles, Agamemnon and Priam. When boats arrive with wine from Lemnos, slaves are one of the goods which the Greek troops use to acquire it, on a par with cattle, hides, bronze and iron. Quite how the troops had surplus slaves available is not explained: if they were war captives they would all be female. Homer simply assumes their presence, referring to them as *andrapoda*, a frequent Greek word for them but used only in this one place in the Iliad.[6] Taken literally, it means 'man-footed beasts'. In Homer's lifetime and for centuries after, nobody contested slavery's existence.

At the top of the pyramid, aristocratic values vary from one age and setting to another. In 1861, the nurse Florence Nightingale praised her aristocratic associate, the second son of the Earl of Pembroke, recently dead, as one who was 'eager and enthusiastic in duty, cared little for the reward, and not at all for the credit. No assertion of self; purity of nature and high principle.'[7] These values are a total contrast to those which Homer's aristocratic heroes exhibited long before Christian teaching and the restraints of a fully developed city-state. Florence Nightingale's hero was Britain's secretary of state for war, but he never fought while holding that position. Homer's heroes are at war and in much of the poem they engage in fighting.

For them, fighting is battle face to face, not a distanced modern war against unseen snipers and weapons fired without sight of their target. This setting is highly relevant to the values which they endorse. Modern study has characterized them as competitive and presented them as taking priority over co-operative values, ones to which the word *agathos*, or 'good', is never applied.[8] Indeed old Nestor recalls how Achilles was charged by his father Peleus 'always to be best and stand far above the others', the epitome of competition.[9] This competitive ideal is one which Achilles heard from his father, just as the campaign to Troy was about to begin. Presumably, it related to being best in battle, thereby winning honour, some of which would be material reward, and glory, *kudos*, to be perpetuated as fame.

Personal fame and honour may seem egotistical ideals: Achilles is the hero who exemplifies them. He withdraws from the fighting and leaves the Greek army to suffer because his own honour has been slighted. He then makes those remarks to Patroclus in book 16 about how he wishes all the other Greek soldiers might die, leaving just the two of them to sack Troy and win glory for themselves alone. I will say more about Achilles in another chapter, but even so, he keeps his own followers, the Myrmidons 'beyond number', out of the battle, so that none of them, his immediate friends and dependants, dies because of his withdrawal. His behaviour also does not go uncriticized. In book 9 when the three envoys come to plead with him, the most effective speaker is Ajax, who tells him he is pitiless, and his heart 'evil', the very word, 'for the sake of a girl, just one', meaning Briseis.[10] As Agamemnon was now offering to give back Briseis, Ajax is referring to Achilles' withdrawal in the first place and calling it pitiless and bad. He and other heroes do not condone such conduct, nor does Homer, whose implicit ethics are not always those stated by his heroes or implied by what they do.

Despite Achilles' selfish behaviour, those who aspire to honour and fame cannot wholly ignore other people: they depend on their estimation and their readiness to commemorate a fame-seeker's deeds. Nor do honour and fame necessarily crowd out co-operative values. On the Trojan side, Hector gives a resounding endorsement of fighting for one's homeland, calling it a better guiding principle than anything implied by dubious omens. As he leaves his wife for the last time, he tells her he cannot skulk away from battle 'like a bad man', a lowly coward, as he has learned always to be 'fine', brave therefore, and to fight among the first of the Trojans.[11] These ideals are ones to be pursued by anyone born 'a good man', but they also involve other people, in Hector's case his fellow Trojans. After hearing of his death, his wife Andromache laments him as Troy's guardian who 'kept [safe] its dear wives and baby children'.[12] Shame for what Troy's men and women would otherwise say of him had driven Hector to go out again and risk his life.

Heroism is not an easy, automatic course. Achilles refers to his sufferings at heart while risking his life in battle and to his many sleepless nights before his bloodied days. Hector says he has learned the ideal of excellence, one, therefore, which did not come naturally. A likely teacher is his father, Priam, because heroes are often impelled by a concern to live up to their fathers and forefathers. To do so, they strive to show bravery, a quality which is enhanced into courage by the fact that they know fear.

As for the Greek army's rank and file, their values are not Homer's primary concern, but fame and glory do not weigh with them to the same degree: in book 2 they have no compunction about pulling out and ignobly heading for home when Agamemnon seemed to be proposing an abandonment of the campaign. Yet, they promptly turn out again, disciplined and in order, marching onto the killing field when the option of return has proved illusory. Loyalty is important for them: during the great struggle to seize Patroclus' corpse, 'fewer by far' of the Greeks die than of the Trojans 'for they were always mindful to ward off sheer death from one another'.[13] Throughout the rest of the poem they obey their leaders and continue to suffer heavy casualties while doing so. During a brief truce to bury the dead, each side, not just the nobles, grieve in their hearts as they work to identify their own, washing off the blood and gore.[14] On the next day, however, they are out fighting all over again.

It is not for them to challenge one of the greats in single combat. In a marvellous passage, Homer relates how the sons of the Achaeans ran to look at great Hector just after Achilles had killed him and how each stabbed him with his spear:

> They gazed at the stature and wondrous form
> Of Hector, and not one of them stood beside him without
> stabbing him.
> So one would say, looking at one beside him,
> 'Well now, softer indeed to handle
> Is Hector than when he burnt the ships with blazing fire.'

The little ones emerge to stab a great one, but only when he is safely dead.[15] They still do.

Male heroes are the poem's main protagonists, but they are not 'ungodly man-killers', as the poet John Dryden called them in the 1690s, nor louts on the loose.[16] Despite the exceptional behaviour of angry Achilles, they are not fighting only for themselves: they win honour if they also protect their *philoi*. These *philoi* are not just a little circle of friends: they are people close to them, and at times extend beyond their own households, even comprising fellow Greeks or fellow Trojans, not only the leaders, either. Heroes, too, value loyalty and good faith.

During lulls in the fighting, they prize the ability to speak well and counsel wisely. When they are off the killing field, they are expected to be generous and to show hospitality to their social equals. They also preside over offerings and prayers to the gods, for the good of one and all. They recognize that one good turn deserves another and that they must give as good as they get, but it is stretching the term 'reciprocity' to claim that it governs their ethics.[17] Revenge is expected of a hero, especially for the death in battle of a brother or close friend, but not every gift a hero gives is made in the primary expectation of a quick return. Heroes are also commended for showing pity, that crucial aspect of the poem. An unpitying heart is not at all to Achilles' credit, as Ajax and, seven books later, Patroclus tell him: ethical terms are indeed applied to parts of a hero's psychology, in this case Achilles' heart.[18]

In times of peace, their values are not solely aggressive. The Iliad implies that they are expected to rule justly and to continue to be generous and hospitable. When dispensing justice, a noble would usually tend to avoid antagonizing another noble, but to avoid strife, a judgement had to qualify as justice in the minds of participants too. As for hospitality, that enduring Greek value, they could extend it widely, without reciprocal expectations. On the Trojan side, Axylos, a rich man, used to be a 'friend to men', Homer says, as he lived by a road and 'would show friendship to everyone'.[19] This fine behaviour is not at odds with other aristocrats' priorities: they too were expected to be kind to travelling strangers whatever their background. Kindness, or being *ēpios*, is an important quality in a hero, one which much modern scholarship elides.

Inside Troy, kindness is shown by Priam and Hector to Helen even though others in the city resented her very presence. In a telling speech, when Patroclus lies dead, Menelaus exhorts other Greek heroes to defend his body, bidding each of them to remember 'kindly, poor Patroclus, as while alive he knew how to be gentle to one and all'. Kindness is not to be shown while fighting, but a hero's kindness and gentleness in other contexts is a reason for fighting to recover him. Heroes are not just thuggish volcanoes, waiting to erupt in anger. As upper class warriors they must fight to deserve their honour, but kindness matters too, away from battle.[20]

In back-stories away from the killing field, there are men who show decidedly uncompetitive priorities and are approved nonetheless. My personal hero in the Iliad is Phylas the Thessalian, the kinsman of a leader of Achilles' Myrmidons.[21] Phylas had a lovely daughter, 'beautiful in the dance', whom the god Hermes saw dancing in a chorus in honour of Artemis. He went upstairs to her in her bedroom and ravished her: she produced a son, Eudorus, as a result. She then married a mortal and left her baby with Phylas, her father: he brought up his little grandson, the future Myrmidon, and cherished him, 'loving him through and through as if he was his own son'. Homer's exceptional word for this exceptional loving is *āmphăgăpāzŏmĕnos*, which occurs only here in the poem and fills the entire first half of a hexameter: surely he dwelt lovingly on it as he performed. It has nothing competitive about it. Nor does the value on which the final direction of the poem depends: Achilles' intense love for Patroclus.

Homer does not say whether this love was also sexual, a point made explicit only many centuries later by the master dramatist Aeschylus and by playwrights and poets after him.[22] Certainly, Homer never presents Achilles and Patroclus as kissing or sleeping together. At the end of book 9, after the Greek envoys depart, Achilles sleeps with fair-cheeked Diomēdē, his slave-captive from Lesbos, while Patroclus sleeps on the other side of the room with fair-girdled Iphis, another slave-captive, one whom Achilles had taken on the island of Scyros.[23] She had been acquired, therefore, before the Trojan war began, and if Achilles gave her then to Patroclus, he had been bedding her for some ten years. Achilles and Patroclus might still have been physical lovers, but Homer says nothing about such a side to their relationship: what matters to him is the over-riding love that binds them anyway. The Iliad follows not just the course of a hero's wrath, but the consequences of his intense love.

21.

Heroes at Play

Despite grandfather Phylas and kindly Patroclus, a widely held modern view of the heroes' values is that their hallmark is to be inherently destructive: 'Homeric ethics gives each person an interest in supporting a system whose effects harm everyone.'[1] If they do, they are not unique or primitive: the ethics of modern industrial societies have done likewise, leading to destructive changes in the climate, affecting everyone. In the war itself, the two pre-eminent warriors, Hector and Achilles, indeed take decisions which put their own fame and repute before the best interests of those on their own side, but they are not to be generalized as an exemplary sort of decision for everyone else. Hector remains outside Troy, out of shame, and dies, to the city's detriment, but his decision is a special tragedy in the poem. Achilles withdraws and lets many of his own side die, but other heroes make it quite clear that this decision is unpitying and bad. In other cases individual heroism, pursuing fame and glory, did not damage the Greeks at all: it enabled them to capture Troy.

To fill out the heroes' values we need to consider them when not on the battlefield. The crucial evidence is in book 23, the funeral games for Patroclus. The heroes are competing, but not always fighting. Here, the Manas poem in central Asia is a telling comparison. It too has a long episode of funerary games and their contests. As in Homer, great heroes wrestle, Manas being one. They too race horses and quarrel over the prizes. Once they even include a live show, when an ageing woman, a 'disgraceful heathen', crouches on hands and knees and lets another hero have sex with her in public. This novel type of four-legged action began in the morning of a hot summer day, shocking Muslim spectators and persisting till noon, 'a scene', the poet tells us, 'that would never leave their minds'. It is a reminder of Homer's decorum. In the Iliad and Odyssey there are only two sex scenes, both of them between a god and a goddess.

In his funeral games, Homer presents many of the heroes for the last time. The context is not wholly unlike battle: 'war minus the shooting', as George Orwell once characterized competitive sport. I will dwell on the values which underlie it and then compare them with those in contests of another sort, duels to the death on the battlefield.

In the games, none of the competitors belongs socially to the rank and file. In the boxing, Epeius admits he falls short in actual battle, but, he says, 'nobody can be expert, after all, in everything'. He describes himself, assertively, as 'the best', the best of boxers, and takes a hold of the first prize, a mule, before he even fights for it.[2] He threatens to break the flesh and smash the bones of anyone who opposes him, but Euryalus stands up to fight him nonetheless, a true prince, 'equal to the gods'. The contest has not pitted a princely amateur against a lower class professional. Epeius is called noble too, though not quite as noble as Euryalus: boxing and sport are activities for the upper class. When they fight, Epeius punches princely Euryalus to the ground, but 'great-heartedly' helps him off, spitting blood with his head hanging to one side.

A wrestling match follows in which there is no doubt about the contestants' standing: they are two major heroes, cunning Odysseus and hefty Ajax. Like the boxers, they wear belts: unlike real competitors in the Olympic games, at least from *c.* 720 BC onward, Homer's heroes do not compete naked. The wrestlers strain almost to bursting point, and after one fall by each of them Achilles intervenes and graciously stops the match, although a third round would have been customary in real life, guaranteeing an overall winner. In an armoured contest, two heroes then compete to draw blood with real weapons and here too they are major heroes, Ajax, again, and Diomede. This time the spectators call a halt, fearing that one of the two will be badly hurt. These aggressive games and real battles are indeed combative, but unlike those on the killing field, the combatants are from the same army, and so the winning boxer helps his victim to his feet and the armed duel is stopped before anyone is wounded.

Throughout the games, intense effort coexists with mishaps, magnanimity with angry protests, giving the contests a variety and human appeal which battle lacks. They are a tribute to Homer's range and empathy. Spectators laugh at failing competitors, but not with the sarcastic laughter with which combatants mock opponents on the battlefield: in the games the recipients of it laugh and smile too. When young Antilochus finishes last in the running race, he smiles and tells the crowd that the gods favour older men, the winner being Odysseus, 'someone who they say is a sprightly older man'. It is hard, he says, for Greeks to contend with him on foot, he adds, 'except for Achilles'.[3] This compliment gives glory to Achilles, who promptly rewards Antilochus with a further half-talent of gold. It caps their previous dispute.

There are no women among the spectators. The watchers are the army, and among them tempers still flare quickly. A heated arguments begins over who is in front in the chariot race, the event narrated at most length. Idomeneus even proposes that Ajax and he should bet a 'tripod or a cauldron' on the truth of the matter 'so that Ajax may learn by paying up': it is the first known offer of a bet.[4] Of course, the contestants are highly competitive, just as on the battlefield, but one way to win in the chariot race, as old Nestor tells his son, is to use cunning intelligence, *mētis*, not brute force. His son takes it to extremes, however, and when the track on which they race narrows, he drives off one side of it and forces Menelaus and his team to hold back: it is the first known example of cheating in a race. It succeeds, but it does not go unchallenged.

While heroes compete in the events, they refer, like warriors, to the shame and disgrace of being seen to lose and to the honour if they win. This honour, or *timē*, is still closely linked to material prizes, but the prizes are personal gifts from Achilles, the host, and so they can, in principle, be re-allotted. His treatment of them is very revealing. Before the chariot race, he announces the prizes and then ranks them in order, but when the race has ended, he wants to award second prize to the driver, Eumelus, who has come last. His reason is simply that Eumelus is known to be the best, as are his horses, but in the race he had been foiled by the vengeful goddess Athena. His excellence, Achilles assumes, deserves a prize despite this temporary setback.

The spectators agree with this allocation of honour, *timē*, even though it is not supported by a competitive result. However, Nestor's son, young Antilochus, objects. As on the battlefield, we wonder whether results will matter after all. He had finished in second place and so he warns Achilles that he will be very angry at the proposed change. Nonetheless, he accepts that Eumelus is a 'good man', one of us. If Achilles pities him, he says, then from his own possessions he should give him something even better than the second prize, or else – why not? – give this extra prize 'here and now, so that the Achaeans may praise you': he too is not locked into a purely competitive ethic. However, he will not give up the pre-announced second prize, a mare pregnant with a mule, as he has won it, and if anyone tries to take it, he says, he will fight them. In reply, Achilles smiles 'because Antilochus was his dear companion', a close *philos*. It is his one and only smile in the poem.[5]

Throughout antiquity, rich donors could be challenged verbally in a public setting to be even more generous there and then: Achilles responds positively to what he calls young Antilochus' 'command' to him to give something extra, using the very verb, *epididonai*, which expresses such extra giving in later usage.[6] It is the first known example of generosity escalating in this way: Achilles promptly gives Eumelus an even more precious prize, a special breastplate from his own battle-spoils.

Achilles' dispute with him has already revealed values beyond simple competition: a respect for pre-existing excellence, a wish to honour it despite a contest's result, and pity and magnanimity, as if winning is not the be-all and end-all. Nonetheless, Antilochus had threatened to fight if an agreed prize was re-allocated. In the poem's first book such a re-allocation had led to Achilles' anger, but here the threat is taken in good heart as a sign of a young man's keen spirit. A fight is avoided by the addition of an extra gift to those already on offer, but the tensions do not end there.

Noble Menelaus, Agamemnon's brother, stands forward, receiving the sceptre from a herald, and claims, correctly, that young Antilochus has cheated against him in the race and has 'shamed' his fine skill. Nonetheless, Menelaus says explicitly that he does not want to be adjudged to prevail just because he has more status and power than the young man: if any of the Greeks were to say he had done so, he implies, he would be ashamed. First, therefore, he proposes that the lords of the Argives should judge the dispute, but then he moves on and says that he himself will have it judged 'and the judgement will be straight': Antilochus, he states, must stand forward and swear by the gods that he has not cheated.[7]

Homer presents this sequence of proposals in Menelaus' own words, one taking over from another just as they do at heated moments in life. They do not expose a general weakness of governance in the Greek army: a racing dispute is never one to be put to a general assembly. In this case, Antilochus, avoiding perjury, defers to Menelaus, saying his mistake was due to youth and inexperience, and that the young should give way to older heroes, especially to avoid resentment from someone as noble as Menelaus. So he offers to give him the mare, saying, however, it was 'one I won', and offers to add other possessions too. Menelaus' rising anger melts, both because Antilochus is so young and also because he, his father and his brother have worked hard for Menelaus' cause, the war against Troy: so 'I will give you the mare, though she is mine.' The blaming of an action on one's youth, rather than apologizing fully for it, the need to respect seniority, the reciprocal claims of past services, all play a role in this fine episode, so different from the quarrel which began the poem. However, artful Homer makes each protagonist continue to refer to the prize as one which he has personally won.

Behind this scene lie the previous relations of Menelaus and young Antilochus, two heroes who have regularly combined in action during the poem.[8] Its sequel, too, shows that results are not all that matter in a hero's values. As the fifth prize is now going spare, Achilles bestows it on old Nestor in memory of Patroclus, though Nestor has not competed at all: he receives it gladly as a tribute to his 'kindliness' towards Achilles and to the 'honour which it is apt that I should receive among the Greeks'.[9]

In the last contest, the throwing of the javelin, the contestants do not even compete. Achilles simply gives first prize to Agamemnon because men know how far he has excelled others and how he has always been the best in power and in spear-throwing. Achilles proposes, however, that part of the prize be given to the other competitor, Meriones, and Agamemnon duly gives him it. So far from being judged only by deeds and results, here too a prize is given according to pre-existing status. One part is then conceded to a rival without demur. Within their own class, heroes can be magnanimous.

There is a sense here of rounding things off as the Greek heroes take a final bow in the poem.[10] Homer wishes to present Achilles as the magnanimous host, reconciled at last with heroes whom he had formerly rejected. He is now the mediator, not the escalator, of a quarrel; he smiles and defers to young Antilochus over the allocation of a prize; he concludes by honouring Agamemnon. It is all such a contrast to the poem's opening episode. Although he commands Agamemnon to give part of the prize to Meriones, he prefaces the order politely: 'if you, that is, wish so in your heart'.[11]

I have dwelt on the values underlying these scenes because they have been criticized as a hopeless muddle: they seem so only to those who class the heroes as combative in all circumstances and driven solely by results. In the games, Homer's presentation of them is more nuanced, but it is still the case that moods can change very quickly and anger and quarrelling are near the surface. They even erupt in the spectators, as two of them exemplify in that argument over who is leading the chariot race: 'the strife between them would have gone further', Homer continues, 'if Achilles himself had not stood up and spoken a word'. This flare-up is not unprecedented in other contexts. In four of the poem's back-stories, a named hero is said to have killed a cousin or a family member and therefore to have had to leave home. A fifth, Patroclus, is repeatedly represented as kindly when not fighting, but in boyhood he had killed a young contemporary while playing knucklebones.[12] He had had to leave his homeland as a result and was taken by his father to Achilles' father Peleus, with whom he grew up. He looks back on the deed and regrets it, but in most modern societies he would have been put into a remand home and prevented from ever bonding with Achilles, someone younger than himself.

The violence and the volatility of these incidents transfer readily to actual battle. On the killing field, unlike the sports field heroes on the same side never compete among themselves for glory. Competition and aggression take over when a hero meets an enemy. They usually exchange insults and boast before they fight: Homer's words for threatening, being vexed and so forth have a range which is often hard to translate.[13] They then throw a spear or spears in close combat at an enemy or rush on and drive a spear or sword through his skin, typically white skin, and on through his flesh and bone. These throws and thrusts would have required exceptional strength and muscle. In modern war, combat with fixed bayonets is the nearest equivalent, though it is very rare outside a soldier's preliminary training. At times, the spear of a Homeric hero is even said to rage madly or to long for blood. This turn of phrase has been considered archaic, but modern users still credit their bayonets with a similar impetus. Like the heroes, when thrusting through flesh and bone, they credit their weapon with a killing impulse of its own.[14]

These battle scenes are not for the faint-hearted. When heroes win, they gloat, sometimes sarcastically at their victim's expense. They never take prisoners, not even suppliants who beg for mercy: suppliants in battle are never spared. Mutilation of an enemy's dead body is not just a threat. When Agamemnon meets Trojan Hippolochus, who has just fallen before him as a suppliant, he cuts off his arms and his head and allows the latter to roll like a stone through the crowd. Ajax does likewise, as does Peneleos, and yet in 480 BC Greeks in their great war against Persian invaders regarded mutilation of the dead as barbaric, the vile practice of their foes.[15]

In the Iliad, heroes who mutilate the dead are usually taking personal revenge.[16] Agamemnon certainly was, as Hippolochus' father had urged the Trojans to kill Menelaus, Agamemnon's brother, when he came on an embassy to the city and had also urged that they retain Helen, hoping personally to receive gold from Paris. In book 17, Trojan Euphorbus too threatens a decapitation. He had just struck the first blow which led to Patroclus' death, but Menelaus comes to stand over Patroclus' corpse, whereupon each tells the other to withdraw rather than be killed. When neither does so, Euphorbus warns Menelaus he will cut off his head and bring it together with his armour to lay in the hands of his own father and mother. It is a grim prospect, but Euphorbus explains that Menelaus had just killed his brother, thereby bereaving them. The severed head, he says, will 'stop their lamentation', an act of revenge indeed, but one which will be well received.[17]

In book 14, Peneleos' actions develop differently. He is stirred by the taunts of Trojan Acamas, who has just killed a Greek, so he rushes at him, as if to take revenge. However, Acamas retreats and Peneleos is left to kill Trojan Ilioneus instead, the only child, Homer tells us, of a father who was especially loved by Hermes. The detail adds pathos, but Peneleos rams his spear through Ilioneus' eye and cuts off his head and helmet with a swipe of his sword. As his spear is still in the eye, he holds up Ilioneus' head on it 'like the seed head of a poppy' and taunts the Trojans to tell Ilioneus' mother and father to prepare a lament in their halls. The beheading relates to an unusual wound and Homer does not disparage it. He simply adds: 'So he spoke, and trembling seized the limbs of them all and each man peered around to see where he might escape grim death.' The words and actions here are meant to seem frightening to Homer's audience too.[18]

Achilles' mutilation of Hector is more straightforward: it is an act of pure revenge, in this case for the killing of his beloved Patroclus. When he drags dead Hector behind his chariot, he might seem to be flouting every Greek norm, but Achilles came from Thessaly and as Aristotle later remarked, Thessalians still dragged the corpses of their enemies round their graves in Aristotle's own day.[19] What makes this 'Thessaly drag' outrageous is that Achilles persists in it day after day.

In my ten selected books, killing predominates in only one, book 16, but my selection obscures its central role in the poem. In nine of the other books it is pervasive, much of it during the plot's longest day. It challenges many modern readers' appreciation, especially as there is a distinctive aspect to it. Unlike other oral heroic poems, the Iliad makes listeners and readers attend to the wounds which its heroes inflict. Their weapons' passage into and through the body is described with a detailed naming of parts.[20] During the longest day, the descriptions are particularly gruesome. In one, Meriones' arrow pierces the retreating Harpalion's right buttock, passes through his bladder and goes under the bone, in modern terms the pubic arch. He falls and lies stretched out on the ground 'like a worm, and the dark blood flowed out and wetted the ground'. Wounded heroes even lose their eyeballs and clutch their gushing liver or their entrails.[21] Their duels are stylized, like gun duels in a western movie, but unlike those shoot-outs, they present blood and guts with detailed physical precision.

This aspect of the poem is Homer's choice, executed in his own voice. He is capable of such empathy and pathos elsewhere: why does he dwell on such details? His descriptions of wounding sometimes transpose effects of a sword or spear thrust to an arrow shot, for which they are impossible. They have evolved, therefore, from sword wounds in earlier poems to arrow wounds by the time of Homer's.[22] It would be wrong, however, to excuse them as a layer which he inherited, whereas deaths full of pathos were introduced into the poem by his genius: he exploited them both, not because tradition obliged him to do so, but because he chose to. The choice reflects not so much on his heroes' values as on his own and those of the audience whose attention he had to retain.

22

Heroism and Hyper-Reality

War is a hallmark of the Iliad, and as a narrator Homer characterizes it in two ways. On the one hand, it is chilling, hateful, full of
tears and a state which nobody would choose for its own sake.
The heroes also express this view in their speeches. In book 14,
during the longest day, Odysseus reminds the wavering Agamemnon that wars are Zeus' hard gift to heroes: 'Zeus has given us the
[task of] winding gruesome wars, like a ball of thread, from youth
to old age.'[1] There is no escaping this destiny, but it is not one to
be relished. In book 13, in a notable speech, the hero Menelaus
refers to things which anyone would hope to enjoy to the point of
satiety, 'sleep and love and sweet song and dancing', rather than
war, which is the Trojans' perverse preference, he protests. Homer
has just given an overview of the fighting, one which bears out
Menelaus' view. He has described it as the 'killer of mortal men'
and as bristling with spears which cut men's flesh. The glare of
bronze from the armour blinded onlookers' eyes, and only if
someone was hard-hearted would he have 'rejoiced at such toil
and not grieved'.[2] This sympathetic view extends beyond the sufferings of upper class heroes: it includes the toil and losses of the
ordinary ranks, Greeks and Trojans alike. Many more were dying,
Homer remembers, than the great and good whom he names in
individual combat.

On the other hand, war, he says, brings glory to men. Twenty-
two times, he uses the word *charmē* in connection with battle and
the prospect of fighting. One modern view is that it always means
'will to fight', but the root of the word relates to rejoicing and that
sense is certainly present in some cases.[3] In book 4, the Achaeans

put on their armour and remembered their *charmē*, promptly exemplified by Agamemnon, who did not just regain a will to fight: he eagerly hastened into battle. In book 13 the god Poseidon touched the two Ajaxes with his staff and 'filled them with mighty strength' and made their feet and limbs seem light. They comment on their renewed eagerness and sense of lightness and then Homer describes them as 'rejoicing', the very word, in the *charmē* which the god put in their heart: more than will was involved here. So too when the goddess Athena and grim Strife intervened, they made battle seem 'sweeter' to the Greeks than 'a return in their hollow ships to their dear homeland', a sweet prospect indeed. When Achilles finally roused his Myrmidons, he reminded them that they used to 'love' battle, using a very strong word which evokes lust.

A similar duality is applied, once, to bodies killed in battle. In the great speech in which Priam begs Hector to pity him and come inside Troy, he implores him not to leave him, old as he is, to die hideously and be devoured by his own dogs when the city falls. An old man's death, he says, is ugly, whereas

> '. . . for a young man all is seemly
> When slain in war, pierced by sharp bronze,
> He lies: dead as he is, all is beautiful that may be seen.'

His point is not that it is fine to die young for one's country: it is that the appearance of a young man's body, dead in battle, is fine, in contrast to an old man's, ugly in his nakedness, mangled by dogs:

> 'But when the grey head and grey beard
> And shameful parts of an old man, killed, are shamed by dogs,
> This indeed is the most piteous thing for wretched mortals.'

It is a highly rhetorical contrast, made in a speech, and as Alexander Pope well realized when translating it, 'the old Man, 'tis certain touches us most'.[4] Homer gives Priam five and a half verses to present his likely death and another three to relate it more generally, concluding his great speech. The young man's death receives only two and half verses, in between.

In the narrative, the beauty of a young man's death is not exactly prominent. When Hector lies dead in the dust, onlookers come to marvel at his 'wondrous form', but they do not comment on his beauty, pierced as he had been in his neck by Achilles' enormous spear: they marvel at his physique, visible in the rest of his intact body.[5] Repeatedly Homer describes the rending and mutilation of the dead in battle, their bodies spattered with blood and dust. The wives and children they have left, their fathers unable to save them, the skills and talents which have not availed them, these are the features which add poignancy to their deaths. The beauty of a young brave death is never mentioned, neither aesthetic beauty nor moral.

Sarpedon's is a fine example. A spear, thrown by Patroclus, strikes him, heroic son of Zeus, full frontally in the chest 'where the lungs are shut in around the dense heart'.[6] No death could have been more glorious and more honourable, but he lies dying in front of his chariot and horses, groaning and clutching at the bloody dust. Homer compares him to a bull, also groaning, which is killed by a lion in its herd, but the bull is tawny and great-hearted, not beautiful in death. Patroclus then stood on Sarpedon's chest and 'drew out the spear from the flesh and the lungs followed with it'. Before long, 'not even a clever man would have recognized' Sarpedon, heightening the pathos of his death, as he 'became wrapped in weapons and blood and dust from his head right down to the soles of his feet'.[7] To restore his looks, the gods had to intervene: Zeus told Apollo to take him away and wash him in a river's streams, anoint him with heavenly ambrosia and clothe him with immortal robes. It takes a rare divine intervention to falsify the physical truth of death in battle.

In later classical art, the warrior-victim is shown frozen before death, a recipient of his enemy's serene gaze. In Homeric combat there is nothing aesthetic about the loser's dying: wounds are often presented in detail, sometimes exact, as with Sarpedon's lungs and their positioning round the heart. How, if at all, are the battle joy and the chilling horror, the glory and the gore, to be reconciled?

Most of Homer's grisliest accounts of wounds are wounds to Trojans. However, he does not give them only to the Greeks' enemies, let alone as if they deserved what they got. Hector, on the rampage, kills a Greek, Coeranus, by 'striking him with his spear beneath his jaw and ear': the spear thrust out his teeth and cut through the middle of his tongue.[8] Homer's scenes of blood and guts are not always partisan.

In one modern view, heroes at Troy are fighting with a constant sense of the pathos which war imposes on them. In book 19, six of them remain with Achilles while he laments for Patroclus and calls the loss the worst thing he could suffer, worse even than news of the death of his own father, who is perhaps weeping even now in Thessaly for his son. As he speaks, weeping, the heroes with him weep too, each remembering what he has left at home.[9] The response is one which will resurface in Achilles and Priam at the climactic end of the poem, but the six who weep here with Achilles are all older heroes, Agamemnon, Menelaus and Odysseus among them. Their emotion for what war has obliged them to leave may not have been shared by younger heroes, Diomede being a prime example. Only the goddess Hera refers to the wife whom young Diomede has left at home and her potential sorrow if he dies.[10] In all his exploits Diomede never mentions her. Heroes were not all toiling at Troy in a perpetual vale of tears, nostalgia and regret.

In 1980, in a profound study, Jasper Griffin redefined the entire poem, putting its scenes of combat in a very different light. He presented the Iliad as a poem not about violence but about life and death. 'Actual duels in it are short, and the greater hero shows his greater stature by killing his opponent, who for his part is usually killed with ease, sometimes without resistance . . . Fate, not fighting technique, is what interests the *Iliad*; the hero, splendid and vital, going down into death.' It is prevented from being 'gruesome, or boring, or unbearable' by the 'light in which the warriors are seen'.[11] Even the lesser ones are given pathos by accompanying details, he remarks, the loss of their youth and their beauty, or the loss which their parents, especially their fathers, will feel, or the fact that their skills in earlier life were of no avail. Prematurely, many of them leave a wife to grieve for them.

Long before Griffin, in an essay prefacing the second volume of his translation in 1716, Alexander Pope had already dwelt at length on these back-stories and their 'wonderful Art', their 'pathetick Circumstances' and their inducement of a 'different Movement in the Mind', one of compassion and pity.[12] The style, Griffin claims, 'preserves the poem from sentimentality on the one hand and sadism on the other'. These brief notices are like little obituaries, he well notes, and can be compared with later Greek epigram-poems, put up by fathers in memory of their dead sons. In the Iliad they allow Homer to present persons close to the heroes who could not otherwise feature in the plot. Importantly he does so on both sides, Greek and Trojan. 'The universality of the Homeric vision . . . led to this highly exceptional device, which confers significance on the victims of the great heroes, who in most warlike epics count for nothing.'[13]

Actual duels are indeed short: 170 battle encounters are described and a further 130 are mentioned, as their expert scholar Hans van Wees has calculated, but 'only 18 involve more than one blow, and a mere 6 of these involve more than a single exchange of blows'.[14] There were obvious poetic reasons for these quick ins and outs. Homer wanted to present plenty of fighting, but he also had to retain listeners and keep the story moving. Nonetheless the pattern is coherent: the most prolonged combats are fought over a loser's dead body, when each side is trying to drag it off.

As for the theme of life and death, two major deaths are indeed accompanied by fine last-minute speeches from the dying man: Sarpedon's and the poignant death of Hector. Another, the death of Achilles, will occur after the Iliad ends, but mentions of its inevitability at a very young age are essential to the poem's effect. However, the pathos of death does not dominate quite as Griffin emphasizes.

The first detailed fighting in the poem extends over some 1100 verses from the end of book 4 to the early parts of book 6, all in a single day. In it fifty-four named individuals are killed. They include

Axylos, that rich man 'who was dear to men, for he used to be friendly to them all, living in a house by the road'. Yet, Homer adds, 'not one of them then kept grim death from him'. Axylos' death is indeed made more poignant by this back-story, one which was justly called very moving by Alexander Pope as he translated it. He compared Axylos' 'manner of keeping house near a frequented highway, and relieving all travellers' with the 'ancient hospitality' of the patriarchs in the biblical book of Genesis and with practices which were current in the Ottoman empire. Diomede also 'took away the life' of Axylos' attendant, who was driving his chariot at the time. Pope considered that the death of Axylos' loyal driver was 'natural' to Axylos' character, a friend to all men.[15]

Axylos' death comes near the end of a long sequence of killings. The majority of them, 46 out of 53, are oriented very differently.[16] Not a word conveys their pathos and nothing is made of the victims' death. In a frequently used description, the hero simply 'fell with a thud and his armour clattered on him'. This part of the Iliad occupied about two hours of the poem's performance at a likely rate of delivery and was its listeners' first prolonged exposure to battle scenes. They are far more concerned with killing and with the passage of weapons into the body than with any tragedy of life and death. In much of this long sequence, the main killer, Diomede, is explicitly being helped to win *kudos*, glory, by the goddess Athena. In another long stretch of the poem, books 15–17, many heroes are killed too. In book 16 the major deaths of Sarpedon and Patroclus certainly have pathos, but the many deaths before and after theirs are narrated without any back-story adding poignancy to them. Some of them occur in the prolonged fighting over the two heroes' bodies, in which plunder and glory are at issue, or the body's rescue for due funerary rites. They do not relate to big questions of life and death at all.

In a powerful essay on the poem, the French thinker Simone Weil, thirty years old at the time, presented it in a rather different light, as a poem not of death but of force: 'the true hero, the true subject matter, the centre of the Iliad is force . . .', she began, 'those who know enough to discern force, today as in the past, at the centre of all human history find in the Iliad the most beautiful, the most pure of mirrors'.[17] Weil was writing in summer 1940, a time when the power of force was all too evident in the Nazi invasion of France. Her reading drew on her own deeply thought ethical convictions, including her sense of mystical experience, but it also related to earlier French presentations of the First World War, one of which had anticipated that war's beginning as 'the great harvest of Force, towards which a sort of inexpressible grace precipitates and ravishes us'.[18] Weil well remarked that on first setting out for Troy, the Greeks had boasted they were the best: while eating and drinking lavishly on the island of Lemnos, they had claimed that they would each stand in battle facing one or two hundred Trojans.[19] Like soldiers in her time and ours, they soon found a prolonged war to be very different.

Weil recognized that 'people in the Iliad are not segregated into the conquered, slaves and suppliants on the one side, and conquerors and masters on the other: every human being may at any moment be compelled to submit to force'. Force's power to transform human behaviour into things, she claims, is twofold 'and works from two sides: it turns to stone differently, but equally, both the soul of those who undergo it and of those who wield it'.[20] Here, her reading goes astray.

Sometimes great heroes are indeed gripped by the force of battle frenzy. Even Hector, kindly to Helen and his wife Andromache, is called a rabid dog by his enemies when he rages in battle and blazes with battle lust. When Achilles returns to fight, he too rages in battle, slaughtering any Trojans who confront him, yet he and Hector still express in words just why they are on the rampage. It is not force which causes Hector to confront Achilles or Achilles to confront Hector. It is shame and honour on Hector's side and on Achilles' side anger and revenge. Throughout the poem's fighting, victors and victims, so far from being objects, wonder what to do and debate alternatives which are open to them.

Rather than force, the poem implicitly addresses a vice of which Greeks were to be acutely aware throughout their history: excess.

Despite its many scenes of killing, notions of going too far or beyond acceptable behaviour underlie the plot. Arrogance and insolence, summed up in Greek as *hubris*, are implicitly resented, although the word *hubris* occurs only twice in the poem, each time in the first book, where it applies to Agamemnon's high-handed behaviour to Achilles, as does its related verb *ephubrizein*, used of that behaviour in book 9.[21] When the offers to Achilles fail, one of the envoys, Odysseus, says that Achilles has become even more intent on acts of excessive arrogance: they are expressed in a word, *agēnoriē*, whose root, at least, has the literal meaning 'too much manliness'. In book 22, fearing that Hector is dead, his wife Andromache uses the same word, speaking of his 'grievous *agēnoriē*' which made him keep running far forward in battle, 'yielding to nobody in his might'.[22] For these speakers, the word conveys that a preferable limit of manly behaviour had not been observed. It was overridden, not by force, but in Achilles' case by anger and a selfish lack of pity and in Hector's by reckless bravery.

Seen through a hero's eyes, battle can inspire eagerness, even passion. It is also hateful and full of grief. Seen through the poet's eyes, it can bring glory to men, but it is also full of pathos and suffering which no onlooker could contemplate unmoved. The Iliad is neither an anti-war poem about war, nor a celebration of violent killing: Homer, as ever, is not one-eyed. He presents war's duality, one which is still 'a troubling and unsettling mystery', as Margaret MacMillan well emphasizes in her important book on how war has shaped us. 'It should be abhorrent, but it is so often alluring and its values seductive. It promises glory and offers suffering and death.'[23] That mystery is already crystal-clear in the Iliad, a powerful reason for engaging with it.

Unlike most of Homer's modern scholars, most of his first male listeners would have been combatants, although only the nobles among them would have engaged in anything like the stylized, heavily armoured duels which the Iliad presents. In my view, the Iliad was first performed to warriors, during or just after a campaign. From their own experience, they could relate to the insults, the boasting, the rushes of battle frenzy: even now, they are familiar elements in soldiers engaged in combat, ones which many of them reflect on subsequently and wonder if they were really being themselves at the time.

In a fine discussion of the poem's violence and the strategies of critics, ancient and modern, who have tried to skirt round it or transfer it to a higher plane, James Porter has proposed that 'Homer uses beauty not to make war palatable but to make it questionable. Homeric epic is always counter-epic . . . Epic attracts by problematising itself.'[24] I doubt if Homer or his first listeners questioned war: they accepted it as a fact of life, and the pathos which frequently went with it. Like the boasting and battle frenzy, the descriptions of wounds made the combat scenes fearsome and, yet again, vivid. Vividness is a quality which ancient critics, centuries later, rightly acknowledged in the poem. They used the word *enargeia* for it, meaning not that it has the 'glare of an unbearable reality', as a great lover of Homer, the poet Alice Oswald, has interpreted the word, but simply that it makes a subject manifest.[25] Homer set his vivid scenes of battle in a frame to which listeners could relate: war's two aspects, its glory and its horror.

Spanning both of them, his battle scenes relate to reality, but they are not a true picture of it. Unlike real warriors, his heroes never die slowly from a protracted wound or remain disabled after a clumsy sword thrust. They are never wounded in their private parts. Their fights follow a stylized series of moves. Like the edited film shots of modern military 'engagements', they purport to be real, but simulate reality. In modern wars, such a presentation has been classed as hyper-reality and considered to be especially convincing to viewers who have become accustomed to digital images.[26] However, long before the digital age existed and hyper-reality was labelled, Homer had exploited it. The wounds and emotions of his warriors seem real, but their stylized encounters are not. Even in the eighth century BC, a hyper-real simulation, in verse, not images, could hold its listeners' attention.

23.

Shame and Glory

Violence becomes war when it is carried out on a large scale by one political unit against another. The Trojan campaign qualifies as one even though part of the Greeks' army had come from areas outside Agamemnon's realm and joined him through its leaders' ambitions and personal ties to one another. It is misleading to present the heroes as mere bandits, a view first exploited by Émile Zola, or as no different from modern *mafiosi*, some of whom use words like 'noble' to characterize their leaders. The heroes are warriors and true nobles, not gangsters whose terms of rank and quality are parasitic on a noble culture far beyond them. The Greeks are not violent bandits, who have simply come to ruin the poor Trojans' peaceful lives. Much more than force has brought and kept them there.

'What, after all is Helen to Odysseus', Simone Weil asked, 'what indeed to him is Troy, filled with riches that will not compensate for the ruin of Ithaca', his home kingdom, which he indeed found being ruined on his return?[1] Homer says little explicitly in answer to this question, one he did not need to pose, but it can be answered nonetheless. Plunder was one of the reasons for coming to fight, but fame and glory were important too, as it would be shaming to fail to join this great expedition when so many other aristocrats were joining it and when heroes' fathers and grandfathers had won fame already in campaigns waged beyond their borders. Heroes often say that they must not fall short of their fathers and forbears.

It is misleading, too, to idealize the Trojans as poor innocent victims. A Trojan, Paris, had stolen the wife of noble Menelaus, king Agamemnon's brother, together with other treasures, although Menelaus had received him honourably as his guest. On arriving at

Troy the Greeks' leaders had sent envoys to try to negotiate Helen's peaceful return, but there were calls from some of the Trojans for them to be killed on the spot.[2] In book 3 of the Iliad the two armies remained apart to let Paris and Menelaus fight a duel. A truce was sworn with solemn oaths, prescribing dire punishments for anyone who broke it, but a Trojan, Pandarus, broke it treacherously when the duel proved inconclusive. In book 7 another duel, between Hector and Ajax, also proved inconclusive and the two sides parted. Inside Troy, in a 'grim and noisy assembly', Antenor, husband of the priestess Theano, then proposed that the Trojans should give back Helen and the treasures Paris had stolen: 'as of now, we are fighting having lied and broken our trusted oaths'.[3] In reply, Paris proposed to give back the treasures and add more besides, but utterly refused to surrender Helen. With king Priam's approval, his offer was sent to the Greeks: they received it in silence until the young Diomede raised the stakes. Neither Helen nor the offer of treasure should be accepted, he said, and 'it is known even to someone who is wholly foolish that all the Trojans' destruction is already sealed'. As so often, the demands in a war escalated: 'all the sons of the Achaeans shouted out, approving the words of Diomede tamer of horses'.[4] The looting of Troy was now the only acceptable war aim. It would lead necessarily to the killing of all males in the city, even the little boys, and the enslaving of all the girls and women, a standard practice in Greek warfare.

Why, though, are so many heroes from elsewhere fighting with the Trojans? They were receiving gifts and food, we learn, but more was involved. In a famous speech in book 12, the Trojans' ally Sarpedon, that Lycian lord from south-west Asia, gives an answer to his colleague Glaucus.[5] Why have we been specially honoured, he asks, 'with a special seat and meat and full cups in Lycia, and all men look on us like gods?' Therefore, he says, they must go and fight among the foremost Lycians so that many of the Lycian warriors may say, 'Not inglorious, indeed, are our lords who rule over Lycia and eat rich sheep and drink choice honey-sweet wine.' In the eighth century BC, Homer's audience still looked on their ruling aristocrats in this way: on the battlefield they were the champions and so they were duly pre-eminent off it. Sarpedon reminds Glaucus that they 'must' go to fight in the front of the battle: the necessity arises not from a social contract linked to the honours they enjoy, but from the glory they must win and the shame in others' eyes if they do not try to do so.[6] However, this argument did not explain why the Lycians must fight so far away from Lycia. The Greeks were to sail home if Troy fell: they would destroy it, but they would not then try to colonize western Asia. Lycia was not directly threatened.

Sarpedon then makes a second, rather different point, whose logic is related to the here and now. If he and Glaucus could be ageless and immortal, he says, escaping from the war, he would not fight in it, nor send Glaucus into the 'battle which brings glory to men':

> 'But now, as the fates of death stand beside us,
> Thousands of them, which no mortal may escape or avoid,
> Let us go . . .'

Glory is present in this stirring exhortation too.[7] In a mortal existence, it is a compelling aim, Sarpedon is saying, now that they find themselves in battle: the hard fact is that men will die anyway, so they may as well enter the fighting. Yet, if he and Glaucus had left Troy and gone home, far fewer fates of death would have been standing beside them. In the heat of the moment, Sarpedon does not make a crucial point, that as allies of Priam it would be shameful for them to arrive at Troy and then withdraw. Four books later he dies, killed at Patroclus' hands.

A constant check on heroes' decisions and behaviour is indeed shame. In a brilliant study, conceived in 1947, E. R. Dodds interpreted Homer's heroes as living in a shame culture, not a guilt culture.[8] The concept has been much discussed since, and as Dodds already observed, the main Greek word at issue, *aidōs*, does not always overlap with our concept of shame. *Aidōs* can also cover modesty or respect: it can inhibit a superior from killing an enemy who entreats him and begs him to be spared. Its general effect is to inhibit someone from uttering a word or doing a deed.[9] It is not applied to being 'ashamed that' something has been done: that sort of shame is present in the Iliad too, but in a different set of words, among which are *aischron*, disgraceful, and *aischynē*, a sense of disgrace.[10]

Shame differs in two under-appreciated ways from guilt. It is not that guilt is a private, internal response, whereas shame always rests on the reactions of others: we can be privately ashamed of ourselves or secretly feel shame inside ourselves before an imagined onlooker. One cardinal difference is that we can be ashamed of something that is done or said by others to whom we relate, whereas we feel guilt only for what we ourselves have personally said or done. Teachers can be ashamed of what some of their pupils have done, but unless they instigated it, they do not feel guilt for it. Captains can be ashamed of some of their team members' conduct, without feeling guilt, as they have not done it themselves. There is also a difference of scope and timing. We feel shame about something we might otherwise do and we are therefore inhibited from doing it. We feel guilt and have guilty thoughts only about something we have actually thought or done (or failed to do). The responses involve our sense of ourselves in different ways. When we feel guilt, we accept that we, our full selves, are fully responsible. We can feel shame, however, when we feel we have acted out of character, our true self, or fallen short of our best.

Homeric heroes indeed conform to distinct features of our concept of shame, all of which are worth following in the poem. Appeals to *aidōs*, 'ashamed to . . .', are uttered by one hero to other heroes in order to make them stand firm on the battlefield and fight: they appeal to their shame, not to guilt. Two good examples occur in book 15.[11] First, Ajax urges the Greeks to be men and to 'put shame in their heart, and to have shame of one another in the mighty battles'. If they are ashamed to let others down, he means, they will stand firm: 'of those who have shame, more are saved than killed'. Soon after these words, Nestor, too, implores the Greeks, this time one by one, to 'put in their hearts shame for other men' and, as a result, not to scatter while the Trojans break in among their ships.

Shame can also shape an individual hero's course of action. In book 6, Hector famously tells his wife Andromache that he cannot stay safely inside Troy, because he feels shame before the men and women of the city if he does so. In book 22, in his fine speech to himself, he says that he cannot retreat inside Troy, because he feels shame before its men and women, this time because he has ruined the army by his folly, persuading them to stay out on the plain. Someone worse than himself, he says, a social inferior therefore, may say as much, a shameful possibility which inhibits him from coming inside the walls. 'It would be far better', he says, 'to go to confront Achilles and kill him, or to die in fair fame before the city.'[12] Shame, in the sense of 'being ashamed to . . .', impels him to his death: strikingly, it is shame not just at what a respected other person may say, but at the words of someone of a lower social class.

A hero can certainly be pained by another's behaviour and what is said of it, just as Hector is pained by the conduct of Paris, his brother-in-law. He refers to his heart's grief when he hears others' shaming reproaches of it, but does not actually refer to his own shame, as we would.[13] No hero in the Iliad ever quite says, 'I am ashamed of you and your behaviour.' They do, however, refer to others as disgraces, exemplified by Priam's berating of his sons as he prepares to go out to plead with Achilles. The implication is that he is ashamed of them. In a deep discussion of shame, the philosopher Bernard Williams has observed that 'the expression of shame . . . [and] the particular form of it that is embarrassment, is not just the desire to hide, or to hide my face, but the desire to disappear, not to be there.'[14] Homeric heroes express this very wish too: 'may the earth gape wide open for me', says Agamemnon, if he and the army ever have to slink back home and a Trojan is able to exult on his brother's grave, two shaming prospects indeed.[15]

'With guilt', Williams suggests, 'it is not like this; I am more dominated by the thought that even if I disappeared, it would come with me.' Whether Homeric characters ever express guilt is arguable. The Iliad has no word for it, but the absence may not be significant, because people can feel more than they express in words.

Helen has been considered a case in point when she repeatedly regrets her elopement with Paris and wishes she had died first. Is she implying a sense of guilt? Achilles, too, wishes he might 'die at once, since I was not after all to defend my comrade when he was being killed'.[16] However, we also speak of dying of shame, and shame can indeed be a motive for killing oneself: Achilles goes on to wish that anger and strife might disappear among gods and men, not that he, guilty of anger, might somehow surmount his guilt. Helen accepts that she is responsible, even guilty, but someone can be considered guilty without feeling inner guilt. I do not think she is wracked by guilt, any more than is Achilles when he feels ashamed at having let Patroclus down.

In the Iliad, I believe, guilt is absent. Its absence does not mean that feelings of guilt were absent in eighth-century life. In the heroes' values, however, shame is the prominent inhibition, with a further, notable emphasis. Aristocrats in other societies are impervious to what many others think of them, not giving a damn except, perhaps, for the opinions of those fellow aristocrats whom they most respect. Homer's heroes, by contrast, worry frequently what others may say of them, even people who are far inferior to themselves.

Are they, then, mere egoists? It is a mistake to regard shame as an egotistical or narcissistic response, as if all that matters in it is what others think of one. Shame is linked to the views of others, real or imagined, but it becomes an inhibition, 'ashamed to', or a reaction, 'ashamed that', only if these others' views relate to actions and qualities which the person subject to shame values too.[17] Elderly Phoenix, Achilles' tutor, gives a good instance in his long speech to Achilles during the embassy to him in book 9. 'I planned to kill him', he says about his own father who had just cursed him, 'with sharp bronze', but one of the gods stopped his anger by 'setting in my heart what the people would say and the many reproaches of men, so that I might not be called "father-killer" among the Achaeans'.[18] Shame at public reproach inhibited him, but only because the reproach, father-killing, was something Phoenix too thought wrong.

Could a real society ever give such preponderance to shame, not guilt? To support the reality of the Iliad's ethics here, scholars have looked to societies far away from Greece, whether in parts of Africa or in modern Japan: a famous post-war study of Japan, Ruth Benedict's *The Chrysanthemum and the Sword*, inspired Dodds's diagnosis of a shame culture in the Homeric poems.[19] Such studies have proliferated, as if honour and shame are values embedded in Mediterranean social groups, especially in modern Greece.[20] More relevantly, shame continued to be prominent after Homer in ancient Greek texts and social groups, from ancient Sparta, very much a shame culture, to tragic plays by Sophocles and Euripides, Sophocles' *Ajax* and his *Philoctetes* being good examples, together with Euripides' *Hippolytus* and *Iphigeneia at Aulis*. Shame is then prominent in Xenophon's account of his march through Asia with 10,000 Greek mercenary soldiers and even in the career of Alexander the Great. It is present, still, in the third Gospel: 'I cannot dig; to beg I am ashamed', says the prodigal son in the parable named after him.

Shame's prominence in the Iliad is not just poetic fiction, carrying its audience into hyper-reality. It held their attention because listeners recognized its power. It also holds ours. The heroes' combative values, their concern for personal face and material reward and their response to shame as a sanction tend to be studied as values far apart from those of modern readers. Yet they still loom large in whole sections of modern life, whether in business leaders when fighting hostile takeovers or being shamed because of their excessive pay or in star sportsmen when at odds with their captain and team. The values of the Iliad are not a remote historical oddity. Shame and fame, honour, rage and disgrace engage us because they are still at large.

24.

Character and Background

These pervasive values in the poem might seem likely to limit individual characterization. So might the recurring phrases which are attached to particular heroes. When Homer refers to his main protagonists, he distinguishes each one with a particular epithet, or adjective: 'Hector of the gleaming helmet' or 'Diomede good at the war cry' are famous examples. They recur even when Hector is not at war and Diomede is not in battle. Recurring epithets also apply to whole peoples, 'horse-taming Trojans', 'bronze-tunicked Achaeans' and so on. They do not give depth to their subjects. They belong to the traditional phrasing which Homer inherited and which helped him to compose hexameter verse in performance. As they recur irrespective of context, they have misled some of his readers into thinking that characterization is rudimentary in the Iliad. In fact Homer characterizes peoples and individuals by a subtle use of speech, thought and action. They are hallmarks of his poem, raising it beyond an undifferentiated series of killings and acts of revenge.

It is evident even when Homer presents peoples far from the killing field. At the beginning of book 13, Zeus turns his shining eyes far off to peoples north-west of Troy, including the 'lordly Horse-milkers who drink the milk of mares', nomadic people, therefore, of the open steppes, and the Abioi, justest of men. In central Asia, fellow nomads were later classed with them and called, collectively, Scythians: they too drank mares' milk.[1] Two characterizations are present here: the nomads are just, and, by implication, the turbulent fighters around Troy are less so. Zeus looks away from the toil and killing he has caused around the Greeks' ships and prefers the faraway nomadic world, as if he were to prefer the sight of Kyr-gyzstan and its summer yurts to contemporary battles in Syria.

Like many later Greek writers, Homer presents an idealized image of distant peoples, the further away the better. In book 1 Zeus and the gods go off on that twelve-day visit to those 'blameless Ethiopi-ans' by the outer Ocean, 'furthest away of men' as the Odyssey remarks, placing them in the east and the west where the sun rises and sets.[2] In their faraway land they meet the gods face to face and entertain them to a banquet. They are far more virtuous than the heroes, whose homes the gods tend to visit, if at all, in disguise. Unlike later Greek authors, Homer does not call them black-skinned, but their name means 'with burnt faces' and refers, therefore, to a skin colour darker than the sun-bronzed Greeks: they are closer to the gods than any others.

He applies similar empathy to the Trojans. Although Homer was composing for Greeks, Hector, Priam, Andromache and Hecuba are among the poem's most memorable participants. When Hector returns to Troy, the Trojans' wives and daughters come running to ask him about their sons and brothers, kinsmen and husbands in that scene which is so poignant. 'In the days of peace, before the sons of the Achaeans came' is one of the poem's most moving phrases, crediting Troy with a prosperous, more fortunate past, which enhances the pathos of its current plight.[3]

Later Greek stereotyping presented people in Asia as womanish and given to excessive luxury. In the Iliad, Priam's kingly family extends to fifty sons and twelve daughters, the results of his poly-gamous marriages. His sons, all fifty of them, live with their wives in rooms in Troy's palace complex while his daughters live with their husbands in rooms on the opposite side of its courtyard.[4] The scale of this royal family and its shared palace was not matched by any Greek heroes in their settlements at home. Priam had bastard chil-dren too, but not because his palace was peopled with concubines whom he visited in rotation during the year: he is never represented as effete. His son, Paris, might seem an exception: he is outstand-ingly handsome, as the plot required, and when first seen is wearing a panther skin on the battlefield, presumably so as to look glamorous. He is an able warrior nonetheless when he chooses to fight. Trojan Euphorbus wears gold and silver finery in his hair, but his death is presented with pathos.[5] Among the Trojans' allies, there is one exception: in book 2's Catalogue of Trojans, Nastes leads the Carians from south-west Asia and is described as going to war 'like a girl' because he is wearing gold.[6] Here indeed an Asian non-Greek is regarded as girlish for being overdecorated. However, the catalogue is by a later poet, not by Homer himself.

On the battlefield, the Trojans are outnumbered by the Greek army, fifty to one, but are afforced by many more allies, who bring the Trojan troops up to half the Greeks' strength. These allies, too, contain heroes with whom the poet empathizes, especially the two Lycians, Glaucus, the grandson of Bellerophon, and Sarpedon, Zeus' son. In general Homer's view of the Greeks' enemies is remarkably impartial, especially when compared with those in other cultures' heroic poems. In its modern versions the Manas poem looks on 'heathen' neighbours from a Muslim perspective. The Qïtay, says the elderly Kökötöy on his deathbed, 'are people with evil intentions, separated from men since the time of Adam, who marry their own sisters and hate their fathers, and for this reason were separated from us'.

Homer stands at the head of a very different Greek attitude to foreigners, one which supposes that they are more like Greeks than they ever were. His Trojans, unhistorically, all speak Greek. Their gods are almost all Greek too, except for their local river god Scamander. They cast living horses into his waters, as Greeks never did into rivers, but they also sacrifice bulls to him, a practice followed by Greeks for river gods of their own.[7]

Traces of a pro-Greek bias in the poem exist, but they are occasional and very slight. Few readers or listeners realize what a close count shows, that in the Iliad's individual combats 189 named Trojans die, but only 43 Greeks. The warriors who abase themselves on the battlefield and supplicate their victors are all Trojans, but when they beg a Greek to spare them, they never succeed. Trojans are also recipients of most of the deadly wounds which Homer describes in grisly detail.

The most obvious contrast comes when the two armies first go out to battle. At the start of book 3 Homer presents the Trojans as advancing with a clamour and a cry 'like birds', albeit orderly cranes flying south to bring death and destruction. The Greeks, by contrast, advance 'breathing might in silence, keen in their heart to defend each other'. In book 4, as battle is still about to be engaged, yet again the Greeks are said to advance in silence, except for the orders of their officers, so much so that 'you would say that such a big army had no voice in its chests, as they feared in silence their commanders'. The Trojans, by contrast, advance in a multilingual clamour, as their army includes so many men from different lands. They sound like ewes in a farmyard waiting to be milked, 'who bleat incessantly hearing the voice of their lambs'. In book 17, during the fight over Patroclus' corpse, Trojans, their allies and Greeks were falling thick and fast, but 'far fewer' of the Greeks were perishing, 'for they remembered always to keep off grim death from one another in the throng'.[8]

The contrast between the two sides is telling, but does not govern the course of the war, as if the Greeks were bound to win because of their better discipline. The Trojans' bleating troops, with Zeus' backing, win major victories and even set upon the Greek ships to burn them, no longer bleating but uttering the very opposite, a loud battle cry. Homer's image of steady, silent, co-operating Greeks reveals his own partiality, but does not determine the poem's plot. When the Trojans are driven back into Troy, they are running scared before the least steady enemy, enraged Achilles and his impassioned onslaught. After the poem's ending, his fellow Greeks take Troy, not by discipline but by a trick, the Wooden Horse.

There are no villains among the heroes, a striking absence. Homer does not characterize his plot as one of vice against virtue. Nor does he delay it with his own long reflections on each hero's thoughts and emotions. Nonetheless, his heroes are not interchangeable. They are differentiated even when he does not make differences explicit. His listeners, like us, were capable of filling in gaps in what they heard and, during the poem's performance, adding feelings, intentions and thoughts to its protagonists' words and actions: this mind-reading is inherent in all human communication, including conversation.[9] The problem is to decide how far we readers should take it. In world literature, explicit discussions of character and its types begin in Greek, but only become prominent with Aristotle and his pupils in the later fourth century BC.

In a brilliant essay, the literary critic Erich Auerbach discussed the absence, in his opinion, of an unexpressed background to Homer's heroes: in their psychological processes 'nothing must remain hidden or unexpressed'. They appear, he believed, in a 'perpetual foreground' in which Homer's use of Greek's small connecting particles, adverbs and so forth relates emotions, arguments and responses with 'never a lacuna, never a gap, never a glimpse of unplumbed depths'. In contrast to Abraham in the Hebrew scriptures, Auerbach considered, the Homeric heroes 'wake every morning as if it were the first day of their lives: their emotions, though strong, are simple and find expression instantly'. They are not 'fraught with background'.[10]

Auerbach's fine presentation did not consider the poem's women or goddesses, counter-examples to it, as we will see. Nor did he consider the poem's oral composition, let alone its composition in performance which makes it so different from the written texts of scripture. Profound disquisitions on inner character in the poet's own voice would have delayed and blunted its impetus and cost it most of its listeners. Hence the perpetual foreground, but most of Homer's heroes had a background nonetheless, one which Auerbach omitted to mention: they featured in other heroic poems now lost to us, some of which can be recovered from bits of later poems and stories modelled on theirs. On the Greek side, especially, Homer presumed knowledge of his main protagonists. Odysseus is presented as 'father of Telemachus', a unique identification of a hero by his son.[11] Telemachus has no role or relevance in the Iliad but the poem's listeners are expected to know him, evidently from other poems. Likewise Patroclus: he was probably a latecomer to Thessalian traditions about Achilles, but as we have seen, Homer presents him simply as son of Menoitios on his first appearance as if listeners already knew who he was and would not be surprised by his presence in Achilles' company.[12]

Pre-existing heroes brought traits of character with them: Cretan Idomeneus is a telling example, worth following in readings of book 13. Homer narrates his brief bout of personal prowess on the longest day and introduces him as 'grey in the middle'. Probably Idomeneus was already known in poetry for this trait, as Homer does not explain it though his word for it occurs only here in the Iliad. It seems to refer to his age, as if grey hairs showed on his head: he is still good in close combat, we later learn, but his feet are indeed no longer light and swift enough for him to run back after throwing his spear or to rush into closer combat.[13] Listeners were expected to know him already, a point which a curious fact about his prowess supports. Several of his victims in battle, all on the Trojan side, have names which link them, oddly, to Crete. It seems that stories about Idomeneus' prowess on his home island were known to Homer, who transposed names in them to Idomeneus' opponents at Troy.[14] He makes him be praised as a good counsellor and show himself in combat to be as valiant as a wild boar, though not exactly the youngest of the Greek heroes, as one of them taunts him.[15] That much sufficed: Homer wanted such a hero in the action and so Idomeneus, from Cretan legends, was brought in for the purpose.

On the Trojan side, Hector, Paris and Priam were surely well known too before the Iliad made them even more famous. However, there was scope for Homer's invention of lesser Trojans and Trojan allies, especially those to whom he gives Greek names. Sarpedon, Zeus' son from Lycia, surely had been the subject of pre-existing tales, but Trojan Polydamas is quite different. He appears in book 12 as an advisor to Hector in battle and on two other occasions gives wise advice which Hector rejects. He is in the poem, therefore, as a foil to Hector, setting off his mistakes at important points in the narrative. Wise advisers became persons for whom later Greek historians also invent a role in their narratives.

Polydamas is presented at first with stock epithets, 'blameless Polydamas' and so forth. A modern narrator would introduce him with his personal qualities, but Homer implies them through what Polydamas goes on to say. He is a man of the people, he says, although it emerges only later that he is not a lowly commoner but the brother of a well-born Trojan. He interprets an omen with great skill and insight, even predicting Achilles' eventual return to battle, a signpost for Homer's listeners, but only when he is about to advise for the third and final time does Homer begin by telling us explicitly that Polydamas knew the past and future and that he had been born on the very same night as Hector. He is not an old adviser, like garrulous Nestor, nor an intemperate young one, like Diomede: he has qualities which Hector, his exact coeval, lacks. Homer is explicit about his age and skill only at this crucial point, before the third speech of wise advice which Hector, fatefully, rejects.[16]

In general, Homer does not introduce his major heroes with a sketch of their physical details or their own family relations. We have to wait until book 11 to learn that Patroclus was older than Achilles and even then the fact emerges obliquely in a speech.[17] The relation of fathers to sons is a recurring theme, whether Priam's to Hector, or Peleus' to Achilles: Phoenix was turbulently related to his own father but stood in a fatherly role to Achilles since childhood. No relationship could have had more depths, but although Homer presents it he does not dwell on this contrast. We also hear, but only in book 19, that young Achilles has a son, Neoptolemos, and has been hoping that if he dies at Troy, Patroclus will bring the boy from the island of Scyros to Achilles' home and show him his property, slaves and high-roofed house.[18] The role of fatherhood, the woman who bore him this boy and the love, or not, for these people are never explored in Achilles' character.

Young Diomede is worth following with similar themes in mind. In book 4 Agamemnon reproaches him and urges him to live up to his great father, Tydeus; he is not inferior to him in council, but he must now emulate him in battle. It is Diomede's companion who answers indignantly: with exquisite skill Homer makes young Diomede rebuke him, for doing so and say only that he does not blame Agamemnon and that he appreciates why he is urging the Greeks into battle. In book 6, we then hear in a very different context that since Diomede was a little boy he had not seen his father, who had died in the great war against Thebes.[19] A modern novelist would relate this fact to Diomede's psychology, but Homer proceeds differently. In book 5 he gives young Diomede exploits of great valour on the battlefield, assisted by the goddess Athena, who stands beside him and lights a glow of fire around his head. With her help Agamemnon's rebuke is implicitly refuted.

Diomede takes on two Trojan opponents at a time, then in a crescendo of heroism attacks the unwarlike goddess Aphrodite, then Aeneas, and then, after further urging by Athena to live up to his father, he wounds Ares, god of war. Eventually he would even have attacked Hector himself, but at last Zeus intervenes and protects the fleeing Trojans by hurling a thunderbolt in front of Diomede's chariot. After these heroics, in books 7–14, we hear Diomede intervening decisively in debates, urging a continuation of battle and twice opposing Agamemnon, as if with battle-won confidence, and rightly opposing his feeble plans to withdraw. In the last such speech he recalls his father's valour, a reason why he should be heeded. In book 9 we also hear that he still remembers Agamemnon's reproach to him about 4000 verses earlier.

Cumulatively, through his deeds, others' words and his own, Homer builds up a portrait of Diomede the young valiant warrior, undaunted in counsel, urging battle when battle is the right course. Composing orally, he lets his qualities emerge as the action proceeds. He has a pool of themes on which he draws and hence those which he develops for Diomede recur for Achilles when he returns to fight from book 18 onwards: Athena's direct aid, the flame around his head, his crescendo of combat, Apollo and Zeus' intervention. So, too, old Phoenix's appeal to Achilles in book 9 contains themes which reappear in old Priam's final appeal to Achilles in book 24.[20]

Nonetheless, Homer can still give heroes individual qualities. He has bundles of knowledge about each one, a store on which he draws in performance. He also uses similes, or comparisons: often he compares a hero's predicament with those of a wild animal in a particular setting, helping us to envisage his mood and temper. I will return to the similes later, but they are secondary to his use of speeches, his great means of individuation.

At least 60 per cent of the Iliad is made up of speeches, frequently paired, sometimes grouped in a three-way exchange. Speakers generally share a level of style and vocabulary, but they characterize themselves and others by what they say. The beginning of book 9, the embassy to Achilles, is a good example. Agamemnon begins by declaring his own folly and thereby reveals his distress and defeatism. Diomede rebuts him, rebuking Agamemnon explicitly for weakness, and shows his own valour and youthful resolution. Old Nestor then emphasizes Diomede's youth too and credits him with being the best counsellor among his young contemporaries. After an interval Nestor addresses Agamemnon again, aware of the tact with which such a king should be addressed but reminding him frankly that his taking of Briseis from Achilles was 'not in accordance with our way of thinking'.[21] Each speaker illuminates himself and others, a process which continues into the scenes with Achilles himself.

In the Anglo-Saxon poem *Beowulf*, only once does the poet allude to his hero's inner thoughts: they occur in the face of a dragon's terrifying destruction, when Beowulf's 'heart within him welled with dark thoughts, as was not usual for him'.[22] These thoughts were simply a fear that he had offended a god. Homer is far more subtle. He gives heroes soliloquies in which they debate alternatives before checking themselves with the words 'why does my heart ponder like this within me?'[23] When Hector sees Achilles bearing down on him outside Troy, his soliloquy is especially fine. It refutes a modern contention that heroes in the Iliad lack a coherent notion of the person and the self. Indeed they address their heart or wits as if they are independent entities, but so at times do we. They have no special word which means to decide, but they are fully capable of decisions. They are not responsive only to threats and assertions, cast at them from outside.[24]

Of all the heroes, old Nestor is the one most obviously character-ized by speech. In book 1 Homer introduces him as a clear speaker, whose voice was sweeter than honey, and as an elderly survivor into the third generation of men from his home, Pylos. His introduction is unusually long, as are most of the speeches which he gives, nine in the poem: Homer cleverly catches an old man's habit of harking back at length to achievements in his past. Nestor speaks with good intentions, giving advice, trying to reconcile quarrels, but Homer is well aware of the gap between spoken words and reality. In Nestor's case he implies the gap between advice and enactment: though speaking well, Nestor is sometimes belied by events.[25]

If Nestor personifies garrulous old age, young Diomede conveys keen aggression in battle, whereas Ajax, a hero of few words, stands for dependable, solid defence. Some of Homer's readers find Mene-laus a lively character too, one prone to be soft-hearted, even with a suppliant before him on the battlefield, but I do not find he is a hero who comes distinctively to life. Others are more varied, so much so that they have seemed to some of their readers to be incoherent.

Composing in performance, Homer might slip for a verse or two into words which are at odds with a hero's earlier priorities in the poem: across such a long span, total coherence would be unlikely. One example, I think, is Achilles' command to Patroclus in book 16 that he must return after driving the Greeks away from the ships they are trying to burn: he himself, Achilles, will then win great honour from all the Greeks and they will send back the 'very beau-tiful girl [Briseis] and give other glorious gifts too'. In book 9 he had rejected these very gifts, Briseis included, but here he seems to be wanting them nonetheless.[26] Many explanations have been suggested, but I think that Homer had swept on in performance here for three verses without too much concern for what he had said seven books before.

Occasional incoherence is one thing, but many-sidedness of

character is quite another, as it is a feature of almost everyone in real life. Heroes' values are not a simple code, and as circumstances vary round them, they have to vary too. Hector is an example. He is a hero with whom it is particularly easy to identify. He is aware of the need for him personally to go out to defend Troy and is aware too of the awful fate of its families if he fails. He is sensitive throughout to what others will say of him and how it may afflict him with shame. He is also aware that one day Troy will fall. However, even he, when fighting, has a phase of battle frenzy, in which his eyes blaze like fire and his ferocity knows no limit. He is said to be wanting to cut off the dead Patroclus' head and impale it on Troy's battlements.[27] His frenzy is not incoherence on Homer's part: fighters indeed become gripped by bloodlust when in action, mild and kind though they may be when not.

Agamemnon shows an inconsistency which is more pervasive. He is a king favoured by Zeus and is often addressed, therefore, with due deference and tact.[28] He too has a phase of battle frenzy while briefly rampaging against Trojans in his path, but in general he is indecisive and prone to despair as a leader. He can also be highhanded: his treatment of Achilles in their quarrel does him no credit. It is Homer who has chosen to present the Greeks' main leader in this flawed but humanly intelligible way: inconsistency is integral to him. Deliberately, Homer made the pre-eminent king among the Greeks very far from being the dominant Greek hero in the poem. It is a striking presentation.

Odysseus raises a different question, his consistency, or not, with the Odysseus of the Odyssey, composed later than the Iliad, but in awareness of it. In the Iliad he is memorably characterized by Antenor the Trojan for his way of speaking, his unprepossessing stance until he begins to speak and then his way of impressing his hearers with a forceful flow of words like winter snowflakes.[29] In the Iliad we see him counselling well and twice expostulating vehemently in reply to Agamemnon. As in the Odyssey, he is 'many-wiled Odysseus', a traditional and metrically apt phrase, but it is in the Odyssey that his wiles and versatility become most evident. The

Iliad's Odysseus gives little sign of them, not because he is inconsistently characterized but because the poem gave him a narrower role, except when wrestling in the games for Patroclus. There is one clear difference. During his great journey home in the Odyssey, Odysseus toils and suffers with his crew and then disguises himself humbly as a beggar. In the very different plot of the Iliad, imperious Odysseus is the hero who thumps common Thersites for daring to speak out and who abuses members of the lower classes who are noisy and slow to attend a meeting. If he had behaved in that way in the Odyssey, his crew would have thrown him overboard.

Modern readers, familiar with long novels, look for characters who develop as a story unfolds. The compressed action of the Iliad covered only four central days and left little scope for such development. In book 19 Agamemnon comes to recognize the folly in his behaviour at the beginning of the poem, but he is not a reformed character as a result: in a long digressive speech he blames it on Zeus, who took away his wits.[30] After this admission he plays no further active part in the poem.

Its central hero, Achilles, is the one who dominates. His presentation is indeed a hallmark of the poem, but first I will consider another, the horses which accompany him and others. Whereas individual heroes are characterized by Homer's art, horses are characterized according to underlying rules which run through the poem. In them, tradition keeps company with exact observation and is used for profound poetic effect.

25.

Equine Poetics

People reveal their qualities not just by what or whom they attack, but also by what they love. In many heroic poems the life and deeds of heroes relate to two beloved items: women and horses. Women have been ever-present, preconditions for men's existence, but horses too have had an age-old relationship with men, long before Homer and his teachers presented them in hexameter verse. Like imperishable fame, mentions of horses can be traced far back to a shared 'Indo-European' past before *c.* 2000 BC when they were already being described as swift and as flying across the ground as fast as the wind.[1] Homer deploys such language, but, as ever, his poetry cannot be reduced to his heritage.

In the ancient tales of Gilgamesh, bulls and wild cows are the prominent animals. Gilgamesh's dear friend Enkidu is a 'wild ass on the run, donkey of the uplands, panther of the wild', but not a stallion running free: in what survives of the poem, horses receive only a passing mention. 'You loved the horse so famed in battle', Gilgamesh says scornfully to the goddess Ishtar, 'but you made its destiny with whip, spur and lash.'[2] An entire dimension of the Iliad is absent. Central Asia, by contrast, is a heartland of horses and the heroic Manas poem in its various dictated versions shows the possibilities.

Manas was born on the same day as his horse, its mother's first foal: when its 'muscly body was gazed on, He had a gorgeous look, He was such a beautiful steed With a flowing tail and mane . . .'[3] Manas's wife was exceptional too. At first, like Achilles, Manas slept with captive girls, but then, aged thirty, he was given a bride. Unlike Achilles' father Peleus, his father sent envoys to find a suitable princess. They discovered one in Bukhara: alone among Bukharan women she knew how to put up a yurt.

Manas's bride changed her name to Kanikei and Manas renamed his horse Ak Kula (Cream-white). When he rode Ak Kula among the yurts, it was at Kanikei's that the horse stopped, confirming that she was the girl for Manas to marry. As he prepared to leave for a great battle against the Chinese, his forty companions came to her yurt to be entertained. She gave them warm clothing and socks made of fox fur, ammunition for their guns and leather belts studded with emeralds. She added gold bridles for their horses and leopard skins to serve as saddles. In Manas's absence she 'showed a mind fit for a man', ruling the young tribesmen who liked to hunt or lie all day in the sun, singing by their yurts of what they had seen in heaven and on earth, while some of them drank fermented mares' milk and danced, wearing hats.[4]

The exploits of Ak Kula and Manas are high points in the poem, never more so than in the story of a great khan's funeral feast, known most fully in an elaborated version dictated and transcribed in the 1920s. It is full of praises of the finest horses, active by 'cherished custom' at Kirghiz games. 'When you saw the [race-horses] on hilly ground,' Daniel Prior's fine prose translation at last allows us to read, 'they were hunched like hungry polecats; when you saw them on the broad steppe they dashed along like hungry wild sheep. The dust billowed up to the sky, the racing jockeys whooped, the galloping race-horses flew along; from the jockeys came a steady, shrill scream.'

On Ak Kula, Manas lived out the rest of his legendary life: in central Bishkek they are still galloping in their huge statue in the main square. Unlike Manas and Ak Kula, a Homeric hero and his horse are never said to have been born on the same day. The Iliad has no story of a hero's taming of a four-legged companion, nothing like eleven-year-old Alexander's taming of Bucephalas, his mount for eighteen years: for once, history was to excel Homeric epic.[5] Nonetheless, Homer's horses illumine two interrelated hallmarks of his genius, his exact observation and his emphasis on a particular boundary, central to his poem. I will begin with the ground rules which govern their role and then I will bring out their poetic effect.

In the Odyssey, horses play almost no role, but in the Iliad they are important. At least twelve heroes have names beginning with the Greek word for horse (*hippos*), a recurrent feature of upper class Greek naming. Almost all of them are Trojans, whose names, being Greek, were probably devised by Homer himself. Collectively, the Trojans' repeated epithet is horse-taming, but it is one which Homer had inherited from long memories of the past, whether or not they went as far back as the later phase of Troy VI and those quantities of horse bones which have suggested to archaeologists that Troy then served as a centre of horse-breeding and trading. In the poem he never mentions the most famous horse in tales of the Trojan war, the Wooden Horse with which the city was eventually captured: it lay beyond the end of his plot. Instead the heroes' horses are harnessed for battles or races, in both of which they pull light chariots. They remain, therefore, above mundane work.

Such work is the business of those other equids, mules. A mare mule, 'six years old and unbroken', Homer correctly says, is the 'hardest to tame': a mule is indeed best tamed when still a foal and an adult mare mule is the most difficult to break. Mules then become 'patient workers', as he also rightly calls them when they drag a load of timber down a stony mountain path.[6] When Priam sets out on his mission to Achilles, he obeys the constraints. He drives a light horse-drawn carriage, but behind him, mules pull the cart on which to bring back Hector's body.

Too noble to drag heavy loads, Homeric horses pull light two-wheeled chariots and compete with them at the funeral games for Patroclus. In the Manas poems, when a young khan stages a race for his dead father, it is prolonged for six months until spring: in the version composed and dictated in the 1920s Manas hits a rival and his horse, the great Ak Kula, gathers speed. As in the Iliad, spectators strain to see who is in the lead, until, in the version dictated earlier to Radloff, Manas and Ak Kula do something last minute and win with a sensational run from the back of the field. In the chariot race in the Iliad, a last-minute run fails to secure second place and the result is disputed by the charioteers.

The 'world of the horse' is notably consistent in the Iliad's narrative, meeting one of Moses Finley's two criteria for the reality of Homeric society. There is no need to assess it against his other criterion, simple societies in places as far away as Borneo. Comparative evidence for it exists from the world of Homer and his audience. His listeners would readily relate to his poem's horses, because they too regarded them as socially significant. In the eighth century BC, bronze figurines of horses were dedicated to the gods in sanctuaries all over Greece, including Olympia, at whose games horse-drawn chariots already competed. In Attica, painters of huge pottery vessels in the Geometric style also showed horses, schematized and spindly-legged, grazing or pulling chariots, evidently in funerary processions.[7]

Among the Athenians, horse ownership defined a high social class, just as on the nearby island of Euboea. There too horses were prominent on big pottery vessels and were once even shown in the act of mating: aristocrats called themselves horse-pasturers (*hippobotai*) because they grazed horses galore, using up productive land.[8] In the broad grass plains of western Asia, Homer lived among horse-pasturers too. He credits an early king in the Troad, Erichthonius, with pasturing as many as 3000 mares in Dardania long before Troy was founded. Dardania included that middle Scamander river valley where marsh parsley grew, the tall, lush plant now known as alexanders on which horses indeed feed contentedly. In his addition to book 2 the poet of the catalogue credited Achilles' horses with eating marsh parsley while they remained withdrawn from the war, together with lotus, probably a sort of clover, another food plant which would grow well in wet ground, perhaps even by the sea.[9]

In real life, as in the poem, horses never pulled heavy loads, because the complex type of collar for such traction had not been invented. There was, however, one major difference: in Homer's lifetime, horses were ridden as well as harnessed. By the later eighth century BC, mounted warriors, wielding spears, were being presented on

Greek painted pottery, just as anecdotes of eighth-century battle also attest. There are no cavalrymen in the Iliad.[10] The closest of bonds between a hero and a horse, the one between Manas and Ak Kula, is missing.

It is not that Homer was ignorant of it. Once, in a simile, he mentions remarkable equestrian skill. At the end of book 15, when Ajax is jumping from ship to ship, warding off Trojan attackers, Homer compares him to a rider who brings four horses into town along a public road, amazing onlookers, he says, by jumping from one horse's back to another as they go.[11] This very special display is still a stunning trick for show-riders. On an Attic cup, *c.* 720 BC, a rider is shown doing something nearly as difficult: he is holding the reins and standing up bareback on a horse while a warrior stands with a shield on the ground below. This image and others have been well understood as evidence that 'as a breeder and trainer of animals the Geometric period aristocrat [*c.* 800–700 BC] embodies a new kind of "Master of Animals" '.[12] Homer knew this mastery, but excluded it from his main plot.

By excluding it he could present the world of his heroes as unlike the world of his hearers. Though consistent, the heroes' use of horses is stylized and unreal: they merely drive to and from the killing field in horse-drawn chariots and disembark from them in order to fight. Unlike real chariot warriors in the Bronze Age past, they almost never shoot and fight from the chariot on the move. Nonetheless, Homer shows a sharp eye for the horses who pull them. When Patroclus routed the Trojans just before his death, their chariot teams 'groaned': as they ran off their noise was as loud, Homer says, as a torrential storm from Zeus and the roar of the rivers which flood down the mountains as a result.[13] The teams here are, notably, mares and their loud groans on the run can be matched to real life. After close study of the Iliad, Édouard Delebecque, a scholar and a horseman, concluded that the phrases which Homer applies to horses are seldom generic and formulaic, but are varied by him to give an exact representation. In Homer, therefore, he saluted a practised horseman.[14]

The line between traditional language and the poet's own observation is not an easy one to draw, but Homer refers to a horse's
sweat on its forehead and on its chest, two well-observed details, the
former being dampness, the latter becoming visible as foam. Such
small, fine details are unlikely to have been passed down to him in a
tradition fixed long before his lifetime.[15] He does not happen to
mention horses pawing the ground in excitement or standing in
pairs head to tail to brush away flies from each other, but he refers
to them shying (*paretressan*) and to their hot breath on the back of a
rival charioteer when their team is racing very close behind his chariot. Most of his epithets for horses relate to their speed, but he also
refers to the din of their hooves when they gallop on the dry killing
field (for Delebecque the *bruit de galop*).[16] It was surely as a spectator
of chariot racing that he had the command of its details which he
shows in book 23: I like to believe even more that at some point in
his life he drove a racing team himself.

The singular bond between rider and horse is absent from the
Iliad, but its heroes' relations with horses are not at all remote.
Patroclus used to wash the long manes of Achilles' immortal horses
'kindly' and rub them with olive oil, an example of the general
kindness with which Homer repeatedly credits him.[17] On the Trojan side, Pandarus, though an archer, is similarly sensitive to horses
and their needs. He explains to Aeneas why he has come on foot to
the war: he did not want the family's horses, he says, to suffer. His
father had eleven fine new chariots in his stables with two horses for
each, white barley for the horses to eat and robes of cloth for each
chariot, but Pandarus ignored his urging to take a team to Troy: he
was afraid that in such a crowd of warriors they might go short of
food. In fact there was a fantastic number of horses there, all being
imagined with enough to eat, but Pandarus is represented as putting the horses' wellbeing before his own status. When Aeneas
invites him to take the whip and drive with him in his chariot, he
still thinks of the horses' needs: Aeneas, he says, must drive because
the horses will respond to his voice and he does not want them to
miss it and be frightened if they have to retreat.[18]

Inside Troy, Hector's wife Andromache is more than a match for Pandarus' thoughtfulness. She never needed to learn to put up a yurt, but she used to mix wine and corn for Hector's horses and feed them before organizing dinner for him. Wine in a horse's feed is not a Homeric fantasy, as inexperienced scholars have sometimes considered, beginning with Aristarchus in the second century BC: it has been given to racehorses to strengthen them quite often in racing's history.[19] Like many sound upper class ladies since, Andromache put the family horses' needs before her husband's.

It was a small step for heroes to talk to their horses and expect to be understood while racing them or driving into battle. Tellingly, they use arguments based on their own human values. Hector goads on his team by appealing to reciprocity: if Andromache has favoured them, so, therefore, must they oblige him.[20] In the chariot race in book 23, Homer does not abide by the stallion-only rule which prevails in subsequent Greek art. He is notably willing to present an all-mare team, Admetus', as far the best in the race and to single out the special effort of a mare in another one too. In the final stage of the contest, 'the might of fair-maned Aithē was increasing' with every stride and if the race had been a little longer she would have taken Menelaus' team to victory.[21] However, he makes Nestor's son Antilochus urge on his all-male team more crudely: he appeals to their shame if they are to be beaten by a team which includes a mare. Stallions, like heroes, are assumed to be sexist and to respond to a shame culture.[22]

In Iliad book 2, at the end of its Catalogue of Ships, a brief, often neglected, Catalogue of Horses begins, listing fine horses which accompanied the Greek heroes to Troy. Like fine women, they were eminently worth fighting for. The Greek army began their siege of Troy because of Paris' theft of a woman, Helen, but long before, Heracles had come from afar to labour for Troy's king Laomedon and kill a hostile sea monster in return for mares from his heavenly bloodline. Heracles obliged, but Laomedon refused to hand over the mares and so Heracles sacked Troy for their sake.[23] The Iliad's heroes still know the power of such rewards. Old Nestor recalls how in his youth he had raided hundreds of horses from one of Pylos' neighbouring kings: now, though past his sexual prime, he urges the Greeks into battle by telling them that when they win, each one of them will sleep beside a Trojan girl. King Agamemnon uses an alternative bait: he exhorts Teucer by promising him two horses and a chariot from Troy's spoils. Like women, horses are prizes which fire up heroes to fight.[24]

As horses and girls were such objects of desire, what were their relative values? In the funeral games for Patroclus, Achilles offers as second prize in the chariot race a mare, six years old and unbroken, who is in foal to a donkey. The fourth prize is two talents of gold, and the first prize is a 'woman to lead away', a slave therefore, who is skilled in handiwork, together with a tripod which holds twenty-two measures. A compelling chain of cross-references and inferences allows the first prize to be calculated as worth eight talents, four for the skilled slave girl and four for the tripod, and the second prize as six talents, four for the mare and two, surely, for the unborn mule inside her.[25] Six years old and unbroken, the mare is especially good to breed from, worth her high value as she can be broken and mated for the rest of her life. For that reason she matches the value put on the skilled slave girl.

This mare-for-girl equivalence cannot be generalized to all horses and girls in the heroes' world: each side of it is a special case. Nonetheless, throughout the Iliad horses are man's trusted companions, far more so than dogs.[26] Whereas dogs would callously eat the flesh of dead men, even of their former masters, Homer's horses remain loose-lipped herbivores. Unlike dogs, they share some of their masters' values and enter the battles with them. When they are out on the killing field, no horse yoked in a chariot team ever dies. The reason is one of plot, not sentiment: heroes have to be taken from the battle after they have fought, and without a living team of horses they would not be able to depart. For that reason a hero sometimes puts the safety of his horses before a recovery of his charioteer who is lying dead on the ground.[27] It is not that he prefers horses to people: he needs the horses for his own retreat.

The exceptions prove the rule, the trace-horses that Homer sometimes presents as tied to one of a chariot's vertical side bars. Twice, trace-horses are killed in battle and have to be cut loose in order to free the main yoked team: Homer probably transferred them from their use in real life on processional or funerary chariots to war chariots, where they fit awkwardly as they contribute nothing to the pulling.[28] When Patroclus drives into battle, he is transported in Achilles' chariot, pulled by his two immortal horses, but a third, mortal Pedasos, is tied to the chariot as a trace-horse. He is there because, unlike the two immortals, he can die in the ensuing battle and enhance the excitement of Patroclus' duel with Sarpedon. In its first round, Sarpedon's spear misses Patroclus' driver but kills Pedasos, who 'groans and gasps', an exactly observed detail of a dying horse. In an exciting variation on a duel's usual pattern his driver has to cut him free. Homer adds another telling detail. Pedasos had become Achilles's property after the sacking of Eetion's city.[29] This provenance recurs for other items in the poem, Achilles' lyre, his lump of iron and women who are central to its plot. Eetion was Andromache's father and in the sack of his city Chryseis was taken too, the girl at the origin of the poem's opening quarrel.

Pedasos' team members relate to a different theme: they are immortal. The gods, too, have divine horses, gold-maned and fed on ambrosia, and sometimes divinity runs in the pedigree of mortal breeds. Before the great chariot race Homer makes old Nestor refer to Arion, another horse 'from the gods by family'.[30] He leaves the full story unspoken, how the goddess Demeter had tried to escape Poseidon and had turned herself into a mare and hidden in a herd, whereupon Poseidon turned himself into a stallion and covered her. Arion, the resulting foal, was a half-brother to Persephone, the goddess Demeter's daughter.

Homer mentions three sets of divine horses in mortal ownership, two on the Trojan side, one on the Greek. In the distant past he recalls the parentage of Erichthonius' foals and their fathering by the divine north wind. This origin conformed to a widespread Greek belief that if mares, when in season, stand tails to the wind, they will be fertilized, unlike girls, by one of its gusts. Because of their paternity Erichthonius' horses could run like the wind.[31] The other divine team, on the Trojan side, belongs to Aeneas. His two horses descend from the immortal stallions which Zeus once gave to his great-grandfather Tros: they were Zeus' recompense, four legs for two, for his lecherous abduction of Tros' young son, gorgeous Ganymede.[32] They exemplify Homer's ability to sustain narrative continuity across a long span of his poem. In book 5 they are abducted by Diomede during his bout of prowess and in book 23 they reappear, still with Diomede, to pull him to victory in the great chariot race.

Aeneas' divinely descended horses contrast with Hector's mortal ones, just as Achilles' divine horses contrast with Agamemnon's. There is a clear hierarchy here. As Agamemnon and Hector are not from a divine bloodline, they rank below Achilles and Aeneas, the sons of divine mothers, and their horses rank lower too, even though Agamemnon's include that valiant mare Aithe whom a rich young man had given him in order to avoid serving in the Greek army. She was a mare from Sicyon in the Greek Peloponnese, a place famous for fine horses in Homer's own time, but she was not from an immortal bloodline.[33]

Hector's horses are mortal too, a team of four according to book 8, and as a result Hector wants to capture Achilles' divine horses and use them instead.[34] However, as Zeus tells us, that wish is excessive. Hector abandons it, but only when Apollo tells him he must. Horses are the first of Hector's misplaced ambitions to be rebuked by the gods. It is soon followed by another, his refusal to withdraw inside the city and avoid Achilles. It leads to his death.

On the Greek side, Eumelus from Thessaly brought a team of mares to Troy which Apollo had raised while working for his father: their special history is presupposed in the chariot race, but is described only in the post-Homeric Catalogue of Horses.[35] Divine rearing was not the same as immortal parentage. Here, Achilles has the supreme team, a gift of the god Poseidon to his father Peleus, presumably at his wedding to Thetis. Called Chestnut and Dappled, they too are foals of the divine north wind. They feature in passages which have drawn great poets to translate them, especially Cavafy, author of an admired modern Greek tribute.

Like Aeneas' horses, Achilles' immortal horses maintain a continuity across several books of the poem, but it has a far more poignant value. In book 16 he lends them to Patroclus to transport him into battle and when Patroclus dies there, they mourn him. In general, Homer's horses make very sparing use of the fantastic: unlike horses in other heroic poems, his horses do not fly, nor do they have magical properties. Their mourning may seem an exception as they begin by dropping their heads to the ground and allowing their manes to be stained in the dust. They are long-maned, therefore, impossibly so, it might seem, to those with only a casual knowledge of horses. However, very long-maned breeds are still present in parts of Greece and in southern Spain, where they carry heroic riders in solo fights against bulls.[36] In Cavafy's poem they simply toss their manes, as if Cavafy could not credit what Homer correctly presented.

The unreality lies not in the horses' long manes, but in their mourning for their master. Unlike dogs, horses do not grieve for individual humans. However, these horses are immortal and mourning horses may have featured in other, earlier heroic poems, known to Homer but lost to us. Certainly, when Manas dies, his horse 'foams and eats no grass. On his ribs black flies gather. He howls and stands by the house, Lies down by the grave of Manas, And is as dried up as a stone image'.[37] Homer too describes Achilles' horses as 'missing their driver, now dead' and experiencing 'longing' for him. It is quite untrue that in the poem's narrative the horses of the Iliad have no life of their own. Deprived of Patroclus, these horses stand stock still on the battlefield, refusing all coaxing and threats, as horses indeed sometimes do. In a fine simile they are compared to a stone, in their case to a grave-marker which stands on the tomb of a dead person. The comparison is with the tombstone's immobility, but it also draws on its link with death.[38]

In Cavafy's poem, the simile is omitted and the horses grieve for

the 'eternal disaster of death', a sorrow far removed from Homer's
text. Instead, Zeus sees the horses' grief and, talking to himself,
asks a rhetorical question:

> 'why did we give you to king Peleus,
> A mortal, whereas you are unageing and immortal?
> (Was it so that you might have painful sorrow among)
>   miserable men,
> For there is nothing more wretched than a man
> Of all that breathes or crawls on earth?'

Zeus knows very well that the horses were not bestowed for that
reason, but he is expressing pity for the consequence of the gift. He
must not be misunderstood here as if he is showing pity for horses,
but not for mortals.[39] In his synoptic gaze mortals are pitiable too,
but the verses express a crucial Homeric theme, the gulf between
mortals and immortals: Cavafy merely makes the horses 'toys of
fate'. In book 23, when the funeral games for Patroclus begin, these
same horses are still standing apart, sorrowing with their manes
trailing on the ground.[40] Homer needs to explain why they and
Achilles will not be competing in the race, and so he returns to their
stationary mourning, a theme six books ago.

Their mourning for Patroclus comes at the end of a powerfully
constructed sequence with a common theme, suited to oral composition in performance. Repeatedly it ascribes words and thoughts
to others. First Homer presents at unusual length unvoiced assumptions which are going through an absent hero's mind: he ascribes
them to Achilles, who is still unaware of what has happened to
Patroclus. Then, he gives words to an unnamed Greek, one of those
in the battle for Patroclus' corpse, and likewise to an unnamed Trojan: 'Friends,' the Trojan says, 'even if it may be our destiny, all of
us, to be laid low beside this man, let none of us withdraw from the
fight.'[41] The scene of the grieving horses follows this sequence and
concludes with another example, the words given to Zeus who is
'shaking his head and speaking to his own heart'. Zeus goes on to

say that he will not allow Hector to take the horses and their chariot: 'is it not enough that he has the armour and helmet?' His pity leads to action nonetheless: he puts strength into the horses, energy indeed, so that they will transport their remaining driver out of the battle. He will not change his general plan, he says: he will continue to give 'glory to the Trojans, to kill until they come to the Greeks' ships and the sun sets'.[42] We know how the action will proceed, but again Zeus does not reveal the sequel.

This scene is brilliantly placed and conceived, but its poignancy is capped by another, even greater. In book 19, after Patroclus' death, Achilles returns to fight, mounting his chariot and goading these same two immortal horses into action. Before they set off, he berates them for leaving Patroclus dead and he tells them this time to bring their driver back safely. Chestnut bows his head so that his mane touches the ground: again it is a sign of mourning. This time, the goddess Hera enables him to speak, a unique event in the poem. In self-defence he explains that Apollo killed Patroclus and there was nothing the horses could do to stop it. Then he predicts, his bowed head expressing sadness:

> 'Now at least we will save you, mighty Achilles,
> But the day of doom is near to you, nor will we
> Be responsible, but a great god and mighty Destiny . . .
> We would run with the breath of the west wind,
> Which they say is the swiftest of all, but for you yourself,
> It is fated to be laid low by a god and a man.'[43]

Once again, a horse, grieving, leads to a prediction, but this time, it is one from the horse's mouth. It takes us even further into the future, beyond the point where the Iliad will end. What is fated is, as usual, a source of extreme pathos and sadness.

Hector's death has already been predicted by his wife Andromache, but Achilles has no wife to predict his. He has these horses, however, who are with him, and so his death and, for the first time, its agents are predicted by one of them. The Erinyes, the Furies, then

284

silence the horse again, perhaps because it had spoken of death, one of their spheres of action.[44] This unique event has a strong emotional impact. Achilles, 'greatly moved', is left to reproach Chestnut for the prophecy. 'Chestnut, why do you prophesy death to me? It is not right for you to do so . . .' The words resonate with anyone who has had horses as close companions.

In ancient myths horses have symbolic links with death, with wind, with sexual lust, with ships or with the sea. Homer can sometimes deploy symbolic associations of objects in his epic, ones which usually derive from their history. Here, the horses are simply horses, but they are not true to life. Their grieving is a touching instance of sentimentality in a poem which is generally considered to be without it. In the Odyssey, it is Odysseus' dog who recognizes him when he first returns home, but then dies. In the Iliad it is horses who mourn, as if they are emotionally close to a human. Talking horses, even mourning ones, have parallels in other heroic poems, but the horse Chestnut even understands the relevant powers in heaven: those responsible for Achilles' imminent death are a 'great god', he says, surely Zeus, and mighty Destiny, surely a divinity with a capital D. He goes on to tell us for the first time that a god and a man will indeed kill Achilles after his crucial decision to rejoin the war. He and his fellow horses are divine, but they have also allowed Homer to emphasize a boundary which is crucial to the entire poem, the one between wretched mortals and ageless immortality. It is a boundary which haunts the words and plight of their owner, Achilles, the hero whose character drives the poem's plot.

26

Swift-Footed Achilles

Achilles, owner of Chestnut and Dappled, is indeed a hallmark of the poem. Whereas the poem's equine background is consistent and its horses usually follow rules in the narrative, Achilles questions rules and transgresses them. For two-thirds of the poem he withdraws in anger after the affront to his personal honour, but even in his absence Homer keeps him in his hearers' and protagonists' minds. Lamenting to Hector her lack of family, Andromache recalls how Achilles killed her father and her seven brothers in a previous foray. When Ajax prepares to fight with Hector, he berates him by telling him that lion-hearted Achilles is lying among the ships because of wrath towards Agamemnon, but nonetheless, there are other warriors among the Greeks as he will now discover.[1] Achilles remains a name to conjure with.

Throughout he is swift-footed Achilles, but only at the end of book 21 does he show his speed, sustaining it into the beginning of book 22. There is so much more to him, most of it surely Homer's own invention. Previous poets, I suspect, had presented him as a young hero who fought as the Greeks' supreme warrior and died young at Troy. In the Iliad he is still young, more of a warrior than a wise counsellor, as other speakers observe, but they add that he needs to curb his quick temper, a feature which Homer may have enlarged and made central to a plot for the first time.[2] His Achilles is indeed capable of fury and frenzy, shown when he almost kills Agamemnon in their opening quarrel or when he cuts loose to avenge Patroclus by killing every Trojan he encounters. His treatment of Hector's body is atrocious, even as an act of revenge. He expresses wishes of monstrous selfishness, that Zeus may favour the Trojans and let the Greeks be killed by their ships, or that all other Greeks should perish except himself and Patroclus so that the two of them could win glory together by taking Troy. He even gives that order to Patroclus, not to go too far in battle as he will detract from 'my' glory if he does so.[3]

Achilles is certainly special. He is the only hero to have been born from the formal marriage of a goddess and a mortal. Uniquely, he was brought up by a centaur, half man, half horse. Even so, his goddess mother, Thetis, has cared for him, like a tender plant in an orchard, she says, and is not at all remote: when he set off for Troy she put a chest on board his ship, 'filling it well with tunics and cloaks and woolly rugs to keep off the wind'.[4] He is especially close to his divine helpers. In book 18, Athena kindles a fire around his head to terrify the Trojans when he emerges to rejoin the battle.

Physically he is an imposing presence. When he speeds towards the Trojans outside Troy, old Priam, watching, remarks that he is huge. As he bears down on Hector, Homer calls him huge too. When Priam finally sits in Achilles' company he marvels at how big Achilles is and how he looks like the gods.[5] In battle he throws and thrusts a spear so large that nobody else can use it. He feels fear when confronting the raging flood of the river god Scamander, but he never feels fear before a mortal.

Despite his pitiless egoism and concomitant savagery, Achilles does not cease to engage the poem's hearers and readers: how does Homer contrive this? Achilles is not just an angry killer. He first appears in a thoughtful role as the summoner of an assembly to find why plague is afflicting the army. He assumes, correctly, that it is due to Apollo's anger. He also shows touches of chivalry. Repeatedly he gives a good welcome to others, even to those whose business is not to his liking, whether they are the heralds who come to take Briseis away or the envoys who come to beseech his help or eventually Priam himself. He is a generous host, especially in the games he gives for Patroclus. Homer even presents him, once, as an oral poet, in that scene when the envoys in book 9 find him playing his lyre. Paris too has a lyre, but Achilles is the only hero in the Iliad who performs with one. He is singing of the famous deeds of men, just what he is denying himself by his withdrawal from the war.

He is unusually self-aware. In the poem's concluding scenes he shows memorable pity. His final action could hardly be less callous, that taking of old Priam by the hand 'in case he might feel fear'. However, he knows that he is doomed to die young while fighting at Troy, knowledge which was given to him by his mother Thetis, who presumably had it from Zeus. He is the one warrior who has such knowledge. It hangs over his decisions and actions, intensifying them beyond any other hero's. My guess is that Homer was the first poet to deploy it in this way: he may even have given it to him for the first time, abstracting it from the wider tale of the Trojan war in which Achilles indeed died.

Achilles also delivers great speeches, whether in the escalating quarrel as the poem begins, in his reply to the envoys in book 9, or during his final meeting with Priam.[6] Homer gives him distinctive ways of speaking. Achilles uses not just similes but ones in which he draws comparisons with female figures, a mother bird or a pleading little girl. He evokes faraway landscapes as no other hero does. When he speaks at length, he tends to pose broad questions and refer to his role in the war in far from glamorous terms. 'I am not tending [my father Peleus] while he grows old,' he tells Priam, 'since far indeed from my homeland I sit around at Troy, causing care and trouble for you and your children.'[7] It is he, and only he, who states that there are two jars from which Zeus gives good or evil to individuals, but it is a statement implicit in the entire plot of the Iliad, one which is crucial to its understanding: Achilles is the one who makes it explicit.

He has no illusions about a hero's life, but it is wrong to see him as an outsider, alienated from its values. Once, he calls himself a 'useless burden on the earth', but only in the context of Patroclus' death, an event he had done nothing to prevent.[8] His moods change memorably, but they do not swing unpredictably from one moment to the next, let alone from elation to depression and back again.

During the poem he changes from rage to extreme grief and then to reconciliation and pity, but his course is, on the whole, coherent. These changes are responses to circumstances which change too. There are reasons for each of them: they are also what moves the plot onward.

In tragedies or modern novels, protagonists sometimes realize the error of their ways and finally change after turbulent experience. Achilles is the one hero in the Iliad for whom the question of such a change needs to be addressed. To answer it, he must be heeded carefully as the poem begins.

During his quarrel with Agamemnon, he already expresses his own relationship to the war: he states that he does not hold the Trojans responsible for wrongs done to him. He is fighting, he says, to win honour for Menelaus, Helen's husband, and for Agamemnon, but not for any personal grievance against Troy. When he loses Briseis it is he who tells Thetis to go to Zeus and beg him to help the Trojans and let the Greeks be killed among their ships 'so that they may profit from their king', Agamemnon, and realize his folly in dishonouring the best of the Achaeans.[9]

In book 9, in answer to Odysseus' speech, he asks, 'Why must the Argives wage war with the Trojans?' He might seem now to be questioning the war's entire validity, but that is to misread his position. He promptly answers his own question, stating that they are fighting for the sake of a woman, Helen: it is much as he has already said in the first book. He then relates this fact to his own predicament, his love for Briseis, who has been taken from him, also as in the first book.[10]

One crucial question is whether he would have accepted the offer made to him if it had been proffered much earlier in the poem, and another is whether he ought to have accepted it in book 9. In book 9 Agamemnon was offering him exceptional presents, including Briseis, far more than Achilles had previously expected: he had also admitted to the Greek elders that he had been gripped by destructive folly, *atē*, when he began the quarrel. In book 1 Achilles had been assured by Athena of the very things Agamemnon was now offering, glorious gifts, and had looked forward to Agamemnon admitting his *atē*. In book 9, however, he refuses to relent.[11]

Has he hardened, or is Homer, composing orally, being inconsistent? At one level there had been an insult which material possessions alone could never resolve: Achilles had fought at intense risk to his life, from which he had won *kudos*. For it, he had been given a special prize, not one of the shares of a venture's plunder which other heroes received too. Material gifts would never quite restore what the loss of that special prize had damaged. There is, however, significant absence. Agamemnon, close readers realize, had not come to apologize to Achilles in person. When he listed the gifts he would give, he ended by saying that Achilles should submit to him 'in as much as I am more kingly' and older.[12] The conflict between being mighty as a king and mighty as a warrior, risking all in the front line, had been central to their quarrel in the first place. When the envoys come to Achilles, Odysseus, the first of the three to speak, omits what Agamemnon had injudiciously said. Homer does not emphasize this omission nor the relevance of Agamemnon's absence; do they account for Achilles' rejection of the offer? At the end of his great speech he alludes to Agamemnon's refusal to look him in the face, but only as one more item in a flurry of anger. I do not think it accounts for his refusal.

Is another reason for it that he has changed since the poem's beginning? When he receives the envoys, he is not in a furious temper. He is singing, and when he stops, he prepares generous food and drink for them. However, anger is still in him: when he speaks 'forcefully', this latent anger becomes overt. The root of it is still an agonizing insult to his honour, and he simply broadens his refusal of Agamemnon's gifts by fine words on the fact that a warrior's life cannot be won back once he dies. In the first book he had stated that his life would be brief, a prospect that his mother Thetis tearfully endorsed. Now, he states that his mother has told him that he has two possible fates, a brief life of glory fighting at Troy, or a long, inglorious life if he returns home. It is the first we have heard of such a choice, but it fits his sweeping speech at this point: in the light of it he asserts that he will leave tomorrow by ship for home.[13] It is a change, but it does not change Achilles' character: he is still impelled by hyper-heroic temper, *thūmos*, as in the first book of the poem.

In answer to the final speaker, Ajax, Achilles replies that Ajax seemed to have spoken 'in accordance with my own feelings', or *thūmos*, but that angry bile is swelling in his heart when he thinks how Agamemnon utterly dishonoured him before the gathered troops.[14] His refusal is impassioned, but even so, it has not driven him to a new extreme: he had been enraged by this slight from the very start. In response, Homer cleverly makes him change his ground. He abandons his remark about sailing off home and ends by saying that he will not fight yet, but will fight when Hector reaches his ships. Again listeners are left to pick up this change: it is not a result of a sudden swing of mood.

The Iliad does not unfold from book 9 onwards as a morality tale. By refusing the envoys' offer, Achilles does not expose himself to punishment from the gods and lose Patroclus as a result. He had his reasons for refusing and the loss of Patroclus had already been foretold by Zeus before the envoys set out: the outcome was already known.[15] From book 16 to book 20, however, two further changes have to occur, each of which is essential for carrying the plot forwards. First, Achilles must relent from his anger with Agamemnon, enough at least to allow Patroclus to go out and fight. Then, when Patroclus is dead, he must set aside anger with Agamemnon and act on a new anger, one directed against Patroclus' killer, Hector. Homer does not imply there are unplumbed depths in Achilles' person which explain these changes: each is brought about by events.

In reply to Patroclus' request Achilles simply says of his anger, 'let us leave these things in the past' and implies that he had anyway intended to resume fighting when Hector began to burn the Greek ships: 'it was not, after all, that I should somehow be angry unceasingly'.[16] When he hears that Patroclus is dead, his grief is intense, but again he says that 'these things', his anger at Agamemnon, must be left in the past: he must control his temper 'from necessity', the necessity being revenge for Patroclus.[17] In book 19 he moves finally from old anger to new, a shift which Homer handles deftly.

When Achilles receives his divine armour, brought by Thetis, he is seized with anger, new anger, however, at Hector, on whom he will take revenge. In a speech to Agamemnon soon afterwards he simply says, 'now I stop my anger; it is not right for me to be angry interminably', meaning his old anger with Agamemnon. He never apologizes for the quarrel and his withdrawal. In book 18 he simply wishes that anger might somehow vanish from the hearts of men.[18] In previous speeches he had already expressed a wish that this or that might be otherwise: nothing has changed in him when he repeats the pattern here.

At each of these points the poem moves rapidly forwards, without any more words on Achilles' change of mood and purpose. When Agamemnon announces he will indeed give the gifts, Achilles even replies:

> 'as for gifts, if you wish to give them, as is proper,
> Or to keep them – that is up to you.'

His new priority, revenge for Patroclus, is in the poem's foreground, and so it supplants the old quarrel.[19] It is not that Homer is being emotionally imperceptive. When Patroclus is reported dead, Achilles has to move from an angry refusal to fight to extreme grief and then to impassioned revenge. He duly moves to the first phase: he rolls in the dust, talks of dying and refuses to eat: the messenger who brings the news to him has to restrain his hands for fear he may kill himself.

In his arresting book *Achilles in Vietnam*, Jonathan Shay compared Achilles' reactions to the loss of Patroclus, 'as dear to me as my head', with the reactions of veterans of the Vietnam War, which they presented to him in subsequent therapy after the loss of very close companions. They too spoke of a desire not to go on living and of an impulse to kill any enemy they could.[20] These emotions are not specific to service in that war, as they have been exemplified by combatants in many places before and since, but they conform very well with Achilles'. Bereaved combatants' grief modulates into intense rage, just as Homer modulates Achilles' grief into rage in books 20 and 21. Battle frenzy possesses his heart; he slaughters Trojan upon Trojan who are trying to hide in the river Scamander; he sets aside twelve young Trojans to be offered later as requital for Patroclus. He then confronts Priam's son Lycaon, a warrior whom he had captured and ransomed in a previous encounter.

Homer sets up this encounter with particular intensity, a sign of its importance. Lycaon is exhausted by his escape from the flooding river Scamander. He is unarmed, having thrown away his helmet, shield and spear. On seeing him, Achilles muses with grim irony that it is as if Trojans whom he has killed have come back from the house of the dead: he had sold Lycaon formerly into captivity, but here he is all over again. Lycaon approaches to implore him as a suppliant and even crawls under the uplifted spear with which Achilles means to kill him. The spear passes into the ground behind Lycaon's back and so he grasps it with one hand and grasps Achilles' knees with the other, the gestures of a suppliant. He makes a fervent plea, begging Achilles to show respect, *aidōs*, and pity. Achilles, he says, has ransomed him previously: he has already killed his brother; Lycaon does not think he will escape, 'as a god brought me to you', and yet he begs in conclusion:

> 'Do not kill me, because I am not the full brother of Hector
> Who killed your companion, kindly as he was and mighty.'[21]

Even a Trojan knows of Patroclus' kindness.

Homer has shaped this encounter in the most affecting way, but Achilles answers without mercy, telling Lycaon, 'fool, do not talk of ransom'. Before Patroclus died, he says, he was minded to take enemies alive and ransom them, but now no Trojan will be spared. He addresses him as 'friend', but in my view with merciless irony:

> 'But, friend, you too must die: why do you lament like this?
> Patroclus died, who was a far better man than you:
> Do you not see what sort of man I too am, how fine and tall?
> I am the son of a noble man and a goddess mother bore me,
> But over me too hangs death and mighty destiny.
> There will be a dawn or evening or noon
> When someone will take my life too in battle . . .'

His words have been admired by some of his most sensitive modern readers, as if 'Achilles' own acceptance of death is the source of the power of the passage' and 'transforms a cliché into a truly tragic insight'.[22] This response is a crucial misreading. Certainly, Achilles accepts he must die, but the acceptance is not the result of a recent change in him. By going to fight at Troy in the first place he had already accepted his life would be brief, just as he had told his sorrowing mother at the very start of the poem. In book 9 he had briefly seemed to waver and try to choose otherwise, but his wavering came to nothing. When he resolved to go out and avenge Patroclus he explicitly accepted, as before, that he would never return home and gladden his father.[23] The force of his encounter with Lycaon is not that Achilles, with a new insight, sees death and killing as blips in a wider pattern of mortality. It lies elsewhere, in its wholly unpitying pursuit of revenge.

Achilles' words to him would be no mitigation if spoken by a modern serial killer. As Shay aptly remarks, 'This so-called "consolation" to Lycaon is nothing but the chilling cruelty of the berserker; a warmer reading of this scene is ruled out by Achilles' gratuitous mistreatment and mocking of Lycaon's corpse.'[24] On hearing these words about mortality, Lycaon's knees and heart fail him and he falls defenceless with his arms outstretched. Achilles runs his sword through Lycaon's neck, takes him by the foot and flings him into the river to be carried away: grimly he tells him to be licked, now, by the fishes as his mother will never lay him out for his funeral.

The encounter's prelude and sequel bear out this reading. Before killing Lycaon, Achilles had just killed fourteen named Trojans, one after another, without passing any comment to them about his own inevitable death. One of them, Tros, had also come to supplicate him and beg for pity and a ransom: he was a 'fool' says Homer, this time in his own person, because Achilles 'was not soft of heart nor gentle of mind'.[25] Indeed he was not: he drove his sword into Tros' liver even as he tried to take hold of his knees. After throwing Lycaon's body into the water, he continues in the same vein: he goes on to kill another eight named Trojan allies without saying anything to any one of them about his own mortality. He blocks the river with the dead he kills, enraging its river god. After escaping from its angry flood, he presses on against the Trojans who are running to their city: 'mighty battle frenzy always held his heart', Homer tells us, 'and he was striving to win glory'.[26]

Achilles' actions are not condoned here by Homer, no more than when he persistently maltreats Hector's body or cuts the throats of those twelve young Trojans and casts them onto his pyre for Patroclus. After his extreme funerary honours for Patroclus, he shows magnanimity to the Greek heroes, even to Agamemnon, in the games, but not because he himself has changed: the plot has moved on and these Greek heroes are no longer the objects of his wrath. Hector, however, is still an object of it, even when dead.

Eventually, Achilles ransoms Hector's body and shows pity and respect for Priam, Hector's father. Pity and respect were exactly what Lycaon and Hector had begged from him, but failed to secure: in Priam's presence, at last Achilles relents. It is a profoundly moving change, as worthy of a hero as the impassioned revenge which had preceded it on the battlefield, but even so, it occurs in particular circumstances. It is shown to one individual, Priam, who reminds him explicitly of his father Peleus, a constant figure of respect and sorrow for him. It is also shown away from all the other Greek leaders. It is a change, but not a conversion. Achilles, we know, will be back on the battlefield within a fortnight, fighting to take Troy though he also knows he will die while doing so.

Was his pity for Priam not just an emotion but the result of a new insight? Suppose Chryseis, not Briseis, had been his prize when the plot began: if her elderly father had come as a suppliant to him and offered him a ransom, would he have already pitied him and given back the girl? I think he would, remembering his own elderly father. In that sense his character did not change in the course of the poem, but events in it surely taught him lessons. It was not the lesson that the gods mix good and evil for men; he already knew when the poem began that he was destined to die young. It was a lesson about asking too much from Zeus. Until book 18 he did not know that Zeus would grant favours for him, but also grant the ultimate woe, the death of Patroclus: in the light of that knowledge he would surely be wary about asking Thetis to implore such favours for him from Zeus again.

When he mentions Zeus' two jars to Priam, he does so not because he himself has learned that truth the hard way, from the death of Patroclus, but because they relate to his father Peleus, an old father like Priam, and about to be bereaved. Peleus, like Priam, was once fortunate, but then he had an only son, Achilles, who calls himself *panaōrios*, a word which occurs nowhere else. Its meaning has been disputed, but I accept the majority view, that it means 'utterly doomed to die young', not 'unlucky in every' way': Achilles goes on to say that he will not tend Peleus in his old age but will die far from his homeland.[27] In context, spoken to Priam, the words about the two jars are not new-won knowledge: they have been true about Peleus ever since Achilles went to fight at Troy and chose to stay there.

What the poem chooses to express is significant. It chooses to follow Achilles' movement from anger to rage and revenge and ultimately to pity and compassion. What follows is outside the poem and does not detract from the movement which is in it. As it closes, events have taught Achilles lessons, but have not changed him or brought him new self-knowledge: he will be out on the killing field again.

In Babylonia's old heroic poem about Gilgamesh, the pursuit of glory had already been memorably explored. Like Achilles, Gilgamesh then lost his dearest companion: he began a quest for immortality, but finally learned that it could not be his. The Iliad too explores through Achilles the boundary between mortality and immortality, but in a very different way.[28] Achilles has a range and scope which the boastful, tyrannical Gilgamesh never does. Achilles has accepted a brief life even as the Iliad starts: he does not come to accept it only when chastened by events. Gilgamesh, by contrast, seeks and learns wisdom about immortality during a quest. In no way is Homer's characterization of Achilles shaped by an awareness of the Gilgamesh poems.

During the Iliad, the major change in him is that he ceases to abuse Hector's body and agrees that he must indeed ransom it. This change is important, but it is not due to a prior change in himself, brought about by experience: it is due to orders from Zeus. In the first book Athena intervened to check his attempt to kill Agamemnon. In the last book Zeus intervenes to stop his anger at Patroclus' killer and make him accept a ransom. Throughout, the Iliad's plot and its characters relate to this essential dimension, the gods, to whom I will now turn.

PART V

Parallel Worlds

27.

The Heavenly Family

The heroes and their prowess intersect with three worlds beyond the battlefield, the world of the gods, the world of women and what, to us, is the natural world. They are already present in the poem's beginning. Achilles is visited by two goddesses, Athena and then Thetis. He addresses the future of two enslaved women, first Chryseis and then Briseis. In his second speech to Agamemnon, he refers memorably to 'the shadowing mountains and the echoing sea'.[1] I will address each of these parallel worlds in turn, just as I have addressed Homer's horses, first setting out their consistent detail, and then their blend of tradition and exactness and Homer's use of them for poetic effect.

'The mind of Zeus is always stronger than a man's', Homer says in his own person as Patroclus goes to his death.[2] My surveys of the poem's highlights, its heroes' values and their individuality have so far paid less attention to the divine, but it is a crucial constituent. The plot is shaped and impelled, not by men, but by gods. Throughout it, Zeus' plan 'was being fulfilled', with inherent twists and turns: Zeus accepts that Troy is to fall, but he permits the Trojans to prevail for a while, fulfilling his promise to Thetis. Achilles is offered even greater gifts as a result, but then loses Patroclus, the sting in Zeus' plan. These twists become known to us through words which Homer gives to the gods, but they are not known to the heroes until they come about. There is an imbalance between their knowledge and ours. It is essential, as we will see, to the poem's power.

The divine dimension is immediately apparent, whether in book 1's sending of a plague by angry Apollo or in Zeus' sending of a deceptive dream to Agamemnon at the start of book 2. In books 3, 4 and 7 divine interventions are integral to the two duels and their consequences. Many other interventions follow, whether at the start of what will become the longest day of fighting, when Zeus sends Strife to rouse the Greek army, or in book 23 in details of the games which Achilles holds in honour of Patroclus. As book 11 begins, Strife lets out 'a loud and terrible shout and casts great might into the hearts of each one of the Greeks'.[3] During book 23's chariot race, Apollo dashes the whip from the hand of Diomede, Athena's favourite, but she promptly speeds off and gives it back to him. Apollo had acted out of resentment, but Athena then does the same, smashing the yoke of Eumelus' chariot and making him crash, though his team was the best in the race: he would otherwise have beaten her favourite, Diomede. So too, in the foot race, Odysseus, another of Athena's favourites, prays to her, whereupon she helpfully lightens his limbs and then makes one of his rivals slip and fall into dung. Gods and goddesses are intensely partisan, showing spite to attain their ends, even on sports day.[4]

They also affect events on the killing field. They join in the battles and even when banned from them by Zeus, they exert a general influence. In a striking image, during the longest day of fighting they 'looped the bond of strife and war and stretched it over both armies', ensnaring them.[5] They themselves never kill a hero, but they can intervene and leave others to finish him off. Frequently they stir anger in a warrior, take away his wits, give him might and courage or force him in a particular direction. Off the battlefield, Aphrodite, goddess of sex and love, works on the woman at the centre of the war, Helen, and powerfully shapes her relations with Paris, the man with whom she had impelled her to elope.

This level of divine direction has caused modern scholars to question whether Homer's heroes really have free will: if the gods send destructive folly or take away a hero's wits, how can mortals be held responsible for what they do? The question is not one which Homer or his listeners ever formulated, nor is it one to which a tidy answer can be given. Homer presents two levels of determination, one divine, one human, and in a pre-philosophic era does not see an inconsistency between them.[6]

In other parts of the poem he proceeds differently: there is no divine intervention, an aspect which has attracted less comment. When heroes debate and plead, Homer allows whole scenes to proceed without direct action by a god. In book 7 the inconclusive duel between Hector and Ajax is followed by debates in the Greek camp and in Troy. No god intervenes in them, not even in Priam's unwise decision at the end of the Trojans' debate. No god guides the two sides to agree to bury their dead or attends them when they do so under a truce. In book 9, the absence is especially striking. Achilles and the three envoys sent to him refer to the gods in their speeches, but the gods play no explicit part in what is said or what results from it. Book 11 has another such sequence, beginning with the wounding of the warrior-hero Eurypylus and his rescue from the battle. Achilles is curious as he sees him being driven past and sends Patroclus to find out more: Patroclus is kind to the wounded man and has a long discussion with old Nestor. Across some 275 verses, this sequence is crucial for the course of Zeus' plan, but it takes place without any mention of a god's role in it.

The most intense scenes in the poem involve Andromache, Hector's wife, but in them too the gods are absent. No god or goddess guides her to him in book 6 when she meets him inside Troy and none influences their profound encounter. None comes to tell her of his death in book 22 or of the return of his body in book 24. One of her persistent themes is that Hector is everything to her and without him she will be totally bereft. It is for this reason, I think, that she is alone, never guided by a god or goddess beside her.

Within this pattern of overall direction and intermittent absence, Homer's gods are certainly not his inventions. Ares and Poseidon, Dionysus, even, and probably Hera are names attested in written records back in the Mycenaean period, *c.* 1300 BC: the name Zeus can be traced back to the name for a sky god in the 'Indo-European' era, *c.* 2000 BC, and one of his wives, Dione, has been persuasively credited with cult at Dodona since time immemorial.[7] Apollo is likely to be a Greek adaptation of the god Apaliuna, active in west Asia and attested in Hittite texts, also *c.* 1300 BC. Aphrodite was pre-Homeric too, but not with such a long past. She originated from Greeks' interactions with Phoenicians and others on Cyprus *c.* 1150–1050 BC.[8] Nonetheless, she pre-existed Homer's lifetime and was entirely familiar to his hearers.

In the Iliad divinities with these ancient names are firmly aligned on one or other side of the war. Hera, Athena and Poseidon are anti-Trojan, whereas Apollo, Ares and Aphrodite, three A's, are pro-Trojan. Homer does not explain these alignments when they first feature, but passing references in the poem clarify them. Poseidon, we eventually learn in book 21, had been cheated by the former king of Troy for whom he had helped to build walls for the city: hence his anti-Trojan hostility. Apollo had helped with those walls too, but he is pro-Trojan, perhaps because he was associated with local cults nearby in western Asia. As for Ares the god of war, he was the son of anti-Trojan Hera but was often associated with barbaric Thracians, allies of Priam, making him a ready ally of Troy despite his mother.

Behind the goddesses' alignment lies something else, better known to us from later authors.[9] Before the Trojan war, a dispute had arisen between Hera, Athena and Aphrodite about which of them was the most beautiful: some said it occurred at the wedding of Peleus to Thetis. This feminine contest was referred to the judgement of the Trojan prince Paris, who was confronted by the goddesses in the inner courtyard of his sheep farm on Mount Ida. Each of them tried to bribe him, but Aphrodite won by promising him Helen, the most beautiful woman in the world. As a result, Aphrodite, winner in the beauty contest, is pro-Trojan, whereas the losers, Hera and Athena, are Troy's implacable enemies, even though the Trojans continued, in ignorance, to honour Athena with a big temple inside their city.

Only at the start of book 24, near the poem's end, is there explicit mention of the connection between the goddesses' hatred for Troy and Paris' destructive folly. The next two verses amplify its link with Paris' prize-giving, but I am one of the many who consider that they are not Homer's and were added by a later performer, perhaps when he was singing only the final stages of the poem as an extract and wanted to make its background clear.[10] However, hints of the judgement of Paris can be traced in earlier books, showing that Homer expected his hearers to know the story. As Auerbach well realized, Homer's mortal heroes are usually presented without hidden depths, but he failed to see that the goddesses are counter-examples. They come with a background which is assumed, not openly stated. Homer had not invented it: he presumed listeners would make the connection from what they already knew. Modern readers need to be aware of it.

Although they stretch far back in time, Homer's gods and goddesses have precise, local connections in space. In the Iliad, they are linked to particular sanctuaries and are sometimes worshipped with epithets which connect them to a place or function. Aphrodite is linked to a temple at Paphos on Cyprus, an important place for her cult in real life, Hera to Argos, likewise, and Poseidon, 'shaker of the earth', is credited with that underwater palace at Aigai by the coast of what is now the Gallipoli peninsula. Zeus, too, has that sanctuary of his on Mount Gargaron, near to the Trojan plain, from which he can watch the battle more closely. Hera is credited with particular fondness for Sparta, Argos and Mycenae, the three cities most dear to her. Even so, she is willing to let Zeus destroy them so long as he lets her destroy hateful Troy.[11] It is a chilling reminder of a goddess's attitude to mere mortals.

These local cult centres are powerful pulls on their gods' loyalties, but they are secondary to a residence which the main divinities share in the poem. They live, speak, feast and drink on Mount Olympus, that high mountain in the north of Greece, on which their home is 'not shaken by winds nor wetted by rain', says the Odyssey, 'nor does snow come near it', a contrast to the real peaks of Olympus and the snowy blanket which settles even in summer on the alpine plants of its nival zone.[12] In this one place Homeric gods assemble and pass beguiling days. At the start of book 4 they are gathered in Zeus' Olympian palace and are drinking nectar from golden cups while they look down on Troy after the duel between Paris and Menelaus. At the start of book 8 Zeus imposes divine distancing and bans them from descending to join the fighting. Nonetheless, partying continues on Olympus throughout the ban.

This concentration on Olympus is a poetic device. No cult of the Olympian gods as a group is known in real life. Modern readers sometimes think of them as twelve, the twelve gods, and indeed a notion of twelve gods needing twelve separate portions of a sacrifice can be found quite soon in post-Homeric poetry.[13] In the Iliad, however, ten divinities, not twelve, are most prominent on Olympus and at least another five can be added. Homer presents his most-mentioned gods, not as a divine dozen, but as a family, and yet not all members of it are on the mountain. Disruptive Dionysus, a son of Zeus, is absent, important though his cults were in real life. So is Demeter, a sister and wife of Zeus. Homer calls her 'blonde Demeter' in a simile in which she is attending a harvest on a threshing floor, the grain being blonde like herself: through the loss of her daughter Persephone she had associations with the underworld which helped to make her an unsuitable presence on Olympus.[14] Artemis, a daughter of Zeus, is called 'mistress of wild animals', a very ancient title, when she descends to join in the battle, but though she too was ubiquitous in cult and myth, she is not prominent in the poem, perhaps because she was most at home in wild nature and because one of her main roles, nurturing young children, was out of place in a poem about war.[15]

Why has Homer concentrated his main gods in a family and on a single mountain? In many other cultures, including those in parts of the Near East, gods live on a high mountain, meet in a council and interrelate, at least in part, as a family. Some of Homer's modern scholars claim, therefore, that he borrowed his presentation of a family and mountain of gods from a Near Eastern prototype.[16] It would have had a strange resonance for his hearers if he himself had borrowed this format for the first time and presented the gods in a newly imported foreign mode. There are indeed a few touches of exotic eastern detail in his presentation of Aphrodite, but they are unsurprising as she was a creation by Greeks on Cyprus in the early dark ages: nothing in the poem implies that other Olympians were to be received in this way.[17] There is no one source known in Near Eastern texts from which Homer's presentation of his heavenly family can be derived, even supposing he could have understood its language.[18]

Across more than a thousand years, the myths and societies known to us in the Near East are many and varied. Rather than specifying a single source, proponents of their influence on Homer's gods sometimes appeal to 'broad streams of international tradition' in which a mass of story patterns floated freely.[19] The notions of a heavenly family, a council and a mountain need no such vague derivation. A mountain is an obvious place for earth-bound worshippers to ascribe to their gods, one which they have chosen in many parts of the world without any contact with 'Near Eastern' stories. As for a family or a council, they are projections onto heaven of social forms on earth, the most ready source for mortals' imagining of their gods. Families and councils were basic social groups in the Greek world, ones which poets before Homer had surely projected already onto heaven. In the Iliad gods gather and debate but they are not explicitly described as a council.

Apart from the main family, many other divinities pay a visit to Olympus, although they do not live there. The greatest gathering in heaven is the one summoned in book 20 when Zeus is about to allow the gods to enter the battle. 'None of the rivers was absent, except Ocean': as Ocean bounded and bonded the world, he could not exactly leave it to fall apart. Nymphs, by contrast, could take time off, so up to Olympus they came, those 'who frequent the fair groves and sources of rivers and grassy meadows': Homer has a mass meeting in mind, a wondrous one to envisage. Mass meetings of gods occur in some of our surviving Near Eastern texts, not least in those from Babylonia about the enthronement of the great god Marduk and his creation of the universe. None is a match for the exquisite beauty of Homer's.[20]

Homer's Olympian visitors could hardly be less like the heavenly family of Christianity. Although Zeus is their ruler, it is a modern misreading of the poem to regard him as a step towards monotheism, as if it is the inevitable end point of mortals' religious experience. Zeus is not an eternal god. He had not created the universe. He was born in time to heavenly parents and had become king only after wars in heaven against cruel Cronos, his father, the previous ruler, in which monsters participated. Homer alludes to these battles, but only incidentally, as events in the past. Stories of such struggles for succession in heaven were indeed very old in the Near East and were told in various languages. For once, we can be specific about points where Greeks made contact with them: north Syria and then, as visitors diffused them, the nearby islands of Cyprus and Crete. During the tenth to ninth centuries BC, they became entwined on those islands with a Greek tale of the birth of Aphrodite and another about the infancy of young Zeus, but Homer gives no space to them.[21] He even ignores a crucial item in them. His epithet for Cronos is 'crooked counselling', but it had developed from an older and more apt one, 'with a crooked sickle', the weapon which Cronos had used to castrate his father in the old stories of succession: Homer and his teachers had modified that epithet and lost its violent implications.[22]

Like Cronos, Zeus might be overthrown one day, but meanwhile his strength remained awesome, on a scale which mere mortals can hardly imagine. Memorably, Homer helps us to do so. At the beginning of book 8, he makes Zeus deter the gods from joining in the battle by warning them that he could hang a golden rope down from the top of Olympus for them to hold on earth below, and if they did, he would then pull them all up, together with the entire world, to show them how overpoweringly strong he is. The remarkable image of this rope was picked up by later readers, including Aristotle, who used it to express the sense of a divine power running through the world. Others imagined that the rope had links and was the great chain of being in which everything has its fixed place.[23] In Homer it had no such connotation.

Zeus is the father of gods and men, but like so many monarchs' families, his is fascinatingly dysfunctional. He is incestuously married to Hera, his natural sister, and is wary of her, his ever-querulous wife. She in turn is wary of him, as marital fidelity is not at all his ideal. He is an uninhibited seducer, sexually harassing mortals even when, in modern terms, they are underage. The other gods do the same. Zeus' family members also quarrel and fight and have sex with mortals who catch their fancy on earth.

Implored by Thetis, Zeus lays a plan which only he fully knows. Within it there are intervals when other gods and goddesses can act independently, in battle in book 5, until Zeus bans their participation in book 8, and in battle again in book 14, if only because Hera has seduced Zeus and sent him to sleep. In book 20 he then gives them permission to re-enter the killing field and to fight among themselves. This device, an overall plan and intervals within it, is Homer's way of sustaining a plot to its conclusion while prolonging it along the way.

It works well because Zeus is so strong. When Zeus bans the gods from participating, they obey, reluctantly, because they fear his superior power. Hera and the other goddesses protest at intentions he announces to them but they never make him change his mind. Their modes of address to him reflect his superiority. He is at the top of the Olympian pyramid. When a god or goddess is insulted or wounded, they fly up to heaven and complain to him, hoping for sympathy or redress: he rebukes wounded Ares before he helps him and he merely listens to wounded Aphrodite with a smile. As the powerful father of a family, he is the natural resort for pained or aggrieved members. Again, a pattern of power and social relations on earth has been projected onto the gods in heaven: there is no need to derive these scenes from approximate prototypes known in texts from the Near East.

Disobedience of Zeus has to be covert, because it brings brutal reprisals, as Hera's experience shows. She has a history of finding devious ways to frustrate her husband: once, she foiled the prospects of a son of his, Heracles, who was to be born from a mortal mother. In return, Zeus punished her by attaching anvils to her feet and a gold bond to her hands and hanging her upside down among the clouds. At another time he laid his 'untouchable hands on her': domestic violence came readily to him.[24] When he wakes in book 15 from her wilful seduction, he tells her he may well lash her with blows, something she averts only by swearing a most solemn oath.

Among themselves, gods and goddesses argue, quarrel, lie and fight, affecting the course of the plot, especially when free to be partisan during the games in book 23. There is humour, both when gods laugh at one of their number and when we, like Zeus, smile at Aphrodite's wounding or at the dialogue between Hera and Sleep. Guided by a Muse, Homer even dares to present the gods' very words. They are such beguiling players in the poem that they may seem to be poetic gods, quite different from those which his hearers took for granted in their own lives. That way of reading them needs more careful consideration.

28.

Sublime Frivolity?

The Iliad's gods and goddesses are manifestly personalities. By arguing, laughing, making love and fighting in battle, they behave as impersonal powers never could. They have individual characters: Hera is the artful, resentful wife, who often uses Athena as her ally, whereas Apollo works on his own, never chivvying Zeus or trying to evade him.

Sometimes Homer refers to a god in a general way as a *theos*, not a particular god by name. When they come down to earth they usually adopt disguises, but these temporary transformations do not displace their personalities from the centre of their identities.[1] He and his speakers also refer to divine powers, Strife being one and the Prayers others, each suited to the contexts in which they are presented. They are personified powers nonetheless: Strife is imagined as shouting, the Prayers as old and wrinkled.[2] An influential modern view considers that outside epic poetry the Greek gods were envisaged as powers, not personalities.[3] I do not draw such a distinction: in art and prayers, in accompanying myths and epithets, Greek gods outside poetry were personalities too. In an important comment the historian Herodotus states that Homer and the poet Hesiod marked out the titles, powers and forms of the gods of the Greeks. He did not think they were poetic fantasies.

Even so, gods in the Iliad intervene in ways which strike us as entirely miraculous. In books 3 and 20 they whisk heroes up and away from duels which they risk losing: Poseidon lifts Aeneas from the ground, away from Achilles, and Aeneas is launched from the god's hand over and above 'many ranks of men and many chariots.' Once, Hera grants Achilles' horses the ability to speak. Once, she alters a day's duration by sending the unwilling sun to set in the Ocean, thereby shortening the day of victories which Zeus has announced for Hector.[4] The poem's speeches and action are so compelling that it is easy to miss the scale of these interventions. The Iliad does not observe laws of nature, a concept which was quite unknown to Homer.

In real life, nobody expected the gods to airlift them from a battle. For poetic reasons the scale of divine intervention is indeed enhanced, but the possibility of it at a lesser level was ever-present in most Greeks' minds. Homer is telling of a time when heroes were not as mortals nowadays: he enhances the gods' interventions for the sake of a plot and a storyline which are his own choices.[5]

He also refers to an external power which seems to be ever-active: destiny, or fate. Twice, Zeus holds up a pair of golden scales and weighs in them two lots, or fates, to see which will preponderate at a time when the death of a hero very dear to him is imminent. It might seem that he is giving way here to an external power, Fate, which is stronger than he is.[6] However, he has pre-announced the deaths of these two dear heroes, Sarpedon and Hector, as part of his plan, and the weighing merely dramatizes an outcome which he has already foreseen. When Homer's speakers talk of *moira*, 'destiny' or 'portion' they do not necessarily mean our Fate with a capital 'F'. They often simply mean death. They are also talking in a poem which Homer is shaping and in which he himself directs what has to happen. Destiny adds to its poignancy, but is not necessarily a power beyond Zeus to which he must conform.

In many other cultures, a notion of fate has coexisted with named personalized gods. It is a powerful element in pre-Islamic poetry with its flexible notion of time and fate, *dahar*. It is implicit in versions of the Manas epic, even when Muslim religion pervades them: in a long retelling of the episode of the funeral feast, transcribed in the 1920s, a young khan is made to tell his counsellor, 'If you are going along single-mindedly on a long journey, do not gallop. To each mortal comes his turn, so do what you do in the time you have.' In an early Babylonian text, the goddess Nintu is called 'creator of destinies', a role she is also credited with in *Gilgamesh*.[7] In

Homer, Zeus could be aptly described likewise, but the scenes of his weighing two fates on scales make the relationship more vivid than any in these Near Eastern texts.

Homer's use of it would not strike his audiences as poetic invention: *moira* was to have a long life in Greeks' thinking, epitaphs and mentality.[8] A precise metaphor occurs in the Iliad with even more force: speakers refer to this or that having been 'spun' for a hero at his birth.[9] In his great reply to Priam's supplication, Achilles refers to the gods as doing the spinning, by which they fix a crucial fact of life, that they themselves live at ease, whereas mortals live among sorrows. Elsewhere, Hera refers to Fate, *aisa*, as the spinner, who has devised an outcome for Achilles at his birth, and likewise Hecuba refers to mighty Fate spinning for Hector, also at his birth, that he should be the prey of dogs far from his parents, beside a mighty man. She is, however, speaking with hindsight when this outcome was already known.

Moira, or a mortal's portion, was not a new notion, introduced into poetry quite recently and sitting uneasily beside an older world in which gods still appeared and intervened in heroes' lives.[10] The two had long coexisted. The notion of a man's destiny as spun for him by Fate was very ancient too. If pressed, there are inconsistencies here, between Destiny and divine intervention, spun *moira* and Zeus' decided plan, but they continue to appear in Greek texts long after the Iliad. Like Homer, readers should live with them.[11]

Meanwhile, nothing spun or fated makes mortals' offerings to the gods pointless. Homer's listeners would certainly not regard the cult paid in the poem as poetic fancy. Heroes make offerings in order to avert misfortune and win favours, aims which remain the mainsprings of cult paid in real life throughout pre-Christian antiquity. In the poem, as in life, the offerings include animals, killed, ceremonially butchered and roasted. There is no hint of guilt about these killings, as one modern theory of sacrifice has postulated.[12] Homer is not suppressing a sentiment which he and others knew to be important for anyone offering a sacrifice in real life. In book 8 Hector forces the Greeks back and threatens their ships with Zeus' support, so much so that Agamemnon prays in distress to Zeus, saying he never passed any fair altar of Zeus in his ship on the way to Troy without burning on it the 'fat and thighs of oxen in my eager desire to sack well-walled Troy'. There is not a trace of guilt here about the killing of these animals and the violence involved. In reply Zeus briefly relents from his plan and gives the Greeks some respite: the gods have no compunction about enjoying the scent of animal offerings which ascends to them as smoke.[13]

As in life, heroes swear oaths, appealing to the gods to uphold them and punish transgressors. In the Iliad, the offerings which accompany oaths are notably precise: Agamemnon cuts hair off the animal to be killed, puts it in the hands of onlookers and then cuts the animal's throat. Its carcase is not roasted and offered to the gods: it is taken away or thrown into the sea.[14] This detailed procedure is distinct from the killing and roasting of animals on other occasions, not because Homer is inventing it, but here too, because offerings linked to oaths indeed proceeded differently in real life.

Throughout the Iliad mortals pray to the gods, even when engaged in battle. These invocations, too, are not Homer's invention. He describes them in terms which match those attested in everyday prayers. There is a pattern to their words, first the invocation of the god, then the claim to his favour and, lastly, the specific request.[15] Libations of wine accompany them and are given with due ceremonial, again as in real life: then too wine was poured away as the simplest and quickest sharing of an offering with a god. At portentous moments in the poem a very special cup is specified, none more so than the cup with which Achilles prays for Patroclus' safe return as he is about to depart to fight. The cup, Homer carefully tells us, is one from which only Achilles ever drank wine and poured libations, and then only to Zeus.[16] The emphasis is poetic, befitting a pivotal moment in the plot, but a preliminary ritual accompanies it which was surely familiar to its hearers. Achilles cleans the cup, first with sulphur, then with clear water, and then washes his hands.

Here and elsewhere, ritual slows the poem and gives it a stately measure.[17] It is not poetic fancy, but as ever Homer has selected what he includes. He omits aspects of everyday cult and belief which would complicate his plot or redirect its focus. In real life, mortals' fear of pollution, or *miasma*, was very important, attaching to dead bodies, among much else, but Homer excludes it, partly because its expiation would have greatly slowed his narrative.[18] So, too, he excludes cult for dead heroes: it would have conflicted with his poem's view of their shadowy, confined existence. In the Iliad he also excludes any mention of a hero putting questions to a god at an oracular site, though such sites were flourishing more than ever in the Greek world during his lifetime. Instead, his gods communicate indirectly through omens sent to the killing field, especially through the flight of birds. Omens were a pervasive element in Greek life. Once only, he mentions an examiner of the innards of a sacrificed animal: they too were indicators of a god's intentions and were frequently studied by experts in real life.[19]

The range of cult and ritual is selective, then, but not poetic fiction. Its recipients have qualities which are not Homer's invention, either. Being immortal gods, they never die. They never even age, the ideal of mortal masters of our digital multi-verse. They act with an ease denied to mortals. With one movement of a hand they can knock down an entire wall or lift a hero up to the sky. They also watch and listen to what happens on earth. Here too Homer was not inventing. Throughout antiquity, prayers and inscribed dedications address gods specifically as 'listeners' and assume their general vigilance over human affairs.[20] In the Odyssey, as in Hesiod's poetry, divine *daimones* are said to range among men, watching for their misdemeanours.[21] The Iliad has no such heavenly Stasi: its gods look on or descend from time to time, but they are spectators, not sneaks.

In the Iliad, what strikes every reader is that the gods are a visible presence, moving among the heroes. Among the faraway, blameless Ethiopians they move and feast even more freely, face to face. Very occasionally they appear directly to a hero too: in book 1, when Athena intervenes in the great quarrel, she is visible, her eyes blazing, to Achilles, but to nobody else. At the beginning of book 4, she is seen, unusually, by one and all. She springs down to the battlefield in order to break a temporary truce in the war. Her descent is compared to a star from which sparks fly, but she has not assumed the form of a star herself. She 'leapt into the middle' between the two armies, and 'amazement came on those who saw her'. Uniquely she appears here to one and all, in an epiphany in her own person. However, she promptly takes on the guise of an individual man and goes to find the one Trojan she wants to address.[22]

Usually, when gods visit heroes they appear as Athena ends by doing here, as if they are a well-known mortal. Then they talk to them directly and touch them. Homer's heroes are explicitly 'not as mortals nowadays': this type of contact is far more direct than any which could be expected in normal lives. However, close encounters with Homeric gods or goddesses follow a general pattern. They appear, concealing their identity. They talk and intervene, and usually only when they are departing does their identity become clear. Intimacy provokes awe and fear, but the god reassures. This pattern is unlikely to be Homer's invention. It also occurs, independently, in parts of the Bible, in the visits paid by angels, whether to Abraham's slave girl Hagar or to Samson's parents, to young Tobias or to Mary and Jesus's apostles.[23] A sense of divine presence proliferated in the ancient world and was expressed and represented in this persistent pattern. It is one which Homer shared.[24]

It was not just a literary device. Homer's hearers had a general sense of a divine presence in real battles, just as their descendants sensed it in their wars against the Persians, or as Christians, later, sensed St James at work in their battles against the Moors in Spain. Close encounters with an individual divinity also befell them at a further degree of distance: in dreams. At night the frontier between gods and men remained wide open. In the Iliad, Zeus sends a dream as a separate entity, which enters a bedroom and speaks to a hero in his sleep. In subsequent centuries, while mortals slept, gods themselves seemed to stand beside them. These visits had a further stimulus, unavailable to Homeric heroes, the personalized statues and images of gods and goddesses which had proliferated in public and domestic spaces. People who lived daily among this forest of images envisioned their subjects and dreamed of them more readily. Images shaped the contours of the gods and helped dreamers to identify their experience when they awoke.

In a famous passage the literary critic Longinus, writing no earlier than the first century AD, remarked that 'Homer has done his best to make the men in the Iliad gods and the gods men.'[25] Longinus disapproved, because he thought this presentation to be unworthy of divinity as he understood it, but his point can be taken further, in each direction. When Homer calls a hero god-like, the term is often poignant: the hero will soon be going to his death. He is like a god in some ways, but not in his mortality, the point that matters most. Nonetheless Homer makes Achilles say that Hector was someone to whom 'the Trojans used to pray as a god'. In his own person he also says that a priest in Troy was honoured by the people 'as a god'.[26]

This honour was not confined to non-Greek Trojans. Mighty Thoas was lord of many Aetolians, 'far the best of them, skilled with the javelin, but a good man in close fighting, and in the meeting place few of the Greeks could excel him whenever young men were competing in speech': this multi-talented hero was 'honoured by the people like a god'. In later Greek history, exceptional men and women were sometimes given honours which were explicitly stated to be 'equal to the gods', even in their lifetimes. Homer's precise words, I believe, already had this force, presenting these exceptional people as recipients of god-like honours while alive. Cult was eventually paid in the Greek world to living rulers, athletes and exceptional female beauties, but its roots were already present, underemphasized, in Homer's poetry. In no way was it, as once believed by some of its scholars, an import from the east.[27]

If heroes can be god-like, members of the Olympian family are human-like in so many ways. When Zeus and Hera, brother and sister, fell in love, they first had sex, Zeus recalls, away from their parents' vigilance: they were like young mortal lovers, therefore, who escape to the privacy of a meadow to do it where they will not be noticed. On the battlefield, when Ares god of war kills a mortal, he stops to strip off his armour. He has no need of armour himself, but he is presented as a victorious hero would be, stripping an enemy he has slain.[28]

To a degree that egalitarian readers still find hard to appreciate, Homer's gods are represented as super-aristocrats. Like upper class heroes, these heavenly super-crats have a keen sense of their *timē*, or honour. Thetis' appeal to Zeus invokes hers most effectively, and when the Greeks build a temporary wall round their ships and camp, Poseidon regards it as an affront to his honour too.[29] Crucially, gods regard mortals much as aristocrats regard the lower classes, a cardinal point in their presentation in the Iliad. In a general way they care for them, as an aristocrat might profess to care for his dependants, but if slighted by one of them, gods are terrifyingly hostile and cruel, as an aristocrat would be to an insolent inferior. Yet gods also respect strangers and suppliants just as a noble would respect them on earth.

Like heroes, gods exist in a shame culture: they feel and acknowledge the restraint of shame, or *aidōs*, and avoid what is *aischron*, disgraceful.[30] They also feel pity. They live in what social anthropologists class as a culture of the gift. On earth the poet Hesiod, Homer's near-contemporary, urged men to be canny and 'give to the giver, not to the one who does not give'. Homer's gods are assumed to recognize that same ethic. On earth, aristocrats would tend to do the maximum good to their friends and the maximum harm to their enemies. Divinities in the Iliad do the same, especially the goddesses Hera and Athena, who pursue vengeance for defeat in a beauty contest even to the point of destroying innocents in an entire city.[31] Spite and jealousy still erupt in the contests of modern beauty queens, but usually only between the competitors themselves.

In their prayers to a god, heroes appeal to reciprocity. They cite the gifts they have given to him as grounds for him to give them favours in return: 'if ever' they have given this or that, a temple perhaps or an animal offering, so the god should now give to them. The Greeks' long-lasting culture of vows and votive offerings, those touchstones of ancient piety, rested on a similar hope, that a giver would be most likely to receive a counter-gift.[32] Like aristocrats, gods have personal favourites, not only the children they father on mortals, but those 'dear' to them, their *philoi*. Here too favours might be reciprocated, but gods being gods, a counter-gift was never certain: the favours of earthly aristocrats were unpredictable too. Gods favour mortals who have favoured them, exemplified in Zeus' hesitation as to whether to save Hector from Achilles because he had offered him so many fine burnt offerings. A god's favour arises from selfish concern for his own respect and privilege, not from concern for the good of a hero's community.

In the Iliad the values of aristocrats have been projected in wide-ranging detail onto heaven's super-crats, the gods. They are a way of imagining them which is so pervasive, so taken for granted that it is not one which Homer newly devised for his poem's sake. It is not peculiar to the Greek dark ages. In Christian society, heaven became peopled by patron saints, projections of the mortal patrons whose power, whims and status dominated Christians' earthly lives. Like a Roman emperor, God came to be imagined as the ruler of a court in which His angels were attendant courtiers, ranked in honorary robes like imperial courtiers on earth. This way of imagining the divine prevails especially among pre-literate peoples, as anthropologists' studies widely attest. In societies where social relations are highly unequal and stratified, those relations of power are projected onto gods in a magnified form. They are collective representations indeed. Illiterate Homer and his teachers did likewise: the gods who struck later ages as immoral and reprehensible made sense in an age when power was aristocratic and unquestioned. Power relations on earth shaped the personalities of gods.

To the gods, mortals are mere mortals, much as the lower classes seemed mere inferiors to aristocrats, the 'fine and fair'. There is no cosmic justice. On Zeus' part, any overt justice in the narrative is decidedly limited.[33] His immoderate promise to Thetis is elicited by her demand for her past favours to be reciprocated and her honour to be respected. Zeus does not grant it because he considers Agamemnon's treatment of Achilles to be unjust. He is a protector of

"JUST"

oaths and strangers, and yet he does not present the imminent fall of Troy as a just punishment for Paris' elopement with the wife of Menelaus, the man who had been entertaining him as his guest. In book 13, Menelaus proclaims over a Trojan whom he has just killed that the Trojans show no lack of insolence and disgraceful behaviour, as they did not fear the harsh anger of Zeus the god of hospitality 'who will one day destroy your steep city'. So Menelaus sees events, but when Zeus discussed Troy's fate with Hera nine books earlier he provoked her by asking what Priam and his sons had done to antagonize her.[34] He even implied that he might encourage a peaceful conclusion and the return of Helen to her husband.

By some of its finest modern critics, the behaviour of the Iliad's gods has been classed as unserious: 'this gay treatment of the gods', Maurice Bowra wrote in 1930, 'was no doubt excellent as far as poetry was concerned'.[35] However, it was not just a fiction for poetry: it was an unquestioning projection of earthly social relations into heaven. It was not Homer's invention, nor was it for light relief. In 1938 Karl Reinhardt referred more subtly to the gods' 'sublime frivolity'. Again, his phrase looks on the gods from a point outside the unquestioning assumptions of Homer himself and his hearers. To aristocrats in his audience the gods' behaviour on Olympus was the realization of an ideal, one in which grief was short-lived and existence a carefree delight. Whereas heroes strive on earth to win glory, *kudos*, Zeus exults in his glory without needing to strive at all. Homer or his audience would never have called it 'frivolous'.

As among aristocrats, even at play, a potential response is ever present among heaven's super-crats: anger. It is not only anger between one another: they can direct it at mortals too. It is not in the least frivolous. Long after the aristocratic age, anger of a god continued to be emphasized in the words of oracles, believed to originate from the gods themselves. Throughout antiquity, therefore, Homer's listeners were aware that gods had anger and spite and might show it in human affairs. Divine anger, they accepted, might lie behind disease or the destruction of a city. It might cause earthquakes or famine. Particular myths about gods and heroes

ANGER

attached the effects of a god's anger to particular places, explaining old ruins, old tombs and features in the landscape. The jealous revenge of Hera and Athena against Troy was not at odds with everyday assumptions.

It was not just a poetic device, nor was the gods' capacity for spite and jealousy: they made sense of human misfortune. The explanation of misfortune is a crucial function of religion.[36] In the Iliad misfortune abounds, not just during war but in the very fact of being human. The heavenly super-crats and their moods explain it, but there are none of the consistently fierce and deadly goddesses known in early Indian religion, none like Kali, bringer of death, famine and disease. Apollo, sender of a plague, has favourites whom he helps and protects. No Homeric god is always the sender of misfortune. It results from a particular god's spite or anger or a quarrel with another god, and so its explanation is often hidden from the earthly protagonists. To them, the favours and enmities of the gods are not just unpredictable: they are inscrutable.

In book 2, Agamemnon calls the older Greeks, six of them, to stand round a bull, a fat five-year-old, which he is about to offer to Zeus. He prays that Zeus will not let the sun go down on this day, the first day of fighting in the poem, until he has cast Priam's palace to the ground and torn Hector's tunic with bronze and made many of his companions fall round him headlong in the dust:

> So he spoke, but the son of Cronos was not yet
>   granting fulfilment.
> He received the holy offerings but increased the
>   grievous toil of war.[37]

The gods look down on the human action, sometimes pitying what they see. Misunderstanding, however, is endemic on the human side of the relationship, crucial, as we will see, to the poem's profound power.

29

White-Armed Women

Like the gods, women in the Iliad inhabit a parallel world to the world of the heroes, but intersect with it, intensifying the poem's effect. Beauty is one of their recurring attributes. In the first book, Chryseis and Briseis are described as fair-cheeked and in book 19 Briseis is even lovelier: she is like golden Aphrodite. In book 3 Helen's beauty receives the finest compliment in all poetry.[1]

In the *Gilgamesh* poem there are no such women. Only one is named, Shamhat the harlot, who seduces wild Enkidu and begins his taming: 'She spread her clothing and he lay upon her / She treated the man to the work of a woman / His passion caressed and embraced her / For six days and seven nights / Enkidu was erect as he coupled with Shamhat.' Since 2015, a newly identified text, an older version, has doubled Enkidu's performance: he keeps it up not for seven nights, but for fourteen. Shimhat had already made love to Gilgamesh, who was the terror of every young bride in Uruk: the night before their weddings he would 'couple with the bride-to-be, / He first of all, the bridegroom after.'[2] No Homeric hero behaves so abominably.

Unlike *Gilgamesh,* the Iliad abounds in women, in back-stories of the heroes' young lives, in similes and especially in the palaces of Troy. They are foils to the heroes and their choices, but without them the poem would be profoundly diminished. First I will explore the social context which Homer's narrative assumes for them, one which ranges across marriage, love and family, work in the household, dress and the public roles which an upper class woman can assume. Then I will follow the poem's three most famous women, Helen, Hecuba and Andromache, whom Homer has immortalized with singular art.

During war, slavery hangs over every woman's future if her city falls. As the poem begins, two enslaved girls, Chryseis and Briseis, are given, swapped and taken away by males, but even in their dire plight, their status is not permanently fixed. Briseis was nobly born and had been married before she was taken captive. While enslaved, she was assured that Achilles, her master, would marry her, freeing her, therefore, if and when they returned to his homeland. When Chryseis was brought back to her father in order to end Apollo's anger, she too underwent a change of status. She was placed in his arms by Odysseus and he 'received his dear daughter joyfully'. She was free again, no longer an enslaved object.[3]

In later life, she would again be an item of exchange: like every free-born girl, she would be given in marriage. The choice of a husband was made by the girl's father, not her mother or herself. In a marvellous scene, crafted on the shield for Achilles, finely dressed boys and girls are dancing, the boys wearing gold daggers on silver belts, the girls wearing beautiful garlands. The action has an exquisite courtesy, but the girls, unmarried, are described as 'worth many cattle', a traditional epithet.[4] Marriage made them so: how was it conducted?

In the Iliad, marriage customs have been read as evidence that the poem has combined customs from different eras, not from social reality at any one time. In my view, they cohere well enough.[5] Girls would be married off when young, 14–16 being a likely age, as later Greek evidence attests. The individual brides, all upper class, almost always marry out of their family and away from their homeland. They pass into their husband's family and become kin to his brother's wives, a relationship which is categorized by a special word of kinship, *einatēr*, whose linguistic root is very old. According to Aristotle, some four centuries later, brides in archaic Greece were bought, but Homer's examples contradict him.[6] In his poems' upper class, marriages involve not sales but transfers of goods in differently named stages.

Gifts, *dōra*, passed between a girl's suitors and her father or male kin, often as a first stage, inclining the girl's father to announce a marriage and then to choose and honour one or two suitors in particular. Those he favoured would then offer him a separate transfer, one of bride-goods, or *hedna*. These offers would probably be competitive, one suitor rivalling another. The chosen bridegroom would then transfer actual *hedna* to the bride's father or, in his absence, transfer them to her male kin in return for the bride: *hedna* were not a dowry, transferred for her use. Her father might also add gifts at this stage, especially if his daughter was marrying above her family's status and needed to be made an even better catch or if, being ugly, she was impossible, without extra gifts, to place at the social level which her family's background deserved. These gifts were not wedding presents as we know them. They were given to the bride's father or nearest male kin, not to the bride or bridegroom.

The masterly classical scholar E. R. Dodds once distinguished these two Homeric exchanges, women with gifts and women for *hedna*, as 'women at a discount' and 'women at a premium'. However, these words imply sale and a market price, terms which do not fit the procedures which Homer implies.[7] Bidding is a more apposite word, one suitor outbidding others.

Both of these exchanges, gifts and *hedna*, could coexist in a single instance of marriage. In order to win over Achilles and repair their quarrel, Agamemnon offers him one of his daughters in marriage without the need for bride-goods from Achilles, but with enormous gifts from himself.[8] This double offer was exceptional in fixing both of its transfers to the bridegroom's advantage. The special context required such generosity, but it rested on customary practice, whose parts are exemplified in less extreme examples. To receive Andromache as his bride, Hector, though a prince of mighty Troy, offered 'countless *hedna*' to her father Eetion, although Eetion was only the king of little Thebe. The implication is that Andromache was exceptionally desirable, expressed, I think, by Homer's adjective for her, *poludōros*, 'with many gifts'.[9] In other cases, the balance between bride and groom was rather different. When elderly Altes, a local little king, married his daughter Laothoe to Priam, he gave very valuable gifts with her: Priam was a far greater king, and although Laothoe was to be only one of Priam's wives, Altes had to give bronze and gold with her to ensure this highly advantageous marriage.[10] Priam is not said to have offered any *hedna*: he was such a catch that he was probably spared the usual procedure. Again, Laothoe had no say in the arrangement.

Comparative evidence shows that the customs of dowry and bride-gifts can indeed coexist in a society at one and the same period. Some of the Homeric references to them are awkward to interpret, especially if those in the Odyssey are included, but they cohere well enough if *hedna* are understood as given by the bridegroom whenever they are mentioned, whereas gifts, or *dōra*, are given by either party at various points in the process.[11]

In two cases in the Iliad, another element is present: a father has no living son and wishes to retain a young outsider in his kingdom because of his physical prowess. He therefore offers him his daughter and residence in his realm. Neither of these cases is set in a Greek context, but, even so, the fullest, involving a nobly born Trojan, follows the usual upper class pattern. Iphidamas had been sent off as a boy to his maternal grandfather in Thrace and was brought up there: in due course his grandfather offered him his remaining daughter in marriage. She was his aunt, but as an heiress she was a very valuable bride and so, despite the family connection and the initiative being her father's, Iphidamas had to give a huge amount, expressed by Homer as a hundred cattle and a promise of a thousand sheep and goats, as *hedna*, all from his own flocks. He received his aunt as his bride, but slept with her only on the wedding night before going off to fight the Greeks at Troy. He was killed there by Agamemnon.[12]

At marriage, Homeric wives might be given separate gifts by their fathers, fine clothing, some jewellery or a slave girl for their own use. Otherwise they had no direct control over property: were they simply regarded as carriers of legitimate children? In *The World of Odysseus*, Moses Finley stressed what seemed, to him, the absence in this 'man's world' of 'romantic attachments' between man and woman and of any 'ordinary words with the specific meanings

FINLEY.

325

"husband" and "wife" '. In no relationship, he concluded, 'between man and mate in the Homeric poems was there the depth and intensity, the quality of feeling – on the part of the male – that marked the attachment between father and son on the one hand, and between male and male companion on the other'.[13]

Homeric brides would indeed be young girls, probably fourteen or so, to judge from later Greek practice. As we saw in the Iliad's very first book, a husband, admittedly Agamemnon, might callously praise in public the attributes of his slave-concubine above those of his wife. In heaven, meanwhile, Zeus used physical force on his wife. Even our primeval parents, Ocean and mother Tethys, could plausibly be said to have had a matrimonial breakdown and to have given up making love.[14] Homer is not starry-eyed about married couples, but he is not one-sided, either: Finley's reading is interestingly mistaken.

Homer's vocabulary distinguishes between having sex with a girl, *opuiein*, and actually marrying her, *gamein*. Both words could be applied to one and the same girl, said to be an *opuiomenē*, but also to be 'called a wife'. Two fine episodes, each with a god, illustrate the point. Hephaestus' relationship with lovely Charis, Grace, is an example of the former: he was simply having sex with her, *ōpuie*, in the continuing imperfect tense, but was not married to her: his wife in the Odyssey is Aphrodite.[15] The god Sleep's longing for another Grace, one of the younger ones, is a memorable example of the latter: Hera promises her to him, specifying she will be 'opuiomenē and called his wife', spelling out the physical detail in order to excite Sleep's desire.[16]

There was no defining ceremony for a marriage, neither in Homer nor in later Greek practice. The new husband might hold a celebratory feast, a *gamos*, but it honoured a change of status which was already constituted by both parties' prior agreement. Such an agreement meant that their children would not be bastards. It brought a desirable, often able, girl from a good family to a hero's bed, and it endured for the rest of her life if the husband so wished. Only he could end it. Meanwhile he was free to father bastards too, and, like many aristocratic wives since, it was his wife who would bring them up.[17]

The line between being an *opuiomenē* and a wife does not in itself contradict Finley's blunt view of Homeric marriage. As he also recognized, Homer's word *alochos* indeed means a bed-mate, not specifically a wife.[18] However, another word, *mnēstē*, is sometimes combined with it, meaning 'wooed', and in the Iliad a separate word, *akoitis*, means 'wife' in every instance. Neither French (*femme*) nor German (*Frau* and *Mann*) has a word used only for a husband or a wife, but matrimonial love is professed very widely by speakers of those languages. Love can certainly exist in a patriarchal context. Hector's profound love for his wife Andromache and hers for him have touched every reader except, in the context of his Odyssey book, Moses Finley. Homer calls Iphidamas 'pitiable' because he dies without 'knowing the *charis*', or graceful recompense, of his bride, that aunt for whom he gave much but slept with for only one night.[19] More than sex was involved in this *charis*, as he could have had sex with any slave girl. The loss of this extra dimension, available from a wife, was what made Iphidamas someone to pity.

The offers to angry Achilles in book 9 bring out the spectrum of sentiment. In an attempt to placate him, Agamemnon cites the number of women, seven, whom he will give Achilles if he relents and returns to the war. These unnamed girls are items in a list which includes fine horses, but they are slave girls, taken from Lesbos.[20] When Agamemnon finally gives his gifts in book 19, these slave girls are deposited with others already in Achilles' huts: in Briseis' absence he had been sleeping with at least one of them, fair-cheeked Diomēdē, whom he had taken as a slave-captive before her.[21] She was also from Lesbos, so the new arrivals could reminisce with her about their shared home. As for the horses given by Agamemnon, they too, all twelve of them, were driven off to join Achilles' herd. Yet, there is more involved for one of the girls, the most important. In reply to Agamemnon's offer, Achilles had already declared in book 9 his 'love from the heart' for Briseis, though she was an enslaved captive girl. 'Whoever is a fine man,' he said, 'a sensible one, loves and cares for the girl who is his': the background emerges only in book 19, that he is likely to marry her if he returns home.[22] In that same book he also says to Agamemnon that he wishes she had been killed by an arrow from Artemis on the day he first took her as plunder, such is the disaster that has followed from his quarrel over her with Agamemnon. In the context of his rapprochement with Agamemnon I do not think these words cancel out his earlier insistence on his love for her from the heart.[23]

Homer is not myopic here. He is aware of the utter horror of enslavement for women when a city falls, but he has no reason to explore it in detail through a victim's own words, because his poem ends before Troy is ravaged and the girls, as he anticipates, are dragged away. If we had a poem by him called 'The Fall of Troy', he would certainly not have imposed silence on the girls and their manhandling. In the Iliad, the girls he leaves in silence are others, those in the brief back-stories which he sometimes attaches to individual heroes. They are not slaves, but there is a reason for their silence, one which is artistic, not sexist. Speeches in these flashbacks, whether by men or women, would greatly delay the main narrative.

Like the young brides, the women in these back-stories are not autonomous agents: they are evoked only for roles connected with men, mourning them or giving them 'bed and bedding', sex. If they are mothers, they are usually left unnamed and are mentioned only because they will grieve when they hear that their son has died far from home without the lament and the funeral which they would otherwise help to give him. Homer mentions them to heighten the pathos of a young man's death, a pattern which is then amplified in the eventual death of Hector, away from his wife and mother's arms. As usual he never specifies their age, but as they are mothers of young warriors they should be envisaged in their mid to late thirties.

In other back-stories, women are evoked for the encounters which caused them to conceive children in the first place. Sometimes they met a man out in the country and became pregnant by him, but in each case they were divine nymphs: they were not mortal girls out walking on their own.[24] Girls never wander freely beyond their city, except in the Odyssey to the banks of a river where young Nausicaa and her girl-friends go for the feminine task of washing clothes. When girls in the Iliad's back-stories were met and ravished by a god, it had to be inside their home city: it was while singing and dancing in honour of Artemis that lovely Polymele was noticed by Hermes, who then went upstairs to her bedroom and made love to her.[25] There is an unspoken rule to such encounters: sex with a god always makes a girl pregnant. If he has sex with her twice in one encounter, she has twins.

The most heavenly sex was Tyro's in the Odyssey, who fell in love with a river god and used to go out to his waters, but was ravished by Poseidon, who had taken on the river god's form. He caused a purple wave to arch over the two of them. and inside it he made divine love to her. Evidently he did so more than once, as he then told her she would have 'glorious children' in the plural, as indeed she did.[26] Heavenly sex did not diminish a girl's value for subsequent mortal suitors. Quite the opposite: countless *hedna* were later exchanged for divinely ravished Polymele by her future husband.[27]

Even so, the lives of such women were strictly constrained. Their dress reflected this fact: Homeric woman wears a big wrap-around robe, sometimes multicoloured and embroidered with figures. It is pinned together, not sewn: it falls into an overhang over her bosom; it is held in by a belt round her waist and it extends to the ground. On her head she wears a head veil, extending down at least to her shoulders: with it she could veil her face.[28] A Homeric woman never enters the battlefield. Her primary place is in the home and her main activities there are spinning and weaving, work, indeed, on which her own impressive style of dress depended. In the Greek world, textiles, mostly lost to us, were women's work, whereas metalworking, which sometimes survives, was the work of men. A woman could exercise some agency away from a loom, but only in ways related to her wifely status. Sex, birth and death involved her directly.

Phoenix —

In a remarkable speech, old Phoenix, Achilles' tutor, recalls how his father once took a slave-concubine, loved her and began to despise Phoenix's mother, who therefore came to Phoenix, went down on her knees in a formal supplication, an extreme act, and begged him to 'have sex first' with the slave girl 'so that she would hate the old man', as the ancients rightly understood the words, not 'be hateful to him' as modern scholars have sometimes misunderstood them.[29] Sex with an old man was abhorred in Greek myth and poetry: after sex with vigorous young Phoenix, the slave girl, Homer means, would loathe the prospect of sex with his elderly father. The wife's initiative enraged the old man, caused him to curse his son, and split the household.

So far from silencing all its women, the Iliad contains speeches by seven of them. Within a household, Homer gives one short speech to a slave, Hector's housekeeper. Women's space in the home was not a world wholly apart from a man: Hector had not hesitated to enter it in his house while looking for Andromache. Then, as he left it, he turned back to ask the slaves and his busy housekeeper. She explains that Andromache has gone out to the city wall 'like a maenad' in her frantic emotion, 'and the nurse is carrying the child'.[30] Her words are a mixture of due deference and emphatic direction, reorienting her owner's search for his wife. They build up the emotion of the meeting before it happens.

When a son or husband dies, women take the lead in an important public role: they lament him openly. When Achilles' immortal horses mourn, they merely lower their manes: women, by contrast, tear their hair, beat their breasts and even lacerate their faces. They weep and deliver heartfelt speeches, praising the dead man and lamenting their own predicament. In later Greek sources there are patterns to a lamentation, one singer leading a dirge, a woman then speaking a lament and then a group of women lamenting in answer as a refrain. Over dead Hector on his return to Troy, there is already such a pattern, but elsewhere Homer gives the lament of one woman and simply adds '*epi de stenachonto gynaikes*', a phrase used several times in the poem. It can mean 'the women lamented in reply', as if in an antiphonal refrain, but it need only mean 'the women lamented in addition'.

The one and only speech given to Briseis is a lament, even though she is still a slave-captive. When restored to Achilles, she delivers it over the dead Patroclus, whose body confronts her in Achilles' encampment.[31] In fine words she refers to her own loss of her husband and three brothers, all killed by Achilles when he sacked their city. She then recalls how Patroclus 'used to say', not once therefore, that he would make her Achilles' wife and that Achilles would prepare a wedding feast among the Myrmidons. It is the first we hear of this significant aspect of her life. She herself says nothing about the prospect of marriage with the very man who had killed her brothers and her former husband: she ends by lamenting Patroclus as 'ever kindly', her final words in the poem. The other slave girls with Achilles then join in the lament: '*epi de stenachonto gynaikes*', whether in addition or in answer. In a superb touch, Homer adds that 'Patroclus was the reason, but each one mourned her own sorrows'.[32] Once again he expresses so much by saying little. In barely two verses he presents the profound wretchedness of women enslaved in war. In performance I imagine him pausing briefly at these verses' end.

Women's other public role is service of the gods, exemplified by Trojan Theano. Mother of ten sons, one of whom was married, she was also bringing up the bastard son of her husband Antenor, wishing, we are told, to please him by doing so.[33] She was therefore in her mid to late thirties at the very least, but is nonetheless called fair-cheeked, a generic epithet for women. As Troy's priestess of Athena it is she who helps to fulfil Hector's orders to pray to Athena in her temple. Her role there is a public one, but is basically an extension of her role in a household. She opens the door of the temple, the goddess's house, no doubt with a key, the usual marker of a priestess in later Greek art, and then lays a robe on the knees of Athena's statue.[34] She is the keeper of the goddess's house, just as at home she is the keeper of her husband's, controlling the key to its storeroom and the women's robes within it. She then leads the

accompanying elderly women in a votive prayer to Athena, typically promising the goddess gifts if she will do what is requested.

The social context of Homer's women is not poetic fantasy. As
wives, spinners and weavers, mothers and priestesses, they are
consistently presented, in roles which match the roles of well-
born women in real life in Homer's own time. Even in the later
classical age, such women continued to serve as priestesses; in
public they wore head-veils; paintings on Greek pottery show
them spinning thread and weaving textiles: they are already shown
lamenting beside men's funerary couches on big Geometric pottery vessels, painted in the eighth century BC. If we knew details
of a grand betrothal, king Agamemnon of Kyme's daughter, perhaps, to king Midas, we would surely find *hedna* and so forth being
transferred. The main difference between Homeric poetry and
real life is that seduction by a god was impossible in the post-heroic
world, although several women claimed it happened to them: in a
fictitious letter, composed under the Roman empire, girls of Troy
were said on their wedding day to go down to the river Scamander, swim and call out, 'Scamander, take my virginity!', a useful
precaution, it might be added, if they happened to have lost it anyway before their wedding night.[35]

Virginia Woolf once claimed that 'Women have served all these
centuries as looking-glasses possessing the magic and delicious
power of reflecting the figure of man at twice its natural size.'[36]
When women in the Iliad lament, they indeed reflect the best of a
man, as a lament was also, typically, a eulogy of him. In the back-
stories, however, what women magnify is not a man's importance
but the pathos of a young man's death. Here, Andromache, Hecuba
and Helen come into their own, the three major women in the
poem. They are presented in ways that are not just enlarged reflections of the men around them. They are hallmarks of Homer's
empathy and emotional intelligence.

30.

Royal Mothers

Hecuba, Helen and Andromache appear in only four of the Iliad's twenty-four books. Even Helen, cause of the war, has nothing more to do to help the Iliad run its course. They are marginal to the plot, but without these royal mothers it would be much less poignant. After Homer, it is no coincidence that they went on to become great heroines of Athenian tragedies, three of which, by Euripides, survive and bear their names.

Each of the three was a foreign bride, married into the Trojan royal family. Material goods were exchanged with them. Following the usual procedures, Hector gave gifts, surely *hedna*, to Andromache's father. As Hecuba's father was greatly inferior to Priam, the suitor, it was surely he who gave Priam *dōra*, reversing the usual practice; Helen eloped, but with her too went treasure, stolen, however, from her husband's household. As usual, Homer never stops to present these women's ages, but there are clues that he was working with a consistent view of them. They span three ages of woman, and readers need to bear them in mind.

Hecuba, wife of Priam and mother of Hector, had no fewer than nineteen sons by Priam, all of them old enough to join the war and all, I believe, mentioned in the Iliad.[1] If she married at the customary age of fourteen or so, and if she bore children uninterruptedly in her fertile years, she would have had the last son in her mid to late thirties. When he was old enough to be fighting, she would be in her mid to late fifties at the very least.

In book 6, as Hector commands, she gathers elderly women in Troy to honour the goddess Athena. When she goes with them, her age, though unstated, enhances the scene: she is an appropriate

Elderly women in epic —

leader of the one and only appearance of elderly women as a group in a Greek epic.[2] Sixteen books later, as Hector hesitates whether to stay outside Troy and confront Achilles, she is on the city walls, and in tears she begs him to come inside. In a fine speech she implores him, 'dear child', dear 'offshoot whom I myself bore', and enhances her entreaty with a powerful gesture. Opening the fold of her dress with one hand, she holds up her breasts ('these') with the other, imploring Hector to respect and pity her who used to give him the breast to make him forget cares.[3] Translating the passage, Pope comments that 'it is a silent kind of Oratory, and prepares the Heart to listen by prepossessing the Eye in favour of the Speaker'. After nineteen children and at least forty years of adult existence, her breasts were long past their prime.

When she then saw that Hector had been killed out on the plain, she

> began to tear her hair, and cast the gleaming covering of her head
> Far from her, and shrieked loudly indeed when she saw her son.

Translating these lines Pope makes her 'rend her tresses, venerably grey': Homer never specifies greyness, but Pope correctly intuited her age.[4]

Hecuba, Helen and Andromache exemplify Homer's grasp of characterization through speeches, their own and others. Women's speech and its patterns have become keen subjects of study by sociologists and philologists: in the Iliad, some think, women protest, whereas men rebuke, replicating a pattern believed to prevail in women's speech in some of modernity's social groups.[5] More generally, men in the poem aim for fame, *kleos*, whereas women practise *goos*, lamentation. Nonetheless, their lamentations have been considered to address great issues of the poem with unexpected authority.[6] I will examine these claims, beginning with their relevance to Hecuba, the oldest of the three.

Hecuba speaks six times in the poem, protesting once, lamenting twice and urging and entreating three times. On three occasions she is presented as weeping, on two as tearing her hair and on two as shrieking loudly. She is never credited with dignity or the composed concern of older age.

Three of her speeches are paired with a man's, Priam's, two of them when he too is entreating and lamenting. They both stand on the wall of Troy, imploring their son Hector to come inside and avoid Achilles, but their pleas differ.[7] Four of Priam's thirty-eight verses dwell on the impact which Hector's safety or death will have on the Trojans, whereas the others address its impact on himself and his piteous old age. In her eight verses, Hecuba, baring her breasts, implores him to pity her and not to leave her and Andromache unable to lament his dead body if he dies beyond the city. Translating them, Pope remarked that 'this is a great beauty in the Poet, to make Priam a Father of his whole country; but to describe the Fondness of the Mother as prevailing over all other considerations, and to mention only that which chiefly affects her'. Here, too, Pope was correct.

When Hector is first seen to have been killed out on the plain, the two speak again.[8] Priam is the one who anticipates the plot, saying he will go out to plead with Achilles, and ending with a lament that Hector has not died in his arms and been mourned by them there. His speech, again, is twice as long as Hecuba's six verses, in which, again, she centres her grief on herself: 'My child, how wretched I am . . .' In neither of her speeches in this book has she addressed great issues of the poem as a whole, let alone with unexpected authority.

On three other occasions, once to Hector, twice to Priam, she speaks, urging a course of action. There is a common theme to these speeches too. When Hector visits her in Troy in book 6, she shows a mother's care: she takes his hand and offers him wine to pour a libation to Zeus, then to drink himself. Skilfully Homer lets her begin with a guess as to why he has returned, to pray to Zeus, a good guess but not a correct one, as he has come to pray to Athena.[9] In book 24 she speaks again. Her husband Priam has just been visited by Iris, messenger of the gods, and encouraged to go out to Achilles and ransom his son: Priam asks Hecuba what she thinks. He receives not a rebuke but a shriek of horror at the idea, followed by a fierce denunciation of Achilles. Hecuba tells Priam he must be mad and she execrates the man who has killed their son. There is no distinctive vocabulary in women's speech in the Iliad, but 'much of this could reflect colloquial idioms', Nicholas Richardson considers, commenting on these verses, 'there is frequent enjambment throughout', a word amplifying one verse's sense at the start of the next, and then a long sentence in conclusion, changing course as Hecuba speaks, 'reflecting her mixture of reasoning, pity and bitter hatred'.[10] Priam overrides her, telling her not to be 'a bird of ill-omen in his halls', a cue for what happens next. When Priam is about to go out nonetheless, Hecuba meets him with wine in a gold cup so that he can pour a libation to Zeus and request an omen, or otherwise 'I at least would not bid you to go'. He pours one and Zeus duly sends a favourable eagle, dark and broad-winged.[11]

Hecuba has indeed protested, but only in reply to her husband's request for her opinion: 'tell me this, how does it seem to your heart?' What unites her pleas to Hector and to Priam is not a comment on the great issues of the poem, but advice related to the gods, indeed an important sphere of upper class women's lives, as they served in public as the gods' priestesses. In her final lament over dead Hector, Hecuba speaks, now with steady dignity, about his dearness, again, to the gods: it is apparent even now, she says, in their preservation of his body with dew-like skin.[12]

Of the three women's, Hecuba's speeches are the ones nearest to a mirror, magnifying the qualities of the men closest to her. Nonetheless, there is variety and implicit characterization of her, making her more than a stereotypical woman bemoaning her plight.

In Helen, Hecuba's daughter-in-law, Homer faced a greater challenge, the most beautiful woman in the world, for whom the entire war had begun. He confronts it at length in book 3, when the Greek and Trojan armies march resoundingly out to battle and his listeners were surely expecting heroic fighting and bloodshed. Instead, he makes the troops put down their arms and prepare for a duel which could end the entire war. He then cuts back to Troy while holding the duel in abeyance and, there, he presents Helen in two sequences of supreme art.

When we first meet her she is weaving a double purple textile into which she is 'working many labours of the horse-taming Trojans and the bronze-tunicked Achaeans which they were suffering at the hand of Ares [god of war] because of her'. Weaving is women's usual work, but Homer uses it here to bring out Helen's sense of her predicament, one which will constantly characterize her words.[13] He never dwells on her life before her elopement. He simply calls her daughter of Zeus and lets her mention only once that she had had a daughter by her husband Menelaus, a little girl whom she had left when she eloped.[14] Unlike Hecuba, she never makes a mother's care central to what she says. The child, however, is an implicit clue to her age. She had spent a number of years before the war and then its nine years with Paris, now her husband: they had had no children. Once, in passing, Homer makes her say that twenty years in all had passed since she left her former home in Sparta, but a ten-year prelude to the ten-year war is hard to credit and he was surely not being exact there.[15] If Helen was fourteen when she first married, sixteen when she eloped with Paris and if ten years passed until the Greek army arrived to retake her, she would be about thirty-six years old at the Iliad's point in the war. Even if the twenty years are reduced to, say, twelve, she would be in her late twenties. Nonetheless she had a beauty which surpassed all others'.

How ever could Homer evoke it, a beauty which excelled even Briseis' likeness to golden Aphrodite? He does not give it specific adjectives. Like other women in the poem, Helen is long-robed, long-haired and, no doubt, white-armed, the arms being the one part of a woman's body which showed from her dress. Homer never calls her fair-haired, the assumption of many later authors. He never refers to her breasts, though they were so beautiful, later poets said, that on exposing them, she stopped her former husband, Menelaus, from running his sword through her during the sack of Troy. Centuries later, a temple at Lindos on the island of Rhodes claimed to have the very cup which Helen had dedicated there: it was shaped like one of her breasts, one of those smooth breast-shaped cups, therefore, which Greek male drinkers used to enjoy stroking and bringing to their lips during real-life parties.[16] The temple of Athena at Lindos was a treasure trove of legendary fakes.

When Helen is summoned from her weaving by the goddess Iris in disguise, she still does not speak. She goes out, veiled, with two attendant slave-maids as befitted an upper class lady. Still silent, she 'sheds a warm tear'. Iris has explained to her that she is to witness a duel between her former and present husbands and that she will be given to the victor, but Iris has also put sweet longing into her for her former husband, city and parents: as usual her daughter is not mentioned. Helen meets us, therefore, already in sadness, pining for what she once abandoned. She is totally unlike Auerbach's Homeric heroes, who, he considered, 'wake every morning as if it were the first day of their lives'. Repeatedly she wishes it was her last day and dwells on her past.

So far, Homer has given no impression of her exceptional beauty. In a marvellously contrived encounter, he does so through its impact on others. As Helen comes to Troy's gate, she passes two old men who are sitting there around Priam and his brothers: one is Antenor, the husband of Theano the priestess, the other is Oucalegon, 'Not-caring', who is mentioned only here in the poem.[17] They are elders of the people, too old to fight but still able to speak well in public 'like cicadas in the forest on a tree', a simile which neatly evokes these old emeriti's voices. 'Quietly', Homer tells us with exquisite imagination, they say to one another:

'It is no disgrace to the Trojans and the well-greaved Greeks
  To suffer such pains for so long for a woman such as her.
  She seems awesomely like the immortal goddesses when she
    is seen face to face.'

Obliquely, Homer says it all, the finest of compliments to female beauty. However, the old men add:

'Even though she is such a one, let her go back in the ships
And not be left as a trouble to our children.'

Helen has still not said a word in the poem. When she and her
slave girls pass on beyond the old men, Priam invites her to sit before
him, 'so that you may see your former husband and dear kin', he
says to her, and tell him about the Greek commanders whom they
can see on the battlefield beyond. In other heroic poems, far from
Homer's in place and time, scenes of recognition of enemy warriors also occur, but Homer makes this one supremely his own. It is
not just a clever device to deepen our awareness of the Greek leaders before the Iliad's fighting begins, nor is it simply a link between
the current stage of the war and events before it was reached: it
gives scope to emotions which Helen has begun to feel about her
past. As an adulteress and a cause of so much suffering, she would
have been blackened by a lesser poet. Instead, Homer activates our
pity for her by compounding our awareness of the sadness which
besets her. He leaves us to pick it up from what she says: his Helen
is a character who invites interpretation. We feel with her, not just
for her.

With exemplary kindness, Priam tells her that he does not hold
her responsible: the gods, rather, are to blame, who 'urged on me
the war of the Greeks with its many tears'. Others around him, his
brothers and the old men, were thinking quite otherwise: she was
an outsider, with a past, who had married into a foreign royal family
and had brought catastrophe on it, reinforcing the distaste with
which members of the royal household already regarded her. Priam
differs, and resets the way we respond to her.[18] She addresses him,
her elderly father-in-law, as a figure of awe, well catching that relationship's blend of distance and intimacy, bridged with contrived
affinity.

In response to Priam's first question about a Greek leader on the
plain below, Helen begins by telling him how 'death, though grim,
should have pleased her' when she followed Paris and abandoned
her former bedchamber and the lovely companionship of the girls

of her own age and, mentioned here only, her daughter too. 'But this did not happen, and for that I have pined away, weeping.'[19] Unhappiness, we learn, has long been her hallmark, compounded by regret. When Priam asks her in successive questions the identity of three of the Greeks who are visible beyond, each provokes an answer in which Menelaus, her former husband, is recalled. Her past, we realize, is present throughout the scene, and she concludes it with a query herself, one about Castor and Pollux, her twin brothers. She cannot see them and wonders if they are avoiding the battle out of fear for all the shame and insults which attach to her. She is unaware that they have died far away in Sparta. Her dialogue with Priam begins with her past and present sadness and evokes the hostility others feel for her. It ends with the prospect of yet more sadness, known to us but not to her.

On one reading of these verses, Priam's asking her about Agamemnon was itself artful: the old man surely recognized him from afar, but wanted to make Helen recall her former brother-in-law, as she duly did.[20] That reading is not excluded by the text: in reply Helen indeed looks back on her past as if it was another world and on Agamemnon as her brother-in-law 'if he [or 'it'] was ever really so'.[21]

Before the duel begins between her past and present husbands, she returns to her room in Troy. She remains there while Aphrodite miraculously saves Paris from death and comes to fetch her to him. The goddess enters, disguised as an elderly slave woman, an extreme reversal of a type more frequent in the Odyssey: she speaks of how Paris is summoning Helen to him while waiting in the bedroom in his full beauty and his gleaming robes. 'So she spoke, and stirred Helen's heart in her breast', not her anger, as some have misread it, but her feelings.[22] Helen is wretched in the plight which she has brought on herself, but her heart can still be stirred for the man for whom she ran away. Homer has implied enough for listeners to realize it without further emphasis.

In a disdainful speech, she reproaches Aphrodite, whose beauty she has just recognized, taunting her as to whether she is deceiving her and planning to take her off to yet another man in another part of western Asia. As for Paris in his bedroom, she tells Aphrodite to go there herself and always fuss about him and guard him and 'call him her bed-mate, or he call you his slave': hers is the poem's only use of the blunt word for slave girl, *doulē*.[23] They are extremely scornful words to address to a goddess and are not at all inhibited by feminine modesty: Helen most certainly utters rebukes, refuting a modern stereotype of feminine gendered speech.[24] She speaks sarcastically.

Herself, she will not follow and go to bed with Paris: that is an action, she says, which the women of Troy would not approve. Presumably she thinks so because her former husband, Menelaus, has won the duel and is about to reclaim her, or so she unknowingly assumes. In reply, Aphrodite turns on her, threatening to show her a hatred as great as the love she has hitherto borne her. Like the gods and goddesses in Greek tragedy, Aphrodite is destructive when crossed, 'and Helen was afraid'. Wrapped in her shining robe she goes with her, unnoticed by the Trojan women, 'and the goddess was leading', three words in Greek which imply so much more than they state.[25]

In the bedroom Aphrodite sets her on a chair before Paris, but Helen begins by rebuking and berating him too. 'You have come from the war: how you ought to have died there', scorning his return from the fighting when he should have been 'killed by a mighty man, who was once my husband'. Again she becomes sarcastic: Paris used to say that he was mightier with spear and sword, so 'go then and challenge him to fight again . . . but . . .' But . . . Homer surely paused here when performing, in the hexameter's penultimate foot.[26] After her 'but', Helen changes tack and bids Paris to do no such thing, but to stop, in case he might be killed. She cannot let that happen: she has eloped with a feckless, shameless bounder, and yet . . . she does not really wish him dead. Aphrodite has enhanced her sexual attraction, and so Paris declares he has never felt such desire for her, not even when he first sailed with her from Sparta and stopped on Rocky island, Kranae, to have sex with her. So he leads the way to bed, 'and with him followed his wife'.[27] Previously she had followed imperious Aphrodite: now she follows her husband to make love.

Homer has brilliantly presented her inconsistency, reviling a man she despises, wishing she was dead, 'and yet . . .' she cannot resist him. In each of her emotional reactions, she has been roused by a goddess, but the responses are her own, those of a woman who has eloped, regretted it and still regrets it, but cannot reject the man with whom she ran away. She is the first inconsistent lady in poetry, beautifully imagined and brought to life.

Three books later, when Hector returns to Troy, he finds Helen with Paris in Paris' house, overseeing the slave girls' fine and splendid works, the weaving, no doubt, of yet more textiles.[28] She ends by inviting him to sit beside her, an offer he declines, tempting though it surely seemed. First, the offer of wine from his mother Hecuba, now the offer of a seat beside lovely Helen, each of the attempts to detain him enhances our sense of Hector's heroic resolve. Speaking to him, Helen laments yet again the fact that she was ever born and her current husband's shamelessness and folly. She laments her own role, 'bitch that I am, deviser of evil', accepting responsibility for her elopement. She ends by referring to her and Paris' role as subjects of song for future generations, as 'Zeus has laid an evil destiny upon us'.[29] In the plot of the Iliad, Helen, cause of the war, has little more to do, but Homer makes her remind us that she will remain a celebrity nonetheless, the enduring subject of poetry, not least his own.

In her speeches Helen is her own severest critic: she even calls herself a chilling bitch. She is not torn by guilt: she is beset, like the male heroes, by shame. In book 2, old Nestor had urged the Greek warriors not to return home until they had requited 'Helen's strivings and miseries'.[30] These miseries are not the miseries 'of' Helen inside Troy, because the Greeks, outside it, could not know of her feelings there: they are their own sorrows 'on account of' Helen, just as she herself goes on to reiterate in person. In the final book, when she laments Hector's death, she expresses yet again a wish to have died before eloping to Troy. This repeated regret at being alive would make her a one-dimensional person, but Homer has far greater art.

At the very end of the poem, when she laments over the dead Hector's body, she recalls his kindness to her, a kindness like Priam's, she repeats, but then she concludes by lamenting for herself, alone now with 'nobody else in broad Troy who is gentle and kind to me, but all of them shudder at me . . .'[31] Like Hecuba's lament, hers centres not on great issues, but on herself. The words pick up her meeting with Priam far back in book 3, but here they have a specially chilling power. They are her last words in the poem, the last to be spoken by a Greek.

The island, Kranae, where Paris and Helen had sex on the rocks, has been claimed by many candidates since, most recently by Marathonisi, a Fennel-Island, while it was still detached from the Maniot coast of Sparta, as if 'that momentous and incendiary honeymoon began among whispering fennel'.[32] The first words spoken to Helen and her last words in lament have had memorable afterlives too. In the eleventh century AD, the Byzantine emperor, Constantine IX, brought a new foreign mistress to his indignant court at Constantinople, a girl from the faraway Caucasus. As she processed with him in the city's hippodrome, a cultured Greek courtier repeated the words of Homer's old men, 'It is no disgrace . . .', and eased the tension of her arrival. She realized their impact, but as an ignorant outsider had to ask him what they meant.[33]

In that pugnacious story of public schooling, *Tom Brown's Schooldays*, set at Rugby school in the 1830s, Thomas Hughes, the author, responds finely to the force of Helen's last words: he honours their 'exquisite pathos . . . the most touching thing in Homer, perhaps in all profane poetry'.[34] Hard-working little George Arthur, thirteen years old and a boy from faraway Devon, is told to translate these lines in class, beyond the point to which his lazier classmates have prepared. Yet, he cannot continue, as he is reduced to tears by verses which come home to him so powerfully, a boy whom the bigger, rougher boys revile.

Neither Hecuba nor Helen appeals to honour, or *timē*, that value of the male heroes. Nor do they talk of courage. Helen can indeed speak as a reflecting mirror, but so far from magnifying Paris she rebukes and belittles him as an item of shame and disgrace. What she most reflects is the pathos of her own situation. In Andromache, Homer was to invest even more of this pathos, expressed in three of the Iliad's finest books.

In book 22, Andromache, too, is weaving a double purple robe, but in her case she is working into it many *throna*, a word which later Greek poets took to mean flowers, but which may have meant animals, the meaning which it was later known to have had in Thessalian dialect.[35] In her fine book *The War That Killed Achilles*, Caroline Alexander remarks that 'the remoteness of this inner world of spinning and weaving from the rending and tearing that is the work of war is also a symptom of its powerlessness'.[36] Nonetheless, the two women's activity presents them with a depth which is implied, not stated. By hers, Helen expresses a major theme even before we hear her speak: her sense of her own responsibility for the suffering in the war. By hers, Andromache shows something quite different, her obedience to her husband Hector's final words to her. Sixteen books earlier, at the end of the harrowing scene of their parting, he had told her to 'go back home and busy yourself with your work, the loom and the distaff'.[37] So indeed she has, but when we hear of her busied there, the context is even more agonizing: she is unaware that her husband has just been killed outside Troy's walls. Powerlessness gives overwhelming power to the poem here.

At the time, Andromache was supervising a bath for Hector on his return from battle, unaware that he had remained alone outside the walls. When a cry of grief sounds, her worst fears are aroused. On going up to the battlements she sees her husband dead, being dragged across the plain behind Achilles' chariot. She faints, throwing away all of her shining headdress, which is specified here only in the poem with four constituent parts: the final one is the *krēdemnon*, surely the head-veil, which golden Aphrodite had given her on the very day when Hector took her from her father's halls as his bride.[38] As so often, a Homeric object enhances pathos.

When Andromache recovers, she delivers a superb speech, ranging from her and Hector's shared misery to the future which awaits their little boy Astyanax, whom she addresses, twice, by name. She concludes with Hector's fine clothes, such a contrast now to his body, which is a prey for 'writhing worms, naked' beyond her care. As she cannot use them for his last rites, she will collect them and burn them, she says, on a blazing fire to give him glory before the Trojans and Trojan women.[39]

Young widows still burn their husband's clothes, to mark tragic finality, and help them move on without painful reminders of their loss. Andromache's reasons for doing so are different, but at every level her speech is overwhelming. Two books later, when Hector's body is finally brought back to Troy, she cradles its head in her hands and laments again. Trained male singers have begun the dirge and the women have answered, but hers is the first solo voice to be heard. She uses at least twelve once-only words, intensifying her lament. She anticipates Troy's fall, inevitable in Hector's absence, and with it the grim aftermath for little Astyanax and especially herself, to whom 'you did not reach your hands while dying on the bed nor speak to me any meaningful word, which I would have recalled night and day while shedding tears'.[40] The bereaved still crave and cherish one.

Andromache is much younger than Hecuba and younger, even, than Helen. Homer never gives her age, but she and Hector have just one child, their son who is still a baby. She was already in Troy, married to Hector, when Achilles sacked her home city and killed her father and brothers. Homer never says in which year of the war that foray had occurred, but sixteen to eighteen is an apt age at which to imagine her. Young though she is, her final laments pick up what has gone before. Across an interval of eighteen books, they evoke her last encounter with Hector by Troy's city gate, the supreme episode of book 6.

For more than a hundred verses, Homer sustained that meeting with exceptional poignancy.[41] It begins with Andromache running to meet Hector, with the nurse carrying their son 'like a fair star'. For the only time in the poem, Hector smiles, 'looking at his son in

345

silence', one of Homer's most powerful expressions of so much so briefly. Meanwhile Andromache, in tears, takes his hand. She speaks to him of her utter dependence on him now that all her family has been killed by Achilles: Hector, she says, is her father, mother, brother and husband. There is a force to her predicament beyond anything in Helen's, whose kin from her two marriages are all alive. Again, the focus of a woman's speech is herself and her predicament. Like Helen she expresses it by relating past facts to the present and looking ahead to an even bleaker future.

Hector replies in a magnificent speech which rises to a climax as he asserts he would wish to be buried beneath the earth before he ever saw her dragged away into slavery: the sight would pain him more than the enslaving of his parents and the death of all his kin. It might seem an impossible speech to follow, but with consummate skill Homer makes him reach for his baby son: the little boy shrinks back to his nurse's bosom, distressed at the sight of his father. He is afraid of the bronze and the horse-hair plume of his helmet. Taking it off, Hector laughs, and so, in her own way, does Andromache: after kissing his son and stroking him Hector prays for him to the gods. He then gives the baby to his mother and takes her hand too, the first time in their meeting that he has touched her of his own accord. He pities her, that crucial emotion for a hero, and speaks his last words to her, about the impossibility of a man escaping his destiny and the need for her to return to work at her loom. She does so, but takes our hearts with her: 'turning and turning again, she sheds warm tears as she goes'.[42] It is a devastating scene, and yet she caps it. Back in their house she starts the lament with her slave girls 'and so they lamented Hector in his own house while still alive'. Sixteen books before his death, she already senses that he will never return to her again.

Almost any discussion of this meeting is bound to fall short of its power for listeners and readers. In 1959, however, the great Homeric critic Wolfgang Schadewaldt published an essay which rose to the challenge, beginning from the correct assessment that it is not that 'Homer's epic resembles a continuous stream, without beginning or end', as if it was an impersonal tradition, linked by 'and then' episodes. It is 'as carefully constructed, as full of tension, as consciously articulated as it could be. In particular Homer creates movement, action: he *directs* his characters'; he 'saves words . . . instead of them he uses restrained gestures', exactly, I believe, as he did in person while performing the poem to its listeners.[43]

Schadewaldt's essay finely presents both the movement towards the meeting of Hector and Andromache in the previous scenes of book 6 and its abiding significance for what will follow in the next eighteen. The meeting enhances Hector as a person, but it is not just a looking-glass to magnify him: through the lens of a wife and child it shows what is at stake in the entire fight for Troy. It strongly implies that Hector's death in battle is now inevitable, though he does not yet know when or how it will occur. It is a first sounding of themes which Andromache's speeches of mourning will sound in books 22 and 24.

Two points in it have puzzled ancient and modern readers. Andromache's first speech to Hector includes some sudden tactical advice, that the Greeks, she says, will try yet again to attack by the fig tree below the wall: he should station the army there, she tells him, and himself remain on the wall inside the city. From Aristarchus onwards, short-sighted critics have deleted these verses as a later insertion.[44] They are not: they are essential to Homer's presentation of her anxious desire. She offers this advice in the hope of retaining Hector inside the walls. He does not even consider it when he replies.

When he takes his son and prays for him, he asks Zeus and the other gods that one day his son may rule in might over the Trojans, and that someone may say he is far better than his father as he returns from battle: 'may he bring bloody spoils, having killed an enemy, and may his mother rejoice in her heart'. This wish has been read as a sign of the gap between Hector's horizons and those of his wife, someone whom the poem never presents as rejoicing in war. Indeed she begs Hector to remain and tells him that 'your might will be the death of you', but just as Helen has shown with Paris, Andromache does not want her man to stay shamefully away from it without reason. In the Iliad 'what a woman wants in a man is the resolution to resist her and go out among the flying spears'.[45] Andromache would wish the same for her son, who would indeed cause her to rejoice if he returned, a grown man, with the spoils of an enemy he had killed in battle.

After his prayer, Hector places his son in his wife's arms and as she receives him in her fragrant bosom, she is 'laughing through her tears'.[46] This heartfelt detail surely moved Homer's listeners to tears just as it still moves us. Here too I believe Homer paused in performance, after these first two words in the hexameter. Once again, he expresses the complexity in a woman's response, tears and laughter together. Empathy and observation convey supreme pathos in two abiding words. 'And her husband noticed, and pitied her', three words in Greek which also say so much: pity was the very emotion Andromache had solicited when she first spoke.

In late summer 44 BC, nearly six months after the murder of Julius Caesar, Brutus, one of the murderers, and his wife Porcia parted in southern Italy, he to go east, she to return to Rome. She was trying to conceal her extreme distress, but a 'painting betrayed her', so Brutus' biographer, Plutarch, well puts it: he presents a story which he knew from a book written later by Porcia's son.[47] The painting was one of Andromache taking her baby from Hector, 'with her gaze, however, fixed on her husband'. When Porcia saw it, she burst into tears and 'visited it many times a day, weeping before it'. Yet she was the daughter of Cato, the most austere Stoic, a woman who would later swallow burning coals to kill herself when she heard the news of her husband's death.

In the Odyssey, the range of female characters is wider than in the Iliad, from Penelope, loyal to her absent husband, to young Nausicaa, beginning to dream of marriage. It shows a sense of what have been called 'women's inscrutable hearts' and a 'mysteriousness which the male characters fail to master'.[48] Yet, the Iliad's women had already intimated as much, whether in Helen's sudden 'but . . .' or in Andromache's laughing through her tears. So far as they are mirrors, they reflect and magnify far more than the figures of men.

31.

The Natural World

As these women exemplify, a combination of observation and empathy runs through the poem, an important part of its power. They extend into its setting, what we now call the natural world. Like the world of women, it is a foil to the main narrative, but it too enhances its effect. Once again I will first survey this parallel world's scope and content and then, in the following chapter, turn to Homer's poetic use of it.

The 'natural' world is treated in two different ways. Homer's main narrative is extremely sparing with details of it: 'nothing is less in the Homeric manner', Jasper Griffin has well remarked, 'than to dilate upon lifelike details for their own sake'.[1] They abound, however, in his similes, the comparisons which run through the poem, especially through the fighting on its longest day. Unlike the main narrative, they present animals, plants and, to us, natural forces. They are supreme distinctions of the Iliad, about 340 in all, eight times as many as those in the Odyssey, and would suffice, if combined, to fill an average book and a half of the poem. Their content, form and distribution bring us particularly close to Homer's genius.

The idea of Nature as an entity with its own patterns and regularities was first formulated by Greek philosophers in the sixth century BC. In its absence Homer presents personalized winds who feast in each other's faraway halls and are solicited with prayers and libations.[2] River gods exist in local rivers and receive vows and prayers too: one of them, Scamander, appears to Achilles in the form of a man, speaks to him and fights him by flooding the plain before Troy. When mothers are said to have borne children 'by' a river, some of them had given birth beside its banks, but others had conceived the child by the river god. This sort of fathering was not just a notion confined to poetry. Children named after rivers continue to be traceable for many centuries in ancient Greek patterns of personal naming.[3]

These ways of looking at what are, to us, natural items might have enhanced their use for pathos, a major quality of the poem. Austerely, Homer never presents the pathetic fallacy that the natural world is sympathizing with the human. Significantly, it reacts only to divine passers-by, whether Poseidon's marvellous progress above the surface of the sea off Lemnos or the parting of the waves around Thetis and the sea nymphs as they come up from the deep to commiserate with Achilles. When the earth quakes and the very roots of Mount Ida shake as the gods enter the battle in book 20, they are impelled to do so by Poseidon. In book 1, by contrast, lovely Briseis is escorted unwillingly along the seashore and Achilles weeps beside it, but as they are mortals, the waves never respond to their emotion.

Homer never fills in details of the coastline. The Iliad differs fundamentally here from the Odyssey, a poem with evocative seascapes, woods and caves. His main narrative presents wildlife very selectively. There are no snakes on the killing field, no rats at work among the dead bodies and not a trace of a fox, even at night. There are no butterflies, though artists have often used them as symbols of the soul or of freedom. There is no birdsong, either, not even a plaintive nightingale. As battle begins in book 2 the troops come out onto a 'flowery meadow', but flowers are never specified or mentioned again.[4] Around Troy, the plains are still scarlet with poppies in early summer, but Homer's narrative never refers to them, not even as a comparison to the blood-red stains of the dead.

In the Iliad, Homer's narrative never describes the weather unless Zeus sends a sudden hazard, rainbows being one. In the biblical book of Genesis, God sets a post-diluvian rainbow in the sky as a 'token of a covenant between him and the earth'. Homeric rainbows are signs of storms and troubles.[5] The father of gods and men did not go in for pacts, let alone with wretched mortals.

The Manas epic is arrestingly different. In its great funeral competitions, the horses parade and a rainstorm besets them, just as in the Kirghiz uplands it still can. 'The mountainsides were all covered with hail; a shimmering haze arose, and the sky blackened in the west, thundering and casting beams of bronze light . . . Eight times the flood from the skies turned to hail and back to drizzle: then an immense blizzard pressed down . . .' The storm heightens the tension of the horses' preparation for the race.

It is not that Homer was blind to such things, as his trees and birds show. He alludes correctly to the great height of fir trees and the smooth trunks of cornels. He mentions the oak, the pine and the aspen poplar. In a fine simile he refers to high-crested oaks on the mountains, 'fixed with extending roots' against the force of the winds, as indeed they remain fixed still on some of Asia's stoniest, driest slopes. By riverbanks he places willows as well as elms and ash. He knows that cardinal fact of Greek and Turkish treescapes, that a poplar or a plane tree will grow best beside a stream or river.[6] These trees are not described in recurring noun-and-adjective phrases, inherited from previous poets: they may indeed be Homer's own choices. He is aware of some very particular qualities, the cedar-like scent of a juniper's wood or the rounded hardness of the wood of a box tree, an apt choice indeed for the rounded yoke on king Priam's mules. His narrative also takes us where Greek poets of the next two centuries never follow, into forests, where warriors, twice, fell trees in order to cremate their dead.[7]

Birds are also distinguished accurately. In traditional, repeated phrases in the narrative, vultures are said to devour the dead, but some of them prey on live items and are distinguished by a separate Greek word meaning 'goat vultures'. They are bearded vultures, therefore, our lammergeiers.[8] Birds are the only items in, to us, the natural world which play individualized roles in the plot, but in the narrative such roles are always related to the gods. Birds are intermediaries between the earth and the sky, and so they appear when gods wish to send messages or are on the move. A travelling divinity is not only like a bird: sometimes one assumes a bird's convenient

shape and it is apt for Homer to specify it.[9] When divine Sleep flies
and hides high up in a tree, he is said to be like a bird which has two
names, both unusual, one among the gods and the other among
humans.[10] Sleep has taken on the appearance of this bird in order to
conceal himself, surely therefore an owl, a Scops' owl being the
neatest match as the dark rings round its eyes give it a decidedly
sleepy look. Homer, I think, had noticed it.

Elsewhere birds feature in the main narrative because Zeus sends
them as omens. Expert bird-interpreters exist, but never ask the
gods for such signs: they appear nonetheless, hinting obliquely at
the future. Among them, different types of eagle are distinguished,
with sufficient detail for us, not Homer, to give them precise names.
One flies into view with a snake between its talons but drops it
when the snake turns and bites it, probably a Bonelli's eagle, indeed
a snake-catcher.[11] When old Priam prepares for his perilous journey
to Achilles, he prays to Zeus for a sign, for 'a bird, the swift messenger, the one dearest to you of birds, whose strength is greatest'.
Zeus duly sends an eagle, the apex of the avian hierarchy, 'the surest
of winged birds' that an omen will be fulfilled: it is a *morphnos*
hunter, 'which men also call *perknos*'. These adjectives made the
bird specific for Homer's listeners, but as they occur nowhere else in
the poem, it is hard for us to be sure of their meaning. The bird's
wings 'spread on either side of its body' and are evoked in a fine
comparison: they are 'as wide as the door of a high roofed chamber,
one of a rich man, fitted well with bolts'.[12] At this crucial point in
the poem, Homer has a particular type of bird in mind. A lesser
spotted eagle has been suggested, despite the white marks on its
upper wings and rump, or even a dark Verrieux eagle, an imposing
bird but not now found in Greek or Trojan territory. A golden eagle
is the likeliest candidate, dark to a viewer, if *perknos* really means
dark, as the gold on its neck is not visible from below. Its wingspan
is indeed awesome, more than two metres across, a third as wide
again as a spotted eagle's.

These details of birds and trees show that despite the austere
setting of his narrative Homer was 'a man who used to notice

such things', as Hardy's fine poem 'Afterwards' says of persons alert to nature. He stands first in the list of such poets, whether Shakespeare or D. H. Lawrence, Sappho or Elizabeth Bishop. Poetry does not depend on this alertness, but in similes it is indeed relevant. 'As when . . .': if Homer's many comparisons were fictional or false, they might sound beguiling, like the faraway geography in some of Milton's similes, but they would fail in their main purpose. They would not help their hearers to pin down the item being compared.

How original are they? Some of them are very brief, 'like fire' or 'like a lion'. Similes of this length were probably traditional before Homer composed. They occur in older texts known in languages to the east of him, from Egypt to Babylon, but Greek poets did not have to derive them from these prototypes: they occur in many other heroic poems which were wholly unaware of Greek or Near Eastern parallels. In the long episode of the funeral feast and games, dictated in the 1920s by an expert singer of the Manas poem, troops muster like billowing waves and Muslim warriors are like wolves, dividing and attacking a flock of sheep when they fall on their heathen enemies. Manas compares himself to a tall poplar, a 'mighty poplar with golden branches rising up to the sky'. These similes occur independently in the Iliad too, but not the Manas poem's comparison of the ears of a fine racehorse to parrots perched in a garden or the nose of a giant warrior to a landslide on a mountain slope. In an earlier version of another episode, a speaker wishes to exalt the girls who are waiting in nearby yurts: he describes them

> With flesh whiter than snow when snow falls on snow,
> With cheeks redder than blood when blood drops on snow,
> Wriggling like musk-deer, squealing like puppies,
> Wantoning like lynxes, languishing in speech.

Who could resist them, even if 'their teeth, large as shovels, show white when they smile'?[13]

Unlike the Manas singers, Homer runs similes over several verses, a prolongation which I like to think was his poetic innovation. His example was then imitated by later Greek poets and philosophers and changed the shape of European epic, influencing Virgil and Dante, Milton and Matthew Arnold. Similes of such length do not feature in oral heroic poems elsewhere, but even so they were not unique to Homer: in his lifetime they were being used by writers of prose. In the mid eighth century BC, both long and short similes were exploited, quite independently, by prophets in northern Israel. 'I will be unto Ephraim as a lion and as a young lion to the house of Judah', says God, at least according to the prophet Hosea: lions abound in Homeric similes, but are never used by Zeus as a comparison with himself. In an especially fine prose simile, Hosea compares the unfaithful hearts of the Israelites to 'an oven heated by the baker; he ceases to stir the fire from the kneading of the dough until its leavening': like its embers meanwhile, the Israelites' hearts lie smouldering. 'The baker sleeps all night, but then in the morning his oven burns as a flaming fire': the Israelites' adulterous hearts burn likewise when they are fired up by a surge of lust.[14] Homer never heard of his contemporary Hosea, that victim of a self-inflicted marriage to a harlot, but he would have much enjoyed his gift for vivid comparisons to illuminate feelings and dispositions.

Like Hosea, Homer can dramatize a movement of the mind by comparing it with the world outside it. Memorably, Nestor hesitates between two courses of action like a swell on the sea which 'forebodes the swift paths of shrill winds' and is waiting to break in one direction or another 'until a decisive blast is sent by Zeus'.[15] Homer does not stop there: unlike Hosea he uses a state of mind to illuminate an event in the world. In a superb comparison, the goddess Hera, flying sideways from Olympus to Mount Ida, is said to move as quickly as 'a thought flashes in the mind of a man who has travelled far: he thinks "I wish I was here, no, I wish I was there . . ."' Brief comparisons to a thought may have been conventional, but a comparison to thoughts as subtle as these is surely Homer's innovation.[16] He is wonderfully alert to our inner life. In Achilles' final pursuit, when Hector tries to run back to the safety of Troy, Achilles keeps on anticipating him and forcing him back onto the plain:

> Just as in a dream a man cannot catch someone who flees
>   before him,
> one unable to escape altogether, the other to pursue,
> so Achilles could not overtake Hector on foot, but neither
>   could Hector escape.[17]

This brilliant simile is both exactly matched to the situation and psychologically true to a dreamer's experience.

Other similes fasten on everyday actions of children, a striking contrast to the poem's main theatre of battle. As each of them is used only once in the Iliad, they are highly likely to be Homer's own, results of that empathetic eye which also picked on Hector's baby son shying away from the plume of his father's helmet. Achilles' Myrmidons swarm out to battle like wasps which boys, in their foolishness, provoke from a nest beside a road, 'always chivvying them'.[18] When Apollo breaks down the Greeks' wall in front of their ships, he does so 'with ease', like

> a child with sand near the sea
> who whenever he has made it into playthings in his childishness
> then confounds it again playing with his hands and feet.[19]

A comparison between the action of a god and the action of a child at play on a sandy beach might seem forced, but this one brings out, not the arbitrariness, but the extreme ease of the god's demolition.

Even a little girl can make a point. When Achilles sees Patroclus shedding tears after discovering the grim plight of the Greek leaders, he compares his crying to a little girl's who

> runs beside her mother and demands to be picked up,
> clutching at her mother's robe, and holds her back as she presses on
> and in tears looks up at her until she takes her up.[20]

This superbly observed simile relates to Patroclus' weeping, not to any girlish role in the two heroes' love.

Similes of sandcastles or a dreamer's nightmare attach us to a long continuity, one which stretches back at least 2700 years. Then too, we realize with awe, people behaved or felt just as we do, and Homer had noticed it exactly. He is not elusive here, as if he was an idea or a tradition or a blend of poets who composed over many centuries. He is an accessible individual, noticing and appreciating such things. His comparisons gain extra power for us as a result. For his first listeners they had no such retrospective force.

Although Homer's similes are set in the present, they describe events or actions which might recur at any time. Only one simile, albeit very famous, refers to a prolonged process, the annual growth, fall and regrowth of leaves on the trees.[21] Otherwise they refer to a precise incident or moment. As for space, many are set in the mountains or in remote places, far from the battlefield, but some of the most striking are set in domesticated settings, a sleeping child watched by its mother or a poor woman at work with threads and wool.[22] Whether far away or domestic, they centre on persons and places which are marginal to the poem's main narrative.

Several of them evoke a garden or an orchard and a person caring for it. When Achilles tries to escape from the flooding river Scamander he is compared to a gardener who goes to guide a watercourse for his plants and garden beds and clears obstructions from its channel with a mattock, but is then overtaken by the rush of water which is released down the hillside.[23] When the fiery god Hephaestus dries up Scamander's flood by setting the river-plain on fire, the effect is compared to a north wind in autumn which is drying a newly watered orchard, much to the delight of the man who tends or rakes it. When Thetis refers to her upbringing of young Achilles, she compares her care for him to care for a tree in a 'rich corner of cultivated ground' and his growth to the growth of a sapling.[24] In 1936, a scholarly reader, Edward Forster, added other famous passages in the Odyssey and concluded that Homer's 'attitude towards plant-life is that of the gardener rather than the lover of wild nature'.[25]

Both can coexist in one and the same simile, but the gardener's work is at its empathetic centre. When Menelaus kills Trojan Euphorbus, he is compared to a wind 'with a mighty swirl' which tears from a ditch the young olive which a man has been tending near water in a lonely place, where it has quivered in the breeze and put out white flowers. Menelaus' wild force is awesome, as the comparison emphasizes, but the carefully tended white-flowering olive heightens the pathos of Euphorbus' death.[26]

Despite Homer's evocations of gardening, specific flowers, apart from a poppy, never feature in similes. There are no roses or narcissi, no hyacinths or violets, the staple flowers of later Greek poets. Even the poppy has caused problems for close readers. It is 'in a garden and heavy with seed and spring rains' and is compared with the head of the dying young Gorgythion, but a stem which supports a poppy's seed head never falls sideways like Gorgythion's head: it is rigid and it sways, at most, in a rainstorm.[27] However, the simile is beautifully observed, because Homer is envisaging, not a poppy's stem, but its petalled flower. Whether it was a corn poppy, an intruder from the fields, or an opium poppy, cultivated for seeds or juice, the petals of either variety turn to one side in rain, forming a fragile right angle with the unbowed stem. It is a very short-lived effect, missed by all but the sharpest observers, of whom Homer, manifestly, was one. Later in the poem, when Peneleos spears the severed head of Trojan Ilioneus, he holds it on high like a poppy head. The comparison is another fine one, because a poppy's rounded seed head, shorn of petals, indeed resembles a rounded human head and top knot.[28]

The tamed settings of gardens, orchards and those who care for them are arresting items for a poet to have chosen to set beside a narrative of battle and loss. Notably, the settings of similes are never battles and their protagonists are never warriors. However, they are not idyllic or a version of pastoral. Winds, storms and floods beset most of their gardens and orchards. With fire or with predatory wildlife those forces are prominent, too, in the many similes set in forests or farmsteads or among mountains: in similes at sea, waves swell and pound the shore. In these similes, the majority, there are constant battles, most of which men are losing, a vivid comparison for the battle in the main narrative.

They are not lyrical interludes. In Greek tragedies, songs by the chorus sometimes evoke a faraway other world, spatially and tonally the very opposite to the play's action, to which the singer may even wish to be transported. These songs are profoundly un-Homeric: no such wish to escape is expressed or encouraged by any simile in the Iliad. In no way are they wistful. In Romania's famous oral poem, the Mioritza, the 'magic lay, and lies', wrote Patrick Leigh Fermor, who knew it by heart, 'in its linking together of directness and the tragic sense, its capture of the isolated feeling that surrounds shepherds and the forlorn exaltation that haunts their steep grazing and forests'.[29] There is no such tragic sense in the similes which Homer sets in wild nature, not even when shepherds are part of them.

Comparisons with winds or forest fires, surging rivers or fierce animals, were surely ones which previous hexameter-poets had exploited, but the longer ones in the Iliad are more likely to be Homer's own, especially if they contain details which he uses only once. Those which involve animals are particularly telling.

In his similes, he works with an implicit animal hierarchy: first I will set it out and then the degree of observation on which it rests. He does not divide the animal world about him into the noble and ignoble: he draws comparisons with buzzing flies no less than with lordly lions. He even adduces locusts who fly from fire into the safety of a river, as indeed they do. Flies, wasps, snakes or worms have no demeaning epithets. The exceptions are dogs. To call a hero a dog is an insult, one which Helen applies to herself, calling herself a bitch. Gods and goddesses use it too, Zeus about his wife Hera, and Hera, in turn, about her stepdaughter Artemis. Whereas flies are simply flies, a dog-fly is a special Homeric insult, combining the boldness of a fly with a dog's shamelessness. Hera even applies it to Aphrodite goddess of sex and love.[30]

This lowly rating may seem surprising. Dogs guard flocks and farms and, unlike horses, join bravely with men in hunts. Sometimes they share their masters' houses and even their food: Achilles

has nine dogs as his table companions and sets two of them, already
killed by him, as his crowning offering on Patroclus' pyre. The crucial point, once again, is that dogs scavenge, eating dead flesh.[31] On
the battlefield they even eat the flesh of dead warriors. They social-
ize with humans, but may end up eating them, a double role which
helps to explain why they are regarded as shameless and why they
are used as a term of abuse.

Sheep, pigs and cattle, by contrast, are animals which men themselves eat. They feature in the poem with generalized epithets,
white-fleeced, horned and so forth, but play only a secondary role in
similes, usually when they are attacked by bigger beasts. Only very
occasionally do they depart from their typecasting: when Achilles
states that wolves and sheep plot evil for one another, he is stretching
a point about sheep, which are elsewhere, correctly, typified by fear.[32]

As for Homer's wild beasts, they were not fantasies: they were a
real presence in landscapes he knew. On the slopes of Mount Ida,
they abounded in the forests and dense covert. Leopards, even,
prowled there, as elsewhere in western Asia: they would bound at a
hunter, Homer knew, when wounded by a spear. Wolves were widespread there too. He always presents them in a pack, whereas he
presents wild boar in splendid isolation, one at a time. Boars proliferated in western Asia and are particularly well observed, turbulently
rooting up trees and crops, charging with their manes upright and
whetting their tusks, as indeed they do by running the tusks in their
lower jaw against the smaller hollow tusks in their upper one, carried for that purpose.

Homer has no idea of the social and familial hierarchies which
groups of wild boar observe, but these patterns of piggish matri-
archy have only been discovered quite recently. His wild boar, always
loners, are engaged by hunters and hounds, whereupon they wheel
round and charge their attackers, as every hunter still knows and
fears. Homer never mentions the loud grunting and squealing
which boars emit. He never refers to the foam which gathers round
their jaws, though it was an item which later Greek poets specified
and which the Roman emperor Marcus Aurelius singled out in his

personal diary because it had such an impressive appearance.[33] Instead, Homer refers to the boar's eyes as blazing like fire when it 'rages in might'. In fact a boar's eyes are small and dark, lacking a reflecting layer in their retinas. In photographs taken at night their eyes can appear to be red, but Homer had no camera film to deceive him. He or his predecessors added this blaze to enhance the animal's ferocity, but it was not true to life.

The lion, by contrast, is the lord of Homer's beasts: it is a predatory carnivore, pre-eminent because of its diet. Boars, though fearsome, are herbivorous and therefore rank below it, a ranking which has a poetic use. In book 16, when Patroclus kills a prime hero, Sarpedon, he is compared to a lion, one which is killing the prime bull in a herd. Soon afterwards, as his own death is near, he confronts lion-like Hector and this time is compared to a boar.[34] These animals will indeed fight each other, and the change of comparison is well judged. Lion-like Hector duly kills boar-like Patroclus, as the similes have implied in advance of their encounter.

Homer's lions and lion hunts are crucial items in the poem, much discussed but also much misunderstood. There are more than forty lion similes in the Iliad, many of which are developed with clever variations over several verses.[35] They have frequently been interpreted as items from a distant past, even as part of a layer from the Mycenaean period when lions were indeed depicted in art and sculpture and are agreed to have been quite widely present in Greece. From the early tenth century BC onwards, lions reappear on Greek painted pottery and metalwork, but only in the seventh century BC do they become beasts carved in stone.[36] Even then the prototypes of these sculptures are Near Eastern, the stone lions which Greeks knew in late Hittite art, probably in or near north Syria.[37] They were carved there with stylized heads and were not drawn from life. Homer's lions have been understood as unreal too: as art historians point out, they never roar.[38]

If this view of them is correct, the effect and relevance of many of Homer's similes are affected. They are evoking items which he had never seen and about which neither he nor his listeners knew anything. However, the silence of his lions does not prove that living lions were unknown to him. His boars are silent too and never foam round their jaws, but they were a widespread presence in western Asia, one which he and his poetic teachers manifestly knew. If closely read, his lion hunts are decidedly un-Mycenaean and not at all Near Eastern in style.

In Mycenaean art, kings and attendants go out to hunt lions as their designated prey. They travel in chariots and shoot them with arrows. In Homer there are no specialized lion hunts of this type. His hunters go out on foot into wild land, not specifically to encounter a lion, but sometimes they happen to put one up while hunting in a general way. In later Greek history, Philip, Alexander and their first Macedonian successors were to be true lion kings who hunted lions face to face on horseback or even on foot.[39] Homer's lion similes are very different. A king or lord is never involved. In many of them, villagers or farm workers rally to confront a lion who is threatening their flocks or who has leapt into one of their enclosures. The hero is compared to the lion, so bold, so fierce, but is never compared to the hunter, a point which troubled the well-born Synesius of Cyrene, a Christian and a passionate hunter in the fifth century AD. Quite often, Homer's hunters and villagers emerge worse from the encounter than do the hounds.[40]

Homer's lion similes, like his boar similes, select from their subjects' habits and tendencies. They centre on them as predators, but, as ever, Homer varies the details with great skill: he presents herdsmen, hounds and hunters in varying actions and he characterizes the outcomes and victims in cleverly differing ways. Accurate observation shows through. Homeric lions jump onto their prey's back in order to break its neck, an exact representation of a real lion's targeted pounce.[41] When Menelaus is forced to retreat from Patroclus' dead body, he withdraws like a 'bearded lion', not a whiskered one, as some scholars imagine: a lion's beard is a conspicuous feature. Replacing Menelaus, Ajax then stands at bay over dead Patroclus

like a lion around its cubs,
whom setters-on have encountered as it is leading its
  young in a forest,
and it exults in its might and draws down its brow,
  hiding both eyes.[42]

The details need to be pinned down here. The word for these setters-on, or *epaktēres*, is only attested in classical Greek in the Homeric poems. They are huntsmen of a particular type, those engaged in setting on the lead hounds, each of whom would be known as an *epagōn*, just as a tracker dog was known as a *paragon* in the hound vocabulary which passed from Greek into Latin.[43] As for the lion's brow, it is exactly observed too: its wrinkling or apparent frowning is a feature famous in modern beauty treatments, the *ride de lion* which begins to show between clients' eyebrows from the late twenties onwards and has become part of the inter-girl canon as a blemish which needs pre-emptive treatment.[44] When a lion furrows its brow, its eyes, like a beauty-conscious young lady's, become narrowed.

These exact details have not somehow been preserved for Homer across at least five illiterate centuries since the lion-conscious Mycenaean age. The words used for the lion's brow and the setters-on among the hounds are not formulaic: they occur only here in the Iliad. Nor has the lion's pounce on its prey's neck or the attacks and defences of villagers passed down to Homer from a distant age of regal Mycenaean hunting. In his lifetime lions were current in north Thessaly and parts of Macedon and remained so as late as the fourth century BC. They are attested in western Asia, bones of lions being known near Mount Mycale and reported, with bones of leopards, from Troy VIII, the one which Homer visited: they survived in western Asia into the modern era.[45] From the seventh century BC onwards a lion's head appeared on the coins of Lydia and then on coins of the island of Samos, where in due course fine images of a lion's frown and narrowed eyes were engraved. These images were based on an existing knowledge of lions at large. Maybe Homer knew exact details about lions from contemporary hearsay, but it is just as likely that he knew them himself. As his similes show, lion hunts were not confined to people of a high social class. An epic poet was not performing every day, all day long. He could perfectly well participate as one of the hunters or as a villager joining the fray. Homer the hunter, I believe, has left even more of a trace in the Iliad than Homer the putative gardener.[46]

Like every other simile, his lion similes are contemporary. There is more at issue here than Homer's grasp, or not, of animal realities. If these similes were Mycenaean survivals, he would indeed have been comparing aspects of the heroic world to items of the distant past, far removed from his own and his hearers' comprehension. Their impact on the audience would have been very different, not one of recognition through likeness, but one of evocation through romance. In fact, being contemporary, they are a telling counterpoint to the main narrative.

The narrative's heroes are 'not as mortals are now' and their material items are indeed a composite mixture culled from very different eras, blending Mycenaean bronze spearheads with those dark age cremations for the very special dead. His similes, however, are exact and, in each case, apt for their listeners' own time. Their language supports this inference: it does not use many formulaic phrases and it makes conspicuous use of words which recur nowhere else in the poem. It has been shown to be consistently late among the poem's linguistic layers. The interplay between these two dimensions, the fantasy setting of the heroes and the contemporary setting of the similes, exactly observed, is an element underlying the Iliad's power.

32.

'As when . . .'

The accuracy of the similes' observations and their siting in Homer's own lifetime exemplify once again his gift for the specific, even while using language rich in generalized, recurring phrases and adjectives. The deeper questions remain of why he uses similes at all and what their poetic effect may be. Homer is a brilliant exploiter of contrasts of tone and setting, not least in his distribution of action and emotion throughout his plot. He also uses metaphors, which are condensed one-word comparisons. Metaphors enabled poets to express the final moment of death, one which was never transmitted in personal memory, but in many other contexts metaphors were not dead for Homer and his audience. The 'strife of war' blazes (like fire), which was perhaps a trite verb for it, but when personal combat is called love talk, in which a participant 'is either killed or saved' it is hard to be sure of the exact force, how far it is ironic or erotic, but the metaphor is not dead at all.[1] It is easier to pin down why the west wind can be goat-butting when it bows the heads of a deep field of corn: its effect is indeed like a goat's thrust with its horns, pushing, pausing and then repeating.[2]

Inside a metaphor there is a simile struggling to get out: why, then, did Greek poets use similes when they had these other resources? One possibility is that similes developed from Greeks' interest in omens, a category for which birds were especially important.

Bird similes in Homer are very sharply observed. At the start of book 3 the cry and clamour of the Trojans, advancing into the poem's first battle, are compared to the clamour of those cranes who fly south, bringing death to the pygmies. Migrating cranes are indeed one of the great sights and sounds of the Balkans, excellently appreciated by Cretan shepherds, who still tell how they fly 'stretching beak to tail from one edge of the sky to the other so high above Mt Ida as to be almost out of sight, but accompanied by a strange unearthly sound like a far-away conversation'.[3]

As for the Greek army, its first advance, too, is compared to the sound of birds, the 'many tribes of geese or cranes or longnecked swans' who settle in the Asian meadow and land 'with a clamour, and the meadow clatters'. In 1906, in India, a lover of Homer, J. Maclair Boraston, heard this very sound from birds alighting: 'To say the meadow "crashed" were modesty,' he recalled, 'but crash is the only word. It was a sound in which there were many parts, each flung down, as it were, to ring like metal and smash like glass.'[4] Plainly Homer himself had heard such a crash-landing.

Observers of omens had to notice details about the bird, its colour, its flight, its actions, and then apply them by analogy to a situation hinted at, but never stated, in what were oblique messages from the gods: 'just as' the bird is, or does, this or that, 'so', by analogy, will this or that befall mortal onlookers. Oracular prophecies, too, were oblique messages from the gods in which animals often symbolized people and what might befall them.[5] Again, an exact awareness of the animal's identity and appearance was necessary for the oracle to be interpreted.

Greek poets' use of similes rested on a similar application of analogy to careful observation, but Homer's differs on a cardinal point: gods are absent from almost all of them. It is particularly striking that gods are left unmentioned in the similes about forest fires, which roar and spread 'ruinously' on mountains and faraway land.[6] Even now, these destructive horrors make observers feel that somehow Zeus and his thunderbolts are causing trees to ignite. Here, Homer's similes contrast with the main narrative, in which almost all that happens is related to the gods.

Homer's narrative contains personified winds, sea nymphs, tree nymphs and river gods, whereas his similes generally present items which have been observed in natural terms.[7] It might seem that the one approach enabled the other, as if the nymphs and tree gods satisfied a Greek's sense of something unfathomable in, to us, natural items, and thereby left poets free in their similes to describe only what they saw. However, this distinction is not absolute: in a few similes Zeus still sends snow or storms, in another gods punish a burning city and, once, a lion turns up, sent by a *daimōn* (a divinity).[8] In the main narrative the earth, the sea and its waves are not always linked to a divinity. The contrast is not between two ways of seeing the world, let alone between one that was appropriate for the time when heroes were 'not as mortals nowadays' and gods prevailed in the world about them, and one in similes, set in the audience's own era when divinity was no longer ubiquitous in 'nature'.[9] The gods show no sign of retreating from nature in texts and inscriptions in the many centuries after Homer. The distinction, rather, is made for poetic effect: comparisons to god-driven items would take them further away from their listeners' immediate apprehension, foiling the similes' main purpose.

Similes are not used simply for variety, as if they offered a welcome change for listeners. In the second book, they proliferate when the fighting is about to begin and has had no chance to become repetitive.[10] They are used because they help listeners to envisage abstract qualities. They begin with the Greek army's effect on the light: its armour gleams like a forest on fire, the first of the forest fire similes.[11] They then convey an idea of its number: the troops are as many as those geese or swans alighting in the Asian meadow. Next they clarify its sound: the ground echoes under the feet of its warriors and their horses like the clatter and clamour of those birds' wings. They then return to the numbers: in the flowery plain of the river Scamander the Greek soldiers are as many as the leaves and flowers in due season or as flies which buzz round a shepherd's farmstead in spring when the pails are wet with milk. Their leaders then separate their units as they muster, just as herdsmen separate herds of goats in a plain. Meanwhile, king Agamemnon presides and is compared to three different gods in sequence and then to a bull 'far the most eminent of all'. The long catalogue of the Greek ships follows, which should be excised as a post-Homeric addition, but it is followed by a simile which picks up the previous ones, the sound and blaze of the ground whenever the monster Typhon is being lashed by Zeus in Arima. This simile is Homer's own. Again it dramatizes noise and gleam.

As the action is about to begin, Homer has framed the sound of the Greek army in two carefully chosen similes which range from the east to the very west of the settled Greek world in his time, first, the Asian meadow in the east near Ephesus, then, in the distant west, faraway Arima, the island of Ischia off the Bay of Naples.[12] They add sound effects to his narrative. A shorter Trojan catalogue then follows, also an addition, but then the Trojan army advances too with a flurry of similes, manifestly Homer's, picking up his similes for the Greeks on the move. Their clamour is like the clamour of those cranes as they fly towards outer Ocean, bringing death to the pygmies. Dust rises from their feet, like a mist which the south wind spreads over a plain, 'dear to a thief but not to a shepherd', a mist which limits a man's vision to only as far as he can throw a stone.[13]

At this climactic moment in the poem, similes have not been multiplied in order to avoid monotony. They present noise and number, visibility, distance and glittering light, abstract qualities which they help listeners to envisage. Elsewhere too they build up a crucial turn in the story, the beginning of its battles or the prowess of one hero in particular. They make comparisons with far-off places and settings, Ischia or the pygmy men, in order to make what is present on the killing field more vivid. They engage the poem's audience by making them compare like and unlike as they listen.

When a major hero embarks on a bout of prowess, he rampages like fire, like a lion, like a wild boar, like a raging wave or, if he is Hector, a storm wind. Opponents fall like trees, making their fall vivid, while killers attack their victims like wild animals pouncing on cattle. Similes are especially prominent in book 15 during Hector's prowess and in book 17 during the prolonged fighting over the dead Patroclus. As the warriors contest his body, thirteen similes are scattered through their efforts, from lions to waves to a forest fire: a cluster of five more concludes the book. Again they are not there to vary monotony. This fighting is a crucial phase in the story and has its own independent drama. Here too, similes build up a significant turn of events and help listeners to envisage its abstract qualities, emotions and action. They focus us on them while holding up the main plot, like a cutaway shot on a cinema screen. Once again, Homer, composing in performance, had hit on techniques later to be deployed in film. Long similes allow him to hold up his story and give it emphasis by focussing on a comparison which is far from the main theatre of war. In similes his text sometimes specifies the posture, heights and positioning of protagonists, like the marks for camerawork which script directors compile, deducing them from the literary works which underlie many of their films.[14]

An absence of similes is also revealing. Similes apply to warriors, but not to the gods, except to the speed, direction or manner of their descent to earth and the supreme ease of their action when they are down there. A simile from the human or natural world would not have been apposite for a god on Olympus. No woman in the narrative attracts a long simile, either, no doubt because women are marginal to the way the plot develops. However, these restrictions do not fully account for the rarity of similes in most of the final books.

After the prolonged fighting over dead Patroclus in book 17, the next book, 18, has no extended similes in its opening scenes, none for Achilles' grief on hearing of Patroclus' death, nor even for the lamenting Thetis and her sea nymphs' emergence from the waves. After the previous deluge of similes, these unmilitary scenes have their own power and movement and it seems that Homer felt they did not need more from a parallel world. Only when he returns to the fighting over Patroclus does a long simile appear. So too in book 22, similes abound during the final pursuit and duel of Hector and Achilles, one picking up another and reapplying it, but then they are absent from the moment of Hector's death onwards.[15] That event, too, has supreme pathos and needs no more from a parallel world. When the scene changes to the women of his family in Troy, they are themselves a contrast to the main heroic action, and like all other women in the poem they receive no extended similes, not even in this crisis.

Similes are almost entirely absent from the competitive games in the next book, except for two which help listeners to visualize a distance and one which clarifies the fading of a hero's anger at being denied a prize.[16] The competitions do not need similes, because they have their own self-explanatory, unfolding drama. In the final book, 24, the opening scenes on Olympus are, as ever, without similes but even thereafter there are only three, one of which relates to Achilles' utter amazement at Priam's arrival, the crucial point in its story.[17] Priam's journey to him had passed without any similes, probably because it, too, was overwhelmingly tense and moving on its own terms.

On the assumption that Homer was orally composing and dictating, his similes' form and distribution are easier to understand. Sometimes they are signposts, anticipating an imminent action which then takes place immediately afterwards in the narrative. At other times, they occur in clusters: like the poet's formulaic phrases, one simile arises out of another. The fighting in book 11 is a good example. In it, Agamemnon is repeatedly compared to a lion as he embarks on a brief phase of prowess. Zeus then rallies the Trojans and as Odysseus and Diomede try to stand firm against the rally, they are repeatedly compared to wild boars at bay and the Trojans to hounds harrying them. The two heroes are wounded and then in a fine triple simile Odysseus is compared to a horned stag, wounded by an arrow: it is surrounded by jackals who wait to prey on it until that lion arrives, sent, for once, by a *daimōn*. Like the lion, Ajax indeed arrives to Odysseus' rescue.[18] The signposting and clustering here moves from a lion to wild boar to a wounded stag and back to a lion. This technique might perhaps be one of a poet who was composing with writing but with an oral performance in mind. It is more readily intelligible as the craft of a poet who was keeping his own text-free performance to an orderly sequence and was working with elements, in this case similes, which arose one from another as he composed live.

This method of composition sits well with the similes' distinctive form. 'As when . . .', Homer often begins, before telling us what in the narrative will be compared and clarified. A simile is not confined to points of exact comparison: read in this limiting way, the majority express only one such point. If a second point is made, it tends to be made in a second sentence appended to the first. Beyond this core, Homer uses further details to enlarge the scene, even if they are at odds with his starting point in the narrative. In this sense only, his similes are sometimes digressive.

In book 4 Menelaus' skin is grazed by Pandarus' treacherous arrow, shot to end the sworn truce, 'and dark blood began to flow from the wound'. Then a simile begins, 'as when a woman stains ivory with scarlet . . .', a Carian or Maeonian woman from western Asia who is presented as making the ivory into a cheekpiece for horses, one which will lie in a treasure chamber and

> Many horsemen pray to wear it, but it lies there as a
>   prestigious item for a king,
> Both an adornment for his horse and a glory for its driver.

Only then does Homer return to Menelaus, explaining that 'such were your shapely thighs, Menelaus, and your legs and fair ankles below, stained with blood'.[19] Menelaus' legs may have been fine, but they were not as inordinately precious as the ivory in the simile which Homer has just elaborated beyond the red stain, the immediate point of comparison.

When the comparison is with an action or emotion, the totality of the simile is what conveys its quality. When Achilles mourns over the dead body of Patroclus, his grief is compared to the grief of a father lamenting the death of a newly wed son.[20] The son's recent marriage is not matched to the situation with which it is compared: Achilles was younger than Patroclus, not a father figure to him, and

Patroclus had not just married. However, it enhances the pathos which propels the simile and the intensity which it illustrates. In book 17, Menelaus' 'bright eyes' search far and wide for young Antilochus, like an eagle 'which, they say, has the sharpest sight of all winged birds under the heavens', which sees from on high a swift hare crouching under a thick bush, swoops on it and kills it. However, Menelaus' aim was to find Antilochus, not kill him: the simile as a whole dramatizes Menelaus' sharpness of sight, not point by point but through a vivid, exact scene.[21]

The final book contains a crucial example of this expansion. It occurs when elderly Priam suddenly appears on Achilles' threshold and goes to kiss Achilles' manslaying hands, the very hands that had killed his son. 'As when blind folly has seized' a man who kills someone in his homeland, and he 'escapes to another people, to the house of a rich man, and amazement seizes the onlookers: so Achilles was amazed when he saw god-like Priam'. Yet Priam was the very opposite of a murderer, nor had blind folly seized him: he was rich, far more so than Achilles, whereas Achilles, not Priam, was the one who had killed. Various attempts have been made to read more into the comparison, but I do not find these readings persuasive.[22] The comparison rests on the amazement, intense in each case.

For literate poets, this technique would miss an opportunity which writing allows: with its help they can linger over the details of a simile, working on each one to fit it exactly to the context. Homer has not done so, not just because he was composing *for* performance, when hearers would probably fail to pick up each matching detail, but also because he was composing *in* performance, when multiple close correspondences were far harder to contrive. This type of composition also helps to explain why some of the similes are repeated partly or wholly in the poem and may even, on their second appearance, be more apt.

At the end of book 8, the Trojans' thousand campfires out on the plain are compared memorably to the stars which appear round the gleaming moon, one of the very few mentions of the moon in the poem. The 'air is windless and all the peaks and high headlands and glades appear', but also 'from heaven the infinite air is broken open'. This breaking open sits oddly with a clear, windless night sky, but in book 16, when the verses appear again, it fits perfectly. First, Zeus 'moves a dense cloud from a high peak' and then 'the air is broken open', and all the peaks and so forth appear. This second simile applies to the Greeks' brief respite after pushing the Trojans back from their ships. The simile seems to have been practised and rehearsed previously and to have surfaced in performance as a block in one context, then later in another which it fitted even better.[23]

As the range of similes is so wide, no generalization can catch the purpose of them all. The life they evoke is very seldom ordinary: a lion or a boar hunt or a gale in a garden are not daily events. However, their human participants are never kings or princes. They belong to a social class quite different from the class of heroes who dominate the main narrative. They present craft-workers or people out in wild nature, herdsmen or woodcutters, though they never specify anyone as a slave. The women in them are the very opposite of queens and princesses. Even the hunters in them are never said to be nobly born: they are young and fit and might simply be farmers' sons. Similes about everyday people are excellently suited to a primary context of live performance addressed to an audience of mixed social standing who have chosen to attend. They compare heroes who are not like men nowadays with people whom these listeners can readily recognize.

Their animals, too, are readily envisaged. Whereas in the main narrative they are typecast with unchanging epithets, in the similes they are presented in individualized action. They come to life in them through their varied responses. A careful reader of Homer's similes, Hermann Fränkel, ended by wondering whether the makers of such similes perhaps 'had already become cool, sedate and orderly town dwellers who, if they wanted to describe the great and sublime, turned their thoughts away from the daily life which surrounded them'.[24] They were quite the opposite. The towns of Homer and his listeners were not separated from an alien expanse called the countryside. They lived and worked, herded and hunted in its presence, among its storms and predatory beasts So do the people in Homer's similes and so did he himself, a hunter-gardener, I believe, as well as a performing poet.

Neil

In her empathetic reading of the Iliad, Simone Weil claimed something more profound, that the similes are where the Iliad expresses 'the ultimate secret of war'. For her, the ultimate secret is that battles are determined not by men who calculate and act on resolutions but by men who are 'fallen to the level . . . of the blind forces of sheer impetus', while their victims sink to 'the level of purely passive inert matter'. The Iliad's conquering heroes are indeed likened, as she sees, to 'fire, flood, wind, fierce beasts and any other blind cause of disaster', whereas their victims are 'frightened animals, trees, water, sand, whatever is affected by the violence of outside forces'. Both the killer and the victim, Weil considered, are presented as transformed and so 'the similes that liken them – victors and victims – to beasts or objects can elicit neither admiration nor scorn but only sorrow that men may be so transfigured'.[25] They go to the very heart of the Iliad as she interprets it.

This powerful statement is a revealing misreading of a complex whole. There are indeed a few similes which support it, especially those in which the victims in battle are compared to young fawns. In book 11, Agamemnon begins a brief burst of prowess by killing two sons of Priam, one born in wedlock, the other a bastard, both in the same chariot, where the bastard is holding the reins. Agamemnon kills them 'like a lion who has broken up the babies of a swift deer and takes away their tender life'. The fawns' mother is not far away but 'trembling seizes her' and she sweats as she runs off.[26] The simile is indeed emotive about the lion's victims, but the lion is not said to be gripped by irrational force: it simply wanted food. Lions are sometimes presented as killing a cow or bull or sheep without any emphasis which elicits pity for the victim. Occasionally a predatory lion or boar is itself the victim, forced into retreat.[27] Victims, like similes, vary.

So do victors. In book 24 Apollo indeed compares Achilles' inhumanity and wildness to a lion which has gone out to kill and feast. In book 22 Achilles himself has told Hector that there can be no agreement between the two of them, any more than there can be between lions and lambs.[28] However, Achilles is explicitly behaving with excess anger and inhumanity here. Homer is not saying that all warriors become beasts in battle, let alone that such a transformation is a matter for our sorrow. His similes compare an aspect shared by two items, but do not identify the two of them as one and the same.

So far from expressing 'the ultimate secret of war', the Iliad's similes for combat apply to varied aspects of the psychology of battle. There is no one ultimate secret: Homer, yet again, is not one-eyed. In book 21, Trojan Agenor is given boldness by Apollo, but it does not result in an instant transformation into Weil's 'sheer impetus'. He sees Achilles nearby, waits and debates many things in his heart. Deciding to stand and oppose him, he is not compared to Weil's 'frightened animal affected by the violence of outside forces'. He is compared to a leopard which hears hounds coming, one which even when struck by a hunter's spear fights on fearlessly and attacks at close quarters.[29] He has not become a passive object.

Heroes' lion-like ferocity in battle is awesome to the poet: it is not, as Weil read it, a matter for sorrow. Plato later compared the passions in our nature to wild beasts and although Homer lacked Plato's theory of parts of the soul, he might agree with modern warriors who refer to a sense of the 'Beast within' when they are fighting for their lives in close combat. He was composing long before philosophers and theorists addressed these inner problems of human nature, but in some of his similes he has already dramatized them in a pre-philosophical way.

Do the similes undercut the war in a different way, by placing it as only one part of a wider, unconcerned world? 'From a non-human perspective,' an admiring literary critic has suggested, 'not subject to our sense of time . . . the erupting on to Troy's plain of a horde of armed men is simply an aspect of life on the planet like the flight of migrating birds or the sudden emergence of a swarm of bees', comparisons which Homer makes for them.[30] Yet these comparisons are specific, resting on the birds' noise and the bees' continuing emergence from a hollow rock. They are made in order to help us envisage these qualities in an army and its mustering for an assembly. Both occur in human time and neither turns the action into just one more incident in the planet's indifferent course, a misreading of Homer which has roots in W. H. Auden's complex postwar poem 'Memorial for the City', composed in 1945.

Through Homer's eyes, Auden claimed, human lives are seen as if through the impassive eye of a bird or a camera: they run their indifferent course, and 'for ever and ever / Plum blossom falls on the dead'. He missed the subjectivity and pathos in much of Homer's narrative. In only one of the Iliad's similes, albeit the most famous and most imitated, does Homer compare the fact of mortals' transient lives to the recurring world beyond them: Glaucus tells his opponent Diomede that the 'generations of men are like the generations of leaves' which pass away, yet reappear when the forest flourishes again in spring. 'So one generation of men is born, but another ceases.'[31] This fine simile for human transience may not be original to Homer but his development of it is singularly powerful: he repeats it fifteen books later, when Apollo reminds Poseidon not to fight with him over mere mortals, who 'at one time flourish in a fiery manner, at another waste away, lifeless'.[32] Both comparisons are made by speakers, not by the poet in the main narrative, where the effect of similes is not at all to imply that 'stuff happens', and that fighting is just one part of it. Sometimes, they express loss and enhance pathos.

In her admired poem 'Memorial', Alice Oswald has paid tribute to the pathos of deaths in the Iliad by giving nothing but short biographies of soldiers, each followed by a simile, repeated. She has devised it, she explains, as 'an antiphonal account of man in his world'. In Homer, too, Euphorbus dies like a carefully tended young tree, uprooted by wind; Agamemnon kills two sons of Priam like those 'babies of a swift deer'. However, pathos is only one of the registers in similes about the dead. In others, deaths merely become more visual through comparisons with, to us, the natural world.

When Homer compares a falling warrior to a falling tree, he is not expressing pity for the tree, not even when it is a victim of a man's axe. Exceptions to the rule are horses, which, twice, he presents as mourning for their masters, but they are immortal horses, different from those in everyday life. When he centres a simile on trees or animals he is not implying that they have an equivalent status with humans as shared participants in life on earth: He was not an eco-warrior before his time, pitying trees as man's companions. Rather, human deaths become more visual through comparisons with, to us, the natural world. The trees are picked on for their height and fall, making more vivid the fall of a great hero greatly slain. In the narrative, heroes and woodcutters go into forests, 'big beyond telling', and saw and cut trees for funerary pyres and timber without any implication that they are destroying a finite natural asset.

'Throughout Homer,' Adam Nicolson has written, 'the world of peace consistently resurfaces as a place of reproach and yearning.' He even considers Homer to be 'in love with the idea of nature as a reservoir of stability'. There is no yearning in the similes, no idea of nature, no pervasive sense of its 'stability'. In this context, however, the poem's supreme parallel world, the scenes on the shield made for Achilles, come into play. For every reader and listener, they are a pinnacle of Homer's craft. Again, there is nothing like them in the Odyssey.

33.

The Shield of Achilles

In book 18 Thetis goes to the craftsman god Hephaestus to beg for a new set of armour for her son Achilles. What follows is a prolonged tour de force which fascinates all who encounter it. Like a simile it evokes a parallel world, but it does so in ten scenes, set one after another. The effect, even the purpose, of this extended episode relates to the poem's impact as a whole.

Thetis arrives when Hephaestus is busy in his smithy, making twenty metal tripods which will run to and fro automatically into gatherings of the gods. A true blacksmith, he wipes his 'mighty' neck and shaggy chest' with a sponge and comes out to meet her, moving lamely, however, on his thin, withered legs. He is supported by a great staff and by 'maids of gold, like living girls'. They have a mind, a voice and strength and are 'busied beneath him' as he moves.[1]

In this marvellous scene Homer begins with two amazing innovations, surely his own: the first attestation of robots and the first examples of artificial intelligence. Hephaestus listens to Thetis as she reminds him how once she had helped to save his life when Hera, his mother, threw him out of heaven in disgust at his disability. She then tells him about Achilles' predicament and begs him humbly as a suppliant, asking him to make new armour. 'If only I could save him from grim-sounding death . . .' Hephaestus tells her, 'as surely as beautiful armour will be available to him . . .'[2] He is going to make lovely armour, therefore, and he knows it: it will be 'such as anyone who sees it, from many peoples, would marvel at'. Through Hephaestus, Homer is promising a wonder for his audience. He goes on to present one, a shield with a surface of bronze, gold, silver and tin onto which Hephaestus works scenes elaborated for us in the poet's own narration. In a captivating sequence, Homer lets us look on this marvel as if from above. While Hephaestus works, Thetis waits elsewhere, apparently in another room. We look on, not through Thetis' eyes but through Homer's.

Nowhere is the Iliad more dazzling or ingenious. First, presumably at the centre of the shield, Hephaestus makes

> The tireless sun and the filling moon
> And all the portents with which heaven is crowned,
> The Pleiads, Hyads, the might of Orion
> And the Bear which men also call the Waggon.

Only here do constellations occur in the poem, but they are marvellously evocative. They are portents because they are signs for mortals and their lives: on one possible translation Heaven has 'crowned itself' with them. Behind the Bear's two names lies a Greek misunderstanding which even Homer did not know. In the Akkadian language, used in Babylon, this constellation was known as *eriqqu*, meaning waggon, but the name had sounded to Greeks like *ark[t]os*, their word for bear, and so both Waggon and Bear became Greek names for it when they first heard the Akkadian name and some, not all, of them learned what it meant.[3] 'It circles in its place', Homer says, 'and watches for Orion, and alone, does not share in the baths of Ocean.' Indeed the Bear never sets, though it is not alone in being constantly visible. When Orion rises in early winter the Bear is very near the horizon: Homer credits it with watching for its rival, another active detail in his presentation of the heavens.

Next, Hephaestus fashions scenes of town and country, peace and war. Perhaps they should be imagined in concentric circles radiating out from the centre, but Homer never specifies, frustrating posterity's many attempts to draw his shield or re-create a version of it.[4] The scenes are wonderfully alive. In one of them a wedding procession escorts the brides by torchlight from their houses, watched by older women in their porches as the singing and dancing pass by. In another, a murderer and his victim's kinsman dispute in public over the compensation to be paid. In a third, a city is under siege but the besieged send out troops to ambush a herd of sheep and cattle, while the old, the women and the children mount guard on their city's walls behind. The herd's two herdsmen suspect no danger: they follow their animals, delighting themselves on reed pipes. They are the first known reference to herdsmen playing music, ancestors of the entire pastoral genre.

Three scenes then show agricultural work: ploughing, the reaping of corn and the harvesting of grapes, a trio of energy and action. Two more scenes show flocks on the move, one of cattle being herded out to pasture, attacked by a lion as they go, another, briefly, of sheep. A final, superb scene shows two lines of dancers, both finely dressed, the girls with fair crowns, the boys with swords of gold and belts of silver, advancing and receding with their 'expert feet' as they dance back- and forwards to each other. Then, round the rim of the shield Hephaestus sets Ocean, the river which, for Homer and his hearers, encircles the earth.

Homer's description of scenes on a work of art is the first to survive in such length and detail in world literature. It has been immensely influential: already in antiquity it fathered other such scenes, primarily in idyllic contexts, in pastoral poetry and romantic novels. Unlike those lesser imitations, Homer presents the actual making in progress, but he goes far beyond a description of what Hephaestus did. Sounds and movement, emotions, wishes and intentions are all set before us. So are songs and speeches. They are effects which poetry can contrive, but metalwork cannot.

Why does he develop this episode at such length and why does he give these particular scenes? He had surely seen finely decorated metalwork in real life. Elsewhere in the Iliad, he is aware that examples of it might be made on Cyprus or by people in Sidon, as indeed they were.[5] However, in this case direct imitation does not underlie what he opts to present. Despite claims to the contrary, his scenes are not much like those on the few Cypriote bronze or silver bowls which have survived. The dates, too, of such bowls are uncertain, but probably too late for Homer, as richly decorated survivors are not earlier than the mid to later seventh century BC.[6]

By Homer's lifetime, Greek craftsmen had indeed begun to paint human and animal figures, albeit in a spindly Geometric style. On big pottery vessels, especially those made in Athens, they too presented actions in sequence, but usually in separate panels, one after another, using what has been well called synoptic convention, as if they were scenes in a modern strip-cartoon.[7] Homer's scenes on the shield are quite different. He narrates them continuously as a poet, not a craftsman, and so they unfold in time, departing from what static metalwork or pottery could contrive. They are moving pictures, the earliest known examples in the world. Within the space of 250 verses, Homer has not only presented robots and artificial intelligence for the first time. So often filmic before films existed, he has invented movies: four centuries later, Plato would invent special effects too, in his famous simile of a darkened cave onto whose wall images of objects were projected, lit from behind their seated viewers.[8] Justly, our word 'cinema' transcribes an ancient Greek word, *kinēma*, meaning movement.

Hephaestus was making his shield for a warrior who is 'not as mortal men are now': what, then, is the presumed era of the scenes shown on it? Its scenes of dancing or herding, weddings or a siege, could belong at any time, but others are more specific. The one set in a city's public gathering place (its *agora*) is the prime example. The details are hard to pin down, but one man, I infer, is shown stating that he has paid compensation, whereas the other says that he refuses to accept it. Both tell as much to the people who have gathered round and are cheering for one or other party. The two protagonists are eager to reach a conclusion from a knowledgeable man, but no such person has yet emerged. Elders, seated on polished seats of stone, are standing forward one by one and expressing their personal judgement, while two talents of gold have been set out, awaiting the man who speaks most straightly. I take him to be the knowledgeable man, who will bring a conclusion and be rewarded accordingly. The scene stops before the episode has reached that point, and so the knowledgeable man is not shown.[9]

This scene does not belong in a distant heroic or royal Mycenaean age: no king or royal official is presiding over it. Whatever its exact procedure, it belongs in a community with a council of elders, in which people can cheer and participate informally. It is no earlier than the ninth to eighth centuries BC, an era of pre-*polis* communities, fledgling citizen-states.

The scene of ploughing belongs then too, though it is seldom fully understood. It shows several teams of ploughmen and animals at work on an expanse of land. They are whirling their ploughs to and fro along straight furrows until they reach the headland and have to swing round. At the headland, other men come forward to bring them honey-sweet wine in cups, to spur them on. The setting is not a royal estate. It is the ploughing of what Homer has mentioned in a simile in book 12: common land.[10] Each ploughman is hurrying to plough furrows on the ground which he will then work: the scene shows a great ploughing occasion, like one of the ploughing days in the calendars of other agrarian societies. No king or noble is present: this scene too is not set in the royal Mycenaean past.

Its common land differs from the land in the next scene, the estate of a *basileus* who looks on in silence, rejoicing inwardly in his heart at the harvesting of the crop, his own. This *basileus* holds a staff or sceptre but he is not obviously a grand monarch. He is more likely to be one of those plural *basileis*, or local lords, whom Homer mentions once in a simile and who are known in Hesiod's everyday poetry as rulers of eighth-century Greek communities.

This same context is implicit in Hephaestus' very metalworking. He goes to heat his metals. He prepares bellows to maintain the heat and brings tongs and a big hammer with which to knock them into shape. However, the shield's bronze, silver and gold would have had to be hammered cold, 'with a light touch adapted to their fragility', as their expert, Dorothea Gray, well explained, realizing the anomaly.[11] Homer was imagining ironworking, a skill which needs heat and heavy hammering: iron was never worked in the distant era of Achilles or the Mycenaean age. Here too Homer had his own times in mind, though he adds a touch of fancy, those two talents of gold in the shield's scene of dispute. Two talents of gold rank as the fourth and last prize in one of the games which are held in book 23: they are not an exorbitant sum in the heroes' world. In Homer's own eighth century, they would be.

Like the contents of the poem's similes, the shield's moving pictures are scenes consistent with Homer's era, not his heroes'. Do they differ from the scenes in similes by taking an aristocratic view of their world? In one scene, the dancers are nobly dressed, with crowns and belts of silver and gold, but in another scene the brides who process through the streets by torchlight need not be so grand. The scenes of ploughing and harvesting are full of young workers' energy and joy. In one, a lord, or *basileus*, indeed looks on in quiet rejoicing, the crop being his own, but meanwhile heralds are preparing a feast under an oak tree: 'having killed a big ox as a sacrifice they are preparing it', while 'the women scatter much white barley, a meal for the workers'. These workers are hired men, Homer specifies, not slaves: opinions vary, but I think the white barley is being scattered not for a segregated supper for the hired workers but on the ox-meat which they too will eat.[12] Their lord is being generous.

Homer's near contemporary, the poet Hesiod, has accustomed us to poetry about the hard, canny grind of agricultural work. The angle of vision he adopted is only one of those possible. Homer's scene of grape picking on his shield shows something quite different, the joy and fun of its workers, manifest in their dancing, sporting and singing. In the scene of dancing too a large crowd watches the dancers' actions in delight. Joy and energy are not emotions which only an aristocratic viewpoint could ascribe to scenes of work. Workers too can find fun when they are together at harvest-time or on a dance floor. As for Homer's scenes of the siege, the dispute and the herds, they are not narrated from an aristocratic point of view at all. Like his similes, the movies on his shield have an empathy with their everyday participants.

Round its edge runs outer Ocean, encircling its scenes like a little world: why does Homer take us through this mini-verse at such length? Achilles is not the only Greek warrior to have armour made by Hephaestus. Back in book 5 Diomede, we are told, has such armour too, but it is never described. In book 11 we have also heard about Agamemnon's shield, on which that fearsome Gorgon and personified Fear and Rout were visible.[13] On the shield for Achilles no scary images are present, though they might seem apt for a shield which was to be carried into battle by a great hero, let alone by one whose voice had just frightened twelve of the Trojans to death. In the shield's one scene of fighting, verses currently in the text refer to Strife and Tumult and deadly Fate in the bloodied action, with Fate dragging off warriors, two alive, one dead, but these verses are widely, and rightly, considered to be additions by a later poet.[14] Elsewhere on the shield Homer gives scenes at odds with the killing which Achilles will conduct with them on his arm.

Homer is too much of an artist simply to have allowed these scenes to run away with him once they began. At one simple level, it was time for a change of tone. For seven books, the action on the longest day of battle had been fierce and lethal, broken only by the lighter scene of Hera's seduction of Zeus. Patroclus had been killed and his body finally rescued from a bloody tug of war, while Achilles and Thetis had just responded with intense grief to the news of his death. There is more, however, at issue than relief from prolonged grimness. Before the episode of the shield, Achilles had just chosen to re-enter the fighting, though he knew it would cost him his life. Outside Troy, Hector had just chosen to stand and fight on, not knowing, however, that the decision would be fatal. Like the clusters of similes, the making of the shield comes at a pivotal moment in the plot.

Unlike the scenes in similes, those on the shield are not explicit comparisons: they are actual representations by a god. Nonetheless, on one modern reading of them, they are implicit comparisons in order to 'make us think about war and see it in relation to peace'.

383

After those crucial decisions by Hector and Achilles, 'the two finest things in the *Iliad* – Achilles and Troy – will never again enjoy the existence portrayed on the shield . . . The shield of Achilles brings home the loss, the cost of the events of the *Iliad*.'[15] In fact, one scene of it, the city under siege, shows battle and killing about to begin. During Homer's performance, listeners had little time to think generally about war and loss while they heard these bewitching scenes. We can, but it helps if we consider them in terms which are more specific, arguably the terms in which they struck their first audiences.

Their latest commentator, Richard Rutherford, well picks on the 'unheroic and unmemorable lives of lesser men, women and even children' in them. Those lives are in the similes too, but 'there is paradox, for these are lives which for all their small significance in history offer more in terms of happiness and fulfilment than the path of heroic warfare brings for Achilles'.[16] Again, the scenes of the city under siege or the herd attacked by a lion do not fit this template, but in other scenes there is indeed a joy and delight which neither Hector nor Achilles feels: the response of the grape-pickers, the bridal procession or the dancers. In similes, participants seldom feel delight at all, and then only at an orchard-garden's recovery from flooding when a wind quickly dries it or at a clear night sky, delighting a shepherd when out with his flocks: in each case these comparisons are with aspects of the battlefield, a place which is never delightful. At a turning point in the plot, the shield presents what similes omit. The effect is not one of 'reproach and yearning', Adam Nicholson's phrase, but it can indeed be fitted to Alice Oswald's idea of the similes as an antiphonal account of man in his world. At a turning point in the plot, the scenes on the shield sound contrasting notes of joy. The effect, however, is to heighten the grimness of the main narrative.

Hephaestus makes other armour too, a breastplate 'brighter than the gleam of fire', a helmet with a crest of gold and greaves of pliant tin. He lifts it all up and sets it before Thetis, who flies off with it like a hawk: she has not assumed the form of a hawk, but the speed of one, swooping down from the peaks of snowy Olympus.[17] As dawn breaks, she sets the pile of armour before Achilles' companions, the Myrmidons, and 'trembling seizes them', not at the wondrous scenes on the shield, but at the gleaming pile of metal.[18] Achilles' first sight of it arouses sharp anger in him, impelling him to take revenge on Patroclus' killer, but then he marvels, the first person to do so, as he looks at the pieces more closely. So once more should we.

In the shield's scene of the grape harvest, its pickers are heedless in their young thoughts. 'Beating the ground together, they skip with their feet and follow with dancing and a cry.' In their midst a boy with a treble voice is singing to a lyre, the sound to which the boys and girls are dancing and shouting. What he sings, however, is the song of Linos. It is the one song in the poem with a probable Near Eastern origin, but its date, too, was not Mycenaean, but nearer Homer's own time, deriving from contact between Greeks and Phoenicians in the ninth to eighth centuries BC. It was a dirge on the death of Linos, its young namesake.[19]

On the shield joy and delight preponderate, but grief, here, is artfully intertwined. In the similes, by contrast, delight is very rare, and fear and struggle proliferate. The great Shakespearean critic A. D. Nuttall liked to refer to Shakespeare as the 'boy from Stratford' and considered that he had come quite quickly to realize that as a poet he had the talent to do anything.[20] So too, I believe, did Homer, perhaps the boy from Chios. On the shield the joyous energy of the girls and boys outdoes the sad song, but its note of pathos is present nonetheless. It is one which the entire Iliad exploits to heart-rending effect.

34.

Ruthless Poignancy

I have argued for a Homer who could neither read nor write, who had practised oral poetic composition since his earliest boyhood and then, *c.* 750–740 BC, performed versions of one long Iliad, culminating in the one which he dictated for his family's future use, whose text, I believe, is the foundation of ours. Behind what we read, I seem to hear Homer's voice performing, modulating his tone to suit the protagonists, changing pace to guide his listeners' attention and gesturing too, the first actor in world poetry.

Such arguments can only be persuasive, as decisive evidence has not survived. The poem, however, has, and so I have selected and explored what I regard as accessible hallmarks, beginning with its highly compressed timescale, its directed plot, and its characterization of heroes and heroines by their own and others' speeches. I have brought out the values by which they live and among which the plot coheres, especially the values of its towering creation, Achilles: heroes are not just driven by competitive, mutually destructive values. Nor is the Iliad merely a poem of killing, nor even one of life and death. It is a poem about anger and loss and about battle seen from two sides, chilling, hateful and fought with brutal physical detail, but also capable of inspiring bloodlust and offering glory to men.

Repeatedly, when quoting or citing verses from it I have been impressed by their small and subtle details and how at times they imply far more than they state. Even when Homer is explicit, he is a master of expressing much by saying little. In a long oral performance he could bring out the force of this eloquent reticence by slowing as he recited its words, pausing as they concluded. His plot is set in a world distinct from the world of its first hearers and is narrated in the past tense. Material objects in it, the bronze, the chariots, were dimly remembered items from a much earlier age, but the social setting and customs, I have argued, evoke those at the edge of his audience's awareness of their past, up to two generations earlier. Yet, Homer contrives a marvellous vividness throughout.

He gives speeches in the present tense and deploys an exact grasp of so much that he includes, a quality I have emphasized not least by studying his horses and places which he interrelates in the terrain round Troy. He combines recurring epithets, a store he inherited from earlier poets, with accurate observation, some of which I have dared to trace to his own eye: Homer the hunter, Homer at the site of Troy. He defies the labels we put on a distant 'dark age': he presents robots and examples of artificial intelligence, and in his account of the making of the shield for Achilles he invents moving pictures. Throughout the poem, when he cuts to and fro between battle scenes, he anticipates techniques of 'that most beautiful fraud in the world', film.

I have also dwelt on three worlds which the poem presents beside its heroes, the world of the gods, those aristocrats writ large in heaven, the world of women, viewed with empathy and insight, and the world of similes, whose times and settings are consistently close to their hearers and are a contrast, therefore, to the poem's narrative, which is 'not as mortals are nowadays'. Compelling though these hallmarks are, they are not why the poem transfixes us and moves us to tears. For an answer we need to go deeper. To find one, I will draw on C. S. Lewis and his masterly *Preface to Paradise Lost*.

Before engaging fully with Milton's epic, Lewis devoted fine pages to the Iliad and the qualities which mark it off from other epics. He referred to two in particular: its unwearying splendour and its ruthless poignancy.[1]

Unwearying splendour relates to the recurrent fineness of the poem's traditional epithets. Every day, Homer's dawn is born of the mist or saffron-robed; the wine is always honey-sweet; the earth is abundantly fertile. These epithets never diminish or darken their subjects. They express what Lewis well called the 'objectivity of the unchanging background', and yet they convey it at its brightest and best.[2] In the foreground, meanwhile, a plot unfolds which is ruthlessly poignant. Lewis's phrase goes to the heart of the Iliad: it can be refined into three parts.

The first is pathos. Sensitive ancient critics of the poem, including Aristotle, emphasized the Iliad as a poem of *pathos*.[3] By it, they meant passion and emotion, whereas we and Lewis mean the suffering which the poem describes and the sadness with which it touches us: pathos 'makes the poem's action pathetic, as the Greeks say', the Italian poet Tasso observed in 1585, 'or, as we say, affective'.[4] Pathos, in this sense, is evoked from the start, in the very first lines on the effects of Achilles' wrath and Apollo's plague and then in the person of poor Chryses, come to beg for the return of his daughter, only to be brusquely rejected by Agamemnon and left to walk in silence by the shore of that booming sea. Recurring epithets present the world at its best, but pathos suffuses with sadness what happens in it at a particular time. This interplay takes us closer to the heart of the Iliad's power.

In book 3 pathos runs through the presentation of Helen and her self-awareness, and in book 6 through the wondrous encounter between Hector and Andromache. The poem's scenes of supplication depend on it, especially the scene in which Lycaon, defenceless, falls before heartless Achilles with his arms outstretched. In book 22 it culminates in Andromache's realization that Hector is dead, and lastly in the mission of old Priam to request Hector's body from Achilles. In each of these episodes the pathos is enhanced by helplessness and previous loss.

It is also enhanced in parts of the battle narrative by those brief obituaries for a warrior which physically detailed combat excludes. The young man dies far from his family and homeland; he leaves a young widow who cannot give him a formal lament; his skills and talents have not availed him, nor have his father's. One of the poem's first obituaries is especially poignant.[5] Scamandrios the Trojan, son of Strophios, was an adept hunter, but Menelaus thrust a spear through his back and killed him, this young man who used to kill all the wildlife which the forest nurtures on the mountains. The goddess Artemis had taught him to be an excellent shot, but 'Artemis who delights in arrows did not help him then, nor the archery in which he formerly excelled'.

The past is a particular source of pathos. When Achilles pursues Hector outside Troy, they pass those water troughs in which Trojan women once washed clothes 'in the days of peace before the sons of the Achaeans came'. Above all, individuals evoke the past in four of the poem's most haunting words: *ei pot'eēn ge*, 'if it/he/I was indeed really so'.[6] They compress so much into so little, whether spoken by Helen on seeing from afar her former brother-in-law, or by elderly Nestor when recalling himself as a valiant young man, or by Priam to Hermes, as yet unrecognized, when he remarks how 'my son Hector, if indeed he was really so', never forgot to honour the gods. No other heroic poem has been capable of a phrase or thought of such transfixing wistfulness: here indeed 'the greatness of Homer's heroes is a greatness not of act but of consciousness'.[7]

In the old Gilgamesh poem Gilgamesh tells his companion Enkidu as they set out on a great exploit:

> 'The days of a man are numbered,
> Whatever he may do it is but wind.'

In versions of the Manas poem, the world is called illusory, in implicit contrast to the Muslim paradise to come. Homer never dwells on the vanity of life's pleasures and achievements. Instead, in four words of profound concision, he makes his heroes express the sense that in a contrasting present the past can seem with hindsight to be almost another world. It still can.

Pathos entwines repeatedly with a second constituent of poignancy: pity.[8] Pity pervades Andromache's meeting with Hector in book 6 and then pervades his parents' appeal to him to come inside Troy as book 22 begins. Throughout, it is a cardinal theme in the story of wrathful Achilles. The envoys in book 9 beg him to feel it, but he refuses. He feels it first for Patroclus when he comes weeping, also in pity, for the wounded Greeks. In book 23 he pities Eumelus, defeated by Athena in the chariot race. He then shows outstanding pity to Priam, the ultimate suppliant in the poem's final book.

Pity is a more detached response than empathy, which attempts to feel what another must be feeling. It also differs from mercy. It is not always related to a potential exercise of power. Unlike mercy, it does not require its subject to be superior to the person pitied: I can pity you, my superior, for losing your place whenever you reopen this book. Homer often links it to that inhibiting response, *aidōs*, especially when a suppliant begs for pity, but, unlike mercy, pity does not entail doing less harm than we otherwise might.

Until the final book, people in the Iliad feel pity only for those on their own side in the war. It is not restricted to family members. In battle, heroes can feel pity and act for unrelated heroes who have been killed or wounded near them. In the final book the range of pity then widens, when Priam solicits pity from Achilles and Achilles duly pities him. A movement from wrath to pity runs through the entire story of Achilles, dignifying the poem.

Pity is a mark of shared humanity, but it also occurs among the gods. Mortals pray to them 'in the hope that' they may show pity, and sometimes gods indeed show it: once again, they are imagined as glorified aristocrats, super-crats in heaven who pity their inferiors and suppliants on earth. However, with one exception, the Olympians feel and express pity only for warriors on the side which they favour in the war. When Apollo and Athena meet by the oak tree on the killing field, they are frank about it: Athena pities Greeks, but Apollo pities Trojans. In book 8, Hera and Athena are angry when Zeus bans them from entering the battle, and even say that they lament for the Greeks who are dying in their absence. Pity in heaven goes together with partisan care.[9]

The exception is Zeus himself. There are times when he pities Greeks and times when he pities Trojans. He pities Agamemnon, the Myrmidons, Patroclus and Achilles' divine horses, but he also pities old Priam and Hector. His pity is not just a blip, an ineffective

390

emotion. Regularly it issues in action. When Zeus pities dead Hector, he sends Thetis to tell Achilles to relent and ransom his body. Even when he expresses pity for Achilles' horses, he goes on to energize them so that they take their driver safely out of the battle. Aristotle later claimed that we feel pity only for something we might perhaps suffer ourselves. The gods of the Iliad refute him, as they pity mortals for suffering what they themselves could never experience. Pity for mortals makes Zeus quite other than a cosmic sadist.[10]

In book 20 he summons all the gods to tell them they may at last go down to the fighting, whereas he will remain sitting in a dell on Olympus. 'They concern me, dying as they are', he says in words of disputed scope: 'sitting here, I will watch and delight my mind.'[11] In book 13, during the fighting's longest day, he had already turned his eyes from the killing field and preferred to gaze on those faraway nomads, milkers of mares. His delight will be in watching the gods engaging: it will not be in watching the consequent slaughter of men. It is when special heroes are near death that he expresses pitying love for them. He grants honour and glory to Hector, one man among many, '*for* he was to live for only a short while'.[12] Imminent mortality provokes Zeus' pity, but seven books later he concurs nonetheless in Hector's death.

Pity and pathos give the poem poignancy, but they are not what makes the poignancy ruthless. In her admired essay Simone Weil stressed the bitterness, *amertume,* she found in the Iliad and defined it as 'the subordination of the soul to force, that is, in the last analysis, to matter', the aspect which she made central to her idiosyncratic reading of the poem. In fact, the bitterness comes from quite a different source. In Greek literature, tragic drama has become famous for its use of irony, but Homer, three centuries earlier, was already its supreme exponent. Irony gives the Iliad's poignancy its hard and ruthless depth.

Ancient critics discussed irony as a figure of speech, linked with deception and with saying the contrary to what a speaker really means. Centuries later Socrates was to make self-deprecating irony a hallmark of his questioning.[13] Homer deploys this device in some of the speeches in the Iliad, whose speakers use irony while expecting their listeners to grasp it. Sometimes it is used in gentle mockery or banter, but at others bitterly, in sarcasm: 'sarcasm between heroes on both sides is a constant battlefield refrain'.[14] Sarcasm assumes that both parties know the underlying, very different truth. One of them, even, is already dead. In book 13, on the longest day, Idomeneus berates Othryoneus, who had been offered one of Priam's daughters in marriage without giving *hedna*, in return for his promise that he would drive the sons of the Achaeans from Troy. Idomeneus tells him sarcastically that he and the Greeks would give him the fairest of Agamemnon's daughters if he would only join with them in sacking Troy: he must 'follow us so that we may agree the marriage by the seafaring ships, for we are not harsh in the matter of *hedna*'. Yet, Othryoneus is already dead, killed by Idomeneus, who is beginning, as he speaks, to drag his body away.

Unlike sarcasm, irony does not have to be harsh. Gentle irony is very rare in the Iliad, but it occurs in the poem's final book, in the scene between Hermes in disguise and elderly Priam on his way by night to Achilles. We know, and Hermes knows, what Priam does not, that he is entertaining divinity unawares. The irony here is not ruthless: it relates to disguise and a consequent absence of recognition. The Odyssey will be rich in this sort of irony, exploiting it while Odysseus goes in disguise among members of his own household.

In the Iliad, irony is usually harder, related to the pathos in its protagonists' ignorance of facts we listeners and readers already know. At its simplest and bleakest the ignorance is that a family member is already dead: examples are Helen's ignorance of the deaths of her brothers, Castor and Pollux, or, as book 22 begins, Priam's ignorance of the deaths of two of his remaining sons. In book 20, we have just heard how one of them died, the youngest son, whom Priam loved most and whom he had tried to prevent from fighting: swift-footed Polydorus was killed on the run by a spear-cast from Achilles. The other son is poor Lycaon, killed as that suppliant, arms outstretched. In book 22, looking out from Troy's battlements, Priam remarks that he cannot see them and wonders if they could be ransomed, or if they have been killed.[15] We know, but he does not, that both of them are dead.

This type of irony is capped 400 verses later. In Hector's house in Troy, Andromache is supervising a bath for Hector before his return from battle: she does not know, though we do, that he is lying dead outside the walls. Here, the irony of ignorance joins with pathos and overwhelms its listeners and readers. Homer calls her *nēpieē*: he had already applied this word to Patroclus during his final foray, when he was pursuing the routed Trojans, 'greatly deluded in his heart'. *Nēpios* there meant unknowing, but also foolishly so: in Andromache's case it is closer to innocence.[16] Patroclus was ignoring Achilles' warning not to attack the walls of Troy, but he was also unknowing of Zeus' plan, that his own end was near. 'But always the mind of Zeus is stronger than men's . . .'

The irony of ignorance becomes especially ruthless when it relates to mortals' ignorance of the gods and their decisions. It is first deployed in book 2 when we know, though Agamemnon does not, that the dream sent by Zeus is deliberately deceptive. It is then intensely poignant in book 6. When Hector returns to Troy, the Trojans' wives and daughters come running to ask him for news of their brothers, husbands and kin and he tells them, all in turn, to pray to the gods: 'but for many of them', Homer tells us, 'sorrows had been sealed'.[17] Irony recurs with even greater force when Hecuba leads the elderly Trojan women to pray to Athena in her temple inside the city. We know, but they do not, that Athena is on the side of the Greeks. Fair-cheeked Theano the priestess leads the prayer to her, promising her gifts of oxen 'in the hope she may pity the city and the wives of the Trojans and their unknowing children. So she spoke praying, but Pallas Athena refused.'[18]

This level of irony is especially ruthless because Homer expresses it in so very few words. It is not open-ended: it confronts us unambiguously. In later Greek drama and history writing, irony relates to mortals' misunderstanding of oracles, those messages inspired by a god in words or signs which are ambiguous. In the Iliad heroes never seek or receive oracles: they receive non-verbal omens, whether thunder or the flight of birds. They may mistake what they signify, but we listeners and readers do not: Homer's split-level poem gives us direct access to the gods. We listen in on them as they express their aims and partialities, and so we know what mortals on earth do not. When we then hear and watch those mortals, we are moved by the pathos of their ignorance: little did they know . . . However, Homer is not being cynical. A cynic always puts an unflattering interpretation on events and others' intentions, whereas Homer shows men and women striving to do their best. They merely do not know, and cannot know, what we already do.

'So far as we can judge . . .', Nick Lowe has well remarked, 'the *Iliad* is the ultimate source of what will prove one of the most persistent ideas in Western literature: that *life itself is plotted*, determined by a relatively tight and comprehensible set of narrative rules.'[19] In learning and applying them 'we submit to an education in the human predicament at large . . . Instead of merely importing our understanding of the outer world to help us make sense of a fictional world, we re-export the fictional world's rules to the world of experience. Yes, we say: that way of seeing the world "fits".' In the Iliad mortals' lives are not just plotted by a set of rules in a narrative: they are presented as plotted by the gods. The Iliad's pervasive irony is not simply a trick to shape and seize its listeners' emotions during its performance. It relates to an entire way of seeing the gods and human lives.

Ruthless to the heroes, it is also ruthless to its listeners and readers. As mortals, we too age, fall sick and die, ignorant of what is in store for us and when, whereas gods in Homer's heaven are immortal and live lives of ease. Repeatedly Homer brings out this poignant contrast: Achilles tells old Priam that the gods have spun it like a thread indeed.[20] Mortals can guess at the gods' intentions and motives in the fabric of their lives, but they cannot know them in advance. Yes indeed, we feel, that way of seeing the world *fits*. Even if we no longer credit Homer's gods, we strive, protest and act on plans of our own, but events then teach us otherwise. We can still export this rule of the Iliad's fictional world to the world of our own experience.

In Homer's heaven there are facts hidden from mortals, the partisan hatreds and loyalties, the interplay between competing divinities and, all the while, the inscrutable plan of Zeus. Zeus can overturn destiny, but if he were to do so, the other gods would rebel in disapproval.[21] He does his bit nonetheless: he mixes good and evil for individuals from the two jars in his halls. What Achilles tells Priam in the final book is not a random flourish: the entire plot of the Iliad exemplifies it. To some of us Zeus gives nothing but good, to others nothing but evil, but to most of us he gives both good and evil, mixed.[22] He gives that mixture to Achilles' father Peleus, to Agamemnon, Patroclus, Hector and to Priam. At first, Zeus seemed to have granted Achilles all he wished for, but he also gave him the death of Patroclus, a fistful of evil indeed from his jar.

In ignorance of the outcome, we too press on like the heroes, but life does not bring us unmixed good: disease strikes a child at random, death takes friends at an early age, accidents cripple those most dear to us. Life has a recalcitrant refusal to conform. From Homer's heaven the gods look down meanwhile on the heroes, caring for some, specially favouring others and pitying those dear to them, but they never let pity cloud their own existence. In a fine hymn to Apollo, composed in the 520s BC, its poet tells how

> all the Muses sing antiphonally with their fair voice
> Of the immortal gifts of the gods and the travails men endure,
> All that they have from the immortal gods
> As they live helpless and with no resort, nor can they find
> A cure for death and a means of keeping off old age.

As the Muses sing this song, the gods and goddesses dance, and among them Apollo plays his lyre.[23]

At the end of the Iliad's first book the Muses also sing antiphonally for the gods on Olympus as they feast and set aside a potential quarrel. We do not hear what they sing, but as the poem unfolds we can justly assume it was a song of similar hardness. In the Iliad, Zeus says, nothing is more wretched on earth than mortal men.[24]

Gods and goddesses can care for mortals, but they ought never to quarrel over them: even their pity and grief for a favourite's death are soon set aside. Meanwhile they enjoy their special food and wine. It is as if they look down from a high table onto a hall of hapless students below, burdened by debt and disease and the trials of imponderable exams. They have individual favourites, but as they dine they listen with pleasure to a song sung by their choir on the woes of those others' lives, people to whom they give inscrutable marks, as it were, for their striving with questions whose answers were never known in advance.

With such gods in heaven, religion's great problem does not arise: the problem of evil. Evil is present because it is mixed by Zeus into individual lives at birth. At any time it can result, too, from the spite or anger of a god or gods. Mortal ignorance of its scope and cause adds to life's poignancy, and readers' and listeners' privileged knowledge makes the Iliad's poignancy ruthless. It pervades the poem, not as a trick but as a view of life.

It comes to a climax in the supreme battle, the one between Hector and Achilles, where it is a touchstone for a just appreciation of the poem. Fair-minded readers have sometimes felt it to be a cheat, the death of Hector after callous deception by Athena. It is so much more than that. It is the supreme example of divine decision and the ruthless concealment which accompanies its execution.

During three circuits of the city, Apollo had been filling Hector's legs with might and keeping him swift.[25] Zeus, looking on, wonders if perhaps he might indeed save Hector, but Athena, the spiteful enemy of all Trojans, protests at such a thing, the freeing from death of a mortal man, long fated by his destiny. Zeus reassures her he was not being serious: 'I want to be kindly to you', not Hector. 'Do then as your purpose indeed was, and do not still hold back.' Athena, already eager, flies down from Olympus to vent her spite.

Zeus weighs two fates of death on his scales and Hector's is the one which sinks down: 'and Apollo left him'.[26] We know, therefore, the divine imbalance and what is about to happen, but on earth Hector does not. Athena goes first to Achilles, standing beside him and telling him that now they will win great glory for the Achaeans and kill Hector, 'even if Apollo goes and grovels before Zeus': her sarcastic word for this grovelling fills the entire first half of a hexameter.[27] Achilles knows, and we know, but Hector does not. She goes to him, disguising herself with the utmost cunning: she appears to him as Deiphobus, his dearest brother.

The irony is ruthless and it transfixes anyone who grasps its full context. Hector welcomes 'Deiphobus', of course, and says he will honour him more than ever as he alone has dared to come out from Troy to help him. 'Deiphobus' continues to deceive him with lies about his own boldness in ignoring others and leaving the city walls. So Hector calls to Achilles that, now, his heart bids him to stand firm and face him, 'whether I take you or am taken'. After a first exchange of spear-throws, Hector stands despondent, because he has no other ashen spear. He shouts to 'Deiphobus of the white shield', an epithet used only here, heightening the effect: he 'was asking him for a long spear, but he was nowhere near to him'.

He was nowhere near . . . *ho d'ou ti hoi enguthen ēen*. Six brief words express the irony: ruthlessly poignant, they strike us to the very heart.[28] Hector then realizes what we already know, that Athena has deceived him and that destiny, *moira*, is come upon him: it was dearer, he recognizes, to Zeus and Apollo than his continuing escape. A hero as great as Hector can only die with the intervention of the gods. Athena deceives him, not as an anticlimax, but as a supreme example of man's ignorance of the gods' decisions.

In book 22 ruthless irony intensifies the plights of Priam and Andromache too, but in book 24 Homer suspends it. Instead he gives us the gentle irony of Priam's encounter with Hermes and contrives supreme pathos and pity, in the scenes of Priam and his departure, Priam and Achilles and, lastly, dead Hector's reception in Troy. It is in book 6, however, that pity, pathos and irony combine, all three.

They first combine in that meeting of Hector with Trojans who ask about their loved ones, then in the older women's prayer to Athena and finally in Hector's parting from Andromache. At first, pathos and pity predominate. Andromache begs for pity and eventually

Hector shows it when, seeing their baby son's reaction, she laughs through her tears. The pathos of their conversation and its conclusion is unsurpassed.

Irony then begins to intensify it: Andromache leaves her husband after this supremely poignant meeting, 'turning and turning again' as she goes. On her return to their home she starts the lament for him in his own household though he is still alive. The poignancy is becoming ruthless: how ever could Homer move his poem forwards in performance after such an overpowering encounter? He responds with a brilliant use of contrast: he cuts away to Paris as he comes down from the citadel to meet Hector just as they had agreed.

Swift movement and bright light entirely change the poem's mood: Paris trusts in the speed of his feet; he races as fast as a stallion which has broken free from its tether to gallop to the pastures of the mares; he gleams in his shining armour like *ēlektōr*, a rare poetic word which Homer reached for in performance and which seems to mean the glistening sun.[29] All shine and movement, Paris finds his brother Hector turning aside from the very place where he had just conversed so lovingly with his wife. Irony then returns, to the poem's surface and to what underlies it.

'So, sir,' Paris chafes him ironically, 'am I indeed detaining you in all your haste and dawdling, have I not come on time, as you commanded?' Nearly 200 verses before, Homer had foreshadowed this remark. When they met in his house, Paris had assured Hector that he would indeed catch him up if Hector went on ahead. Unsure of him, Hector had told Helen to rouse him to do so, 'so that he may overtake me while I am still inside the city'. Hector had not known then what would detain him, nor now, at their re-meeting, does Paris. So there is more irony, carefully prepared, behind Paris' ironic words: Hector, we know, but Paris does not, is the one who has been lingering and Paris is the one who has hurried. It is the very opposite of what Hector had assumed would happen.[30]

There is a further irony, even deeper: we know, but Paris does not, what has been detaining Hector and what has occurred in the very place where they meet. Through an ignorant third party Homer is moving the poem forwards from the intensely emotional encounter between Hector and his wife, one which might have brought it to a halt.

In *Anna Karenina*, Tolstoy, his only equal, deploys a similar skill.[31] Levin and young Kitty withdraw from the others at an evening party, to a table on which they write capital letters to each other in chalk. Each catches the other's meaning in Levin's cryptic invitation to marry and Kitty's response: 'in her lovely eyes, suffused with happiness, he saw all he needed to know. And he wrote down three more letters, but before he had finished writing she read them over his arm, and herself finished and wrote the answer, "Yes".'

How ever could Tolstoy move his story beyond this shining moment? He too has his Paris, a third party, unaware:

> 'Playing secrétaire?' said the old prince, coming up to them. 'But we ought to be going if you want to be in time for the theatre.'
>
> Levin rose and escorted Kitty to the door'.

Hector, too, escorts Paris: he takes him to the gate of Troy. However, he does not go in silence. Homer makes him respond neatly to Paris' chafing and, then, to add that by refusing to join the battle Paris grieves his heart. He hears such shameful things on his behalf, but, he concludes, 'let us go: we will settle this later':

> 'If ever Zeus grants the heavenly ever-living gods to set a
>   mixing bowl of freedom in our halls,
> When we have driven the well-greaved Achaeans from Troy.'

Like Levin, Hector says nothing of what has just passed in the very place where he is standing. Out he and Paris go to the bridges of war and the battle which brings glory to men, but he half knows, and we know fully, that the Achaeans will never be driven from Troy: that bowl of freedom will never be set in their halls.

Bibliography

Adkins, A. 1960. *Merit and Responsibility: A Study in Greek Values* (Oxford).

—. 1969. 'Threatening, Abusing and Feeling Angry in the Homeric Poems', *JHS* 89: 7–21.

—. 1972. 'Homeric Gods and the Values of Homeric Society', *JHS* 92: 1–19.

—. 1997. 'Homeric Ethics', in I. Morris, B. Powell, eds., *A New Companion to Homer* (Leiden) 694–713.

Alden, M. 2005. 'Lions in Paradise: Lion Similes in the *Iliad* and the Lion Cubs of *Il.* 18. 318–22', *CQ* 55: 335–42.

Alexander, C. 2010. *The War That Killed Achilles: The True Story of the Iliad* (London).

Alexiou, M. 2002. *After Antiquity: Greek Language, Myth, and Metaphor* (Ithaca, NY).

Allan, W. 2005. 'Arms and the Man: Euphorbus, Hector and the Death of Patroclus', *CQ* 55: 1–16.

—. 2006. 'Divine Justice and Cosmic Order in Early Greek Epic', *JHS* 126: 1–35.

Anderson, J. K. 1985. *Hunting in the Ancient World* (Berkeley).

Andrewes, A. 1961. 'Phratries in Homer', *Hermes* 89: 129–40.

Andronicos, M. 1984. *Vergina: The Royal Tombs and the Ancient City* (Athens).

Arena, E. 2015. 'Mycenaean Peripheries during the Palatial Age: The Case of Achaia', *Hesperia* 84: 1–46.

Arthur, M. B. 1981. 'The Divided World of Iliad VI', in H. P. Foley, ed., *Reflections of Women in Antiquity* (New York) 19–64.

Auden, H. W. 1896. 'Natural History in Homer', *CR* 10: 107.

Auerbach, E., trans. W. R. Trask. 1953. *Mimesis: The Representation of Reality in Western Literature* (Princeton).

Bachvarova, M. 2016. *From Hittite to Homer: The Anatolian Background of Ancient Greek Epic* (Cambridge).

Ballesteros, B. 2021. 'On *Gilgamesh* and Homer: Ishtar, Aphrodite and the Meaning of a Parallel', *CQ* 71: 1–21.

Barker Webb, P. 1844. *Topographie de la Troade ancienne et moderne* (Paris).

Barnes, T. G. 2011. 'Homeric *androtēta kai hēbēn*', *JHS* 131: 1–13.

Bartlett, R. 2022. *The Middle Ages and the Movies: Eight Key Films* (London).

Baudrillard, J. 1991. *La Guerre du Golfe n'a pas eu lieu* (Paris).

Baynes, N. 1955. *Byzantine Studies and Other Essays* (London).

Beaton, R. 2016. '"The National Epic of the Modern Greeks"? – *Digenis Akritis*, the Homeric Question and the Making of a Modern Myth', in S. Sherratt, J. Bennet, eds., *Archaeology and Homeric Epic* (Sheffield) 156–63.

Bibliography

Beckman, G., T. Bryce, E. Cline. 2011. *The Ahhiyawa Texts* (Atlanta).

Beecroft, A. 2011. 'Blindness and Literacy in the *Lives* of Homer', *CQ* 61: 1–18.

Beissinger, M., S. Tylus, J. Wofford. 1999. *Epic Traditions in the Contemporary World: The Poetics of Community* (Oakland, California).

Bennet, J. 2014. 'Linear B and Homer', in Y. Duhoux, A. M. Davies, eds., *A Companion to Linear B: Mycenaean Greek Texts and Their World*, vol. 3 (Louvain–Walpole) 187–234.

[Bentley, R.] 1713. *Remarks upon a Late Discourse of Free-Thinking* (London).

Bernard, P. 1995. 'Une légende de fondation hellénistique: Apamée sur l'Oronte d'après les *Cynégetiques* du Pseudo-Oppien . . .', *Topoi* 5: 353–408.

Binek, N. M. 2017. 'The Dipylon Oinochoe Graffito: Text or Decoration?', *Hesperia* 86: 423–42.

Blackwell, N. 2021. 'Ahhiyawa, Hatti and Diplomacy: Implications of Hittite Misperceptions of the Mycenaean World', *Hesperia* 90: 191–231.

Bloom, P. 2016. *Against Empathy: The Case for Rational Compassion* (London).

Blundell, M. W. 1989. *Helping Friends and Harming Enemies: A Study in Sophocles and Greek Ethics* (Cambridge).

Bonnet, C. 2017. 'Les dieux en assemblée', in G. Pironti, C. Bonnet, eds., *Les Dieux d'Homère: Polythéisme et poésie en Grèce ancienne* (Liège) 87–112.

Booth, W. C. 1974. *A Rhetoric of Irony* (Chicago).

Bowie, A. M., ed. 2019, *Homer: Iliad Book III* (Cambridge).

—. 2021. 'Fate and Authority in Mesopotamian Literature and the *Iliad*', in A. Kelly, C. Metcalf, eds., *Gods and Mortals in Early Greek and Near Eastern Mythology* (Oxford) 243–61.

Bowie, E. L. 2022. *Essays on Ancient Greek Literature and Culture*, vol. 1 (Cambridge).

Bowra, C. M. 1930. *Tradition and Design in the Iliad* (Oxford).

—. 1935. *Early Greek Elegists* (Cambridge, Mass.).

—. 1952. *Heroic Poetry* (London).

—. 1960. 'Homeric Epithets for Troy', *JHS* 80: 16–23.

—. 1972. *Homer* (London).

Bridges, M. 2008. 'The *Eros* of *Homeros*: The Pleasures of Greek Epic in Victorian Literature and Archaeology', *Victorian Review* 34(2): 165–83.

Burgess, J. S. 2001. *The Tradition of the Trojan War and the Epic Cycle* (Baltimore–London).

—. 2017. 'The Tale of Meleager in the *Iliad*', *Oral Tradition* 31: 51–76.

Burkert, W. 1985. *Greek Religion* (Oxford).

—. 1992. *The Orientalizing Revolution* (Cambridge, MA).

—. 1995. 'Lydia between East and West, or How to Date the Trojan War', in J. B. Carter, S. P. Morris, eds., *The Ages of Homer: A Tribute to Emily Townsend Vermeule* (Austin) 139–48.

—. 1997. 'From Epiphany to Cult Statue: Early Greek *Theos*', in A. B. Lloyd, ed., *What is a God?* (Swansea) 15–34.

Burt, R. L. 1990. *Friedrich Salomo Krauss (1859–1938): Selbstzeugnisse und Materialien zur Bibliographie des Volkskunsdlers, Literaten und Sexualforschers* (Vienna).

Cairns, D. L. 1993. *Aidōs: The Psychology and Ethics of Honour and Shame in Ancient Greek Literature* (Oxford).

Bibliography

Carlier, P. 2006. 'Anax and Basileus in the Homeric Poems', in S. Deger-Jalkotzy, I. S. Lemos, eds., *Ancient Greece: From the Mycenaean Palaces to the Age of Homer* (Edinburgh) 101–10.

—. 2007. 'Are the Homeric *Basileis* "Big Men"?', in S. P. Morris, R. Laffineur, eds., *Epos: Reconsidering Greek Epic and Aegean Bronze Age Archaeology* (Austin) 121–8.

Carr, B. 1999. 'Pity and Compassion as Social Virtues', *Philosophy* 74: 411–29.

Carter, J. B. 1995. 'The Occasion of Homeric Performance', in J. B. Carter, S. P. Morris, eds., *The Ages of Homer: A Tribute to Emily Townsend Vermeule* (Austin) 285–312.

Chaniotis, A. 2010. 'The "Best of Homer": Homeric Texts, Performances and Images in the Hellenistic World and Beyond The Contribution of Inscriptions', in E. Walter-Karydi, ed., *Homer: Myths, Texts, Images: Homeric Epics and Ancient Greek Art* (Ithaca, NY) 257–78.

Clarke, H. 1981. *Homer's Readers: A Historical Introduction to the Iliad and the Odyssey* (Newark, Del.).

Clarke, M. J. 2019. *Achilles Beside Gilgamesh: Mortality and Wisdom in Early Epic Poetry* (Cambridge).

Clarke, M. 1995. 'Between Lions and Men: Images of the Hero in the *Iliad*', *GRBS* 36: 137–59.

—. 2006. 'Achilles, Beowulf, and Cú Chulainn: Continuity and Analogy from Homer to the Medieval North', in M. J. Clarke, B. G. F. Currie, R. O. A. M. Lyne, eds., *Epic Interactions: Perspectives on Homer, Virgil, and the Epic Tradition Presented to Jasper Griffin by Former Pupils* (Oxford) 263–81.

Cline, E. H. 2013. *The Trojan War: A Very Short Introduction* (Oxford).

Coccagna, H. A. 2014. 'Manipulating *Mastoi*: The Female Breast in the Sympotic Setting', in A. Avramidou, D. Demetriou, eds., *Approaching the Ancient Artifact: Representation, Narrative, and Function* (Berlin–Boston) 399–411.

Čolaković, Z. 2019. 'Avdo Međedović's Post-Traditional Epics and Their Relevance to Homeric Studies', *JHS* 139: 1–48.

Coldstream, J. N. 1976. 'Hero-Cults in the Age of Homer', *JHS* 96: 8–17.

—. 1977. *Geometric Greece* (London).

—. 1986. 'The Geometric Lion-Fighter from Kato Phana', in J. Boardman, C. E. Vaphopoulou-Richardson, eds., *Chios: A Conference at the Homereion in Chios, 1984* (Oxford) 181–6.

—. 1998. 'Light from Cyprus on the Greek "Dark Age"?', 19th J. L. Myres Memorial Lecture, Ashmolean Museum, Oxford (Oxford).

Colebrook, C. 2009. *Irony* (London).

Colonna, G. 1980. 'Graeco more bibere: l'iscrizione della tomba 115 dell'Osteria dell'Osa', *Archeologia Laziale* 3: 51–5.

Connelly, J. B. 2007. *Portrait of a Priestess: Women and Ritual in Ancient Greece* (Princeton).

Cook, J. M. 1973. *The Troad: An Archaeological and Topographical Study* (Oxford).

Crielaard, J. P. 1995. 'Homer, History and Archaeology: Some Remarks on the Date of the Homeric World', in J. P. Crielaard, ed., *Homeric Questions: Essays in Philology, Ancient History and Archaeology* (Amsterdam) 201–86.

—. 2003. 'The Cultural Biography of Material Goods in Homer's Epics', *GAIA* 7: 49–62.

—. 2016. 'Living Heroes: Metal Urn Cremations in Early Iron Age Greece, Cyprus and Italy', in F. Gallo, ed., *Omero: quaestiones disputatae* (Milan–Rome) 43–78.

Crisp, R. 2013. 'Homeric Ethics', in R. Crisp, ed., *The Oxford Handbook of the History of Ethics* (Oxford) 1 – 19.

Csapo, E. 1991. 'An International Community of Traders in Late 8th–7th c. BC Kommos in Southern Crete', *ZPE* 88: 211–16.

Cullhed, E. 2021. 'The Dipylon *Oinochoē* and Ancient Greek Dance Aesthetics', *CQ* 71: 22–33.

Currie, B. 2012. 'The *Iliad*, *Gilgamesh* and Neoanalysis', in F. Montanari, A. Rengakos, C. Tsagalis, eds., *Homeric Contexts: Neoanalysis and the Interpretation of Oral Poetry* (Berlin–Boston) 543–80.

—. 2016. *Homer's Allusive Art* (Oxford).

Dalley, S. 2016. 'Gilgamesh and Heroes at Troy: Myth, History and Education in the Invention of Tradition', in S. Sherratt, J. Bennet, eds., *Archaeology and Homeric Epic* (Oxford) 116–34.

Dalrymple, W. 2006. 'Homer in India', *New Yorker* (20 Nov.): 48–55.

Danek, G. 1988. *Studien zur Dolonie* (Vienna).

—. 2002. 'Traditional Referentiality and Homeric Intertextuality', in F. Montanari, P. Ascheri, eds., *Omero tremila anni dopo* (Rome) 3–17.

Danek, G., S. Hagel. 1995. 'Homer-Singen', *Wiener Humanistische Blätter* 37: 5–20.

Delebecque, É. 1951. *Le Cheval dans l'Iliade* (Paris).

Demetriou, T. 2015. 'The Homeric Question in the Sixteenth Century: Early Modern Scholarship and the Text of Homer', *Renaissance Quarterly* 68: 496–557.

Des Courtils, J. 2003. 'Xanthos en Lycie: Nouvelles données sur la romanisation d'une ancienne cité indigène', *REG* 116: 1–16.

Dickie, M. 1995. 'The Geography of Homer's World', in Ø. Andersen, M. Dickie, *Homer's World: Fiction, Tradition, Reality* (Copenhagen) 29–56.

Dickie, M. W. 1984. 'Fair and Foul Play in the Funeral Games in the *Iliad*', *Journal of Sport History* 11(2): 8–17.

Dickinson, O. 2006. *The Aegean from Bronze Age to Iron Age: Continuity and Change between the Twelfth and Eighth Centuries BC* (London).

—. 2010. 'Was There Really a Trojan War?', *The Anglo-Hellenic Review* 41: 18–22.

—. 2011. 'Catalogue of Ships', in M. Finkelberg, ed., *The Homer Encyclopedia* (Chichester) 150–55.

—. 2016. 'The Will to Believe: Why Homer Cannot be '"True" in Any Meaningful Sense', in S. Sherratt, J. Bennet, eds., *Archaeology and Homeric Epic* (Oxford) 10–19.

Dodds, E. R. 1951. *The Greeks and the Irrational* (Berkeley).

—. 1968. 'Homer [parts i–iii]', in M. Platnauer, ed., *Fifty Years (and Twelve) of Classical Scholarship* (Oxford) 1–49.

Douglas, M. 2007. *Thinking in Circles: An Essay on Ring Composition* (New Haven, Conn.).

Dover, K. J. 1978. *Greek Homosexuality* (London).

Dowden, K. 2007. 'Olympian Gods, Olympian Pantheon', in D. Ogden, ed. *A Companion to Greek Religion* (Oxford) 41–55.

Drews, R. 1976. 'The Earliest Greek Settlements on the Black Sea', *JHS* 96: 18–31.

Bibliography

Dryden, J., G. Fracastoro, N. Tate. 1693. *Examen poeticum: Being the third part of miscellany poems containing variety of new translations of the ancient poets, together with many original copies by the most eminent hands* (London).

Dué, Casey, ed. 2009. *Recapturing a Homeric Legacy: Images and Insights from the Venetus A Manuscript of the Iliad* (Washington, DC, and Cambridge, Mass.).

Dunbabin,T. J. 1957. *The Greeks and Their Eastern Neighbours* (London).

Düntzer, H. 1872. *Homerische Abhandlungen* (Leipzig).

Duplouy, A. 2006. *Le Prestige des élites: Recherches sur les modes de reconnaissance sociale en Grèce entre les Xe et Ve siècles avant J.-C.* (Paris).

Easterling, P. E. 1991. 'Men's *kleos* and Women's *gōos*: Female Voices in the *Iliad*', *Journal of Modern Greek Studies* 9: 145–51.

Easton, D. F., J. D. Hawkins, A. G. Sherratt, E. S. Sherratt. 2002. 'Troy in Recent Perspective', *AS* 52: 75–109.

Edwards, M. W. 1980. 'Convention and Individuality in *Iliad* 1', *HSCP* 84: 1–28.

—. 1992. 'Homer and Oral Tradition: The Type–Scene', *Oral Tradition* 7: 284–330.

Ellis-Evans, A. 2019. *The Kingdom of Priam: Lesbos and the Troad between Anatolia and the Aegean* (Oxford).

Elmer, D. F. 2010. '*Kita* and *Kosmos*: The Poetics of Ornamentation in Bosniac and Homeric Epic', *Journal of American Folklore* 123: 276–303.

Elmer, D. F. 2013. *The Poetics of Consent: Collective Decision Making and the Iliad* (Baltimore).

Farron, S. 1979. 'The Portrayal of Women in the Iliad', *Acta Classica* 22: 15–31.

Fielding, N., ed. 2020. *Selected Works of Chokan Valikhanov: Pioneering Ethnographer and Historian of the Great Steppe* (Kazakhstan Embassy, UK, and Cambridge).

Finkelberg, M. 2007. 'More on *Kleos Aphthiton*', *CQ* 57: 341–50.

Finley, M. I. 1954. *The World of Odysseus* (1st edn, New York).

—. 1957. 'Homer and Mycenae: Property and Tenure', *Historia* 5: 133–59.

—. 1979. *The World of Odysseus* (rev. edn, London).

—. 1981. *Economy and Society in Ancient Greece* (London).

Finnegan, R., L. Mulvin. 2022. *The Life and Works of Robert Wood, Classicist and Traveller, 1717–1771* (Oxford).

Fisher, N., H. van Wees. 2015. '*Aristocracy*' in Antiquity: Redefining Greek and Roman Elites* (Swansea).

Flaig, E. 1994. 'Das Konsensprinzip im homerischen Olymp: Überlegungen zum göttlichen Entscheidungsprozess Ilias 4. 1–72', *Hermes* 122: 13–31.

Foley, J. M. 1999. *Homer's Traditional Art*.

—. 2004. 'Epic as Genre', in R. Fowler, ed., *The Cambridge Companion to Homer* (Cambridge).

Forrest, W. G. 1966. *The Emergence of Greek Democracy: The Character of Greek Politics, 800–400 BC* (London).

Forster, E. S. 1936. 'Trees and Plants in Homer', *CR* 50: 97–104.

Fowler, R. 2011.'Hellenes', in M. Finkelberg, ed., *The Homeric Encyclopedia*, vol. II (Chichester) 338–9.

Fraenkel, E. 1957. *Horace* (Oxford).

Fränkel, H. 1921. *Die homerischen Gleichnisse* (Göttingen).

Fraser, P. M. 1972. *Ptolemaic Alexandria I–III* (Oxford).

Fredouille, J.-C. 1993. 'Deux mauvais souvenirs d'Augustin', in G. W. Most, H. Petersmann, A. M. Ritter, eds., *Philanthropia kai eusebeia: Festschrift für Albrecht Dihle zum 70. Geburtstag* (Göttingen) 74–9.

Frei, P. 1978. 'Die Lykier bei Homer', in E. Akurgal, ed., *The Proceedings of the Xth International Congress of Classical Archaeology* (Ankara–İzmir) 819–27.

—. 1993. 'Die Bellerophontessage und der Alte Testament', in B. Janowski, K. Koch, G. Wilhelm, eds. *Religionsgeschichtliche Beziehungen zwischen Kleinasien, Nordsyrien und dem Alten Testament* (Freiburg–Göttingen) 39–65.

Friis Johansen, K. 1967. *The Iliad in Early Greek Art* (Copenhagen).

Gagné, R., M. Herrero de Jáuregui, eds. 2019. *Les Dieux d'Homère II: Anthropomorphismes* (Liège).

Gaskin, R. 1990. 'Do Homeric Heroes Make Real Decisions?', *CQ* 40: 1–15.

Gennep, A. van. 1909. *La Question d'Homère: Les poèmes homériques, l'archéologie et la poésie populaire* (Paris).

George, A. 2018. 'Enkidu and the Harlot: Another Fragment of Old Babylonian Gilgameš', *Zeitschrift für Assyriologie* 108: 10–21.

—. 2020. *The Epic of Gilgamesh: The Babylonian Epic Poem and Other Texts in Akkadian and Sumerian* (2nd edn, London).

Gernet, L. 1955. 'Jeux et droit (remarques sur le XXIIIème chant de l'*Iliade*)', in his *Droit et société dans la Grèce ancienne* (Paris) 9–18.

Gigante, M., A. Nava, et al. 2021. 'Who was Buried with Nestor's Cup? Macroscopic and Microscopic Analyses of the Cremated Remains from Tomb 168', in *PLoS One* 16 (10) (web).

Gill, C. 1984. 'The *Ēthos/Pathos* Distinction in Rhetorical and Literary Criticism', *CQ* 34: 149–66.

Gill, C., N. Postlethwaite, R. Seaford, eds. 1998. *Reciprocity in Ancient Greece* (Oxford).

Giovannini, A. 1969. *Étude historique sur les origines du Catalogue des Vaisseaux* (Bern).

Gomme, A. W., A. Andrewes, K. J. Dover 1981. *A Historical Commentary on Thucydides*, vol. 5, book VIII (Oxford).

Gonzáles, J. M. 2013. *The Epic Rhapsode and His Craft: Homeric Performance in a Diachronic Perspective* (Washington, DC).

Gottlieb, P. 1992. 'The Complexity of Socratic Irony: A Note on Professor Vlastos' Account', *CQ* 42: 278–9.

Gould, J. 1991. 'Give and Take in Herodotus', J. L. Myres Memorial Lecture, New College, Oxford.

—. 2001. 'The Idea of Society in the *Iliad*', in his *Myth, Ritual, Memory and Exchange: Essays in Greek Literature and Culture* (Oxford) 335–58.

Grafton, A. 1981. '*Prolegomena* to Friedrich August Wolf', *Journal of the Warburg and Courtauld Institutes* 44 (1981) 101–29.

—. 1983. *Joseph Scaliger: A Study in the History of Classical Scholarship*, vol. I: *Textual Criticism and Exegesis* (Oxford).

Bibliography

Grafton, A., J. Weinberg. 2011. *'I Have Always Loved the Holy Tongue': Isaac Casaubon, the Jews and a Forgotten Chapter in Renaissance Scholarship* (Cambridge, Mass.).

Graver, M. 1995. 'Dog-Helen and Homeric Insult', *CA* 14: 41–61.

Gray, D. H. F. 1954. 'Metal-Working in Homer', *JHS* 74: 1–15.

—. 1958. 'Mycenaean Names in Homer', *JHS* 78: 43–8.

Graziosi, B. 2002. *Inventing Homer: The Early Reception of Epic* (Cambridge).

Graziosi, B., J. Haubold. 2003. 'Homeric Masculinity', *JHS* 123: 60–76.

—. 2005. *Homer: The Resonance of Epic* (London).

—. 2015. 'The Homeric Text', *Ramus* 44: 5–28.

Grethlein, J., L. Huitink. 2017. 'Homer's Vividness: An Enactive Approach', *JHS* 137: 67–91.

Griffin, J. 1976. 'Homeric Pathos and Objectivity', *CQ* 26: 161–85.

—. 1977. 'The Epic Cycle and the Uniqueness of Homer', *JHS* 97: 39–53.

—. 1978. 'The Divine Audience and the Religion of the Iliad', *CQ* 28: 1–22.

—. 1980A. *Homer on Life and Death* (Oxford).

—. 1980B. *Homer* (Oxford).

—. 1986. 'Homeric Words and Speakers', *JHS* 106: 36–57.

—. 1990. 'Achilles Kills Hector', *Lampas* 23: 353–69.

—, ed. 1995. *Homer. Iliad Book Nine* (Oxford).

Griffin, J., M. Hammond. 1982. 'Critical Appreciations VI: Homer, *Iliad* 1.1–52', *G & R* 29: 126–42.

Griffith, M. 2006A. 'Horsepower and Donkeywork: Equids and the Ancient Greek Imagination. Part One', *CP* 101: 185–246.

—. 2006B. 'Horsepower and Donkeywork: Equids and the Ancient Greek Imagination. Part Two', *CP* 101: 307–58.

Grote, G. 1888. *A History of Greece* (London).

Hainsworth, J. B. 1991. *The Idea of Epic* (Berkeley).

Hall, E. 1989. *Inventing the Barbarian: Greek Self-Definition through Tragedy* (Oxford).

Hammer, D. 1998. 'The Politics of the *Iliad*', *CJ* 94: 1–30.

—. 2002. 'The *Iliad* as Ethical Thinking: Politics, Pity and the Operation of Esteem', *Arethusa* 35: 203–35.

Hardie, C. 1956. 'In Defence of Homer', *G & R* 3: 118–31.

Haslam, M. 1997. 'Homeric Papyri and Transmission of the Text', in I. Morris, B. Powell, eds., *A New Companion to Homer* (Leiden) 55–100.

—. 2011. 'Text and Transmission', in M. Finkelberg, ed., *The Homer Encyclopedia*, vol. III (Chichester) 849–55.

Hatto, A. 1990. *The Manas of Wilhelm Radloff* (Wiesbaden).

—. 2017. *The World of the Khanty Epic Hero-Princes* (Cambridge).

Haubold, J. 2007. 'Homer After Parry: Tradition, Reception and the Timeless Text', in B. Graziosi, E. Greenwood, eds., *Homer in the Twentieth Century: Between World Literature and the Western Canon* (Oxford) 27–46.

Haug, D. T. T. 2015. 'Tmesis in the Epic Tradition', in Ø. Andersen, D. T. T. Haug, eds., *Relative Chronology in Early Greek Epic Poetry* (Cambridge) 96–105.

Bibliography

Haugen, K. L. 2011. *Richard Bentley: Poetry and Enlightenment* (Cambridge, Mass.).

Heath, J. 1992. 'The Legacy of Peleus: Death and Divine Gifts in the Iliad', *Hermes* 120: 387–400.

Heath, M. 2000. 'Do Heroes Eat Fish?', in D. Braund, J. Wilkins, eds., *Athenaeus and His World* (Exetes).

Heide, N. van der. 2008. *Spirited Performance: The Manas Epic and Society in Kyrgyzstan* (Amsterdam).

Heitsch, E. 2008. 'Neoanalytische Antikritik: Zum Verhältnis I Lias–Aithiopis', *Rh M.* 151: 1–12.

Hitch, S. 2009. *King of Sacred: Ritual and Royal Authority in the Iliad* (Washington, DC).

Hodges, Paul. 2008. 'They don't like it up 'em!: Bayonet Fetishization in the British Army during the First World War', *Journal of War & Culture Studies* 1: 123–38.

Hollis, A. S. 1994. '[Oppian], Cyn. 2,100–158 and the Mythical Past of Apamea-on-the-Orontes', *ZPE* 102: 153–66.

Holoka, J. P. 1973. 'Homeric Originality: A Survey', *CW* 66: 257–93.

Honko, L. 1998. *Textualising the Siri Epic* (Helsinki).

Hood, S. 1995. 'The Bronze Age Context of Homer', in J. B. Carter, S. P. Morris, eds., *The Ages of Homer: A Tribute to Emily Townsend Vermeule* 25–32 (Austin).

Horden, P., N. Purcell. 2000. *The Corrupting Sea* (Oxford).

Horn, F. 2018. 'Dying is Hard to Describe: Metonymies and Metaphors of Death in the Iliad', *CQ* 68: 359–83.

Howard, K., S. Kasmambetov. 2011. *Singing the Kyrgyz Manas: Saparbeck Kasmambetov's Recitation of Epic Poetry* (Leiden).

Hunter, R. 2018. *The Measure of Homer: The Ancient Reception of the Iliad and the Odyssey* (Cambridge).

Hunter, R., I. Rutherford, eds. 2009. *Wandering Poets in Ancient Greek Culture: Travel, Locality and Pan-Hellenism* (Cambridge).

Hutchinson, G. O. 2017. 'Repetition, Range and Attention: The *Iliad*', C. Tsagalis, A. Markantonatos, eds., *The Winnowing Oar – New Perspectives in Homeric Studies* (Berlin–Boston) 145–70.

Hutton, C. A. 1927. 'The Travels of "Palmyra" Wood in 1750–51', *JHS* 47: 102–28.

Huxley, G. L. 1959. 'Hittites in Homer', *P del P* 14: 281–2.

—. 1969. 'Aigai and Alkaios', *GRBS* 10: 5–11.

Immerwahr, S. A. 1990. *Aegean Painting in the Bronze Age* (Philadelphia).

Irwin, T. 1989. *Classical Thought* (Oxford).

Jacquesson, S. 2020. 'Claiming Heritage: The Manas Epic between China and Kyrgyzstan', *Central Asian Survey* 39: 324–39.

Jamil, N. 2017. *Ethics and Poetry in Sixth-Century Arabia* (Oxford).

Janko, R. 1982. *Homer, Hesiod and the Hymns: Diachronic Development in Epic Diction* (Cambridge).

—. 1998. 'The Homeric Poems as Oral Dictated Texts', *CQ* 48: 1–13.

—. 2015A. 'From Gabii and Gordion to Eretria and Methone: The Rise of the Greek Alphabet', *BICS* 58: 1–32.

—. 2015B. 'proton te kai hystaton aien aeideim: Relative Chronology and the Literary History of the Early Greek Epos', in Ø. Andersen, D. T. T. Haig, eds., *Relative Chronology in Early Greek Epic Poetry* (Cambridge) 20–43.

Jebb, M. 2010. *Patrick Shaw Stewart: An Edwardian Meteor* (Wimborne Minster).

Jeffery., L. H. 1961. *The Local Scripts of Archaic Greece* (Oxford).

Jensen, M. S. 2017. 'The Challenge of Oral Epic to Homeric Scholarship', *Humanities* 6: 97–110.

Johnston, A. W., A. K. Andriomenou. 1989. 'A Geometric Graffito from Eretria', *ABSA* 84: 217–20.

Johnston, S. I. 1992. 'Xanthus, Hera and the Erinyes (*Iliad* 19.400–418)', *TAPA* 122: 85–98.

Jong, I. J. F. de, ed. 2012. *Homer: Iliad. Book XXII* (Cambridge).

Josefowicz, D. G. 2016. 'The Whig Interpretation of Homer: F. A. Wolf's *Prolegomena ad Homerum* in England', in A. Blair, A.-S. Goeing, eds., *For the Sake of Learning: Essays in Honor of Anthony Grafton* (Leiden) 821–41.

Jousse, M. 1981. *Le Style oral: Rythmique et mnémotechnique chez les verbo-moteurs* (1925) (repr. Paris).

Jumaturdu, A. 2016. 'A Comparative Study of Performers of the *Manas* Epic', *Journal of American Folklore* 129: 288–96.

Kagan, D., G. F. Viggiano. 2013. *Men of Bronze: Hoplite Warfare in Ancient Greece* (Princeton).

Kanigel, R. 2021. *Hearing Homer's Song: The Brief Life and Big Idea of Milman Parry* (New York).

Karageorghis, J. 2005. *Kypris: The Aphrodite of Cyprus. Ancient Sources and Archaeological Evidence* (Nicosia).

Karageorghis, V. 2006. 'Homeric Cyprus', in S. Deger-Jalkotzy, I. S. Lemos, eds., *Ancient Greece: From the Mycenaean Palaces to the Age of Homer* (Edinburgh) 665–75.

Kelly, A. 2006. 'Homer and History: *Iliad* 9.381–4', *Mnem.* 59 (2006) 321–33.

—. 2008A. 'The Ending of *Iliad* 7: A Response', *Philorgus* 152: 1–17.

—. 2008B. 'The Babylonian Captivity of Homer: The Case of the Dios Apate', *RhM* 151: 259–304.

—. 2012. 'The Mourning of Thetis: "Allusion" and the Future in the *Iliad*', in F. Montanari, A. Rengakos, C. Tsagalis, eds., *Homeric Contexts: Neoanalysis and the Interpretation of Oral Poetry* (Berlin–Boston) 211–56.

Kenzelmann Pfyffer, A., T. Theurillat, S. Verdan. 2005. 'Graffiti d'époque géométrique provenant du sanctuaire d'Apollon Daphnéphoros à Erétrie', *ZPE* 151: 51–83.

Kerschner, M. 2014. 'Euboean Imports to the Eastern Aegean and Eastern Aegean Production of Pottery in the Euboean Style: New Evidence from Neutron Activated Analyses', in M. Kerschner, I. S. Lemos, eds., *Archaeometric Analyses of Euboean and Euboean Related Pottery: New Results and Their Interpretation* (Vienna) 109–40.

Kim, J. 2000. *The Pity of Achilles: Oral Style and the Unity of the Iliad* (Lanham).

Kimmel-Clauzet, F. 2013. *Morts, tombeaux et cultes des poètes grecs* (Bordeaux).

King, C. 1970. 'The Homeric Corslet', *AJA* 74: 294–6.

Kinglake, A. W. 1844. *Eothen, or Traces of Travel Brought Home from the East* (London).

Kirk, G. S. 1962. *The Songs of Homer* (Cambridge).

Kolb, F. 2014–15. 'Phantom Trojans at the Dardanelles', *Talanta* XLVI–XLVII: 27–50.

Konstan, D. 2001. *Pity Transformed* (London).

Kraft, J. C., I. Kayan, O. Erol. 1980. 'Geomorphic Reconstructions in the Environs of Ancient Troy', *Science* 209: 776–82.

Kramer-Hajos, M. 2012. 'The Land and the Heroes of Lokris in the *Iliad*', *JHS* 132: 87–105.

Krauss, F. S. 1881. *Artemidoros aus Daldis: Symbolik der Träume* (Vienna).

—. 1908. *Slavische Volksforschungen: Abhandlungenüber Glauben, Gewohnheitrechte, Sitten, Braüche und die Guslarenlieder der Südslaven* (Leipzig).

Kucewicz, C. 2020. *The Treatment of the War Dead in Archaic Athens: An Ancestral Custom* (London).

Lane Fox, R. 1986. *Pagans and Christians* (London).

—. 1991. *The Unauthorized Version: Truth and Fiction in the Bible* (London).

—. 1994. 'Literacy and Power in Early Christianity', in A. K. Bowman, G. Woolf, eds., *Literacy and Power in the Ancient World* (Cambridge).

—. 2008. *Travelling Heroes* (London).

—. 2015. *Augustine: Conversions to Confessions* (London).

—. 2020. *The Invention of Medicine* (London).

Lang Ying. 2001. 'The Bard Jusup Mamay', *Oral Tradition* 16: 222–39.

Langdon, S., ed. 1993. *From Pasture to Polis: Art in the Age of Homer* (Columbia, Miss.).

Latacz, J. 2004. *Troy and Homer: Towards a Solution of an Old Mystery* (Oxford).

Lévêque, P. 1959. *Aurea catena Homeri: une étude sur l'allégorie grecque* (Paris).

Lewis. C. S. 1942. *A Preface to Paradise Lost* (Oxford).

Lipinski E. 2004. *Itineraria Phoenicia* (Leuven).

Llewellyn-Jones, L. 2003. *Aphrodite's Tortoise: The Veiled Woman of Ancient Greece* (Swansea).

Lloyd Jones, H. 1971. *The Justice of Zeus* (Berkeley).

Lohmann, D. 1970. *Die Komposition der Reden in der Ilias* (Berlin).

Lohmann, H. 2012. 'Ionians and Carians in the Mycale: The Discovery of Carian Melia and the Archaic Panionion', in G. Cifani, S. Stoddart, eds., *Landscape, Ethnicity and Identity in the Archaic Mediterranean Area* (Oxford) 32–50.

Long, A. A. 1970. 'Morals and Values in Homer', *JHS* 90: 121–39.

Lonsdale, S. H. 1990. *Creatures of Speech: Lion, Herding and Hunting Similes in the Iliad* (Stuttgart).

Lord, A. B. 1948. 'Homer, Parry and Huso', *AJA* 52: 34–44.

—. 1991. *Epic Singers and Oral Tradition* (Ithaca, NY).

—. 1995. *The Singer Resumes the Tale* (Ithaca, NY).

—. 2000. *The Singer of Tales* (2nd edn, Cambridge, Mass.).

Lorimer, H. L. 1948. 'Homer and the Art of Writing: A Sketch of Opinion between 1713 and 1939', *AJA* 52: 11–23.

—. 1950. *Homer and the Monuments* (London).

Lowe, N. J. 1996. 'Tragic and Homeric Ironies: Response to Rosenmeyer', in M. S. Silk, ed., *Tragedy and the Tragic: Greek Theatre and Beyond* (Oxford) 520–33.

—. 2000. *The Classical Plot and the Invention of Western Narrative* (Cambridge).

Luce, J. V. 1978. 'The *Polis* in Homer and Hesiod', *Proc. Roy. Irish Acad.* 78: 1–15.

—. 1998. *Celebrating Homer's Landscapes: Troy and Ithaca Revisited* (New Haven, Conn.).

Ludwig, E. 1931. *Schliemann of Troy: The Story of a Goldseeker* (Boston).

Luraghi, N. 2021. 'Sounds, Signs and Boundaries: Perspectives on Early Greek Alphabetic Writing', in R. Parker, P. M. Steele, eds., *The Early Greek Alphabets: Origin, Diffusion, Uses* (Oxford) 32–57.

Mackie, C. 2013. 'Iliad 24 and the Judgement of Paris', *CQ* 63: 1–16

Maclair Boraston, J. 1911. 'The Birds of Homer', *JHS* 31: 216–50.

Macleod, C., ed 1982. *Homer. Iliad: Book XXIV* (Cambridge).

MacMillan, M. 2020. *War: How Conflict Shaped Us* (London).

Macrakis, A. L. 1984. 'Comparative Economic Values in the *Iliad*: The Oxen-Worth', in K. J. Rigsby, ed., *Studies Presented to Sterling Dow on His Eightieth Birthday* (Durham, NC) 211–15.

Mac Sweeney, N. 2017. 'Separating Fact from Fiction in the Ionian Migration', *Hesperia* 86: 379–421.

—. 2018. *Troy: Myth, City, Icon* (London).

Malkin, I. 1998. *The Returns of Odysseus* (Berkeley).

Malouchou, G. E. 2006. 'Nea epigraphē genŏa', in G. E. Malouchou, A. P. Matthaiou, eds. Chiakon symposion eis mnaēmēn W. G. Forrest' (Athens) 81–90.

Manguel, A. 2007. *Homer's The Iliad and The Odyssey: A Biography* (London).

Markoe, G. 1985. *Phoenician Bronze and Silver Bowls from Cyprus and the Mediterranean* (Berkeley).

Mason, H. A. 1972. *To Homer through Pope: An Introduction to Homer's Iliad and Pope's Translation* (London).

Mayer, A. 2018. 'Conflicting Interpretations of Artemidorus' *Oneirocritica*: Freud, Theodor Gomperz, F. S. Krauss and the Symbolic Language of Dreams', *Psychoanal. Hist.* 20: 89–112.

Meadows, A. 2021. '*Tout ce qui brille* . . .: Electrum and the Origins of Western Coinage', *RN* 178: 443–70.

Meillet, A. 1923. '*Les origines indo-européennes des métres grecs* (Paris).

Mellink, M. J. 1995. 'Homer, Lycia and Lukka', in J. B. Carter, S. P. Morris, eds., *The Ages of Homer: A Tribute to Emily Townsend Vermeule* (Austin) 33–43.

Minchin, E. 2007. *Homeric Voices: Discourse, Memory, Gender* (Oxford) 23–51.

—. 2010. 'From Gentle Teasing to Heavy Sarcasm: Instances of Rhetorical Irony in Homer's *Iliad*', *Hermes* 138: 387–402.

—. 2020. 'Visualizing the Shield of Achilles: Approaching Its Landscapes via Cognitive Paths', *CQ* 70: 473–84.

Mitchell, S. 1990. 'Festivals, Games and Civic Life in Roman Asia Minor', *JRS* 80: 183–93.

Moorhead, A. 1959. *Gallipoli* (London).

Morris, I. 1986. 'The Use and Abuse of Homer', *CA* 5: 81–138.

—. 1997. 'Homer and the Iron Age', in I. Morris, B. Powell, eds., *A New Companion to Homer* (Leiden) 535–59.

Bibliography

Most, G. W. 2004. 'Anger and Pity in Homer's *Iliad*', in S. Braund, G. W. Most, eds., *Ancient Anger: Perspectives from Homer to Galen* (Cambridge) 50–75.

Muecke, D. C. 1970. *Irony* (London).

Muellner, L. 1990. 'The Simile of the Cranes and Pygmies: A Study of Homeric Metaphor', *HSCP* 93: 59–101.

Muhly, J. D. 2011. 'Gold', in M. Finkelberg, ed., *The Homer Encyclopedia*, vol. I (Chichester) 320–23.

Murko, M. 1929. *La Poésie populaire épique en Yougoslavie au début du XXe siècle* (Paris).

Murray, G. 1907. *The Rise of the Greek Epic* (Oxford).

Murray, O. 1993. *Early Greece* (London, 2nd edn).

—. 2008. 'The *Odyssey* as Performance Poetry', in M. Revermann, P. Wilson, eds., *Performance, Iconography, Reception: Studies in Honour of Oliver Taplin* (Oxford) 161–76.

Myers, T. 2019. *Homer's Divine Audience: The Iliad's Reception on Mt Olympus* (Oxford).

Mynott, J. 2018. *Birds in the Ancient World: Winged Words* (2018).

Nagy, G. 1992. 'Homeric Questions', *TAPA* 122: 17–60.

—. 2003. *Homeric Responses* (Austin).

—. 2013. 'Hour One: The Homeric *Iliad* and the Glory of the Unseasonal Hero', in his *The Ancient Greek Hero in 24 Hours* (Cambridge, Mass.) 26–47.

Nicolaides, G. 1867. *Topographie et plan stratégique de l'Iliade* (Paris).

Nicolson, Adam. 2014. *The Mighty Dead: Why Homer Matters* (London).

Nilsson, M. P. 1933. *Homer and Mycenae* (London).

Nimis, S. A. 1999. 'Ring-Composition and Linearity in Homer', in E. A. Mackay, ed., *Signs of Orality: The Oral Tradition and Its Influence in the Greek and Roman World* (Leiden–Boston) 65–78.

Notopoulos, J. A. 1949. 'Parataxis in Homer: A New Approach to Homeric Literary Criticism', *TAPA* 80: 1–23.

—. 1960. 'The Genesis of an Oral Heroic Poem', *GRBS* 3: 135–44.

Oliver, G. J. 2007. *War, Food and Politics in Early Hellenistic Athens* (Oxford).

Onians, R. B. 1951. *The Origins of European Thought* (Cambridge).

Ormand, K. 2014. *The Hesiodic Catalogue of Women and Archaic Greece* (Cambridge).

Oswald, A. 2011. *Memorial* (London).

Page, D. L. 1959. *History and the Homeric Iliad* (Berkeley).

Palamidis, A. 2019. 'Des souris et des hommes: Une réinvention érudite du culte d'Apollon Smintheus à l'époque hellénistique?', *Kernos* 32: 191–236.

Papadopoulos, J. K. 2016. 'The Early History of the Greek Alphabet: New Evidence from Eretria and Methone', *Antiquity* 90: 1238–54.

Parker, R. 1983. *Miasma: Pollution and Purification in Early Greek Religion* (Oxford).

—. 2011. *On Greek Religion* (Ithaca, NY).

Parker, R., P. M. Steele, eds. 2021. *The Early Greek Alphabets: Origin, Diffusion, Uses* (Oxford).

Parry, M., ed. A. Parry. 1971. *The Making of Homeric Verse: The Collected Papers of Milman Parry* (Oxford).

Bibliography

Parry, M. 1971. 'The Distinctive Character of Enjambement in Homeric Verse', in A. Parry, ed., *The Making of Homeric Verse* (Oxford), 251–65, esp. 262.

Patzek, B. 1992. *Homer und Mykene: mündliche Dichtung und Geschichtsschreibung* (Munich).

Petrović, I. 2016. 'On Finding Homer: The Impact of Homeric Scholarship on the Perception of South Slavic Oral Traditional Poetry', in A. Efstathiou, I. Karamanou, eds. *Homeric Receptions across Generic and Cultural Contexts* (Berlin–Boston) 315–27.

Petrovic, R. 1965. 'The Oldest Notation of Folk Tunes in Yugoslavia', *Studia Musicologica Academiae Scientiarum Hungaricae* 7: 109–14.

Pfeiffer, R. 1968. *History of Classical Scholarship: From the Beginnings to the End of the Hellenistic Age* (Oxford).

Pierattini, A. 2022. *The Origins of Greek Temple Architecture* (Cambridge).

Pirenne-Delforge, V., G. Pironti. 2022. *The Hera of Zeus: Intimate Enemy, Ultimate Spouse* (Cambridge).

Pironti, G., C. Bonnet, eds. 2017. *Les Dieux d'Homère: Polythéisme et poésie en Grèce ancienne* (Liège).

Plumtree, J. 2021. 'A Telling Tradition: Preliminary Comments on the Epic of Manas, 1856–2018', in S. C. Thomson, ed., *Medieval Stories and Storytelling: Multimedia and Multi-Temporal Perspectives* (Turnhout) 239–301.

Pöhlmann, E., M. L. West. 2012. 'The Oldest Greek Papyrus and Writing Tablets: Fifth-Century Documents from the "Tomb of the Musician" in Attica', *ZPE* 180: 1–16.

Popham, M. R., L. H. Sackett. 1980. *Lefkandi I: The Iron Age Settlement* (London).

Pormann, P. E. 2007. 'The Arabic Homer: An Untold Story', *Classical and Modern Literature* 27: 27–44.

Porter, A. 2019. *Agamemnon the Pathetic Despot: Reading Characterization in Homer* (Washington, DC).

Porter, J. I. 2021. *Homer: The Very Idea* (Chicago).

Potter, D. 2012. *The Victor's Crown* (London).

Powell, B. B. 1991. *Homer and the Origin of the Greek Alphabet* (Cambridge).

—. 1992. 'Homer and the Origin of a Greek Alphabet', *CAJ* 2: 116–18.

Pratt, L. 2009. 'Diomedes, the Fatherless Hero of the Iliad', in S. R. Hübner, D. M. Ratzan, eds., *Growing Up Fatherless in Antiquity* (Cambridge) 141–61.

Prior, D. 2022. *The Memorial Feast for Kökötöy Khan: A Kirghiz Epic Poem in the Manas Tradition* (London).

Pucci, P. 2018. *The Iliad: The Poem of Zeus* (Berlin–Boston).

Pulleyn, S. 1997. *Prayer in Greek Religion* (Oxford).

Raaflaub, K. A. 1997/8. 'Homer, the Trojan War and History', *CW* 91: 386–403.

—. 1998. 'A Historian's Headache: How to Read "Homeric Society"', in N. Fisher, H. van Wees, eds., *Archaic Greece: New Approaches and New Evidence* (London and Swansea) 169–93.

—. 2006. 'Historical Approaches to Homer', in S. Deger-Jalkotzy, I. S. Lemos, eds., *Ancient Greece: From the Mycenaean Palaces to the Age of Homer* (Edinburgh) 449–62.

—. 2011. 'Riding on Homer's Chariot: The Search for a Historical "Epic Society"', *Antichthon* 45: 1–34.

Rabel, R. J. 1989. 'The Shield of Achilles and the Death of Hector', *Eranos* 87: 81–90.

Radloff, W. 1990. 'Samples of Folk Literature from the North Turkic Tribes', *Oral Tradition* 5: 73–90.

Ready, J. L. 2011. *Character, Narrator and Simile in the Iliad* (Cambridge).

—. 2015. 'The Textualization of Homeric Epic by Means of Dictation', *TAPA* 145: 1–75.

—. 2017. 'The Epiphany at *Iliad* 4.73–84', *Hermes* 145: 25–40.

—. 2018. *The Homeric Simile in Comparative Perspectives: Oral Traditions from Saudi Arabia to Indonesia* (Oxford).

—. 2019. *Orality, Textuality, and the Homeric Epics* (Oxford).

Redfield, J. 1975. *Nature and Culture in the Iliad* (Chicago).

Reichl, K., ed. 2000. *The Oral Epic: Performance and Music* (Berlin).

—. 2016. 'Oral Epics into the Twenty-First Century: The Case of the Kyrgyz Epic *Manas*', *Journal of American Folklore* 129: 327–44.

Richardson, N. J. 1987. 'The Individuality of Homer's Language', in J. Bremer et al., *Homer: Beyond Oral Poetry. Recent Trends in Homeric Interpretation* (Amsterdam) 165–84.

—. 1991. 'Homer and Cyprus', in V. Karageorghis, ed., *The Civilizations of the Aegean and Their Diffusion in Cyprus and the Eastern Mediterranean, 2000–600 BC* (Larnaca) 83–94.

Ridgeway, W. 1885. 'The Homeric Land System', *JHS* 6: 319–39.

Rix, M. 2002. 'Wild About Ida: The Glorious Flora of Kaz Dagi and the Vale of Troy', *Cornucopia* 26: 56–75.

Robb, K. 2019. '*Xenia, Hiketeia* and the Homeric Language of Morals: The Origins of Western Ethics', in *Logoi and Muthoi: Further Essays in Greek Philosophy and Literature*, W. Wians, ed. (Albany) 17–53.

Robert, L. 1978. 'Les Conquêtes du dynaste lycien Arbinas', *JS* 1–2 : 3–48.

Roisman, H. M. 2005. 'Nestor the Good Counsellor', *CQ* 55: 17–38.

Rollinger, R., M. Korenjak. 2001. 'AddikrituSu: ein namentlich genannter Grieche aus der Zeit Asarhaddons (680–669 v. Chr.) *AF* 28: 325–37.

Rose, C. B. 2014. *The Archaeology of Greek and Roman Troy* (Cambridge).

Ruijgh, C. J. 1995. 'D'Homère aux origines proto-mycéniennes de la tradition épique', in J. P. Crielaard, ed., *Homeric Questions: Essays in Philology, Ancient History and Archaeology* (Amsterdam) 1–96.

—. 2011. 'Mycenaean and Homeric Language', in Y. Duhoux, A. M. Davies, eds., *A Companion to Linear B*, vol. 2 (Louvain) 253–98.

Rutherford, R. B. 1982. 'Tragic Form and Feeling in the *Iliad*', *JHS* 102: 145–60.

—. 1991–3. 'From the *Iliad* to the *Odyssey*', *BICS* 38: 37–54.

—, ed. 2019. *Homer. Iliad: Book XVIII* (Cambridge).

Saunders, K. B. 1999. 'The Wounds in *Iliad* 13–16', *CQ* 49: 345–63.

Schadewaldt, W. 1997. 'Hector and Andromache', Eng. trans. in G. M. Wright, P. V. Jones, *Homer: German Scholarship in Translation* (Oxford) 124–42.

Schäfer, M. 1990. *Der Götterstreit in der Ilias* (Stuttgart).

Bibliography

Scheid-Tissinier, É. 1994. *Les Usages du don chez Homère: Vocabulaire et pratiques* (Nancy).

Schofield, M. M. 1986. 'Euboulia in the *Iliad*', *CQ* 36: 6–31.

Schironi, F. 2018. *The Best of the Grammarians: Aristarchus of Samothrace on the Iliad* (Ann Arbor).

Schnapp-Gourbeillon, Annie. 1981. *Lions, héros, masques: Les représentations de l'animal chez Homère* (Paris).

Scott, M. 1979. 'Pity and Pathos in Homer', *Acta Classica* 22: 1–14.

Scott, W. C. 1974. *The Oral Nature of the Homeric Simile* (Leiden).

Seaford, R. 1994. *Reciprocity and Ritual* (Oxford).

Shay, J. 1994. *Achilles in Vietnam* (New York).

Sheppard, J. T. 1933. 'Helen With Priam (Homer's Iliad, III)', *G & R* 3: 31–7.

Sherratt, F. S. 1990. ' "Reading the Texts": Archaeology and the Homeric Question', *Antiquity* 64: 807–24.

—. 2004. 'Feasting in Homeric Epic', *Hesperia* 73: 301–37.

—. 2010. 'The Trojan War: History or Bricolage?', *BICS* 53: 1–18.

—. 2016. 'Homeric Epic and Contexts of Bardic Creation', in S. Sherratt, J. Bennet, eds., *Archaeology and the Homeric Epic* (Sheffield) 35–52.

Shipley, G. 1987. *A History of Samos, 800–188 BC* (Oxford).

Sienaert, E. R. 1990. 'Marcel Jousse: The Oral Style and the Anthropology of Gesture', *Oral Tradition* 5: 91–106.

Snodgrass, A. M. 1974. 'An Historical Homeric Society?', *JHS* 94: 114–25.

—. 1998. *Homer and the Artists: Text and Picture in Early Greek Art* (Cambridge).

Sourvinou-Inwood, C. 1981. 'To Die and Enter the House of Hades: Homer, Before and After', in J. Whaley, ed., *Mirrors of Mortality: Studies in the Social History of Death* (London) 15–39.

Spencer, N. 1995. 'Early Lesbos between East and West: A 'Grey Area' of Aegean Archaeology', *ABSA* 90: 269–306.

Spivey, N. 2018. *The Sarpedon Krater: The Life and Afterlife of a Greek Vase* (London).

Starke, F. 1997. 'Lukka', *Der Neue Pauly*, 7: 505–6.

Stinton, T. C. 1965. *Euripides and the Judgement of Paris* (London).

Strauss, B. 2006. *The Trojan War: A New History* (New York).

Strauss Clay, J. 2011. *Homer's Trojan Theater: Space, Vision and Memory in the Iliad* (Cambridge).

Strawn, M. 2012. 'Homer, Sentimentalism, and Pope's Translation of *The Iliad*', *SEL* 52: 585–608.

Szempruch, B. 2019. 'Literary Commemoration in Imperial Greek Epigram: Niobe in the Living Landscape SGO 05/01/55', *AJP* 140: 227–53.

Taplin, O. 1980. 'The Shield of Achilles within the *Iliad*', *G & R* 27: 1–21.

—. 1990. 'Agamemnon's Role in the Iliad', in C. Pelling, ed., *Characterization and individuality in Greek Literature* (Oxford) 60–82.

—. 1992. *Homeric Soundings: The Shaping of the Iliad* (Oxford).

Tate, A. P. 2011A. 'Matija Murko, Wilhelm Radloff and Oral Epic Studies', *Oral Tradition* 26: 329–52.

—. 2011B. 'Collecting South Slavic Oral Epic in 1864: Luka Marjanović's Earliest Account', *Oral Tradition* 26: 159–74.

Temir, A. 1955. 'Leben und Schaffen von Friedrich Wilhelm Radloff (1837–1918)', *Oriens* 8: 51–93.

Thomas, R. 1989. *Oral Tradition and Written Record in Classical Athens* (Cambridge).

Thompson, H. A. 1952. 'The Altar of Pity in the Athenian Agora', *Hesperia* 21: 47–82.

Thonemann, P. 2006. 'Neilomandros: A Contribution to the History of Greek Personal Names', *Chiron* 36: 11–43.

Tritle, L. A. 1997. 'Hector's Body: Mutilation in Ancient Greece and Vietnam', *AHB* 11: 123–36.

Tsagalis, C. 2008. *The Oral Palimpsest: Exploring Intertextuality in the Homeric Epics* (Washington, DC).

Tsagalis, C., A. Markantonatos, eds.. 2017. *The Winnowing Oar: New Perspectives in Homeric Studies* (Berlin–Boston).

Turner, D. 2007. 'Schliemann's Diary: Greece and the Troad, 1868', *ABSA* 102: 345–91.

Vail, K. 2018. *Reconstructing the Shield of Achilles* (Los Angeles).

Vámbéry, H. 1911. *Jusuf und Ahmed* (Budapest).

Verdan, S. 2018. 'Counting on Pots? Reflections on Numerical Notations in Early Iron Age Greece', in J. Strauss Clay, I. Malkin, Y. Z. Tzifopoulos, eds., *Panhellenes at Methone: Graphē in Late Geometric and Protoarchaic Methone, Macedonia (ca. 700 BCE)* (Berlin–Boston) 105–22.

Verdelis, N. M. 1977. 'The Metal Finds', in P. Åström, ed., *The Cuirass Tomb and Other Finds at Dendra*, Part 1 (Göteborg) 28–65.

Vermeule, E. 1979. *Aspects of Death in Early Greek Art and Poetry* (Berkeley).

Vernant, J.-P. 1965. *Mythe et pensée chez les Grecs*, vol. I (Paris).

—. 2001. 'A "Beautiful Death" and the Disfigured Corpse in Homeric Epic', in D. L. Cairns, ed., *Oxford Readings in Homer's Iliad* (Oxford) 311–41.

Versnel, H. 2011. *Coping with the Gods: Wayward Readings in Greek Theology* (Leiden).

Vidan, A. 2003. *Embroidered with Gold, Strung with Pearls: The Traditional Ballads of Bosnian Women* (Cambridge, Mass.).

Villing, A. et al. 2019. *Troy: Myth and Reality* (London).

Wachter, R. 2000. 'Grammatik de homerischen Sprache', in J. Latacz, ed., *Homers Ilias: Gesamtkommentar: Prolegomena* (Munich–Leipzig) 61–108.

Wade-Gery, H. T. 1952. *The Poet of the Iliad* (Cambridge).

Wecowski, M. 2014. *The Rise of the Greek Aristocratic Banquet* (Oxford).

Wees, H. van. 1994. 'The Homeric Way of War: The *Iliad* and the Hoplite Phalanx (I)', *G & R* 41: 1–18.

—. 1996. 'Heroes, Knights and Nutters: Warrior Mentality in Homer', in A. B. Lloyd, ed., *Battle in Antiquity* (Swansea) 1–86.

—. 1999. 'The Homeric Way of War: The *Iliad* and the Hoplite Phalanx', in I. J. F. de Jong, ed., *Homer: Critical Assessments*, vol. II (London) 221–38.

—. 2002. 'Homer and Early Greece', *Colby Quarterly* 38: 94–117.

—. 2004. *Greek Warfare: Myths and Realities* (London).

—. 2006. 'From Kings to Demigods: Epic Heroes and Social Change, *c.* 750–600 BC', in S. Deger-Jalkotzy, I. S. Lemos, eds., *Ancient Greece: From the Mycenaean Palaces to the Age of Homer* (Edinburgh) 363–80.

Wees, H. van. 2011. 'Shield', in M. Finkelberg, ed., *The Homer Encyclopedia*, vol. III (Chichester) 792–3.

—. 2021. 'Heroic Benefactors? The Limits of Generosity in Homer', in M. Domingo Gygax, A. Zuiderhoek, eds., *Benefactors and the Polis: The Public Gift in the Greek Cities from the Homeric World to Late Antiquity* (Cambridge) 15–43.

Wees, H. van, N. Fisher. 2015. 'The Trouble with "Aristocracy"', in N. Fisher, H. van Wees, eds., *'Aristocracy' in Antiquity – Redefining Greek and Roman Elites* (Swansea) 1–57.

Weil, S., ed. and trans. J. Holoka. 2003. *Simone Weil's The Iliad or The Poem of Force: A Critical Edition* (New York).

Weinreich, O. 1912. 'Theoi epēkooi', *MDA* 37: 1–62.

Wemhoff, M., ed. 2022. *Schliemanns Welten: sein Leben, seine Entdeckungen, sein Mythos* (Berlin).

West, M. L. 1981. 'The Singing of Homer and the Modes of Early Greek Music', *JHS* 101: 113–29.

—. 1988. 'The Rise of the Greek Epic', *JHS* 108: 151–72.

—. 1995. 'The Date of the *Iliad*'. *MH* 52: 203–19.

—. 1997A. *The East Face of Helicon: West Asiatic Elements in Greek Poetry and Myth* (Oxford).

—. 1997B. 'Homer's Meter', in I. Morris, B. Powell, eds., *A New Companion to Homer* (Leiden) 218–37.

—. 1999. 'The Invention of Homer', *CQ* 49: 364–82.

—. 2001. *Studies in the Text and Transmission of the Iliad* (Munich–Leipzig).

—. 2003. 'Iliad and Aithiopis', *CQ* 53: 1–14.

—. 2004. 'Man, Fate and Death in Indo-European Tradition', *Letras Clássicas* 8: 49–66.

—. 2007. *Indo-European Poetry and Myth* (Oxford).

—. 2010. 'Rhapsodes at Festivals', *ZPE* 173: 1–13.

—. 2011A. 'The Homeric Question Today', *Proc. Amer. Philosophical Soc.* 155: 383–93.

—. 2011B. *The Making of the Iliad: Disquisition and Analytical Commentary* (Oxford).

West, M. L., S. R. West. 1999. 'Dividing Homer', *SO* 74: 68–73.

Whitley, J. 1991. 'Social Diversity in Dark Age Greece', *ABSA* 86: 341–65.

Wiener, M. H. 2007. 'Homer and History: Old Questions, New Evidence', *Aegaeum* 28: (2007) 3–33.

Willcock, M. M. 1973. 'The Funeral Games of Patroclus', *BICS* 20: 1–11.

—. 1983. 'Antilochos in the Iliad', in *Mélanges Édouard Delebecque* (Aix-en-Provence) 477–85.

Williams, B. 2008. *Shame and Necessity* (2nd edn, Berkeley).

Wilson, D. 1970. *The Life and Times of Vuk Stefanović Karadzić, 1787–1864: Literacy, Literature and National Independence in Serbia* (Oxford).

Winkler, M. M. 2007. 'The *Iliad* and the Cinema', in M. M. Winkler, ed., *Troy: From Homer's Iliad to Hollywood Epic* (Oxford) 43–67.

Bibliography

Wohl, V. 2012. *Euripides and the Politics of Form* (Princeton).

Wood, R. 1776. *An Essay on the Original Genius and Writings of Homer* (Dublin).

Youtie, H. C., J. G. Winter. 1951. *Papyri and Ostraca from Karanis*, Michigan Papyri vol. VIII (Ann Arbor).

Zafeiropoulou, F., A. Agelarakis. 2005. 'Warriors of Paros', *Archaeology* 58: 30–35.

Zanker, G. 1978. 'Beyond Reciprocity: The Akhilleus–Priam Scene in Iliad 24', in C. Gill, N. Postlethwaite, R. Seaford, eds., *Reciprocity in Ancient Greece* (Oxford) 73–92.

Zanker, P. 1996. *The Mask of Socrates: The Image of the Intellectual in Antiquity* (Berkeley).

Zieliński, K. 2019. 'Women as Victims of War in Homer's Oral Poetics', *Humanities* 8: 141.

Zirkle, C. 1936. 'Animals Impregnated by the Wind', *Isis* 25: 96–130.

Notes and References

Publications on Homer proliferate and my notes which follow give only a fraction of what is available. I have cited most of what I consulted or had in mind while writing, knowing that it will direct interested readers to even more. Richard Rutherford's *Homer* (Cambridge, 2013) is an excellent survey of work until 2012, accompanied by judicious discussion and by examples of the author's own approach to reading particular passages in the Iliad and Odyssey. Among recent prose translations into English, Martin Hammond's Penguin one (Harmondsworth, 1987) is a very good way of gaining a sense of the entire Iliad's plot and contents. Among translations into English verse, Richmond Lattimore (Chicago, 2011) is recommended, as is Peter Green's *The Iliad: A New Translation* (Berkeley, 2015).

Jasper Griffin's *Homer on Life and Death* (Oxford, 1980) and his very short introduction, *Homer* (Oxford, 1980), are exceptionally fine appreciations. The first chapter of E. R. Dodds, *The Greeks and the Irrational* (Berkeley, 1951) is a classic too. There are many other short introductions, but M. S. Silk, *Homer: The Iliad* (2nd edn, Cambridge, 2004) is outstandingly good, and Martin Mueller, *The Iliad* (London, 1984), is an excellent complement. I enjoy engaging with Barbara Graziosi and Johannes Haubold, *Homer: The Resonance of Epic* (London, 2005), which also includes some new ideas. At a more detailed level Oliver Taplin, *Homeric Soundings: The Shaping of the Iliad* (Oxford, 1992), remains a landmark in close readings in English, justly remarking that work of that nature in German had thitherto been more profound. W. Schadewaldt, *Von Homers Welt und Werk* (4th edn, Stuttgart, 1965) remains a classic example.

Among books at a simpler level for a Greekless public, Caroline Alexander, *The War That Killed Achilles: The True Story of the Iliad* (London, 2010), is a good running summary of the Iliad, drawing, as she acknowledges, on interesting scholarly work on Thetis by Laura Slatkin, which is necessarily speculative. Adam Nicolson, *The Mighty Dead: Why Homer Matters* (London, 2014), has reached a wide public, but his claim that Homer composed *c.* 1200 BC, that the world he presented is shaped by a world *c.* 1800 BC and that his poem was preserved accurately until it began to be written down *c.* 700 BC or later is mistaken. The poem's language, social setting and religion refute it: no scholar would accept such a dating. He writes, however, as an impassioned lover of Homer and I have gained by being made to think why his finely written judgements on the poem do not always fit it or fully cover it.

Companions to Homer are also proliferating. The outstanding one is *The Homer Encyclopedia*, edited by Margalit Finkelberg in three volumes (Chichester, 2011), with very clear articles by specialists on all the topics I discuss and more. The bibliography is an excellent aid. Ian Morris and Barry Powell, *A New Companion to Homer* (Leiden, 1997), is a valuable single volume, especially for topics of the poem's date, means of composition and context. *The Cambridge Companion to Homer*, edited by Robert Fowler (Cambridge, 2004), covers a wide range and uses twenty-two experts who write accessibly, but it tends to prefer an early-seventh-century BC date for Homer, crisply and rightly rejected by Barry B. Powell, whose own *Homer* (2nd edn, Oxford, 2007) is vigorous and helpful. C. O. Pache et al., eds, *The Cambridge Guide to Homer* (Cambridge, 2020), is one of several recent surveys of Homer's reception in later ages.

In the past thirty years or so, new commentaries on the Iliad have greatly illumined it. For those taking Greek at school or as novices, the Joint Association of Classical Teachers' Reading Greek series is well aimed, exemplified most recently by *Reading Homer: Iliad Books 16 and 18* by Stephen Anderson, Keith Maclennan and N. Yamagata (Cambridge, 2022). The Cambridge green-and-yellow-bound series is aimed at more-accomplished readers of Greek but its notes and fine introductory sections include much for Greekless readers too. Among its volumes, Colin Macleod's *Iliad XXIV* (1982) set a very high standard, one which has been maintained by recent successors, especially A. M. Bowie's *Iliad III* (2019) and Richard Rutherford's *Iliad XVIII* (2019). My constant resort is the big Cambridge series, *Homer's Iliad: A Commentary*, under the general editorship initially of G. S. Kirk, especially the four volumes covering books 9–24, published between 1991 and 1993. Whenever I cite a Homeric verse, particularly from my chapter 21 onwards, I recommend consulting these commentaries' notes, which are a guide to alternative interpretations and much more bibliography. Their introductions are extremely valuable, even for Greekless readers, and range beyond the particular books being commented on in any one volume.

The major current commentary is the Basel one, beginning with *Prolegomena* (3rd edn, Berlin–London, 2009) under the general editorship of Joachim Latacz, which is excellent on the poem's language, metre and much else. Its volumes, with English translations, are still in progress under the general title *Homer's Iliad: The Basel Commentary* and are full of important detail which is essential reading. I owe a particular debt, even more than I express in my notes, to two major scholars whose main views I do not share, Gregory Nagy and his many writings on the formation and transmission of Homer's poems into an eventual script and M. L. West and his views that Homer (or in his view an anonymous poet 'P') was literate and personally revised the text of his first version of the Iliad, that it owed an important ultimate debt to poems in Near Eastern languages and that 'P' wrote *c.* 640 BC. I certainly do not believe these contentions, but I remain grateful for West's many writings and for conversations in which he often corrected me with characteristic terseness and kindness. The second half of his *The Making of the Iliad: Disquisition and Analytical Commentary* (Oxford, 2011) has notes on the poem which have particular value, apart from his theories of its origin.

I have mostly followed the style of abbreviated references to journals which is laid out yearly in volumes of *L'Année Philologique* and to ancient authors in S. Hornblower and A. J. Spawforth, eds., *The Oxford Classical Dictionary* (4th edn, Oxford, 2012).

When I address the perennial questions of the poem's composition and possible analogies for it, I have profited greatly from the specialist journal *Oral Tradition* and its global range. I have referred most often to the Manas poem still current in Kyrgyzstan and the Kyrghyz diaspora, albeit in a language I cannot read. I find recordings and reports of its composers in performance to be a most seductive analogy when I try to imagine Homer composing and performing. With his fine command of many languages, including Russian, C. M. Bowra was unique among British classicists in citing many details of the Manas poem in his admirable *Heroic Poetry* (London, 1952). I used to skip them, thinking they were a distraction, but no longer.

In his recent prose translation of one version of one part of that poem, *The Memorial Feast for Kökötöy Khan* (London, 2022), Daniel Prior asks in his final note: 'should not then the world's lovers of Homer . . . be beating a path to the Kirghiz epic tradition's door? If that happens, I believe that its unique panorama can reveal something more than the history of an epic tradition: it can point to something deeply, disquietingly human about heroism, one of our oldest and most misunderstood ties between art and life.' Independently, while he was working, I have been beating just such a path, on horseback in the poem's homeland and at home in an amateurish way with its English translations, learning to appreciate its momentum.

Prologue

1. Haslam (1997) 55–100, esp. 60–61. **2.** Xenophanes F2 (Diels–Kranz). **3.** John S. Thomas with video and narration by Jane Masséglia; theconversation.com/rutland-roman-villa. Posted 7 December 2022. **4.** Leon Trotsky, *My Life: An Attempt at an Autobiography* (ET, repr. 2007, New York) 134 and Trotsky, *The Young Lenin* (ET, repr. 1972, Newton Abbot) chap. IX. **5.** Pormann (2007) 27–42. **6.** Manguel (2007) 6. **7.** Graziosi (2002) 93–124. **8.** Paus. 9.9.5; West (1999) 377. **9.** I wonder if Çalainos is in fact a scribal error for Kallisthenes, as in mss. of Strabo 14.4.3. **10.** West (1999) 364–82, esp. 374–6;

West (1997A) 622–3, qualified, however, by West (2000) 374 n.29.   **11.** *A Lexicon of Greek Personal Names*, vol. II (ed. P. Fraser, E. Matthews, Oxford, 1994) 351.   **12.** G. Vico, *La discoverta del vero Omero*, ed. P. Cristofolini (repr., 2006 Pisa).   **13.** Youtie, Winter (1951) nr. 1100 lines 10–11: they aptly remark 'the history of the cult of Homer remains somewhat vague'.   **14.** Pind. F 264 (SM); Stesimbrotus *FGH* 107 F22; Graziosi (2002) 72–7.   **15.** *Hymn. Hom. Ap.* 165–73; Pind. F 264 (SM); Graziosi (2002) 62–6; West (2002) 369–71.   **16.** Hom. *Od.* 8.63–4; Graziosi (2002) 138–46; Grote (1888) 80 n.1 for more recent blind performers; Beecroft (2011) 1–18 for blindness in later 'lives' of Homer.   **17.** *SEG* LXIV (2014) 2178 for a list of these inscriptions; Kimmel-Clauzet (2013) 285–318 for all the epigraphic evidence; Chaniotis (2010) 257–78 for later evidence of Homer's impact.   **18.** P. Zanker (1996) 162–72, esp. 164.   **19.** Arist. F 76 (Rose).   **20.** *IG* XII 5 15 with *SEG* LV (2005) 940; Paus. 10.24.2.   **21.** Hom. *Il.* 4.130–33; 20.251–5; 4. 130–33.   **22.** Hom. *Il.* 18.491–6.   **23.** Hom. *Il.* 22.490–504.   **24.** Hom. *Il.* 22.496–8.

PART I: HOMER AND HIS ILIAD: WHERE?

1. 'When first they quarrelled . . .'

1. Hdt. 2.116.2 and 117; West (1999) 68–73.   **2.** I disagree with Vernant (1965) 80–107.   **3.** Hom. *Il.* 1.34: Griffin, Hammond (1982) 126–42 give a fine appreciation of lines 1–60; Mason (1972) 19–40 is excellent on book 1's structure and Edwards (1980) 1–28 on its relation to convention.   **4.** Hom. *Il.* 1.56.   **5.** Hom. *Il.* 1.70–72.   **6.** Hom. *Il.* 1.125, 365–7, 392; Taplin (1992) 60–62, on 9.334 and 367–8 as a 'rhetorical device', not a counter-example.   **7.** Whitley (1991) 341–65, esp. 348–64, does not discuss this sort of *dasmos*.   **8.** Hom. *Il.* 1.196.   **9.** Lane Fox (1986) 104–23.   **10.** Hom. *Il.* 1.259–303.   **11.** Hom. *Il.* 1.348.   **12.** Hom. *Il.* 1.352.   **13.** Hom. *Il.* 1.365.   **14.** Hom. *Il.* 1.407–10.   **15.** Hom. *Il.* 1.423–4; *Od.* 1.22–3.   **16.** Hom. *Il.* 1.441 and 447.   **17.** Hom. *Il.* 1.488–92.   **18.** Hom. *Il.* 1.503–4.   **19.** Arist. *Eth. Nic.* 1124B15–17.   **20.** Hom. *Il.* 1.505.   **21.** Hom. *Il.* 15.598–9.   **22.** Hom. *Il.* 1.515–16 and 528–30.   **23.** Hom. *Il.* 1.586–9, 113–15.

2. Doing Things with Words

1. Hom. *Il.* 1.307.   **2.** Hom. *Il.* 1.348–50.   **3.** Hom. *Il.* 1.177, 560, 541.   **4.** Hom. *Il.* 1.204–5, 212.   **5.** Hom. *Il.* 1.225, 230, 302–3.   **6.** Hom. *Il.* 1.525–7.   **7.** Hom. *Il.* 1.268, 272.   **8.** Matthew Arnold, *On Translating Homer* (London, 1861) 9.   **9.** Lewis (1942) 19.   **10.** Strauss Clay (2011) 43–95.   **11.** Hom. *Il.* 2.404; 7.73, 159; 9.301; 19.193; are examples.   **12.** Hom. *Il.* 9.478; 16.595–6; Fowler (2011) 338–9.   **13.** Hes. *Op.* 653.   **14.** Hom. *Il.* 16.234.   **15.** Hom. *Il.* 14.225–30: the snowy peaks of the Thracians are not Athos itself: they are indeed those in Bisaltia and on Pangaion. Thence she turns due south to Athos: her route is accurately presented.   **16.** Hom. *Il.* 21.142 and 154–60, with two brilliant studies of its reception, Hollis (1994) 153–66 and Bernard (1995) 353–408, esp. 364–82.   **17.** Hom. *Il.* 9.150, 292.   **18.** Hom. *Od.* 6.44.   **19.** Hom. *Il.* 1.37–40 and 452–5.   **20.** Strabo 13.1.48; Cook (1973) 231–5.   **21.** Hom. *Il.* 1.34–9.   **22.** Cook (1973) 232.   **23.** Callinus ap. Strabo 13.1.48, though Palamidis (2019) 191–236 wants to limit Callinus' role here.   **24.** Palamidis (2019) 191–236, but the archaeology on site is still evolving promisingly.

3. Tracking Homer

1. Easton, Hawkins, Sherratt and Sherratt (2002) 75–109, esp. 98–100; doubted, unconvincingly, by Kolb (2014–15) 36 n.26.   **2.** Latacz (2004) 95–100.   **3.** Arr. *Anab.* 1.12.1; Plut. *Vit. Alex.* 15.7–9.   **4.** Bowra (1960) 16–23.   **5.** *The Complete Letters of Lady Mary Wortley Montagu*, vol. I, 1708–20, ed. R. Halsband (Oxford, 1965) 420; Cook (1973) 20 is unbecomingly sceptical: the admirable lady used such books while travelling and the 1766 (posthumous) publication of (some of) her letters collected ones she had written, and dated, much earlier.   **6.** Lord Byron, Letter, 3 May 1810.   **7.** Hom. *Il.* 7.435–41; ignored in 11.311, 569, 601, 803, 823–4, with J. B. Hainsworth, *The Iliad: A Commentary* (gen. ed. G. S. Kirk), vol. III: *Books 9–12* (Cambridge, 1993) 260–61.   **8.** Hom. *Il.* 13.11–14.   **9.** Kinglake (1844) 25 and 29; West (1995) 217 n.43 was perhaps unaware of this, as he 'sat amid the ruins of Troy on a beautifully clear day in September 1994 and surveyed the landscape – the Dardanelles, Imbros with Samothrace towering behind it, Tenedos and a very obvious Batieia on the horizon, halfway to the hidden beach of Beşik Bay – the conviction grew stronger: *he composed it here*'.   **10.** Huxley (1969) 5–11; Moorhead (1959).   **11.** Hom. *Il.* 13.23–30.   **12.** Hom. *Il.* 11.166, 372, and thereafter: *Il.* 2.793; Luce (1998) 126–34.   **13.** Strabo 13.1.36.   **14.** Nicolaides (1867).   **15.** Turner (2007) 393–408, esp. 388 quoting Schliemann's diary.   **16.** Kraft, Kayan, Erol (1980) 776–82.   **17.** Luce (1998) 140–48.   **18.** Strauss Clay (2011) 103–4 with fig. 4.   **19.** West (2011B) 25: 'pacing out the shore of the bay, he determined . . .'   **20.** Hom. *Il.* 20.74; 5.36.   **21.** Luce (1998) 71–9.   **22.** Hom. *Il.* 21.350–52.   **23.** Hom. *Il.* 12.283, for lotus-plains in general.   **24.** Wood (1776) 281–3; Finnegan, Mulvin (2022) on Wood himself.   **25.** Ellis-Evans (2019) 82; Nicolaos of Damascus FGH 90 F 134.   **26.** Turner (2007) 386, quoting Schliemann.   **27.** Hom. *Il.* 24.350–51.   **28.** Hom. *Il.* 12.20–22.   **29.** Hom. *Il.* 5.773–7.   **30.** Hom. *Il.* 22.149–52.   **31.** Hutton (1927) 102–28, esp. 112.   **32.** Cook (1973) 140–45, in great detail; Luce (1998) 65–9.   **33.** Luce (1998) 159–63, esp. 161, proposing 'the poet visualized the course of the chase as an extended ellipse, not a circle'.   **34.** Hom. *Il.* 22.153–6; Cook (1973) 145.   **35.** Hom. *Il.* 20.53.   **36.** Edwards (1991) 293.   **37.** Luce (1998) 76–8.   **38.** Alexander Pope, *Poems*, vol. VII, *The Iliad of Homer* (ed. M. Mack, 1967) book 20, lines 75–80, 83.   **39.** Cook (1973) 166 on Kesik Tepe; 166–7 on the man-made cut near it: Luce (1998) 145–7 rightly calls Kesik Tepe itself 'a natural limestone outcrop or butte', so it was visible to a visiting Homer *c.* 750 BC.   **40.** Hom. *Il.* 20.215–18.   **41.** Hom. *Il.* 8.47; 14.283; 15.151.   **42.** Hom. *Il.* 12.19; 8.170, 410.   **43.** Cook (1973) 257–8, but he inclines, implausibly, to believe that this peak was only identified as Homer's Gargaron by people at Methymna 'across the strait' after the Iliad became known.   **44.** Ellis-Evans (2019) 100–106 lists the flora of Ida mentioned in Theophrastus.   **45.** Hom. *Il.* 14.346–9.   **46.** Cypria F5 line 3.   **47.** Rix (2002) 56–7; Barker Webb (1844) 137, a Harrovian but botanically very alert, championed the wrong crocuses, *Colchicum autumnale* and (to him) *variegatum*, at the wrong season, late summer, on the wrong peak, Kasdagh.   **48.** Hom. *Il.* 20.307–8.   **49.** Strabo 13.1.52–3; Ellis-Evans (2019) 151 n.156 for the later coins.   **50.** Cook (1973) 302.

4. Homer's Heartland

1. Hunter, Rutherford, eds. (2009).   **2.** R. Janko, *The Iliad: A Commentary* (gen. ed. G. S. Kirk) vol. IV (Cambridge, 1992) 8–19, a lucid survey.   **3.** West (1981) 113–27.   **4.** Lane Fox (2008) 45–120.   **5.** Hom. *Il.* 2.780–85; Lane Fox (2008) 41, 335–7.   **6.** Hom. *Il.* 4.463–9.   **7.** Janko (2015A) 1–32, esp. 25–7.   **8.** Lane Fox (2008) 63–4, 356.   **9.** Wood (1776) 23.   **10.** Hom. *Il.* 2.144–6.   **11.** Hdt. 6.95; Shipley (1987) 11–12 n.32.   **12.** Hom. *Il.* 20.390–92; Hdt. 1.148.   **13.** Hom. *Il.* 2.459–68.   **14.** Hom. *Il.* 24.602–17; Szempruch (2019) 227–53.   **15.** Hom. *Il.* 24.616 with West (2001) 280.   **16.** Hom. *Il.* 20.392.   **17.** Lane Fox (2008) 351–2.   **18.** Hom. *Il.* 5.478–86.   **19.** Hom. *Il.* 17.144–55.   **20.** Mellink (1995) 33–43; Starke (1997) 505–6.   **21.** Hom. *Il.* 5.173 does not, strictly, make Pandarus a Lycian too.   **22.** Hom. *Il.* 6.150–211; 5. 627–62.   **23.** Frei (1978) 819–27 and esp. (1993) 39–65.   **24.** Hom. *Il.* 16.675.   **25.** Robert (1978) 3–48, a tour de force on Tlos; West (2011B) 23 for a possible visit to Lycia by Homer; Kolb (2014–15) 27–50 proposes Lycian involvement in wars in Lydia / Ionia in the early seventh cent., irrelevant, however, to Homer's time and unattested.   **26.** Spivey (2018).   **27.** Hdt. 1.147.

5. Unstitching the Iliad

The 'Homeric question' is lucidly presented by Dodds (1968) 1–49, ably answered by Hardie (1956) 118–31; West (2011A) 383–93 is a more recent survey, from another angle.   **1.** Pollianos, *Anth. Pal.* XI.130:

I take him to be referring to 'one thing after another', not just to an archaic Homeric borrow-ing. **2.** Hom. *Il.* 8.70–72. **3.** Nilsson (1933) 258–9. **4.** Hom. *Il.* 9.182–9, with J. B. Hainsworth, *The Iliad: A Commentary* (gen. ed. G. S. Kirk) vol. III: *Books 9–12* (Cambridge, 1993) 85–7, for six possible explanations. **5.** Joseph. *Ap.* 1.12–13. **6.** A. Grafton (1983) 102–3. **7.** Grafton, Weinberg (2011) 13–14, on Casaubon and Homer. **8.** G. Murray (1907) 125. **9.** G. Murray (1907) 238, 241, 256–8. **10.** Lowe (2000) 106 for a list. **11.** Hom. *Il.* 6.241. **12.** Plumtree (2021) 239–301, for the scope of the Manas epic. **13.** Hom. *Il.* 2.301–29. **14.** Hom. *Il.* 1.352. **15.** Hom. *Il.* 7.421–37. **16.** Hom. *Il.* 2.3–5; 8.471–7. **17.** Hom. *Il.* 15.53–68 and 71.

6. Plotting an Epic

1. Lowe (2000) 275. **2.** Lowe (2000) 103–4, 128, 259–60. **3.** Hom. *Il.* 9.650–52. **4.** Hom. *Il.* 16.46–7, 252, 685–93, 785–7. **5.** Hom. *Il.* 18.9–11. **6.** Hom. *Il.* 15.68. **7.** Hom. *Il.* 15.612–14. **8.** Hom. *Il.* 16. 799–800, 851–4; 17.201–8. **9.** Hom. *Il.* 9.410–16. **10.** Hom. *Il.* 16.709;18.464–5; 19.416–17; 21.275–8; 23. 59–60; 24.84–6, 104–5, 131–2. **11.** H. de Balzac, *La Comédie humaine*, vol. 1, 'Avant-propos', ed. La Pléi-ade (Paris, 1976) 11: 'le hasard est le plus grand romancier du monde'. **12.** Hom. *Il.* 12.387–90 and 16. 510–13, but he was still fighting at 14.426, surely a slip by Homer. **13.** Hom. *Il.* 11.251–74; 19.51–3. **14.** Hom. *Il.* 12.110–41, esp. 139–41, with 13.384–92, 506–8, 545, 567–75. **15.** D. Lohmann (1970) 96–102. **16.** Nimis (1999) 65–78; Minchin (2007) 43 is cautious about structural ring-composition in the speeches; Douglas (2007) on ring-composition in general. **17.** Danek (1988) and (2002) 3–17. **18.** Johansen (1967) 70–75; Snodgrass (1998) 120–21, 131 on his 'running pose', albeit in very un-Iliadic company; Burgess (2001) 226 n.141, denying, however, that the Iliad preceded this image. **19.** Dickinson (2011) 150–55 is a valuable critique. **20.** Giovannini (1969) and the adjustments by West (2011B) 112–14. **21.** *Epikē poiēsis* occurs in Dion. Hal. *Comp.* 23, but *epopoiia* is earlier, e.g. Ar. *Poet.* 1449B 9. **22.** Foley (2004) 171–87, for a survey and an alternative view; Hainsworth (1991) 1–10 is a sensible survey too. **23.** Beissinger, Tylus, Wofford (1999) 2. **24.** Bowra (1952) 27, 43–4. **25.** Wecowski (2014). **26.** O. Mur-ray (2008) 161–76. **27.** Bowra (1952) 410–20; Sherratt (2016) 35–52. **28.** G. Murray (1907) 187–92 is an eloquent supporter of a festival venue; Taplin (1992) 28–9 and 39–40 is another; Lord (1960) 152–3 is sceptical: 'there is too much going on at a festival'. **29.** *Hom. Hymn. Apollo* 146–50, where *agōna* may mean 'gathering', not 'competition'. **30.** Mitchell (1990) 183–93, esp. 184–5. **31.** Hor. *Epist.* 2.1.232–4; Plut. *Vit. Alex.* 29.1–3; Ath. 13.595 E. **32.** H. Lohmann (2012) 32–50: of course, festival gatherings on Mycale may have preceded the Meliac war and these probable traces of it.

PART II: COMPOSING THE ILIAD: HOW?
7. 'Sing, o goddess . . .'

1. West (1981) 113–29. **2.** Hom. *Il.* 9.186–9. **3.** Carter (1995) 285–312, esp. 295–6 and nn.40–42 crediting L. D. Mc Callum. **4.** West (1981) 113–29, with Danek, Hagel (1989) 5–20 and also at www.oeaw.ac.at/ kal/sh/. **5.** West (1988) 151–72. **6.** Hom. *Il.* 6.447–8; Plb. 38.22.1–3. **7.** A. H. Clough, *Amours de Voy-age*, Canto II.VIII lines 218–22. **8.** Haugen (2011) 182–6 is excellent on the history of study of the digamma. **9.** West (1988) 151–72. **10.** Haugen (2011) 96–105. **11.** *The Complete Letters of Lady Mary Wortley Montagu*, vol. III, ed. R Halsband (Oxford, 1967) 117–18. **12.** [Bentley] (1713) 26, answering the view that Homer 'design'd his poem for Eternity, to please and instruct mankind'. **13.** Dué, ed. (2009). **14.** H. Clarke (1981) 156–61; A. Grafton (1981) 101–29. **15.** Grote, II (1888) 56–137: Lorimer (1948) 11–23 on opinions from 1713 to 1939 is still worth reading. **16.** Wachter (2000) 62–106 is an excel-lent summary. **17.** Düntzer (1872). **18.** Wood (1776) 20. **19.** Petrović (1965) 109–14.

Notes and References

8. Homeric Fieldwork

1. Wilson (1970); Tate (2011B) 159–74. **2.** Petrović (2016) 315–27, esp. 318 and 321. **3.** Petrović (2016) 315–27, esp. 324. **4.** Fielding, ed. (2020); van der Heide (2008) 167–173 with the fine fig. 3.1 of a memorial to his work. **5.** Temir (1955) 51–93 on Radloff; Hatto (1990) translates Radloff's Manas transcription. **6.** Hom. *Il.* 13.3–7. **7.** Reichl (2016) 327–44; van der Heide (2008). **8.** Radloff (1990) 89–90. **9.** Hom. *Od.* 8.73–83, 266–366. **10.** Hom. *Od.* 22.347–9. **11.** Radloff (1990) 87; van der Heide (2008) 110–26 on inspiration and the singers. **12.** Plumtree (2021) 239–301, esp. 257–8. **13.** Tate (2011B) 159–74, esp. 165–6. **14.** Krauss (1881). **15.** Krauss (1908) 177–80. **16.** Van Gennep (1909), esp. 52–3. **17.** Sienaert (1990) 91–106. **18.** Jousse (1981); Kanigel (2021) 154–6 is helpful, but it is not clear when Parry first read Jousse. A. Parry, ed. (1971) xxii suspects an influence in the late 1920s, but the first mention is in a paper published in 1930, well after the doctoral viva in 1928: A. Parry (1971) 270.

9. Singers of Tales

I wrote this chapter before Kanigel (2021), a fuller account of Parry, and have checked it against his where we overlap. **1.** M. Parry, ed. A. Parry (1971) 428. **2.** M. Parry, ed. A. Parry (1971) xx, 6. **3.** Meillet (1923) 61, with A. Platt, *CR* 38 (1924) 22. **4.** Tate (2011A) 329–52. **5.** Murko (1929) 15–16; on weddings, 13. **6.** M. Parry, ed. A. Parry (1971) 439. **7.** M. Parry, ed. A. Parry (1971) 239. **8.** M. Parry, ed. A. Parry (1971) 269. **9.** Murko (1929), planches 1–69, a fine archive. **10.** Kanigel (2021) 157. **11.** Kanigel (2021) 180–83, with a photo. **12.** M. Parry, ed. A. Parry (1971) 378. **13.** Lord (1948) 34–44, esp. 40. **14.** Lord (1991) 57–71; Kanigel (2021) 220–29. **15.** Lord (1991) 98 on Međedović dictating 18–20 ten-syllable verses a minute; Murko (1929) 20 noted down 13–38, averaging 16–20. **16.** Lord (1991) 69–71. **17.** www.Russian-Records.com: items 3590 and 3591 for recent examples. **18.** Reichl (2016) 45–63. **19.** Lang Ying (2001) 222–39, esp. 237 on the 'modern Homer'. **20.** Jacquesson (2020) 324–39, for the cultural rivalries between Beijing and Bishkek here. **21.** Hom. *Od.* 17.383. **22.** Petrović (2016) 315–27. **23.** M. Parry, ed. A. Parry (1971) xli, 404–7. **24.** Kanigel (2021) 233–49 for a full recent discussion. **25.** Lord (1991) 71. **26.** Lord (1995) 102; Jumaturdu (2016) 288–96 for recent Manas singers who have orally composed and improvised while being literate.

10. The Uses of Analogy

1. Beaton (2016) 156–63. **2.** Hatto (2017). **3.** Ps.-Hdt. *Vita Hom.* 5–6: ps.-Plut. *Vita Hom.* 1.4 is less specific and implies he began being a poet while a younger man. **4.** Vámbéry (1911) 6–7 **5.** Pl. *Ion.* 535 B–E. **6.** Radloff (1990) 73–90, esp. 85; on recent *manaschi*, Howard, Kasmambetor (2011) and esp. Reichl (2016) 327–44 and van der Heide (2008), a fine first-hand study. **7.** Hutchinson (2017) 145–70 addresses audiences' attention helpfully; for a repetition, Hom. *Il.* 4.163–5; 6.447–8. **8.** Hom. *Il.* 16. 856–7; 22.362–3; Barnes (2011) 1–13. **9.** Čolaković (2019) 1–48, Importantly answered by Elmer (2010) 276–303. **10.** Hom. *Il.* 11.690–91; 4.249–55; 11.668–761; 6.158–206; 9.527–99, with Burgess (2017) 51–76. **11.** West (2002) 1–14, esp. 4–5, and Currie (2016) for surveys; Heitsch (2008) 1–12 for a defence of the approach. **12.** West (2002) 1–14, esp. 3 and 5; Kelly (2012) 211–56 is rightly sceptical. **13.** Hom. *Il.* 18.90–100. **14.** Will cock (1983) 479–85. **15.** Ready (2019) 164–5. **16.** *P.Oxy.* 33.2673 lines 34–5 with Lane Fox (1994) 126–48, esp. 144. **17.** Dalrymple (2006) 48–55. **18.** Rutherford (1991–3) 37–54. **19.** Currie (2016) 16–17, 39–47. **20.** Janko (1982), well defended by Janko (2015B) 20–43. **21.** Meadows (2021) 443–70, esp. 445–54, 464–7. **22.** Wade-Gery (1952) 40. **23.** West (2011B) 13–14 assumes the opposite, but I cannot agree. **24.** West (2011B) 10–14, esp. 14 on 'cutting and pasting'. **25.** Gomme et al. (1981) 400–401. **26.** Lord (1991) 38–48, esp. 43, an acute riposte to Bowra and to Wade-Gery. **27.** Lane Fox (2015) 2–3.

11. A Great Dictator

1. Nimis (1999) 65–78. **2.** M. Parry, ed. A. Parry (1971) 251–65. **3.** Hom. *Il.* 6.496. **4.** Hainsworth (1993) 233; on type scenes more generally, Edwards (1992) 284–330. **5.** Nilsson (1933) 258–9. **6.** West (2011B) 52–3, 101–2. **7.** Ready (2019) 101–82; Hatto (1990) 159–225; Honko (1998); Prior (2022) xxi–xxii and 3–238. **8.** Choerilus, *PEG* I (ed. A. Bernabé) 191 F 2. **9.** Ruijgh (2011) 253–98 and (1995) 1–96, esp. 85–8 on Hom. *Il.* 7.166, but see also Barnes (2011) 1–13, esp. 1 n.2. **10.** Janko (1998) 1–13, esp. 5. **11.** Strauss Clay (2011) 118–19, on mnemonics, however, which I do not think apply to Homer composing orally. **12.** Strabo 13.1.36. **13.** Hom. *Il.* 18.396. **14.** Hom. *Il.* 3.243–4; Bowie, ed. (2019) 139, on v. 243. **15.** Čolaković (2019) 1–48, importantly answered by Elmer (2010) 276–303, esp. 283–9. **16.** M. Parry, ed. A. Parry (1971) 324. **17.** Ready (2015) 1–75 and (2019) 101–82. **18.** Chap. 9 n.15, supra: I give a low average number. **19.** Janko (1998) 1–13, esp. 5 and 12. **20.** George (2020) xvii–xxxii. **21.** Dalley (2016) 116–34. **22.** Currie (2012) 543–60 and (2016) 173–83, esp.173, 184–200 discusses possible borrowings in detail and stresses the 'large historical imponderables'; Rutherford (2019) 231–6 doubts any such borrowings by Homer; so do I. **23.** West (1997A) 587 and 627; West (1995) 203–19; Lane Fox (2008) 352–3 and 447 n.14 dissents. **24.** Janko (1998) 1–13, esp. 13. **25.** Forrest (1966) 60 and 103–4. **26.** Plut. *Quaest. Graec.* 11 is one example, datable to 733 BC. **27.** Lane Fox (2020) 66–8: *SEG* 28.631 for public scribes on Crete. **28.** Pind. *Nem.* 2.1–5: Graziosi (2002) 208–16; Malouchou (2006) 81–90 is important. **29.** Pind. F265 S–M; Graziosi (2002) 186–93 for discussion. **30.** Krauss (1908) 180–81, 185–7.

PART III: COMPOSING THE ILIAD: WHEN?

12. Problems of Literacy

1. Hom. *Il.* 7.185–92. **2.** Hom. *Il.* 6.168–9. **3.** Powell (1991) 198–200. **4.** Csapo (1991) 211–16. **5.** Lane Fox (2008) 60–62, 127–9, 165–7. **6.** Kenzelmann Pfyffer, Theurillat, Verdan (2005) 51–83. **7.** Kenzelmann Pfyffer, Theurillat, Verdan (2005) 75. **8.** Kenzelmann Pfyffer, Theurillat, Verdan (2005) 76–7, queried by Janko (2015A) 12. **9.** Popham, Sackett (1981) 89–93. **10.** Lane Fox (2008) 136–7; Janko (2015A) 14–15. **11.** Verdan (2017) 105–22. **12.** Janko (2015A) 17–19, not invalidated by Papadopoulos (2016) 1238–54. **13.** Also emphasized by Malkin (1998) 263. **14.** Powell (1991). **15.** Powell (1992) 116–18, at 118. **16.** Powell (1991) 158–69; Janko (2015A) 3. **17.** Janko (2015A) 3, with the fascinating suggestion that the cup's owner, Akesandros, may have been a doctor. **18.** Binek (2017) 423–42; Cullhed (2021) 22–33. **19.** Gigante, Nava et al. (2021). **20.** Kerschner (2014) 109–40, esp. 109–10, a major discovery. **21.** Johnston, Andriomenou (1989) 217–20, for a Rhodian bowl at Eretria *c.* 735 BC. **22.** Hom. *Il.* 11.632–723. **23.** J. B. Hainsworth, *The Iliad: A Commentary* (gen. ed. G. S. Kirk), vol. III: *Books 9–12* (Cambridge, 1993) 292–3. **24.** Pöhlmann, West (2012) 1–16: note, however, Wade-Gery (1952) 11, on *byblinos* in Hom. *Od.* 21.300–301; on prices, Jeffery (1961) 56–7, esp. 57 n.1 on *IG.*I².374 lines 279–81. **25.** Gonzáles (2013) 135–44, esp. 144. **26.** Johnston, Andriomenou (1989) seems to refer to a female drinker; Colonna (1980) 51–5, another *c.* 630 BC. **27.** Mimnermus F14 with Bowie (2022) 467–9 and Hom. *Il.* 4.370–400. Alcaeus F 44 with West (2011B) 16 n.6. **28.** Tyrtaeus F 10.21–30. **29.** Hom. *Il.* 22.74–6. **30.** Bowra (1935) 54–5; West (2011B) 385 is wholly unpersuasive. **31.** Hes. *Theog.* 39. **32.** Snodgrass (1998) is excellent here: Burgess (2001) is fuller, but favours a long evolution of the Homeric epics into the seventh century BC (49–53). **33.** Snodgrass (1998) 33–5, doubting Helen and Paris but rightly seeing a legendary reference. **34.** Burgess (2001) 20 fig. B. **35.** Snodgrass (1998) 20–21 figs. 7–8, 26. **36.** Snodgrass (1998) 91–6 is too sceptical; Burgess (2001) 101 and fig. U is also too wary. **37.** Snodgrass (1998) 91–3 and fig. 37. **38.** Coldstream (1977) 349. **39.** V. Karageorghis (2006) 665–75, an important rethink.

13. Trojan Wars

The 'Trojan war' continues to be much discussed: recent helpful treatments include Cline (2013), the best short introduction to the problems, Villing et al. (2019) and Sherratt (2010) 1–18. Mac Sweeney

(2018) is a readable summary, extending into receptions of Troy in later media. Latacz (2004) gives a fine survey of M. Korfmann and others' recent finds but inclines to the view that the historicity of a Trojan war is still an open question, perhaps with a positive answer. Strauss (2006) is a lone scholarly believer in such a war: nonetheless his re-creations of fighting in it are vivid and well based. **1.** Beckman, Brice, Cline (2011) 1–6, esp. 6; Blackwell (2021) 191–231. **2.** Beckman, Brice, Cline (2011) 45–6, 136; on Lazpa, 193–4. **3.** Latacz (2004) 117–18, also suggesting adoption of a son from a Greek concubine. **4.** Latacz (2004) 105–12, with English translation. **5.** Cline (1996) 137–53. **6.** Latacz (2004) 123–4. **7.** Beckman, Brice, Cline (2011) 125; 129, on Walmu. **8.** Ludwig (1931) 233–4. **9.** Turner (2007) 345–91, at 346. **10.** Rose (2014) 17. **11.** Rose (2014) 19 and n.43. **12.** Latacz (2004) 38; Easton, Hawkins, Sherratt and Sherratt (2002) 75–109. **13.** Rose (2014) 30; Latacz (2004) 286. **14.** Rose (2014) 37 and n.138. **15.** Burkert (1995) 139–48. **16.** Hood (1995) 25–32. **17.** Hom. *Il.* 5.640–42. **18.** At Hom. *Od.* 11.521, Huxley (1959) 281–2 suggested that the variant reading *Chētaioi* indeed refers to Hittites. **19.** Hom. *Il.* 24.543–6. **20.** Spencer (1995) 269–306. **21.** Dickinson (2016) 13. **22.** Raaflaub (2011) 5 elaborates this point. **23.** Bowra (1960) 16–23. **24.** Latacz (2004) 43. **25.** Rose (2014) 47–9. **26.** Rose (2014) 49 n.18; Bachvarova (2016) 367–73 favours cross-cultural dialogue here. **27.** Coldstream (1976) 8–17; Rose (2014) 50. **28.** Ion. *FGH* 392 F1; Wade-Gery (1952) 6–7. **29.** Arist. F 611.37; Poll. IX.83; Wade-Gery (1952) 65. **30.** Wade-Gery (1952) 7; the name *e-ko-to* is known in a Linear B tablet, Page (1959) 199, but I do not consider this blunts the possibility that Homer and predecessors took Trojan Hector's name from the Hector previously on Chios: *e-ko-to* is not certainly 'Hector', either, as Page rightly warns.

14. 'Not as mortal men are now . . .'

Bennet (2014) 187–234 is an exceptionally full and fine review of Homer and the evidence related to Linear B; Wiener (2007) 3–33 is a very helpful survey of even more archaeological material than I could address here. O. Murray (1993) 35–68 is a particularly penetrating account of Homer's poems in an eighth-century context. **1.** Bartlett (2022). **2.** Hom. *Il.* 13.665–70. **3.** Hom. *Il.* 9.150, 292. **4.** V. Petrakis, speaking on 17 Nov. 2021 at www.bsa.ac.uk. **5.** Hom. *Il.* 9.380–84. **6.** Gray (1958) 43–8. **7.** Muhly (2011) 321–3. **8.** Wiener (2007) 10 nn.37–8 for other examples. **9.** Hom. *Il.* 19.360–62. **10.** King (1970) 294–6. **11.** Van Wees (2011) 792–3; Lorimer (1950) 132–93. **12.** Hom. *Il.* 15.638–44. **13.** Hom. *Il.* 6.117–18; 7.219–23; 11.485; 17.128, with Lorimer (1950) 182–3, 297. **14.** Van Wees (1994) 1–18 for a summary. **15.** Hdt. 5.113; Sappho F 16.19–20. **16.** Coldstream (1977) 110–11. **17.** Immerwahr (1990). **18.** Llewellyn-Jones (2003) 29–33. **19.** Bowra (1972) 93. **20.** Lane Fox (2008) 55–9 gives a summary. **21.** Finley (1957) 133–59, at 159. **22.** Finley (1954) 35 and 51–2 on social content in older formulas; 68 with n.19 and 70 with n.23 appeal to evidence from other simple societies, though 58 n.8 and 116 n.58 are warnings against importing direct analogies in other instances. **23.** Hes. *Op.* 38 with M. L. West's commentary (1978) 151. **24.** Pl, *Resp.* 404B–C; Heath (2000) 342–52. **25.** Thomas (1989) 126–7. **26.** Whitley (1991) 341–65, answered by Carlier (2007) 121–8. **27.** Carlier (2006) 101–10. **28.** Hes. *Op.* 38, 202, 248, 263. **29.** Wade-Gery (1952) 6–7. **30.** Forrest (1966) 78–86, 121; Hom. *Il.* 16.384–93; Hes. *Op.* 256–62, esp. 260–61. **31.** Plut. *Vit. Lyc.* 6 whose date has been much discussed. **32.** Hom. *Il.* 18.497–508; Finley (1979) 35; Seaford (1994) 2–6, a clear sequel. **33.** Finley (1979) 85–9; Hom. *Il.* 1.368, 9.367 for booty. **34.** Hom. *Il.* 7.171; 24. 400; 15. 189–92. **35.** Luce (1978) 1–15; Finley (1979) 110–14; Hdt. 5.99.1, which I take to be based on relations of *xenia c.* 710 BC; Meiggs, Lewis, *GHI* no. 4 for a later *proxenia* and a 'fascinating tension between . . . Homeric echoes and the political circumstances of a new age'. **36.** Luce (1978) 1–15; Gould (2001) 335–58 stresses the poetic dimension of Homeric 'society'. **37.** Finley (1979) 68 with n.19 comparing Trobriand islanders, 105–10. **38.** Hom. *Il.* 6.230–36; 7.301–5. **39.** Crielaard (2003) 49–62. **40.** Gould (1991). **41.** Hom. *Il.* 7.467–75: Finley (1981) 291 excludes it, unconvincingly.

15. Dating Homer

Crielaard (1995) 201–86 is a full and helpful discussion of many items used to date Homer's poems with the help of archaeological evidence: he inclines to a later date, however, than I and others accept. **1.** Sherratt (1990) 807–24. **2.** Notopoulos (1960) 135–44. **3.** Hom. *Il.* 23.826–35. **4.** Hom. *Il.* 9. 63–4; 2.362–3; Andrewes (1961) 129–40. **5.** Sherratt (2004) 301–37, at 324–6 and esp. Wecowski (2014), but I do not believe that Hom. *Il.* 1.597, *endexia*, implies awareness of sympotic practice. **6.** Zafeiropoulou, Agelarakis (2005) 30–35; Cleomachus in Plut. *Mor.* 760E–761B with the monument preserving his historical identity. **7.** Kagan, Viggiano (2013). **8.** Hom. *Il.* 4.422–8; 13.795–800; 15.380–83; 17.263–8; compare 14.390–402. **9.** Van Wees (2004) 153–8 with, however, Raaflaub (1997/8) 386–403, (2011) 15–16. **10.** Van Wees (1994) 1–18 and 131–55. **11.** I still lay weight on the much-discussed Hdt. 2.152.4–5. **12.** Pierattini (2022) 12–55. **13.** Coldstream (1998) 14–15. **14.** Coldstream (1998) 14 n.61. **15.** Hom. *Il.* 11.32–40; Lorimer (1950) 189–92. **16.** Hom. *Il.* 5.740–43. **17.** Burkert (1992) 83–7. **18.** Lorimer (1950) 190–91 and esp. 481, 'the certainly interpolated mention of the Gorgoneion in the description of Agamemnon's shield'. **19.** Rose (2014) 39–42; Hom. *Il.* 3.184–90. **20.** Hom. *Il.* 18.289–92. **21.** Rose (2014) 42: Hecuba as a Phrygian 'makes sense only as an eighth-century BC reference'. **22.** Lane Fox (2008) 22–4, 60 with much bibliography. **23.** M. Dickie (1995) 29–56, but his arguments for a late seventh-cent. dating can all be countered; Hes. *Theog.* 337–45 shows awareness of Black Sea rivers *c.* 710 BC; for more, Drews (1976) 18–31. **24.** Rollinger, Korenjak (2001) 325–37, esp. 331–5. **25.** Muellner (1990) 59–101, esp. 99–101 for the question of the location. **26.** Hom. *Il.* 6.291; 23.743; Lipinski (2004) 13–18 and 36. **27.** Hom. *Il.* 9.381–4. **28.** Lane Fox (2008) 347–8 with 446 n. 35: Burkert himself abandoned his contention, as he kindly confirmed to me. **29.** Kelly (2006) 321–33 stresses the possibility of a Mycenean input nonetheless. **30.** Hom. *Il.* 9. 404–5. **31.** Lorimer (1950) 450, 481. **32.** Hom. *Il.* 11.696–702; Potter (2012) 41 and 101–2 sees the potential relevance. **33.** Hom. *Il.* 2.780–85 with Lane Fox (2008) 41, 316–17, 335–7. **34.** Hdt. 2.53; 2.75.4 contrary to Graziosi (2002) 112 and n. 57. **35.** Hdt. 2.42.2; Wade-Gery (1952) 27 and n. 66.

16. In Transmission

1. George (2020) 105, 186, 205–6 for examples. **2.** Dalley (2016) 116–34 is clear on this point. **3.** Nagy (2003) 11. **4.** Pind. *Nem.* 2.1–5; Graziosi (2002) 208–17. **5.** The Asclepiads and doctoring are a comparable case : Lane Fox (2020) 67–8. **6.** Heraclitus F42 D–K. **7.** Hdt. 5.67.1. **8.** Pl. [*Hipparch.*] 228B5–C1. **9.** Gonzáles (2013) 907–20; *SEG* LXVI (2016) 975. **10.** West (2001) 11–15, on minor interpolations. **11.** Hippoc. *On Joints* 8. **12.** Plut. *Vit. Alc.* 7.1. **13.** Xen. *Symp.* 3.5; Xen. *Hell.* 2.3. 39–40. **14.** Xen. *Symp.* 3.6. **15.** Aeschin. *In Tim.* 128, 144 and esp. 147–150 with N. Fisher's ed. and notes (Oxford, 2001) 268, 290–93. **16.** Aeschin, *In Tim.* 147. **17.** Plut. *Vit. Alex.* 8.2; Pfeiffer (1968) 71; Schironi (2018) 20 n.64, 41–2 on the scope of the word *diorthōsis*. **18.** Strabo 13.1.27. **19.** Pfeiffer (1968) 72. **20.** Fraser (1972) 476–8; Haslam (1997) 55–100. **21.** Schironi (2018) 35–45. **22.** Schironi (2018) 41–2. **23.** Schironi (2018) 41–2; Fraser (1972) 328. **24.** Fredouille (1993) 74–9. **25.** West (2001) 11; Haslam (2011) 849–55, a good brief survey of the text's transmission.

PART IV: HEROIC HALLMARKS

17. Heroism: the Highlights

1. Dodds (1951) 16; Horn (2018) 359–83; Sourvinou-Inwood (1981) 15–39, on Hades. **2.** Hom. *Il.* 23.100–101. **3.** Coldstream (1976) 8–17; Parker (2011) 287–92, esp. 291. **4.** Lane Fox (1986) 38, 95, 111. **5.** Hom. *Il.* 3.278–80; 19.258–62. **6.** De Jong, ed. (2012) 110, 134–5. **7.** Hom. *Il.* 6.355–8. **8.** Hom. *Il.* 9.413; West (1988) 151–72, at 152, despite the questioning of Finkelberg (2007) 341–50. **9.** Hom. *Il.* 22.393 **10.** Hom. *Il.* 1.515–16. **11.** Hom. *Il.* 3.200–202; Schofield (1986) 6–31. **12.** Hom. *Il.* 3.454. **13.** Hom. *Il.* 6.236–7. **14.** Hom. *Il.* 9.119. **15.** Hom. *Il.* 9.406–9, 410–16. **16.** Hom. *Il.* 9.497; Burgess (2017) 51–76. **17.** Hom. *Il.* 9.605. **18.** Hom. *Il.* 14.157–8. **19.** Hom. *Il.* 14.216–17. **20.** Hom. *Il.* 11.798–801. **21.** Hom. *Il.* 9.650–55. **22.** Hom. *Il.* 16.84–5. **23.** Hom. *Il.* 16.100. **24.** Hom. *Il.* 16.398. **25.** Allan (2005) 1–16, relating this sequence to wider questions of tradition and originality. **26.** Hom. *Il.* 16.853–4.

18. 'Not ingloriously may I die . . .'

1. Hom. *Il.* 18.121–4.   **2.** Hom. *Il.* 18.170–72.   **3.** Hyder E. Rollins, *The Keats Circle: Lettters and Papers*, vol. II (Cambridge, Mass., 1948) 277.   **4.** Jebb (2010) 175–81.   **5.** Hom. *Il.* 18.311–12.   **6.** Hom. *Il.* 18. 466–7.   **7.** Hom. *Il.* 19.86–94, 134–7; Taplin (1992) 206–9.   **8.** Hom. *Il.* 20.443–4.   **9.** Hom. *Il.* 20.502– 3.   **10.** Hom. *Il.* 21.544–9.   **11.** Hom. *Il.* 22.199–201.   **12.** Hom. *Il.* 22.159–61.   **13.** Hom. *Il.* 22. 304–5.   **14.** Hom. *Il.* 22.393–4.   **15.** Hom. *Il.* 22.401–2.   **16.** Hom. *Il.* 22.410–11.   **17.** Hom. *Il.* 22.418– 23.   **18.** Hom. *Il.* 23.34.   **19.** Lowe (2000) 108.   **20.** Hom. *Il.* 23.142–51.

19. 'If it must be so . . .'

1. Hom. *Il.* 24.7–8.   **2.** Hom. *Il.* 24.107–11.   **3.** Hom. *Il.* 24.116–9.   **4.** Hom. *Il.* 24.130–31.   **5.** Hom. *Il.* 24.160–65.   **6.** Hom. *Il.* 24.171–85; 23.90.   **7.** Hom. *Il.* 24.226–7.   **8.** Hom. *Il.* 24.260–64.   **9.** Joseph Spence, *Observations, Anecdotes and Characters of Books and Men*, vol. 1, ed. James M. Osborn (Oxford, 1966) no. 529, p. 223.   **10.** Hom. *Il.* 24.265–9, with the fine observation by Strawn (2012) 585–608, esp. 598.   **11.** Hom. *Il.* 24.334–5; Versnel (2011) 332–48 on sociable Hermes, more generally.   **12.** Hom. *Il.* 24.347–8; E. Fraenkel (1957) 248 n.1 and 249 related it notably to Hor. *Od.* 1.2.41–4.   **13.** Hom. *Il.* 24. 504–6.   **14.** Hom. *Il.* 24.507–12.   **15.** Hom. *Il.* 24.527–33.   **16.** Hom. *Il.* 24.568.   **17.** Hom. *Il.* 24.629– 32.   **18.** Hom. *Il.* 24.667.   **19.** Hom. *Il.* 24.676.   **20.** Hom. *Il.* 24.720–22.   **21.** Hom. *Il.* 24.795–8.   **22.** Hom. *Il.* 12.32; van Wees (2006) 363–80 is important here.   **23.** Hor. *Epist.* 1.2.

20. Heroic Ethics

1. Van Wees and Fisher (2015) 1–57 and also Duplouy (2006) for a contrary view which I do not share.   **2.** Hom. *Il.* 6.382–9; 2.225–42.   **3.** Hom. *Il.* 2.270.   **4.** Hom. *Il.* 2.188–206.   **5.** Adkins (1960) 30–39 is fundamental here still.   **6.** Hom. *Il.* 7.475, rightly included in the text, as Kelly (2007) 5–17 also argues.   **7.** E. T. Cook, *Life of Florence Nightingale*, vol. I (1913) 368–73.   **8.** Adkins (1997) 694–713, well summarizing his views.   **9.** Hom. *Il.* 11.784.   **10.** Hom. *Il.* 9.636–8.   **11.** Hom. *Il.* 6.443–5.   **12.** Hom. *Il.* 24.730.   **13.** Hom. *Il.* 17.364–5.   **14.** Hom. *Il.* 7.427–9.   **15.** Hom. *Il.* 22.370–74.   **16.** Dryden (1693).   **17.** Several fine contributions to Gill, Postlethwaite, Seaford, eds. (1998), esp. 4–5, 51–72, 93–102, emphasize a rather elastic 'reciprocity' (contrast 73–92, which I endorse); Seaford (1994) 7–72 relates it to household and community, gifts, meals, marriage and much else.   **18.** Hom. *Il.* 9.629; 16.35.   **19.** Hom. *Il.* 6.14– 15.   **20.** Hom. *Il.* 17.670–72.   **21.** Hom. *Il.* 16.180–92, esp. 190–92.   **22.** Aeschin. *In Tim.* 1.142; Dover (1999) 196–9.   **23.** Hom. *Il.* 9.663–8.

21. Heroes at Play

1. Irwin (1989) 18.   **2.** Hom. *Il.* 23.669.   **3.** Hom. *Il.* 23.792.   **4.** Hom. *Il.* 23.485–7.   **5.** Hom. *Il.* 23.555.   **6.** Hom. *Il.* 23.559; Oliver (2007) on *epidosis*.   **7.** Hom. *Il.* 23.580; M. W. Dickie (1984) 8–17 on 'fair' play; Gernet (1955) 9–18 on 'rules'.   **8.** Hom. *Il.* 15.568–72; Willcock (1983) 477–85.   **9.** Hom. *Il.* 23.648–9.   **10.** N. Richardson, *The Iliad: A Commentary*, vol. VI: *Books 21–24* (Cambridge, 1993) 202.   **11.** Hom. *Il.* 23.894.   **12.** Hom. *Il.* 23.84–90 with 18.694–7, 15.430–32 and 437–9, 16.570–76 .   **13.** Adkins (1969) 7–21.   **14.** Hodges (2008) 123–38.   **15.** Hom. *Il.* 11.145–7; 13.204; 14.496–500; Hdt. 9.79.   **16.** Kucewicz (2020).   **17.** Hom. *Il.* 11.122–30 and 138–42; 17.34–42.   **18.** Hom. *Il.* 14.494–505 and esp. 506–7.   **19.** Arist. F166 (Rose).   **20.** Lane Fox (2020) 12–16 gives examples; Saunders (1999) 345–63 for more detail.   **21.** Hom. *Il.* 13.650–55, with Saunders (1999) 352–4; 13.615–18; 13.506–8.   **22.** Saunders (1999) 347, 361.

22. Heroism and Hyper-Reality

1. Hom. *Il.* 14.85–7.   **2.** Hom. *Il.* 13.634–9, 340–44.   **3.** G. S. Kirk, *The Iliad: A Commentary*, vol. II (Cambridge, 1990) 262–3 but I cite Hom. *Il.* 4.222; 13.59–61 and 82–3; 11.10–14; 16.208.   **4.** Hom. *Il.* 22.71–3, 74–5; Alexander Pope, *Poems*, vol. VIII: *The Iliad* (ed. M. Mack, 1967) 456–7 n.102.   **5.** Hom. *Il.* 22.369–71, with de Jong, ed. (2012) 154: I do not consider *agēton* to mean 'beautiful' specifically, though many do, following Vernant (2001) 311–41, a fine study which overplays 22.71–5, out of context.   **6.** Hom. *Il.* 16.481, with Onians (1951) 26–7, a shrewd observation.   **7.** Hom. *Il.* 16.638–40, 677–83.   **8.** Hom. *Il.* 17.616–18.   **9.** Hom. *Il.* 19.338–9.   **10.** Hom. *Il.* 5.412–15.   **11.** Griffin (1980A) 143.   **12.** Alexander Pope, *Poems*, vol. VII: *The Iliad* (ed. M. Mack, 1967) 255.   **13.** Griffin (1980A) 139.   **14.** Van Wees (1996) 38.   **15.** Hom. *Il.* 6.12–19; Pope, Vol. VII; *Iliad* (n.12) 323 n.16 and the 'Introduction' ccxxvii, quoting Pope on his own house in Twickenham being 'like the house of a Patriarch of old, standing by the highwayside and receiving all travellers'.   **16.** Hom. *Il.* 4.457–6.11.   **17.** Weil (2003) 19, in my translation.   **18.** MacMillan (2020) 141, citing E. Psichari, *The Call to Arms* (1913).   **19.** Hom. *Il.* 7.228–35.   **20.** Weil (2003) 51.24; 35.61, in my translation.   **21.** Hom. *Il.* 1.203, 214; 9.368; *hybristai*, of Trojans, but in a speech, 13.633.   **22.** Graziosi, Haubold (2003) 60–76; Hom. *Il.* 22.455–9.   **23.** MacMillan (2020) 163.   **24.** J. I. Porter (2021) 205.   **25.** Oswald (2011) ix.   **26.** Baudrillard (1991).

23. Shame and Glory

1. Weil (2003) 59.55.   **2.** Hom. *Il.* 11.138–42.   **3.** Hom. *Il.* 7.345–353.   **4.** Hom. *Il.* 7.403–4.   **5.** Hom. *Il.* 12.310–12.   **6.** Hom. *Il.* 12.315, *chrē*, with 318, *aklees*.   **7.** Hom. *Il.* 12.325–8.   **8.** Dodds (1951) 17–18, with n.19 below.   **9.** W. S. Barrett, ed., *Euripides: Hippolytos* (Oxford, 1964) 206–7; Cairns (1993) 1–147.   **10.** Cairns (1993) 54–60.   **11.** Hom. *Il.* 15.561–3 and 659–66.   **12.** Hom. *Il.* 22.108–10.   **13.** Hom. *Il.* 6.523–5.   **14.** Williams (1993) 89.   **15.** Hom. *Il.* 4.182.   **16.** Hom. *Il.* 18.98–9.   **17.** Williams (2008) 78–82.   **18.** Hom. *Il.* 9.458–61.   **19.** Dodds (1951) 17–18, with 26 n.106 as he stressed to me in summer 1974.   **20.** Horden, Purcell (2000) 488–99.

24. Character and Background

1. Hom. *Il.* 13.3–8.   **2.** Hom. *Il.* 1.423–4; *Od.* 1.22–3.   **3.** Hom. *Il.* 22.156.   **4.** Hom. *Il.* 6.244–50.   **5.** Hom. *Il.* 17.50–60, esp. 51; Nicolson (2014) 200 oddly compares his hair braided with gold and silver to 'the body of a beautiful wasp'(!).   **6.** Hom. *Il.* 2.872.   **7.** Hall (1989) 14–15, 20, 22–31; Hom. *Il.* 21.130–32.   **8.** Hom. *Il.* 17.364–5.   **9.** Auerbach (1953) 6.   **10.** Auerbach (1953) 6, 11, 6–7, 12.   **11.** Hom. *Il.* 2.260.   **12.** Hom. *Il.* 1.307; Kramer-Hajos (2012) 87–105, esp. 97–102.   **13.** Hom. *Il.* 13.361, 512–13.   **14.** R. Janko, *The Iliad: A Commentary* (gen. ed. G. S. Kirk), vol. IV (Cambridge, 1992) 94, 390.   **15.** Hom. *Il.* 4.257; 13.470–76.   **16.** Hom. *Il.* 12.60–81, 109; 210–50; 13.723–53; 18.249–313; 22.100–103.   **17.** Hom. *Il.* 11.785–6.   **18.** Hom. *Il.* 19.328–33.   **19.** Hom. *Il.* 6.222–3; Pratt (2009) 141–61.   **20.** Hom. *Il.* 5.565–75; 15.568–72; 17.684–99; 23.514–613; Willcock (1983) 477–85.   **21.** Hom. *Il.* 9.108.   **22.** *Beowulf* 2329–32.   **23.** Hom. *Il.* 11.407; 21.562; 22.122.   **24.** Williams (2008) 21–49, on 'centres of agency'; Gaskin (1990) 1–15 on heroes making decisions.   **25.** Roisman (2005) 17–38.   **26.** Hom. *Il.* 16.86.   **27.** Hom. *Il.* 18.177.   **28.** Hom. *Il.* 2.284–8; 4.404; 9.32; 14.82–7; Taplin (1990) 60–82.   **29.** R. B. Rutherford, ed., *Homer. Odyssey: Books XIX and XX* (Cambridge, 1992) 16–27 on Odysseus in Iliad and Odyssey; Hom. *Il.* 3.216–24.   **30.** Hom. *Il.* 19.78–144, with Taplin (1992) 206–10, rightly stressing the need to assess it in its dramatic context.

25. Equine Poetics

1. West (2007) 465–7; Nicolson (2014) 158–60.   **2.** George (2020) 63, on Tablet VIII.50; his pp. 47 and 48 on Tablet VI.20 and 52–3.   **3.** *Manas*, trans. Walter May (2004), vol. I 2.30.   **4.** Hatto (1990) 233–5 and

Prior (2022) 55.   **5.** Plut. *Vit. Alex.* 6.   **6.** Hom. *Il.* 17.740–47; Griffith (2006A) 185–246 and (2006B) 307–58.   **7.** Coldstream (1977) 213–14, 254–5.   **8.** Lane Fox (2008) 170–71 and 451 n.19.   **9.** Hom. *Il.* 2. 773–7.   **10.** Zafeiropoulou, Agelarakis (2005) 30–35; chap. 15 n.6, above.   **11.** Hom. *Il.* 15.679–86.   **12.** Langdon, ed. (1993) 65–6.   **13.** Hom. *Il.* 16.384–93.   **14.** Delebecque (1951) 47–55, compelling on Homer's own observations of horses.   **15.** Hom. *Il.* 11.282.   **16.** Delebecque (1951) 52.   **17.** Hom. *Il.* 23.279–84.   **18.** Hom. *Il.* 5.192–205 and 232–5, also noticed by Freya Stark, *The Lycian Shore* (London, 1956) 119–20: 'of all the heroes in the *Iliad* he appears most knowledgeable about horses'.   **19.** Hom. *Il.* 8.185–90, with R. T. Hallock, *Persepolis Fortification Tablets* (Chicago, 1969) 49–50, on wine rations for horses.   **20.** Hom. *Il.* 8.186: *apotineton.*   **21.** Hom. *Il.* 23.523–7.   **22.** Hom. *Il.* 23.407–9.   **23.** Hom. *Il.* 2.763–79; 5. 638–43; 21.442–52.   **24.** Hom. *Il.* 2.354–6; 8.290–91.   **25.** Hom. *Il.* 23.262–70, 652–6, 700–705 with Macrakis (1984) 211–15.   **26.** Hom. *Il.* 1.225, on dogs' eyes and 6.344 as an insult; Graver (1995) 41–61 on possible explanations; I think shamelessness, shown in eating human flesh, is always the underlying one.   **27.** Hom. *Il.* 8.124–9, 316–19.   **28.** Hom. *Il.* 8.87; 16.152–4, 467–77.   **29.** Hom. *Il.* 16.467–77, 153–5.   **30.** Hom. *Il.* 23.347–8.   **31.** Hom. *Il.* 20.219–29, unconvincingly considered to be an Athenian interpolation by Griffin (1977) 39–53 at 41 and n.23; Zirkle (1936) 96–130; Nicolson (2014) 171–3 is good on 228–9.   **32.** Hom. *Il.* 5.265–6.   **33.** Hom. *Il.* 23.295–9.   **34.** Hom. *Il.* 8.185; 17.485–90.   **35.** Hom. *Il.* 23. 532–6; 2.763–7.   **36.** Hom. *Il.* 17.439–40; cf. 19.405–6: https//www.skyrian.horses.org on long-maned horses on Skyros, no less.   **37.** Hatto (1990) 138–9.   **38.** Hom. *Il.* 17.426–40.   **39.** Hom. *Il.* 17.443–7; I disagree with Macleod (1982) 15.   **40.** Hom. *Il.* 23.283–4.   **41.** Hom. *Il.* 17.420–22.   **42.** Hom. *Il.* 17. 453–5.   **43.** Hom. *Il.* 19.405–18; West (2007) 465–7 and esp. n.70 for talking horses in other cultures' epics; Versnel (2011) 167 is acute on Moira here.   **44.** Johnston (1992) 85–98 for discussion, not all of which is convincing. I disagree with her over *audēenta* at 19.407.

26. Swift-Footed Achilles

1. Hom. *Il.* 7.226–32.   **2.** Hom. *Il.* 9.255–60.   **3.** Hom. *Il.* 16.87–90.   **4.** Hom. *Il.* 16.223–4.   **5.** Hom. *Il.* 24.629–30.   **6.** Hom. *Il.* 1.149–71 and 225–44; 9.308–429; 24.518–51.   **7.** Hom. *Il.* 24.540–42.   **8.** Hom. *Il.* 18.104.   **9.** Hom. *Il.* 1.410.   **10.** Hom. *Il.* 9.337–9; 1.159–60; 9.340–43; 1.336.   **11.** Hom. *Il.* 9.121–34; 9. 115–16, with 2.378; 1.212–14 with 1.410–12.   **12.** Hom. *Il.* 9.160.   **13.** Hom. *Il.* 9.410–16; 1.352.   **14.** Hom. *Il.* 9.646–8.   **15.** Hom. *Il.* 8.473–6.   **16.** Hom. *Il.* 16.60–61.   **17.** Hom. *Il.* 18.112–13.   **18.** Hom. *Il.* 19. 67–8; 18.107–10.   **19.** Hom. *Il.* 19.147–8.   **20.** Shay (1994) 52–3.   **21.** Hom. *Il.* 21.34–96, esp. 95–6.   **22.** Hom. *Il.* 21.99–113, esp. 108–12; Griffin (1980A) 191.   **23.** Hom. *Il.* 18.101.   **24.** Shay (1994) 94; Hom. *Il.* 21.120–35.   **25.** Hom. *Il.* 20.466–7; at 21.99 it is Achilles who calls his victim *nēpie.*   **26.** Hom. *Il.* 21. 542–3.   **27.** I am disagreeing with Macleod (1982) 27 on 'insight'; Hom. *Il.* 24.540–42.   **28.** Clarke (2019) compares Gilgamesh and Achilles in great detail and concludes that 'elements of the *Epic of Gilgamesh*' have 'become embedded in the narrative of Achilles' (329). I disagree: they have not.

27. The Heavenly Family

1. Hom. *Il.* 1.157.   **2.** Hom. *Il.* 16.688.   **3.** Hom. *Il.* 11.10–12.   **4.** Hom. *Il.* 23.770–77.   **5.** Hom. *Il.* 13. 358–9; Onians (1951) 317–22, explaining it well.   **6.** Versnel (2011) 163–79, esp. 173.   **7.** Ballesteros (2021) 1–21, esp. 8–12.   **8.** J. Karageorghis (2005) esp. 6–7, 19–20, 226–7.   **9.** Stinton (1965) 1–12, 72.   **10.** Hom. *Il.* 24.27–30 on which I agree with West (2011B) 412, not Mackie (2013) 1–16.   **11.** Hom. *Il.* 4.51–7   **12.** Hom. *Od.* 4.554.   **13.** Dowden (2007) 41–55, esp. 43–5; *Hymn. Hom. Hermes* 128.   **14.** Hom. *Il.* 5.499–502.   **15.** Hom. *Il.* 21.470–71.   **16.** West (1997A) 108, 112–13 with 177: 'Homer's treatment of the gods is in general much more similar to what we find in Near Eastern narrative poetry than to anything warranted in normal Greek religious conceptions.' I disagree.   **17.** Richardson (1991) 83–94.   **18.** Against wider claims of 'Near Eastern' influence in scenes with Aphrodite, Kelly (2008B) 259–304 and in general, Ballesteros (2021) 1–21, with full bibliography. **19.** West (1997A) 401; Bonnet (2017) 87–112, on gods' assemblies, esp. 108–12 on the differences in Near Eastern texts. **20.** Hom. *Il.* 20.4–11; on Ocean here Onians (1951) 316. **21.** Lane Fox (2008) 282–3, 363–4. **22.** Lane Fox (2008) 350. **23.** Hom. *Il.* 8. 18–27; Leveque (1959) for a fine study of its afterlife. **24.** Flaig (1994) 13–31 on consensus in a divine assembly; Pirenne-Delforge, Pironti (2022) on Hera; Hom. *Il.* 19.96–124; 15.16–28; 1.567.

28. Sublime Frivolity

1. Burkert (1997) 15–34, esp. 20–21. **2.** Hom. *Il.* 9.503–4. **3.** Vernant (1965) 267–82, answered in Gagné, Herrero de Jáuregui, eds. (2019) 7–42 , esp. 25–7, and Burkert (1997) 20–21. **4.** Hom. *Il.* 20.326–7; 19.407; 18.239–40. **5.** Lane Fox (1986) 104–7, 165. **6.** Hom. *Il.* 8.69; 22.209; also, mighty Fate at 19.410. **7.** Jamil (2017) is worth comparing with Homeric 'fate' and its relation to the gods; Bowie (2021) 243–61 on differences from Near Eastern texts: Prior (2022) 74–5 on Manas. **8.** Versnel (2011) 166–7, esp. nn.38–40. **9.** Hom. *Il.* 20.127–8. **10.** I disagree with Graziosi and Haubold (2005) 91–5, who consider the concept of 'fate' was in the making when the Iliad was composed; Onians (1951) 378–94 rightly relates very ancient concepts to *moira* and *moros*. **11.** Versnel (2011) 166 and esp. n.39. **12.** Parker (2011) 160–65, a shrewd rebuttal of modern theories of sacrifice belied by Homer's poems; Hitch (2009) is an excellent survey of sacrifices actually practised in the poem. **13.** Hom. *Il.* 8.238–41. **14.** Hom. *Il.* 3.271–311. **15.** Hom. *Il.* 1.37–42; Pulleyn (1997). **16.** Hom. *Il.* 16.225–7. **17.** Lewis (1942) 20–21. **18.** Parker (1983) 66–70, 130–43: pollution is surely not implicit in the *thambos*, amazement, at the killer's arrival in *Il.* 24.480–84. **19.** Hom. *Il.* 24.221, which I do not take to refer to the smoke from a sacrifice: *Od.* 21.145; 22.315. **20.** Weinreich (1912) 1–68 is still classic. **21.** Hom. *Od.* 17.485–7; Hes. *Op.* 122–3, 249–54, 259. **22.** Hom. *Il.* 4.74–80, and only afterwards 86–93; Ready (2017) 25–40. **23.** Gen. 16.7–12; Judges 6.11–23 and esp. 13.3–23; Tobit 5.4–6.16 and 21; 6.3–17: Luke 1.26–38; John 20.11–14. **24.** Lane Fox (1991) 369–74. **25.** Longinus, *Sublime* 9.7. **26.** Hom. *Il.* 22.393–4; 5.76–8; 16.604–5 with Connelly (2007) 105–8. **27.** Hom. *Il.* 15.281–4; 13.216–18, where R. Janko, *The Iliad: A Commentary* (gen. ed. G. S. Kirk) vol. IV (Cambridge, 1992) 74 claims an old linguistic phrase which 'suggests the Myc. attitude to kingship': I disagree. Finley (1979) 150–51 states Homer 'never confused "godlike" with "divine" '; indeed, but 'godlike honours' could be actual cult. Versnel (2011) 460–61 with n.81 favours 'different meanings for different people who used' the phrase, but whereas 9.155, 297, 302 link being honoured with gifts in general to being 'like a god', a rather loose usage, other passages strike me as being stronger, esp. 22.434, spoken by Hecuba about Hector. Others disagree. **28.** Hom. *Il.* 14.294–6; 5.842–4. **29.** Hom. *Il.* 7.446–53. **30.** Adkins (1972) 1–14. **31.** Hes. *Op.* 355; Blundell (1989). **32.** Burkert (1985) 68–70. **33.** Allan (2006) 1–35 with Versnel (2011) 160–61 and esp. n.27; Lloyd Jones (1971) 21–7 is unconvincing; Dodds (1951) 32 is still right: 'I find no indication in the narrative of the *Iliad* that Zeus is concerned with justice as such.' **34.** Hom. *Il.* 13.620–29; 4.31–3. **35.** Griffin (1980A) 199, quoting K. Reinhardt with approval; Bowra (1930) 224; well rebutted by Dodds (1951) 18. **36.** Lane Fox (1986) 230; E. E. Evans-Pritchard's many works presented religion as an 'explanation of misfortune'. **37.** Hom. *Il.* 2.419–20; Griffin (1980A) 187.

29. White-Armed Women

1. Hom. *Il.* 1.143, 184; 19.282; 3.156–60. **2.** George (2018) 10–21. **3.** Hom. *Il.* 1.446–7. **4.** Hom. *Il.* 18.593. **5.** Snodgrass (1974) 114–25. **6.** Finley (1979) 84 on *einatēr*; Arist. *Pol.* 1268B 40 on brides of old being *bought*. **7.** In notes to his Oxford lectures in the 1950s. **8.** Hom. *Il.* 9.119–57. **9.** Hom. *Il.* 6.394; 22.88. **10.** Hom. *Il.* 22.51. **11.** Scheid-Tissinier (1994) 83–114 takes a similar view, inc. of *Od.* 1. 277–8, a complex question (93–4). I differ from Ormand (2014) esp. 52–85, a clear alternative view. **12.** Hom. *Il.* 11.241–5. **13.** Finley (1979) 140, 141. **14.** Hom. *Il.* 14.301–6. **15.** Hom. *Od.* 8.266–366. **16.** Hom. *Il.* 14.269. **17.** Hom. *Il.* 5.70–71. **18.** Finley (1979) 140, noting Hom. *Il.* 9.340; Finley (1981) 233 does note *mnēstē* and translates the phrase as 'wooed bedmate'. **19.** Hom. *Il.* 11.241–3. **20.** Hom. *Il.* 9.128–30. **21.** Hom. *Il.* 9.664–5. **22.** Hom. *Il.* 9.342–3; 19.297–9. **23.** Hom. *Il.* 9.340–43; 19.59–60. **24.** Hom. *Il.* 6.21; 14.444; 20.384. **25.** Hom. *Il.* 16.179–86. **26.** Hom. *Od.* 11.248–9. **27.** Hom. *Il.* 16.187–92. **28.** Llewellyn-Jones (2003) 25–33. **29.** Hom. *Il.* 9.451–2. **30.** Hom. *Il.* 6.389. **31.** Hom. *Il.* 19. 282–300. **32.** Hom. *Il.* 19.301–2. **33.** Hom. *Il.* 5.69–71. **34.** Hom. *Il.* 6.297–304; Connelly (2007) 92–104. **35.** Ps.-Aeschin. *Epist.* 10.3. **36.** Virginia Woolf, *A Room of One's Own* (repr. 1984, London,) 33; Farron (1979) 15–31 on Homeric women in general.

30. Royal Mothers

1. Hom. *Il.* 22.44–5. **2.** Hom. *Il.* 6.286–7. **3.** Hom. *Il.* 22.79–80. **4.** Hom. *Il.* 22.405–7. **5.** Minchin (2007) 143–281. **6.** Easterling (1991) 145–51. **7.** Hom. *Il.* 22.38–89. **8.** Hom. *Il.* 22.416–36. **9.** Hom. *Il.* 6.254–62. **10.** N. Richardson, *The Iliad: A Commentary*. vol. VI: *Books 21–24* (Cambridge, 1993) 294. **11.** Hom. *Il.* 24.299–321. **12.** Hom. *Il.* 24.748–59. **13.** Hom. *Il.* 3.125–8. **14.** Hom. *Il.* 3.175. **15.** Hom. *Il.* 24.765–7. **16.** Plin. *HN* XXXIII.23.8; Coccagna (2014) 399–411. **17.** Hom. *Il.* 3.146–60, esp. 148. **18.** Hom. *Il.* 3.164–5. **19.** Hom. *Il.* 3.172–6. **20.** Hom. *Il.* 3.178; Sheppard (1933) 31–7. **21.** Hom. *Il.* 3.180. **22.** Hom. *Il.* 3.395. **23.** Hom. *Il.* 3.409. **24.** Minchin (2007) 143–251 for such stereotypes. **25.** Hom. *Il.* 3.420; Mason (1972) 36: 'as a human being Helen is extinguished'. **26.** Hom. *Il.* 3.428–36. **27.** Hom. *Il.* 3.447. **28.** Hom. *Il.* 6.323–4. **29.** Hom. *Il.* 6.334, 357–8. **30.** Hom. *Il.* 2.356. **31.** Hom. *Il.* 24.774–5. **32.** Patrick Leigh Fermor, *Mani: Travels in the Southern Peloponnese* (London, 1958) 309. **33.** Baynes (1955) 22–3. **34.** Thomas Hughes, *Tom Brown's Schooldays* part 2, chap. 5 (London, 1857). **35.** Hom. *Il.* 22.441; *Schol. Theocr.* 2.59–62 on *throna*, esp. Thessalian. **36.** Alexander (2010) 51. **37.** Hom. *Il.* 6.490–92. **38.** Hom. *Il.* 22.468–72; Llewellyn-Jones (2003) 28–33. **39.** Hom. *Il.* 22.510–14. **40.** Hom. *Il.* 24.743–5; Richardson (1987) 165–84. **41.** Hom. *Il.* 6.392–493. **42.** Hom. *Il.* 6. 495–6; for similarly placed *entropalizomenos*, *Il.* 11.547 (Ajax), 17.109 (Menelaus), 21.492 (Artemis), each case being in battle. **43.** Schadewaldt (1997) 124–42; Mason (1972) 163–78, making good use of Dryden and Pope. **44.** Hom. *Il.* 6.433–9, with B. Graziosi and J. Haubold, eds., *Homer. Iliad. Book VI* (Cambridge, 2010) 45–6; **45.** Griffin (1980B) 30; I disagree with Graziosi and Haubold (n. 44 above) 31–2. **46.** Hom. *Il.* 6.482–4. **47.** Plut. *Brut.* 23. **48.** Griffin (1980B) 70 and 66.

31. The Natural World

1. Griffin (1980A) 141. **2.** Hom. *Il.* 23.194–5. **3.** Hom. *Il.* 4.473–9 for birth beside a river; Thonemann (2006) 11–43 for other beliefs. **4.** Hom. *Il.* 2.467. **5.** Prior (2022) 128; Hom. *Il.* 17.547–52; 11.27 is not so specific. **6.** Hom. *Il.* 4.482–7; 12.133–4. **7.** Hom. *Il.* 23.127–8; 24.784. **8.** Hom. *Il.* 17.460; Maclair Boraston (1911) 216–50, esp. 230–32 and 239 on carrion-eating *gypes*. **9.** Hom. *Il.* 7.58–61. **10.** Hom. *Il.* 14.289–91. **11.** Hom. *Il.* 12.200–207, with Maclair Boraston (1911) 236, who regards the small-toed eagle as not a high flier (Mynott (2018) 252 n.1 passes over this) and therefore, compellingly to me, opts for Bonelli's eagle. **12.** Hom. *Il.* 24.314–19; MacLair Boraston (1911) 237–8. **13.** Prior (2022) 101; Hatto (1990) **14.** Hosea 5.14; 7.4–6. **15.** Hom. *Il.* 14.16–22. **16.** Hom. *Il.* 15.80–83. **17.** Hom. *Il.* 22. 199–201. **18.** Hom. *Il.* 16.259–67. **19.** Hom. *Il.* 15.361–4. **20.** Hom. *Il.* 16.7–11. **21.** Hom. *Il.* 6.146–8. **22.** Hom. *Il.* 4.130–31; 12.433–6. **23.** Hom. *Il.* 21.257–64. **24.** Hom. *Il.* 18.56–9. **25.** Forster (1936) 97–104, at 103. **26.** Hom. *Il.* 17.53–60. **27.** Hom. *Il.* 8.306–8. **28.** Hom. *Il.* 14.499–500. **29.** Patrick Leigh Fermor, *Between the Woods and the Water* (London, 1986) 205. **30.** Schnapp-Gourbeillon (1981) ably detects the hierarchy; Hom. *Il.* 21.394, 421, applied by Ares to Athena and then Hera to Aphrodite. **31.** Hom. *Il.* 23.173–4; Graver (1995) 41–62. **32.** Hom. *Il.* 22.262–7. **33.** M. Aur. *Med.* 3.2: he is also impressed by a lion's furrowed brow. **34.** Hom. *Il.* 16.487–9, 751–3, 823–9. **35.** Lonsdale (1990) with the review by J. Griffin, *CR* 41 (1991) 293–5; M. Clarke (1995) 137–59. **36.** Coldstream (1986) 181–6, esp. 184–5. **37.** Dunbabin (1957) 46–8. **38.** Dunbabin (1957) 46 n.2. **39.** Anderson (1985) 1–16, for

Mycenaeans, Assyrians and Homeric heroes; for Macedonians, Andronicos (1984) 104–16. **40.** Synesius, *Epist.* 148.79–85. **41.** Hom. *Il.* 5.161; 11.174 with Auden *CR* (1896) 107, a valuable note. **42.** Hom. *Il.* 17.132–7. **43.** Grattius, *Cyneg.* 209. **44.** www.lorealparis.co.in/so-what-is-a-lions-wrinkle-how-to-get-rid-of-your-forehead-wrinkles. **45.** Alden (2005) 335–42, esp. 336 n.13. **46.** Sayakbay Karalaev, a great Manas singer, also kept golden eagles and hunted expertly with them on horseback.

32. 'As when . . .'

1. Hom. *Il.* 17.227–8 with Vermeule (1979) 101–3; for metaphors for the experience of death, Horn (2018) 359–83. **2.** Hom. *Il.* 2.147–8. **3.** Patrick Leigh Fermor, *Mani: Travels in the Southern Peloponnese* (London, 1958) 13–7. **4.** Maclair Boraston (1911) 216–50, at 249–50. **5.** Hdt. 1.55.2 for an example. **6.** Hom. *Il.* 2.455–6; 11.155–7. **7.** Graziosi, Haubold (2005) 87–8. **8.** Hom. *Il.* 19.357–61; 11.480–81; 21.522–5. **9.** Graziosi, Haubold (2005) 87–9 suggest a contrast between the narrator and the world he presents in similes. **10.** Hom. *Il.* 2.455–83. **11.** Hom. *Il.* 2.455–8. **12.** Hom. *Il.* 2.780–85; Lane Fox (2008) 335–6. **13.** Hom. *Il.* 3.10–14. **14.** Winkler (2007) 43–67 is excellent here. **15.** Hom. *Il.* 22.25–32, 93–7, 139–43, 162–6, 189–93, 199–201, 308–11, 317–21. **16.** Hom. *Il.* 23.597–600, 692–4, 759–64. **17.** Hom. *Il.* 24.480–83. **18.** Hom. *Il.* 11.473–84. **19.** Hom. *Il.* 4.141–7. **20.** Hom.*Il.* 23.222–5. **21.** Hom. *Il.* 17.673–81. **22.** Hom. *Il.* 24.480–83. **23.** Hom. *Il.* 8.555–61; 16.297–302. **24.** H. Fränkel (1921) 113–14. **25.** Weil (2003) 35.6.60; 40.79. **26.** Hom. *Il.* 11.113–15. **27.** Hom. *Il.* 11.548–57; 16.823–9; 17.108–13, **28.** Hom. *Il.* 22.261–7. **29.** Hom. *Il.* 21.573–82. **30.** Gabriel Josipovici, in the *Independent* newspaper 20 Feb. 1993. **31.** Hom. *Il.* 6.146–9. **32.** Hom. *Il.* 21.462–6.

33. The Shield of Achilles

1. Hom. *Il.* 18.414–21. **2.** Hom. *Il.* 18.464–7. **3.** J. B. Hainsworth, in A. Heubeck, S. West, J. B. Hainsworth, *A Commentary on Homer's Odyssey* vol. I (Oxford, 1988) on *Od.* 5.272–7. **4.** Vail (2018) is the most convincing attempt. **5.** Hom. *Il.* 11.19–20; 23.741–5. **6.** Markoe (1985). **7.** Snodgrass (1998) 57–8, 64–6. **8.** Pl. *Resp.* 514A–515C. **9.** Hom. *Il.* 18.497–508. **10.** Hom. *Il.* 12.421–3, where Finley (1981) 228 is disinclined to see truly 'common land': contrast Ridgeway (1885) 319–39. **11.** Gray (1954) 1–15, esp. 12–13. **12.** Hom. *Il.* 18.558–60. **13.** Hom. *Il.* 11.36–7. **14.** Hom. 18.535–40; Taplin (1980) 1–21, esp. 7 with nn.20–21; Rutherford (2019) 208–9. **15.** Taplin (1980) 1–21, at 15. **16.** Rutherford (2019) 28: for this to work, 18.535–40 must indeed be excised. **17.** Hom. *Il.* 18.615–16. **18.** Hom. *Il.* 19.14. **19.** Hom. *Il.* 18.570. **20.** A. D. Nuttall, in conversations with me in 2005–7.

34. Ruthless Poignancy

1. Lewis (1942) 22. **2.** Lewis (1942) 25. **3.** Gill (1984) 149–66 and Griffin (1976) 161–87. **4.** Tasso, *Discorso . . .* (Ferrara, 1585) 112, cited by Strawn (2012) 588 and n.19. **5.** Hom. *Il.* 5.49–58. **6.** Hom. *Il.* 3.180; 11.762; 24.426: I disagree with Bowie, ed. (2019) 128–9, who considers that the *ge* 'underlines the certainty' and that there is no wistfulness in the phrase. **7.** Redfield (1975) 101. **8.** Griffin (1980A) 182–3; Macleod (1982) 14 and n.1; Hammer (2002) 203–35 and esp. Kim (2000), the fullest analysis, which even gives pity a structural role in the entire poem. **9.** Hom. *Il.* 8.464–5. **10.** Arist. *Rhet.* 1386A 4–28 with Carr (1999) 411–29; Konstan (2001), but the Altar of Pity in Athens needs to be added (Thompson (1952) 47–82 for all the evidence); Bloom (2016), on empathy, but compassion is different; Most (2004) 50–75 is less specific; Strawn (2012) is excellent; Wohl (2015) 40–49 on pity in Euripides' Trojan plays. **11.** Hom. *Il.* 20.21–3. **12.** Hom. *Il.* 15.612. **13.** Weil (2003) 38.72 and esp. 81.42. Irony is not much mentioned in Griffin (1980A) 102–204, though he was properly aware of it of course, but writes on it mostly in the

Odyssey (Griffin (1980B) 59, 72–4); Rutherford (1982) 145–60 well discusses ignorance and knowledge in Homer and tragedy; so does Lowe (1996) 520–33; Gottlieb (1992) 278–9 on irony's meaning for Plato's Socrates; Booth (1974) and esp. Colebrook (2009) on irony more generally; Shay (1994) 160–61 even considers the 'love' of Zeus for men to be meant as bitter irony! **14.** Minchin (2010) 387–402, esp. 398: I go on to cite Hom. *Il.* 13.374–82. **15.** Hom. *Il.* 20.407–22; 21.115–19; 22.46–53. **16.** Hom. *Il.* 22.437–46; 16.685. **17.** Hom. *Il.* 6.241. **18.** Hom. *Il.* 6.311. **19.** Lowe (2000) 127. **20.** Hom. *Il.* 24.525. **21.** Hom. *Il.* 16.440–43; 22.178–81. **22.** Hom. *Il.* 24.527–33; I do not think the recipient of unmixed evil is a sinner: he is '*lōbētos*', not punished; Achilles' point is bleak about inscrutable hostility of the gods to e.g. a disfigured, or handicapped, man. **23.** Griffin (1978) 1–22 is superb; *Hymn. Hom. Ap.* 182–6, but I disagree with Griffin (1980A) 192 and n.39 that the song implied at Hom. *Il.* 1.604 was very different. **24.** Hom. *Il.* 17.446–7. **25.** Hom. *Il.* 22.202–4; Griffin (1990) 353–69 for the sequel. **26.** Hom. *Il.* 22.213. **27.** Hom. *Il.* 22.221. **28.** Hom. *Il.* 22.293–5. **29.** Hom. *Il.* 6.513. **30.** Hom. *Il.* 6.518–19, 340–41 and 363–4. **31.** L. N. Tolstoy, *Anna Karenin* (trans. Rosemary Edmonds, Harmondsworth, 1954) 423.

List of Illustrations

Every effort has been made to contact all copyright holders. The publisher will be pleased to amend in future printings any errors or omissions brought to their attention.

1. Lyre Player and Bird Fresco from the Throne Room of Nestor's palace in Pylos, *c.* 1300 BC, Archaeological Museum of Chora, Messinia, Greece. Watercolour reconstruction by Pylos Piet de Jong, Department of Classics, University of Cincinnati, painting no. 530. Photograph: Wikimedia.
2. Red-figured neck-amphora (storage-jar) with Rhapsode reciting the beginning of a poem, *c.* 490 BC–480 BC. Photograph copyright © The Trustees of the British Museum.
3. Head of Homer in profile, coin, Ios, *c.* 350 BC. Photograph: Andrew Meadows.
4. *Crocus gargaricus* on Mount Gargaron. Photograph: author.
5. Smintheion, Chryse. Photograph: Andrew Meadows.
6. Sarpedon's body carried by Hypnos and Thanatos (Sleep and Death), while Hermes watches, *c.* 515 BC. Formerly in the Metropolitan Museum of Art, New York (L.2006.10); returned to Italy and exhibited in Rome as of January 2008. Photograph: Jaime Ardiles-Arce / Wikimedia.
7. Tuz Golu (Salt Lake) near Suvla on the Gelibolu. Photograph: author.
8. Milman Parry. Courtesy of the Milman Parry Collection of Oral Literature, Harvard University.
9. Friedrich Wilhelm Radloff. Photograph: G. F. Lokke, copyright © Bibliothèque Nationale de France
10. Avdo Mededović. Courtesy of the Milman Parry Collection of Oral Literature, Harvard University.

11. Sayakley Karalaev. Photograph: Wikimedia.
12. The embassy to Achilles: Phoenix and Odysseus in front of Achilles. Attic red-figure hydria, *c.* 480 BC. Staatliche Antikensammlungen (Inv. 8770). Photograph: Bibi Saint-Pol / Wikimedia.
13. Fragment of an attic black-figured cauldron (dinos) depicting funeral games held in honour of Patroclus, Pharsala (Palaiokastro), 580–570 BC. National Archaeological Museum of Athens (A 15499).
14. Drinking cup (skyphos) with the departure and recovery of Helen, *c.* 490 BC. 13.186, Bartlett Collection, Museum of Fine Arts Boston; purchased with funds from the Francis Bartlett Donation of 1912.
15. Thetis gives her son Achilles his weapons newly forged by Hephaestus. Detail of an Attic black-figure hydria, *c.* 575–550 BC. Photograph: near the Tyrrhenian Group / Wikimedia.
16. The silver Philoktet-cups (Dnf. 10/20) from Hoby. Both goblets are signed by the craftsman Cheirisophos, who made them. Photograph: CC BY-SA, Roberto Fortuna & Kira Ursem, National Museum of Denmark.
17. Marble relief depicting the Apotheosis (elevation to divine status) of the poet Homer, with Zeus, Apollo and the Muses, signed by the sculptor Archelaus of Priene, *c.* 225–205 BC, found in Italy, now in the British Museum, but thought to have been sculpted in Egypt. Photograph: Carole Raddato / Creative Commons.
18. *Eurybates and Talthybios Lead Briseis to Agamemmon* by Giovanni Battista Tiepolo, *c.* 1757. Photograph: Wikimedia.
19. *The Death of Hector* by Peter Paul Rubens. Museum Boijmans Van Beuningen, Rotterdam, Donation: D. G. van Beuningen 1933. Photograph: Wikimedia.

Index

Robin Lane Fox is an emeritus fellow at New College, Oxford. His books include *The Invention of Medicine*, *Augustine* (winner of the major Wolfson History Prize), and *The Classical World*. He lives near Oxford, England.

30 Apollo "mouse god"
79 - Homer "amputated"
89 - Bishlcofe - MANAS
162 - Citizens' rights - first example * 670 scc
215 - Gods - Pity *
220 - Lear - Priamm - Hector - Cornelia
233 "Kindness"
237 gods - running "older men" > See 302 -
278 - HORSES *, 282. 284 ⊙ / chanting
302 t. - Free will.
322 Helen's beauty - Book 3.
377 Homer - A.1. !!